Springer Texts in Business and Economics

For further volumes:
http://www.springer.com/series/10099

Mark K. Pyles

Applied Corporate Finance

Questions, Problems and Making Decisions in the Real World

Springer

Mark K. Pyles
Associate Professor of Finance
College of Charleston
Charleston, SC, USA

ISSN 2192-4333 ISSN 2192-4341 (electronic)
ISBN 978-1-4614-9172-9 ISBN 978-1-4614-9173-6 (eBook)
DOI 10.1007/978-1-4614-9173-6
Springer New York Heidelberg Dordrecht London

Library of Congress Control Number: 2013949157

Printed on acid-free paper

Springer is part of Springer Science+Business Media (www.springer.com)

Preface

One may question why I would choose to write a book involving issues in corporate finance, given the large number of excellent texts that already exist in the academic marketplace. It is my hope that the answer to this question will be largely self-evident upon review of the text. My intention is to complete a work that is unique in the field. Many existing texts do an excellent job of helping readers learn about issues in corporate finance, so my intention is not to simply recreate these products with a different cover. The theory underlying this text is that any specific area of education is a tool, much like any other type of tool in any other facet of life. And, as important as the characteristics defining these tools certainly are, it is application in a real world setting that is of most importance. The attainment of knowledge has very little merit in the workplace without an accompanying understanding of the uses. Perhaps the best way of stating the motivation behind completing this text is that I want students to learn corporate finance as though it is a *verb*, rather than as a noun. As something you *do*, rather than something you *know*.

These words; however, without an accompanying plan of implementation, are nothing more than noble thoughts. Thus, the reader will notice a two-pronged attack. First, the text is written in a different voice than most. Many instructors subconsciously teach finance as though all students learn the "finance way," meaning they have quantitative minds and enjoy working with numbers. However, this is certainly not true in many instances and creates a disconnect between the way we teach and the way many students learn. The intent is to have a text that is readable and understandable; even if that means sacrificing some of the time-honored beliefs regarding the serious and stoic tone that often define academic texts.

The second prong of attack is changing the process for which material is presented. This text is not based upon a modular structure. Instead, we make a very concerted effort to create a continuous stream of events so that the reader can best understand the evolving processes that define corporate finance. The end goal is that the student will have a comprehensive understanding of how the corporate financial cycle works. Extraneous details will often be sacrificed for the sake of brevity and flow of information. Should a reader be seeking a text that covers the width and depth of the minutiae involved in the discipline, I admit this book is not for you.

The elimination of this surplus material will provide space to create a fictional company by the name of *Hack Back, Incorporated* that will guide readers in an understandable and entertaining fashion. The motivation is that students should have some interest in the "story" and will transfer this to interest in the topics.

The text is comprised of nine chapters. In each, material is presented in a streamlined presentation and includes numerous examples to help illustrate the concepts. In addition, when appropriate, the text includes "LOOK IT UP" boxes that encourage the reader to go outside the book and examine how the material being covered is relevant in the world around them. "TECH HELP" boxes spread throughout the text help the reader learn how to use modern technology to help streamline problem solving. The text will include (at the completion of each chapter) possible alternative endings of the *Hack Back, Inc*. storyline, which are designed to encourage creative thinking and facilitate flexibility of instruction.

At the completion of each chapter is a series of CONCEPT QUESTIONS, which test the reader's understanding of important topics covered. Care is given to asking not only pure definitional questions. Rather, the intent is to present thought-provoking questions so that an accurate answer will help ensure the reader goes beyond simply memorizing the material. A set of PROBLEMS are also presented at the end of each chapter which involve mathematical components. The difficulty of the problems ranges from relatively simple to relatively complex.

Charleston, SC, USA Mark K. Pyles

Acknowledgements

Thanks to all the students that I have taught. It is your support, suggestions, and criticisms that provide the basis for the materials in this text. I look forward to teaching several thousand more just like you.

My understanding of finance is a derivative of the teachings of wonderful people that imparted their wisdom upon me. I applaud them of their knowledge and thank them for their time. I particularly am appreciative of the real "Dubarb Freeman," without whom I would never be where I am today and the thought of writing a textbook would be laughable.

Special thanks goes to Pasha Sadeghian for valuable proofreading assistance. Finally, and most importantly, I thank my wife Miranda and two sons, Stone and Dex. You are my favorite things about life.

Contents

Chapter 1
In the Beginning…

This chapter sets the stage for all others to come, which is unsurprising given its placement. In this introductory chapter, we will cover two topics, both of which are crucial in preparing the reader for the topics upcoming throughout the text. The first step in understanding how a corporation operates is to understand how one begins. While the specific steps of a company's start-up can take many forms, there are several things that generally happen. First is the decision of the type of firm the owners choose to create. As you will see in the upcoming pages, this is much more than just a name or a classification. In fact, the company type will determine how the company operates, from day-to-day activities to long-run projects designed to facilitate growth and generate potential stockholder benefits.

Once the decision of firm type is made, the firm then can turn attention to their desired objectives. This starts with the discussion of the appropriate goal of the firm. Further, we dissect the actual steps that must be taken in order to reach that goal and introduce the basic financial questions faced in a corporate setting. As a suggestion, it would be wise to treat this chapter as the first 15 minutes of a movie. While the topics of discussion are far from the most difficult we must face, a failure to understand the materials presented in this chapter would be analogous to coming late to the movie. To do so would result in missing the basic premise behind and motivation for the entire story.

1.1 Types of Business Organizations

1.1.1 Sole Proprietorships

We'll start with the simplest of all business structures, the **sole proprietorship**. The name really says it all. The word "sole" means you can do it yourself, while "proprietorship" indicates you have some type of proprietary skill that you can

M.K. Pyles, *Applied Corporate Finance: Questions, Problems and Making Decisions in the Real World*, Springer Texts in Business and Economics,
DOI 10.1007/978-1-4614-9173-6_1, © Springer Science+Business Media New York 2014

offer the entire population or at least some segment of the population. A sole proprietorship comes into existence when the owner (i.e., the sole proprietor) decides he/she has an idea they believe will provide a needed service to a consumer base. They also likely desire to make money off this idea. It is beneficial to note that a sole proprietorship can be owned by more than a single individual, something the name does not suggest.

There are several advantages to this type of business. First, it is by far the easiest type of company to start. You simply have to wake up one morning with an idea. To illustrate, let's say you want to open a hot dog stand. In order to get going, you simply have to buy the equipment and start selling dogs to whomever will buy. This leads to a second advantage of sole proprietorships: less regulation. While there are likely to be certain permits or licenses required to operate the hot dog stand, in relation to other business types (which we will get to shortly), the regulation is much less burdensome, both monetarily and in time required to satisfy guidelines. Sole proprietorships also have the advantage of the owner keeping all the profits. There are naturally costs associated with any business and the owner may have employees to pay. However, the point is that there need not be additional shareholders or stakeholders, with which you would normally have to split profits.

Of course, as with most things in life, there are also certain disadvantages associated with being a sole proprietor, and they can be very significant if not accounted for and understood. First, the life of the business is limited. It is important to understand that with a sole proprietorship, there is *not a real distinction between the owner and the business*. The easiest way to practically see this is around March or April of each year, when tax returns are filed. As a sole proprietor, any income generated by business operations must be declared on the individual's tax return. More specifically, there is not a separate tax return filed for the business. A worthy note is that a sole proprietorship cannot exchange hands. The property or equipment used in the creation and activities of the firm may be bought and sold, but should someone else start using the hot dog stand, a new sole proprietorship is formed. Therefore, *the business dies with the owner*. Of course, the owner may just choose to stop operations, but that's not as catchy to remember.

A second, and direr, disadvantage associated with sole proprietorships is known as **unlimited liability**. Liability is a contractual obligation to future business proceeds or, in layman terms, debt. Therefore, when the word "unlimited" is attached to this, problems can quickly arise. This indicates there is no limit to the monetary damage the owner can suffer should something happen to increase liability. A point that has not been directly spoken to as of yet is that when a sole proprietorship is started, there is generally no requirement for things such as insurance or accident protection. Therefore, if the owner decides these issues aren't of concern, there is no protection for the owners should something adverse happen. For example, say some poor soul got a bad hot dog from our stand and was stricken with *salmonella*. Then, say this poor soul survives and sues us for negligence. To cut to the chase, should we lose, the entire liability is ours. Hopefully, we had the foresight to protect ourselves with some type of contingency plan, such as an insurance policy (which is required in many instances). However, if we don't have enough money, they can take our house. If that's not enough, they can take our car. If that's not enough, they can take our puppy. Okay, maybe not the puppy, but the point is made.

There are other potential disadvantages to being a sole proprietor. For example, it is likely more difficult to raise funds to promote growth. This is due to several reasons, not the least of which being that shares of the company cannot be sold. As we move forward in the text, this disadvantage will become particularly important, as successful corporate financial policy generally requires money and often large amounts of it.

1.1.2 Partnerships

A second basic type of business organization is a **partnership**. The term partnership automatically evokes thoughts of two people, but this is not necessarily the case. A partnership can have any number of owners, with a minimum of two. Therefore, it is important to remember that a partnership is a type of business, not a pairing of kindred souls. A partnership is actually very much like a sole proprietorship, only there is more than one owner. In other words, to borrow from our earlier example, two or more people have to wake up one morning wanting to sell hot dogs for a living. Therefore, they would open a stand together. To be realistic, it is a bit more difficult than this, as there is a certain amount of paperwork that must be completed. For example, partners may have a partnership agreement or a declaration of partnership.

> LOOK IT UP: What does this declaration of partnership entail? What does it look like and what does it mean to each participant? Try looking it up on the web.

The advantages and disadvantages of a partnership are very similar to sole proprietorships. However, there is at least one very important caveat that needs to be addressed relating to the specific type of partnership. A **general partner** is one that shares proportionally in gains and losses of the business and has unlimited liability for the partnership's debt obligations. In other words, being a general partner is very much like being a sole proprietor, only you have others in it with you. Should something happen, each general partner assumes responsibility for the firm's entire liability base.

An alternative type of partner is known as a **limited partner**. As you can probably deduct, a limited partner has limited liability. In fact, their liability is limited to the amount of capital they contribute to the partnership. On the other hand, their portion of the profits is often a correspondingly smaller percentage as well. If all the partners in a business partnership have, to some degree, limited liability, it is known as a limited liability partnership (LLP).

It is important enough to reiterate: the most important disadvantage of both a sole proprietorship and a partnership is the unlimited liability issue. Therefore, to move on with our discussion of business types, the natural transition is to one that mitigates this considerable problem.

1.1.3 Corporations

The last type of business entity is a **corporation**. The distinction between a corporation and other types of business organizations is that a corporation is *distinct* and *separate* from the owners. That is a big issue, so let's make sure we have it straight before moving on. Once a corporation originates, it becomes a living, breathing thing all on its own. The point is you can consider the business without considering the owners, and vice versa. Following our earlier illustration, you would have to pay your accountant more at the beginning of each year in this case because you would have to file both an individual return and a corporate return. This separation of ownership and control actually creates the potential for substantial problems, which we will discuss a bit later.

A corporation originates with **articles of incorporation**, which are pretty much as they sound. These articles, which are registered with the government, lay out the basic ownership structure of the firm, including the owners and general business purpose. Once a business becomes incorporated, they then become that separate and distinct entity that is redefined as a corporation. To illustrate, consider an example we're all aware of. We've all shopped at Walmart. In fact, you may not ever shop anywhere else. Most of you also probably know that Walmart was founded by Sam Walton in Arkansas a long time ago (1962, if you're into details). However, when you go into Walmart, you never see Sam or any of his descendants. In fact, you really never hear anything about the family, unless it's about their fortunes. The reason for this is they aren't the people who actually run Walmart on a day-to-day basis.

> LOOK IT UP: So, who are the people who run Walmart? Are their last names really not Walton? Compare Walmart's history with their current administrative structure. Try looking both at Walmart's website (http://walmartstores.com) and the Yahoo! Finance site (http://finance.yahoo.com).

Ownership in a corporation may be a bit difficult to understand, particularly the first time you hear about it. If a corporation is a public company, owners can take numerous forms. The owners of a public company are anyone who owns shares of stock in that company. Therefore, Walmart has millions of owners. In fact, you may be an owner or your parents may be owners.

There are some considerable advantages of the corporate form of business organization. First, you no longer have the problem of unlimited liability. In fact, your liability is now very similar to that of a limited partner in that you can only lose the amount you put in. If you buy \$1,000 worth of Walmart stock, then you can lose a maximum of \$1,000 and you can only do that if the stock price goes to \$0, which is highly unlikely.

Another advantage of being a corporation is that the life of the company is not limited. This is due, of course, to the fact the company no longer has to be critically linked to the owners. Therefore, as the owners either decease or choose to stop participating, the firm can continue. As another example, Henry Ford passed away in 1947, yet Ford Motor Company is still alive and well. This indicates ownership is easily transferred. In fact, today ownership in a publicly traded company is transferred as easily as a few clicks of the mouse.

LOOK IT UP: Don't believe me? Check out a few of the online trading sites and see what they allow you to do (for a nominal fee of course). Try www.tdameritrade.com or www.etrade.com, for example.

Alas, nothing is perfect and there are disadvantages associated with corporations as well. In fact, there are two major issues that need to be discussed. The first is something called **double taxation**. This means, logically, that the same money may get taxed at two different levels. As a company makes money, it gets taxed (remember that corporate tax return we spoke of). While that is unfortunate for the company, the real disadvantage is that funds that get dispersed to shareholders (i.e., dividends) also get taxed; only this time it is the individual shareholder who bears the burden. Thus, you have the potential for the same \$1 of revenue to be taxed more than once, and if the shareholder is also an owner, it is effectively paid twice by the same person.

LOOK IT UP: You probably don't remember President Bush's tax cut bill from 2003, but you may recall the debate over (and ultimate approval of) an extension of the cuts at the end of 2010. The bill had interesting ramifications for double taxation and taxation of dividends in general. See if you can find out what they are.

The second disadvantage of a corporation is a deeper issue. The fancy way of describing the difference between a corporation and its owners is that there is a "separation of ownership and control." This has the potential to lead to something referred to as **agency problems**. The basic notion is that the company's operations should be designed to generate wealth for the owners. This is a fairly straightforward proposition for a sole proprietorship, but not as much for a corporation. The separation between ownership and management of the company provides the opportunity for a disconnect. Agency problems occur when management (i.e., the people who run the company) fails to do their best to generate income for the shareholders (i.e., the people who own the company). When these agency problems pop up, they lead to **agency costs**, which are costs incurred to eliminate, or at least mitigate, these issues.

Agency costs can also be defined as those used to prevent agency problems. In 2002, due to agency problem monstrosities at corporate giants such as Enron and WorldCom, the **Sarbanes-Oxley Act** (SOX, for short) was enacted. SOX has resulted in the implementation of an extremely complex regulatory system, designed to ensure that shareholder abuse is eliminated to the extent possible. The effectiveness and necessity of SOX is always a popular debate topic, but one point is not in question; SOX has drastically changed the corporate landscape. A successful firm must learn to incorporate all parts of SOX into their operations.

LOOK IT UP: These are just the three primary types of business organizations. In actuality, there are many others which represent business entities that combine characteristics from the three primary types. For example, see what you can find out about limited liability companies (LLCs) and S-corporations.

IN THE REAL WORLD

Tyler Bryant was born in a suburb of Nashville, TN, in 1981. His father grew up in Chattanooga, Tennessee, before attending the University of Memphis on an athletic scholarship and earning a degree in civil engineering. His mother, a Boston native, obtained a master's degree in Early Childhood Education and then moved south to ply her trade in the rural community of Camden, SC. These two distinct skill sets merged to create a quiet, intelligent lad who would much rather play board games than shoot hoops. Excelling, both in class work and on standardized tests, allowed Tyler to attend Stanford on an academic scholarship. He followed his father's path and majored in mechanical engineering.

Lillian O'Grady was born in Seattle, WA, a mere 3 months after Tyler came into the world. Dubbed Lilly very early on, she did well, but not great, in school. Her real passion was athletics and she played virtually every sport offered by her school. Junior All-American soccer and All-Region basketball accolades led to countless scholarship opportunities. However, her true love (and talent) lies in the game of golf. Her father, a successful insurance salesman, found the game very conducive to obtaining clients. Further, he found it an opportune way to bond with his daughter, so he taught her the game from an early age. Lilly's mother was a world-class track athlete in college who, after failing to qualify for

the 1972 Olympic games, retired from competition to open a small gym in Seattle. Both parents' outgoing personalities were gracefully passed on to young Lilly, and she had no problem finding friends. Despite her petite 5-foot-4 frame, she routinely drove a golf ball in excess of 250 yards during high school, and this, combined with proficient grades, allowed her to play college golf at the University of Arizona. Majoring in Kinesiology, she graduated in four years, but her primary plan was always to earn her card on the LPGA tour.

So, to what event can we attribute these two twains converging? During the spring semester of Lilly's senior year, 2003, an unfortunate event occurred. A routine seven iron from the rough left her with more than the normal amount of twinge in her left elbow. After finishing the round and going through a battery of medical exams, a fracture to the distal humerus was identified as the culprit. After 6 months of rehab and countless hours of practice, the inevitable conclusion was finally accepted. The drives of 260 yards were now 220 and the professional game was not to be.

It was during the summer of 2003, shortly following Tyler's graduation, that he was visiting Tucson for a job interview at an architectural design corporation. Like many high-powered executives, the interviewing vice president preferred to do as much work as possible on the golf course. Therefore, Tyler found himself waiting to hit on the 14th hole, feeling fairly inept as he watched the young lady in the next tee box line a drive straight down the middle of the fairway. Eight minutes later, he followed by slicing a ball deep into the trees that separated the 14th and 15th fairways. Grateful for the momentary break, he excused himself to find his ball. He did so, somewhat to his angst, in the middle of a clump of snarly grass, and attempted to swat it back into play. As he inevitably failed to do so and watched the ball skitter a few feet in front of him, it occurred to him that one could injure themselves with such a shot. Using his analytical mind, he followed that thought with possible solutions. Perhaps if the club had this... or was made like that... or if you had this bracing your arm....

Thirty yards away, in the middle of the 15th fairway, Lilly was (for the millionth time) frustrated at still being 210 yards from the pin. As she pulled a five wood from her bag, she happened to glance over and see a skinny, awkward fellow kneeling intently before a clump of grass and then critically examining his club. Curiosity getting the best of her, she approached him and said, "What on earth are you doing?"

And thus, Hack Back, Inc., was born.

At first, the idea was only that, an idea. A simple club designed for the hacker that occasionally found themselves in the trash (i.e., deep, snarly grass). The club had specially designed vertical grooves that helped cut the grass as it slashed through it and allowed for more of the club head to get to the actual ball. Tyler, with his father's help, created the first prototype in his garage and used it for a couple of rounds. However, the real test would take a real golfer. Thus, Lilly received the second such club. Skepticism remained high as she looked down into the deep rough at her ball on the fourth hole the following Saturday. Glancing around to make sure no one was watching, she took the "Slash" club out of the

bag and gave it a rip. Where she was expecting the normal twinge of pain from her old injury, she actually felt nothing. This was so amazing in itself that it took a full 10 seconds to realize the ball was on the green, 150 yards away. It took another 20 seconds for Lilly to decide she had found a career.

With Lilly's personality leading the way, a local pro shop in Tempe, Arizona, agreed to allow their professionals to try the club. Again, the results were completely unexpected and unanimously supportive. Word traveled quickly and soon the club was being sold in every golf shop in the Southwest. The original club was a stock seven iron. Soon, other clubs followed—all of them, in fact. Then, left-handed and lady's "I-Lash" clubs followed. This led to other ideas related to helping golfers out of the rough stuff. The focus soon shifted away from a simple escape tool to a new way of golf safety and recovery. A new line of arm and elbow braces, specifically designed to reduce the shock from attacking a ball surrounded by heavy grass, added to the product line. In the course of a year, Lilly and Tyler found their names, along with their merchandise, everywhere.

Roughly 6 months into the development of the first club, Tyler approached Lilly with the idea of becoming incorporated. He had taken a basic finance class in college and understood the idea of "unlimited liability." They briefly considered becoming a partnership, sharing equally in both gains and liabilities, but the advantages and safeguards afforded by the corporate framework led to the decision to incorporate. Lilly was the first to suggest Hack Back as the company name. She felt the name summed up the products perfectly in that they finally provided a "weapon" for the average golfer to fight back against the forces of nature.

1.2 Primary Markets and the Going-Public Process

Once a company makes the decision as to the type of firm it wishes to be, the decisions truly begin. In order to effectively understand the essentials of corporate finance, it becomes conducive to primarily examine *public* companies. There are several reasons for this that will be covered throughout the upcoming chapters, but to put it simply, ideas and theories just work better if we assume companies are large and publicly traded. However, don't take this to suggest that the material covered only applies to that segment of the business world. In fact, everything we will discuss applies to any company, just with varying caveats dependent on firm type. To move forward, a good first step is to learn a bit about the process that goes into taking a firm public.

1.2.1 Primary Versus Secondary Markets

When you hear the words "stock market," your mind most likely turns to thoughts associated with buying and selling stocks in some well-known corporation. If so, what you would be thinking of is something known as the

secondary market. It is on this market that the buying and selling of securities is carried out. However, those shares of stock have to come from somewhere. That "somewhere" is technically known as the **primary market**. The primary market is where shares of stock are first brought to the market and offered for sale to the public.

It is perhaps best explained with an analogy. Consider a bucket of water. The water level in the bucket is the number of shares of a publicly traded firm. That level is determined by the primary market. In other words, the primary market offers a stream of water that runs into the bucket but at irregular intervals. When it is finished, the level of water represents the market position of the firm. Then secondary market actions take over. Individual buyers and sellers can trade shares anyway they wish. In the example, this will cause the drops of water to move around in the bucket. However, no matter how much or how often each drop moves, there is still the same amount of water in the bucket. There is still the same number of shares outstanding. Therefore, to conclude, the primary market is where the shares and the value of the firm initially come from, while the secondary market determines how those shares (and the corresponding value) are spread out over various shareholders at any subsequent point in time.

While most of this book will be concerned with secondary markets, we first must address the origination of stock shares. The most popular method of primary issuance is an **initial public offering (IPO)**, which is, much as it sounds, a process that results in shares being offered to the public at large for the first time. Although it is not always the case, IPOs are often a result of a firm that is suffering from excess success. That's right, you read it correctly. The firm is simply doing too well. The firm's resources cannot keep up with the excessive demand for the firm's product. Firms that cannot produce at the level required by customer demand face several distinct options. First, they can borrow money privately through a bank or some other like-minded financial institution. However, this likely does not generate enough capital at a reasonable expense. A second option is that the firm can solicit private equity investments, which are equity arrangements that allow the firm to maintain private status.

IPOs represent an option of obtaining capital on a much grander scale. Throughout the next sections, we will detail this process.

> LOOK IT UP: A firm can issue stock multiple times. However, they only "go public" once. Any equity issuances after this point would be from an already public firm. Look up the term seasoned equity offerings (SEOs) to get more information.

1.2.2 Venture Capital

Firms that wish to go public often need financial help in the going-public process. They often receive this help through a third-party intermediary, known as a **venture capitalist**. Venture capital funds represent a type of private equity. These funds create an investment vehicle that pools funds to invest primarily in projects that are too risky for the standard capital markets or bank loans. One of the primary functions of a venture capitalist is to provide capital to the firm to assist in the process of going public, which is a costly undertaking. Venture capitalists can take several forms, from individual investors to a large corporate entity, but the basic idea is the same throughout.

The funding provided generally does not come free of charge, of course. Venture capitalists often offer funds to relatively young, growing firms in exchange for shares of the company stock. Often, since they are so heavily invested in the company, the venture capitalist also takes an active role, such as assuming seats on the board of directors of the company. However, the investments are typically not long term, and the venture capitalist usually sells their shares or "exits" the company shortly following the IPO.

1.2.3 Underwriters

In most instances, firms don't actually take themselves public. Rather, they use another intermediary, known as an **underwriter**. In fact, they often use more than one underwriter, but there is usually one "lead" underwriter and others join them in creating an underwriting syndicate. An underwriter is a financial institutional that specializes, among other things, in taking companies public. The firm makes their desire to be a publicly traded company known to one or more underwriting companies, who then vie for their services. Then, the issuing company chooses whom they want to issue their shares. Often the quality of the issuing company is related to the quality (or reputation) of the underwriter. As in most businesses, more reputable organizations are in higher demand, and issues subsequently "backed" by those organizations are perceived as higher quality by potential investors.

LOOK IT UP: Notice it says above that the firm *usually* doesn't take the firm public themselves. Usually isn't the same as never. In fact, there is a specific name for an offering done without the guidance of an investment firm. It's called a direct public offering (DPO). See what you can find about the differences between an IPO and a DPO.

Once the company chooses their underwriter, they actually sell the shares to the underwriter. The company must determine the amount of capital needed to maintain a level of production that satisfies consumer demand. In simpler terms, the firm must decide the market value of the firm. This total amount is then divided in chunks called **shares**. Therefore, each share of stock represents fractional ownership in the firm. These fractional pieces of ownership are sold to the underwriter at a predetermined price. This price is carefully negotiated to ensure the issuing firm receives a satisfactory price while being reasonably assured the shares can be sold to the public at a price above this negotiated price.

Once the firm sells the shares to the underwriter, they sit back and wait. Obviously, that is a vast simplification, but the point is crudely made. The underwriter is then responsible for marketing the firm and the upcoming IPO, gauging public demand, and using this to come up with a value per share they can charge when the firm goes public.

This type of process where the underwriter pays the firm a negotiated fixed amount is called a **fixed (or firm) commitment**. In this situation, the underwriter takes the risk that the shares will not sell or will sell at a lower value than desired. On the other hand, a **best efforts** offer is much as it sounds in that the underwriter must make their best effort to sell as many shares as possible at a stated issue price. Therefore, strictly speaking, these types of issues aren't underwritten; however, that detail is often overlooked. Relative to fixed commitments, the number of best efforts issues is very small. Of late, there has been considerable discussion of a third option, known as a **Dutch Auction** offer. With this type of offering, potential investors submit bids of what they would pay for a share of the company's stock (and for how many shares they would pay it). The issue price would then be the highest price at which all shares would be sold. A unique feature of the Dutch Auction process is that some bidders will actually end up paying less than they bid. This method of going public is still relatively uncommon in the US equity markets; however, it is used regularly in issuing treasury debt securities.

LOOK IT UP: You may wonder why there has been considerable discussion of the Dutch Auction IPOs over the last several years. Try to figure out why. Here's a hint: you will likely have your answer as fast as you can "Google" it.

1.2.4 IPO Paperwork

The first piece of paperwork required in an IPO is the declaration to the **Securities and Exchange Commission** (SEC) of the desire of the firm to issue public shares. The SEC is the federal agency charged with regulating US securities markets. The SEC must then agree to the issuance. A major hurdle for the company in this process is getting their **prospectus** accepted. This document details the operations and financial condition of the firm. Also, the firm's need for public funds must be justified in this document. The SEC makes no judgment about the quality of the firm or the value of the stock, but rather ensures the document follows rules pertaining to full disclosure and many other issues.

LOOK IT UP: Want to know what a prospectus looks like? The SEC makes every prospectus available and free to the public at http://www.sec.gov/edgar.shtml. The form number the SEC attaches to a prospectus always starts with 424. See if you can find Google's prospectus from 2004.

While awaiting SEC approval, the next step is for the firm to issue a **red herring**. The red herring is so named because the cover page is stamped in red ink, which indicates the details are preliminary and final approval to offer has not been obtained. The red herring contains information about the issuance but excludes specifics, such as the exact price, along with select other pieces of information. The goal is to generate interest in the stock offering. The underwriter circulates this document to potential investors, particularly large institutional investors who may wish to buy large blocks of shares. This preliminary prospectus will be updated prior to issuance in response to changing market conditions and information obtained from the process of gauging demand. Upon SEC approval, the prospectus will be finalized and the underwriter can begin selling shares to the public.

The issue is usually formally announced in mainstream newspapers and other outlets with a **tombstone**. Once you've gotten to this point, the SEC has approved all registration materials, and the underwriters have arrived at the price at which they feel the shares should be sold. The tombstone is named appropriately in that it looks like... a tombstone. It is generally sparse on details and directs the reader to the full prospectus or red herring. The actual price at which the shares will be first sold, called the **offer price**, is detailed on this document, along with the number of shares issued, the date of issuance, and the underwriters. As a note of interest, the tombstone is often made public after the issuance has occurred.

The difference between the price the company receives for the shares from the underwriter and the offer price is called the underwriter **spread**. This spread represents the profit for the underwriter. There used to be considerable uncertainty surrounding the level of the spread, but for the last several years, the spread has become relatively uniform at 7 % of the offering price.

1.2.5 After Issuance

An underlying concern with a private firm turning public is that the original ownership's contribution to the firm's direction may be marginalized. However, it is often the case that the existing ownership structure (i.e., the founders or private owners) retain a large number of the public shares. In fact, they most often retain controlling ownership in the firms by holding more than 50 % of outstanding shares and often significantly more than that.

While an in-depth analysis is outside the purview of this text, what happens after issuance is very interesting. Since the early 1980s, average first-day returns have been significantly positive. In fact, to be precise, first-day returns have, on average, had significant positive *excess* returns in relation to the market. This indicates the offer price is lower than the market-determined value. Why is this? Well, that's a detailed questioned with a detailed answer, but let's just leave it with this fulfilling solution: we really don't know.

Newly issued stocks are very sensitive to market pressures and investor sentiment. That's pretty much just a fancy way of saying that recently issued securities are very volatile when faced with something the market doesn't expect. An example of this would be when "insiders" sell the stock shortly after issuance. Consider the following scenario. A greedy owner of firm going public retains 60 % of the shares. If he sells 5 %, he can still retain a majority ownership while probably pocketing a large amount of money. However, the real issue is that other investors can see this transaction and interpret it, justifiably, as a negative signal. If the owner feels the need to sell, why shouldn't the average investor who has no knowledge of the inner workings of the firm? Therefore, this has the potential to create a massive sell-off of the stock, which is not a good thing.

The end result of this is that most issues have something called a **lockup agreement**. A lockup agreement stipulates that the "insiders" of an issuing firm must not sell any part of their position for a period of time. This effectively ties the motivations of the original owners of the firm to the firm's performance. Although this period of time has also become somewhat standardized at 180 days following the underwriting, there are exceptions to this.

IN THE REAL WORLD

The year-end income statement for Hack Back, Inc., in 2006 was a puzzle to Tyler and Lilly. Demand had never been higher. Their new line of "Mash and Bash" hybrid clubs had debuted to incredible demand, while a new gel-enhanced wrist brace had been a hit with the over-60 customers. Overall, sales had increased by 241 % over 2005. However, their net income was barely surviving in the black. It didn't make sense to the two entrepreneurs, so they decided to call in help. They realized that to compete in the competitive world of commercial golf equipment, they had to have financial expertise. Therefore, they hired their first CFO.

Thus entered Mr. Dubarb Freeman. "Dube" Freeman, as he was known to his few close friends, was an old-school advisor. He had graduated from Ohio State with an MBA in 1974. Since then, he had held many positions, ranging from staff accountant to CFO of a midsized logging firm. Freeman's eccentricities provided cover for the fact that he harbored a wealth of financial knowledge inside his graying head. His daily uniform consisted of khaki shorts, untucked golf shirts, and an ever-present scruffy beard. He had only four loves in his life: LSU baseball, his wife, and his two Skye Terriers. Tyler had taken the unenviable

task of interviewing a binder full of applicants and was impressed with Freeman's credentials but more so with his attitude. He had never met anyone who tried so hard to downplay his potential contributions to the firm. It seemed he did everything he could to talk his way out of the job.

He was hired on the spot.

Freeman's first task with Hack Back was to carefully examine the accounting statements in order to determine the cause of the low profits. It was less than a week before he asked for a meeting. They met in Lilly's office on Friday afternoon. Mr. Freeman began with a quizzical statement.

"Well folks, it's simple really. You're growing yourself broke."

Tyler and Lilly looked blankly at each other.

"You're going to have to elaborate, I'm afraid," Lilly said, after realizing there was no additional information forthcoming.

"Well, it's like this…," the financial guru began to patiently explain.

Over the next 2 hours, Freeman carefully laid out the reasons for the poor bottom-line results following a high-demand year. First, he illustrated with an example. In May of 2006, a golf dealership in Boca Raton, FL, ordered 400 complete sets of the "Mash and Bash" hybrids. There were nowhere near that many completed sets at the headquarters in Arizona, so a search began in earnest. The 400 sets were found: 100 borrowed from a club in Indianapolis, IN; 50 from a warehouse in San Diego, CA; 25 from a private dealer in Key Largo, FL; 75 from a large corporate retail sports store in Clearwater, FL; and the remaining 150 from corporate headquarters. The order was completed and the Boca Raton dealership was very pleased with the product. However, Freeman found that 40 % of the profit from the sale was offset by the scramble to fill the order.

In another example, Hack Back was asked to deliver 2,000 elbow braces to a large retail center in Detroit, MI. The company quickly kicked manufacturing into overtime to produce the braces, but still could not meet the deadline and was then forced to get rid of the braces at less than market value. In yet another example, Hack Back missed out on a grand opportunity to promote a product during a nationally televised golf tournament due to a communication failure in the obsolete computer system.

"In short," Freeman finished, "you simply do not have the resources to keep up with the demand for your product."

"Well, that shouldn't be a problem," Lilly chimed in, "we'll just call Phil at the bank and get a loan. We have strong credit. How much do you think we need?"

"I estimate somewhere around $80 million, minimum," Freeman deadpanned.

Tyler choked on his half-swallowed gulp of coffee while Lilly started mentally second-guessing Tyler's hiring practices. However, Freeman quickly assured them he was very serious about the amount and went on to explain the incredible sum. It was Mr. Freeman's belief that the company should avoid patchwork fixes that would only work for the short run. The firm had a product base the public was eagerly seeking, and if the firm wanted to meet its potential, they needed a complete system upgrade. In order to keep up with customer demands and maximize profits, he believed production plants needed to be overhauled,

upgraded, and expanded. Also, additional workforce needed to be hired, existing office space needed to be renovated, the firm's public image needed a marketing makeover, and virtually all existing equipment needed to be replaced. That, along with various regulatory fees and overhead costs, added up to approximately $80 million.

"How on earth can we get that kind of money?" Tyler stammered.

"You could go public," Freeman responded, staring intently at his young boss to judge his response.

"What are you talking about? We already sell to the public," Lilly said.

"I think he's talking about being a publicly traded company, Lilly," Tyler corrected, turning to Freeman. "Do you really think we could do that?"

And so, Dubarb Freeman spent the rest of the afternoon telling them why he indeed thought they could. Then, for the rest of the evening, he answered their questions and assuaged their fears. Then, for the rest of the night, he instructed them on the mechanics. And finally, as they ate breakfast on Saturday morning, they decided to take the leap.

Two months later, they had an investment banker, who suggested they issue six million shares of stock. Of those, four million would be retained by Tyler and Lilly, thus ensuring they maintain control of the firm. Six months later, they had the approval of the SEC to issue common stock. A bit over 1 year later, they issued the common stock at $40.00 per share. They were assigned the ticker HBCK and began trading on the NASDAQ exchange at 9:00 A.M. on December 14, 2007. Eight hours later, Freeman met with Tyler and Lilly in the conference room of the Arizona corporate offices. A bottle of Krug 1982 champagne was uncorked, glasses were filled, and a toast was performed.

Then Freeman cleared his throat and spoke, "We better start working. There's a lot to do."

ALTERNATE ENDINGS

1. ***Why do you think Tyler and Lilly brought in Dubarb Freeman? What advantages does expertise in finance bring to a young, rapidly growing company? Or, put differently, what are the dangers of not incorporating financial knowledge in business operations.***
2. ***What would happen if Tyler and Lilly decided to not go public? What would change about their future prospects? For example, what if they decided to become a private partnership or just stay a private corporation? What limitations would they face?***
3. ***What if the firm was unable to find an underwriter that would agree to do a fixed offering? Does Hack Back have any other options? If so, what are the strengths and weaknesses of these options?***
4. ***What might happen if Tyler and Lilly failed to retain majority ownership?***
5. ***Imagine for a moment that you were a fly on the wall during the all-night conversation regarding going public. Suppose at around 1:30 A.M. Freeman***

said "Okay, now it's time to bring up a very important issue. Let's talk about SOX and the effect this should have on your decision."

How do you imagine that conversation went? What were the positives and negatives that would have been brought out in discussion?

1.3 The Goal of the Firm

1.3.1 The Only Appropriate Goal

Those who manage the activities of the firm are responsible for generating income for those that own the firm. This is a fairly straightforward process in certain types of firms, such as sole proprietorships, because those two parties are generally the same. Thus, there is no chance for a disconnect between benefits and those who benefit. However, this is generally not the case with corporations, particularly those that are publicly traded. Therefore, we need to take a closer look at how this fairly straightforward notion plays out in a corporate setting.

The appropriate goal of the firm can be summed up simply with the following: ***maximize shareholder wealth***. To fully understand, consider one word at a time. First, "maximize" simply means to make as big as possible. "Shareholder" refers to anyone that has a monetary commitment to the firm and serves to benefit from firm profits and suffer from firm losses. Simply put, they are the owners of the firm. Finally, "wealth" represents the owners' amount of money. So, putting it all together: *the goal of the firm is to make the owners as rich as possible*.

There are two cautionary statements to remember. Please don't confuse simple with unimportant. The three words that made up the goal and the supporting understanding of the concept is the guiding light in finance, the holy grail of all corporate financial concepts. Our utter existence within a firm is to constantly make decisions that ensure this notion is upheld. While the specific details may be much more complicated, throughout the remainder of this text, it is crucial that we relate every decision we make to the appropriate goal of the firm. Therefore, we have an uncomplicated decision rule. If the decision results in making the shareholders better off, we follow through. Otherwise, we do not.

We also must be careful to not associate an uncomplicated goal with an uncomplicated attainment of that goal. In fact, the objective of maximizing wealth is actually impossible to *directly* accomplish. It is akin to asking how tall the tallest thing could ever be. Without parameters or a tangible model, actually finding the point of maximization is impossible. Thus, a large part of our journey through the corporate finance process will be finding a way to actually transform an impossible-to-answer question into a solvable problem.

1.3.2 Other Goals

Before we move on, it is prudent to examine other goals commonly misused as the primary objective of the firm. This is not to insinuate these are "bad" goals, but rather that each has shortcomings not found in the true goal of maximizing shareholder wealth. Perhaps the most common goal publicly announced is "**profit maximization**." While this sounds like a very worthwhile and noble goal, it is important to take a closer look. First of all, *profit* is a difficult concept to definitively define. While everyone knows the general meaning, it is much more difficult to come up with a mathematical definition. For example, net income is probably the most often defined income measure, but it is certainly not the only possibility. Others include operating cash flow, gross profits, and *EBIT* (all of which will be covered in Chap. 2).

Also, these values are derived from accounting statements, and accounting statements are similar to snowflakes in that no two are exactly alike. The point is this: there is no consistent, clear-cut definition of profit. Therefore, when using it as the focus of the firm, it is easy to imagine managers of the company attempting to hit a moving target.

Now, should we convince every company in the world to accept a common definition of "profit," then perhaps the goal would become appropriate. Of course, that is unlikely to happen. Also, profit maximization is largely a short-term goal. Profits are most often reported on a quarterly or yearly basis. As we will discuss at length a bit later in this chapter, a successful firm likely needs to examine goals over a longer period of time.

Another goal often adopted is to maximize **earnings per share (EPS)**. EPS is the profit the company generates for each share of stock over a period of time. An issue with this goal is that it is also a short-term goal. More importantly, the number is easily manipulated. EPS is an accounting ratio, most often calculated as net income divided by the number of shares outstanding. As with any ratio, there are two ways to increase the quotient. The first is an increasing net income, which is generally a good thing and should be consistent with maximizing shareholder wealth, although that is not always the case. However, EPS also increases as the number of shares outstanding decreases.

Therefore, a possible method for manipulating this quotient is for a firm to implement a stock "buyback," which results in the company reducing the number of shares outstanding. By doing so, the company has effectively concentrated the earnings value by spreading it over fewer shares while artificially making the company appear healthier financially. This process is an example of earnings manipulation, which often arises due to the extreme pressures on firms to meet their earnings estimates. Failure to do so is usually interpreted as a negative signal to the market at large and a decrease in stock value may result.

LOOK IT UP: What is described above is actually just scratching the surface of the larger issue of earnings manipulation, which can result in serious penalties for both the firm and shareholders. For example, look up the case of Gateway's upper-level management being charged with manipulating earnings in 2000. More recently, there was considerable coverage of the General Electric and the SEC contention that they artificially inflated earnings for the majority of the decade beginning in 2000. See if you can find how that situation was resolved.

There are many other potential goals a company may adopt. Some are very ambiguous, such as growth, success, or remaining ethical. Again, there is certainly nothing wrong with having these goals intertwined in the fabric of the firm. In fact, a company would most likely fail without having these aspirations. However, maximizing shareholder wealth encompasses all of these goals and allows us to skip all of those ambiguous, happy-sounding words.

Some other goals are relative in nature, such as beating competitors or the industry average. Again, such motives are admirable, but a company that gets overly distracted in beating other companies will eventually start making decisions that are not in the best interest of shareholders. Not to be a broken record, but, again, if the firm continually maximizes shareholder wealth, it is highly likely they will also outperform at least the majority of their comparison groups.

1.4 Ownership and Control

Let's next examine the two parties of concern a bit more in depth. First, we will discuss the owners of the firm. As we know by now, in a publicly traded firm, any individual who buys at least one share of stock in the firm is an owner of the said firm. Therefore, it is possible that a single firm can have millions of owners. Each of those owners has an expectation of the firm and has invested with the desire to experience some degree of monetary gain.

On the other hand, those who manage may have a variety of their own motivations. The management structure begins at the top with the **board of directors**, which is elected at annual shareholder meetings. Whether you own one share or one million shares, you have the right to attend these annual shareholder meetings and vote to elect the directors of the firm. This addresses the notion of the goal of the firm. Since the appropriate goal is to benefit shareholders, it would stand to reason that those shareholders have some measure of control over the activities of the firm. The election of directors is the vehicle through which the shareholders can exercise control over the activities of the firm.

Unfortunately, from the shareholder's viewpoint, this control isn't as helpful as you may think. On the surface it seems fair to vote for those who control the company just as citizens get to vote for political leaders that control the country. However, there is one very important difference. In political elections each person gets one vote, while in corporate elections each *share* gets one vote. In other words, the size of ownership is of paramount importance in these types of elections. Therefore, the majority owners almost always get the directors they want elected. As a simple example, let's assume you own 50 shares of stock in Home Depot, while Mr. Rich Moneypants owns 38 million shares. You can take the time out of your life to catch a flight to Atlanta for their annual meeting if you like, but your 50 votes are highly unlikely to matter when put next to Mr. Moneypants' 38 million votes.

Continuing along those lines, it's also important to know there are a couple of ways that voting can take place. One is known as **cumulative voting**, which means all directors are elected at once. Let's assume the company in question needs to elect five directors at this particular annual meeting. If voting is cumulative, this means the top five vote getters will be those elected to the board. The alternative approach is **straight voting**, in which the directors are elected one at a time. Therefore, if five directors are to be elected, in essence five separate elections are held, with the top vote getter in each separate election obtaining the seat on the board.

LOOK IT UP: Want to know what the board of some major companies look like? All major public companies elect their directors at annual meetings, just as we say. Prove it to yourself by looking up the board of directors of General Electric and Toyota. You should be able to find them on each firm's corporate website: www.ge.com and www.toyota-global.com.

These two voting systems have interesting implications for the involvement of minority shareholders or those who own a relatively small portion of the company. If a corporation uses straight voting, minority shareholders have essentially no voting power. The majority ownership will simply use their very large number of shares to elect their favorite in each separate election. Cumulative voting is a bit more favorable for the small shareholders. It is possible that one of the latter directors could be of their choosing, particularly if there are a large number of seats available. However, as a practical matter, neither voting style gives minority shareholders substantial control over the management structure. Of course, it could be argued that this isn't necessarily an injustice since it provides the most control to those who have the most at stake.

There is one other thing that needs to be discussed related to shareholder voting. **Proxy voting** is used sometimes as the small shareholders' response to being effectively denied the right to control the direction of the firm at annual meetings. Proxy voting means that individuals can sign away the right to vote their shares to someone else. Therefore, if that individual can get enough shareholders to give them the right to vote their shares, it may become possible to get a director elected without all these small shareholders having to attend the annual meeting. Naturally, the majority shareholders aren't particularly fond of this happening, so proxy voting sometimes leads to **proxy fights**, which are fairly self-explanatory.

LOOK IT UP: There have been several examples of juicy proxy fights. For example, check out the debate that ensued when a large institutional investor, Relational Investors, LLC, threatened a proxy fight with Home Depot in late 2006. The issue is not specific to just large, well-known firms, however. See if you can find out what happened to Hebron, KY-based Pomeroy IT Solutions, Inc., when their largest shareholder was unhappy with the current leadership structure.

IN THE REAL WORLD

Shortly following Hack Back's IPO, Tyler and Lilly began to take a more active role in the activities of the entire corporation. The first major undertaking was to create a management organization that could handle the day-to-day activities. Hack Back had become, in the course of months, one of the leading companies in their segment of the retail golfing industry. Therefore, it became important to run the company in a more corporate fashion. Tyler and Lilly both understood their strengths very well, and it was an easy decision to put Lilly as the most prominent face of the organization. It was her job to design and implement the corporate image to the marketplace. Tyler preferred to stay in the background and, as such, oversaw internal operations such as the design of products and all administrative issues. As always, major decisions regarding the firm would require both of their inputs and approval before moving forward.

Early in the life of Hack Back, Lilly and Tyler had created a board of directors to help guide the firm. The first director was Steven Austin, Ph.D., who had previously been president of Northwestern Arizona University for nearly a decade. The second, Susan Harding, had an MBA from Harvard and had been in the executive structure at Apple for 12 years. Bobby Dennison was elected third, following 8 years as CFO of Calloway Golf. He had learned early on that retirement didn't suit his personality, so he was all too happy to take the position. Finally, Edward Collison, Ph.D., was elected after choosing to leave a very lucrative position as manager of Vanguard's Capital Value Mutual Fund and downsized with his wife to Tucson. Their two children had recently departed to colleges of their choosing, so the quiet life of Arizona appealed to them immensely.

These four individuals, along with Tyler and Lilly, made up Hack Back's board of directors. After the firm went public, Dubarb Freeman was retained as the company's CFO, and he quickly hired four others to round out the finance department of Hack Back. All other areas of the company, from marketing to human resources, quickly took form, and by mid-2008 they were running

relatively smoothly. On August 28, 2008, Tyler and Lilly called a meeting of the five members of the finance team to discuss the direction and goals of the firm.

"We are getting some pressure from the board to give the shareholders some kind of indication of what we are doing for them," Tyler began. "They feel we need to come up with some type of goal that we can announce. We're here today to go over some of their suggestions."

"If I may," Freeman interrupted, "there is only one appropriate goal."

"Which is?" Lilly asked.

"We have to make them as rich as we can."

The two primary owners were, by now, well accustomed to Freeman's no-nonsense approach to things, but they still failed to find a quick enough response. So, again, Mr. Freeman broke into lecture mode. He spent 15 minutes detailing the dangers of misplaced goals before concluding.

"So, the only appropriate goal of any firm is to maximize shareholder wealth. My suggestion is this. We wait to make projections until we have a better idea what we are dealing with. We have many decisions to first make that will be crucial to the longevity and financial success of Hack Back. If you must make a statement, make it broad and similar to what I have just discussed. Say that we will make every decision based upon what is best for the shareholder over the long run."

After a thoughtful pause, the other six individuals in the room looked at each other and collectively shrugged. Then Lilly took the initiative.

"Okay, Dube. So, what are these crucial decisions you're talking about?"

ALTERNATE ENDINGS

1. *Suppose Hack Back made their goal to obtain EPS of $.50/share. At the end of the year, however, they had net income of only $2.5 million dollars. What is their EPS? Should they choose to be unethical, how could they manipulate this figure to make it look better? What specifically must they do to reach their "goal"? What about the same question, only they make the goal to reach profits of $4 million? Why is that not good enough?*
2. *Two days later, Tyler reports to the board of directors that Hack Back is going to wait before issuing any statements of goals. Dr. Austin waves his hand to speak:*

   > *"I certainly understand the sentiment, Tyler," he says. "However, the unfortunate reality of the public corporate world is that analysts are always hard at work making goals for us. When they project our earnings, we automatically have to try to reach them or the market will punish us.*

   He has a point. Discuss how the firm should view professional analyst estimates and the resulting effect of meeting (or failing to meet) these "goals."

1.5 The Corporate Finance Process

The process of running a corporation is not a short-run issue. It starts as such, of course, but soon the company has to start focusing on long-term financial planning. As such, there are a couple of major questions that must be answered repeatedly. You will learn throughout the text that the real-world financial process is rather complicated. However, the basic ideas behind it are not and the logical first step is to introduce the major questions that must be addressed.

1.5.1 Capital Budgeting

Which projects do we want to undertake? is the first question that needs to be answered. Before we get specific on the motivation behind this question, let's take a moment to discuss the term "project," which we will use many times throughout the text. A project is simply anything the company chooses to spend money on in the desire to improve the firm. This could be just about anything, from buildings to machinery or even employees. In other words, it's anything the company invests in with the motivation of generating income for the firm and its shareholders.

The question of which project in which to invest is succinctly known as **capital budgeting**. Capital budgeting requires many steps, but at the end of it all, the objective is to simply look for projects that meet one criterion: *they are worth more than they cost*. On the surface this seems a very straightforward proposition, but unfortunately there are significant complexities involved in the financial definitions for the terms "worth" and "cost."

In order to find projects that are financially beneficial for the firm, each project must be examined in several ways. For example, you certainly have to consider the expected returns of the project, but we must also evaluate the risk associated with those estimated returns. Our task for much of this text is to create a mathematical framework through which the true "worth" of the project can be compared to the true "cost."

1.5.2 Capital Structure

There is a natural follow-up question to capital budgeting. Once the firm chooses the projects they want to take on, they must then find a way to pay for them. Therefore, the second question is this: *where do we get the money to fund the projects?* Obviously one option is to use internal funds. However, for most firms the available amount of internal funds will be insufficient to meet the monetary demand of large projects. In addition, any firm is reluctant to exhaust all excess reserves in the event they may be needed to offset any unforeseen financial shortfalls.

Therefore, the company must look elsewhere for sources of external funding. There are two general sources of this funding.

The first is through debt markets. A firm can either choose to go the traditional route of borrowing money and approach a bank. This is called private debt. However, many firms would still have a difficult time raising the large amounts of money needed to fund certain projects. Therefore, an alternative is to issue public debt. This means, in a very basic sense, that the firm wants to borrow money from outside public investors. These investors can be individuals or other institutions, and there are typically a large number of them.

The other general funding option is through equity markets, something we've already covered a bit. Should a firm that has already gone public decide they need additional funding, they can choose to issue additional shares of stock. This can take several forms, but the most prevalent by far is predictably known as common equity. Issuing equity is vastly different from issuing debt. While both have the same end result of the company obtaining capital, the resulting obligations to the firm are very different. Public debt represents a *contractual* obligation to the firm's future cash flows. In other words, the money must be paid back. This is not necessarily true with equity. In exchange for buying shares, each buyer expects a financial return on their investment, but it is more of a *promissory* relationship than a contractual one. It then becomes the issuing firm's responsibility to provide this return, and if they fail, the investors will likely retrieve their money and invest it elsewhere. Of course, the resulting decrease in demand for the firm's stock will certainly do very little to maximize shareholder wealth.

Both debt and equity have to be closely examined because the specific mixture of the two is the firm's **capital structure**, which is just a fancy way of answering the question of where the money comes from. Therefore, this becomes one of the, and perhaps the biggest, decisions the company must undertake.

1.5.3 Working Capital Management

There is a third aspect to corporate finance. **Working capital management** describes how a company manages their day-to-day operations. In other words, once a firm has decided which projects to take and how to pay for them, it then has to ensure the projects are implemented properly. Working capital management covers things such as the appropriate amount of inventory to maintain, accounts receivable levels, and net working capital. Capital budgeting and capital structure are long-term financial decisions, while working capital management is a series of short-term decisions. Since the focus of this text is primarily on long-term financial planning, less emphasis will be given to working capital management, at least directly. Rather, discussion of short-term financial concerns will be intertwined into our discussions of long-term decisions throughout the entire process.

IN THE REAL WORLD

Dubarb Freeman took a drink from his "World's Greatest Grandpa" mug, then sat back and crossed his right leg over his left.

"In order to accomplish our goal of maximizing shareholder wealth, we have to do one basic thing," he said. "We have to continue to ensure the company grows. We cannot simply relax and assume the current level of sales will continue, and even if they do, it is not enough. We owe it to those people who have invested in Hack Back to generate a return on their investment. And this is going to benefit you as well. Don't forget that you are the two largest shareholders in this company. As the company goes, so goes your net worth."

"Well, while that is comforting to hear," Tyler said, "we are more concerned about the specific steps needed in this process you're talking about. It's all well and good to talk about grand visions and turning them into money, but we need to know exactly what has to happen."

"Well, that's where we come in," Freeman said, sweeping his arm towards the other four employees in the room. "I have taken the initiative of separating our team. Stewart and Marilyn will work on one aspect of the plan, while Brandon and Jane will take the other. I, of course, will oversee the entire process."

"Okay, we don't have a problem with 'divide and conquer'," Lilly spoke up, "but we don't know what you're dividing and what we're trying to conquer."

"Marilyn, why don't you tell them about what you and Stewart will be working on?" Freeman responded.

Marilyn Kramer was slim and elegant, with deep auburn hair and a slightly nasal voice. She was outgoing and had more friends than time for them. Her shortcoming included impatience and a weakness for designer clothing. More importantly, she had graduated at the top of her class from the University of Maryland and had been lured to Hack Back over several other opportunities.

"Sure," she said. "We are working on the capital budgeting aspect of our financial plan. That just means we are actively looking for investment opportunities that will benefit the company. We all know the company has overgrown its current structures and machinery."

Tyler and Lilly nodded in agreement and Marilyn paused for a breath before continuing.

"We also need more employees to keep up with demand. It is our job to identify the best investment opportunities to meet those needs and allow us to grow as an organization. And this is not a one-time thing, but rather is an ongoing process, as we will constantly be evaluating potential projects trying to identify those that will most benefit the firm."

"That makes sense, abstractly," Lilly said, "but can you give me specifics of what goes into this?"

"Sure," Stewart Madick chimed in, not to be completely overshadowed by his pit bull partner. He was her elder by nearly a dozen years, having worked his way up the ladder at a local hardware firm in his native Boise, Idaho. The allure of going to warmer weather had been enough to get him to pack his bags and his girlfriend when offered the job. While not nearly as outspoken as the younger

Marilyn, he had a quiet confidence bolstered by his years of experience. His receding hairline and slight paunch also spoke of his years of experience, but he preferred to let his knowledge obtained on the job speak for itself.

"The first step is to identify areas where the firm needs the most urgent attention. Then, the actual selection of projects first requires understanding all the available options. Once we're through with that, we will then examine the expected benefits and costs associated with each option. Finally, we will use well-established capital budgeting techniques to obtain, accept, or reject decisions for each potential project."

"Then Jane and I take over," Brandon interjected.

"And what exactly is your part in this?" Tyler questioned, as he and Lilly both turned their attention to the other duo.

"Well, we have the hard part," Brandon answered, grinning good naturedly at the other team. "Jane and I have to find the money to pay for those projects they are going to identify as the best."

Brandon Kennedy was an All-American Lacrosse player at Duke University. He had majored in communication and had worked for 3 years in a marketing firm. Then he realized his temperament would fit much better in the business world, so he went back to Duke to get his MBA, where he had excelled as a leader of his cohort. Having just graduated the past spring, he couldn't believe his luck in climbing aboard the new public firm. His time spent working in the marketing world put his age somewhere between Marilyn and Stewart's. Of the four, he was easily the most comfortable in front of a crowd and had a natural ability to pull the audience into what he was trying to communicate. He stood just a shade over 6 ft and had the manicured good looks befitting his upper-class roots.

"What are our options?" Tyler asked. "I thought that was the whole reason for going public, to get money to make the firm more formidable."

"Well, that was certainly part of it," Jane answered, "but that money is not without cost. Also, it is going to run out sooner or later, and the way we expect this company to grow, sooner is the better guess. Therefore, we also have to think about alternative options."

Jane Middleton rounded out the team and it was appropriate that she was the last to speak. Born a certifiable genius, her 164 IQ had always put her in a class with those much older. It also didn't help that she had the perpetual cherub face that made her appear younger than she actually was. As such, she had grown up with few close friends. After running from her intelligence for years, she finally accepted it as a gift. She had graduated from high school in Des Moines at age 16 and then from the University of Iowa at 20. She had been planning to go back for her Ph.D. when she ran across the ad for the position at Hack Back. For the first time in her life, she went with instinct and applied. Freeman had immediately recognized her unique talents, particularly in analyzing quantitative data, and had hired her immediately. Jane turned 21 the day after she had moved to Arizona and had spent her birthday unpacking boxes. She was still making adjustments, but her coworkers had been welcoming, and she was getting more comfortable in her surroundings daily.

"I'm guessing that banks aren't the best option, given how Dube responded to that suggestion last year," Lilly quipped with a thin smile.

"Well, banks are certainly an option for smaller amounts," Brandon spoke up, "but, smaller doesn't mean ten thousand anymore. It means a million. However, that will still likely not be enough for larger projects either. We are probably going to be talking about tens of millions of dollars fairly soon."

Mr. Freeman quickly threw a glance at the two young owners. However, Tyler and Lilly appeared nonplussed.

"Don't worry, Dube," Tyler said. "We've accepted the fact that we are way in over our heads. We'll freak out on our own time."

"Anyway," Brandon interjected, "there are other options for getting funds, including to issue more equity."

"Another IPO?" Lilly asked.

"Sort of," Brandon responded, "but that's getting ahead of ourselves. We will cross that bridge when and if we get there. Right now, it is our job," he toggled his thumb between himself and Jane, "to identify potential sources of funds, paying particular attention to the costs associated with each."

"And then we pick one to go with when they identify suitable projects?" Tyler queried, pointing at Marilyn and Stewart.

Jane answered. "Each project will likely draw from more than one capital source, but you have the general idea."

Freeman roused himself from deep in his chair and spoke.

"Then, it becomes my job to put the teams and their decisions together. They can go a long way individually, but eventually, the two decisions... of where to get money and where to spend it... have to be decided upon simultaneously."

Alternate Endings

1. ***What if the finance team at Hack Back decided to forego the processes outlined and simply takes the first decent option? What could happen in that case and why would it not be advisable?***
2. ***What if Lilly said, "I think we should just focus on what we are already doing and just do it better. Let's forget about trying to do new stuff!" What do you think of this comment?***

Concept Questions

1. **Corporations** Name at least two advantages associated with a corporation. What are the primary disadvantages?
2. **Sole proprietorships and partnerships** What are the primary disadvantages to both the sole proprietorship and partnership forms of business organizations? What are potential benefits?
3. **Agency problems** Bob Thomas is the manager of MLP, Inc., a publicly traded firm. Last year, he chose to forego a valuable project so he could give himself a

larger bonus. What did Bob create? How do you think issues such as Bob's selfishness at the expense of shareholders can be mitigated?

4. **Agency problems** Publicly traded companies are likely to have many different owners. Private companies, however, have relatively few owners. Does this mean that agency problems do not exist for privately held corporations? If so, why? If not, give specific examples of how agency problems could occur in this setting.
5. **Sarbanes-Oxley** What is the motivation behind the legislation? What does its implementation mean to publicly held corporations?
6. **Primary markets** What is the difference between primary and secondary markets? Give an example of each.
7. **Initial public offerings** What are the primary "ingredients" in the IPO process? Describe each in detail.
8. **Venture capital and underwriters** Describe two financial intermediaries that often help the issuing firms in the going-public process. What roles do each play?
9. **Initial public offerings** Discuss the paperwork that is involved in an IPO. What is included in each and what purpose does it serve?
10. **Initial public offerings** Johnny Quickset sits three seats across from you in finance class. After class he approached you and asked the following question: "How do underwriters make money?" How do you answer that question?
11. **Lockup agreement** Scotty Blow's lamp store went public on July 14, 2010. Three weeks later, Scotty sold 47 % of his shares for a profit of $2 million. Why is this a bad thing? Discuss the mechanism designed to eliminate this type of activity.
12. **Goal of the firm** What is the only appropriate goal of the firm? Why?
13. **Goal of the firm** Name at least four other potential goals of the firm and discuss what those goals lack in relation to the true goal.
14. **Goal of the firm and agency problems** Suppose the CEO of a Fortune 500 firm superficially inflates year-end earnings reports to increase his bonus. What is this an example of? How does this influence the goal of the firm?
15. **Director voting** What is the primary difference between cumulative and straight voting? How does this affect minority shareholder participation?
16. **Proxy voting** Discuss how proxy voting affects shareholder influence over the ownership structure. What potential benefits of proxy voting come to mind? Can you think of any potential disadvantages?
17. **Capital budgeting** How important is capital budgeting in corporate finance? What types of issues have to be addressed in capital budgeting?
18. **Capital structure** How important is capital structure in corporate finance? What types of issues have to be addressed in capital structure?
19. **Capital structure** Suppose you are the CFO of a company that just built a $40 million dollar plant. What are your options for paying for this plant?
20. **Capital structure and capital budgeting** Your friend is having trouble grasping the concepts of capital structure and capital budgeting, so you decide to explain it to her in terms of her personal financial situation. How can you do

this? How do we, as individuals, incorporate capital structure and capital budgeting into our lives?

21. **Working capital management** How does working capital management fit into the equation? What types of things need to be considered in working capital management?
22. **Capital budgeting, capital structure, and working capital management** Suppose you are the CFO for a pencil-making firm that is in need of a new machine. Discuss the basic steps that you must go through to make this happen. Discuss each of the three aspects and the decisions that must be made for each one.

Chapter 2
Financial Statement Analysis: What's Right, What's Wrong, and Why?

This is what can be referred to as a bridge chapter in the sense that it provides the setup for what comes from this point forward and builds upon the introduction from the previous chapter. It is sometimes easy to shortchange such topics because they are ancillary to the primary focus of the text. However, although bridges are the means to the destination rather than the destination itself, it is impossible to get there without them. The same is true of this chapter. The materials covered are necessary in laying the groundwork for understanding the purpose of finance in a corporate setting.

We have two topics of concern. First, we will briefly review the primary accounting statements, specifically focusing on how the discipline of finance views and uses the documents. Second, we will dig into methods using accounting statements to make financial decisions. The motivation behind both areas of concern is to provide a clear picture of where efforts need to be focused to improve the financial performance of the firm. It is this motivation that provides the bridge between understanding what we generally want to do in corporate finance (Chap. 1) and the implementation of that understanding (Chap. 3 and beyond).

2.1 Finance and Accounting

The disciplines of finance and accounting are often confused for one another and for logical reason. From the financial perspective, accounting is a support discipline. This is not meant to belittle or minimize the contribution in any way; in fact, finance views accounting as a perfect discipline. More specifically, in finance, accounting information is used as though it is always 100 % perfectly calculated and reported. Accountants are always happy to hear such statements, but they are not made flippantly. As will become obvious as we continue our journey through corporate finance, you will see that virtually everything that is done is based upon accounting in some fashion.

M.K. Pyles, *Applied Corporate Finance: Questions, Problems and Making Decisions in the Real World*, Springer Texts in Business and Economics,
DOI 10.1007/978-1-4614-9173-6_2,

That being said, however, it is necessary to detail the differences between the two disciplines. While many details will emerge, virtually all differences are rooted in philosophical and definitional differences. Accounting is, by necessity, primarily a *past-focused* discipline. In other words, they are tasked with evaluating an immense amount of information pertaining to periods which have ended. Personally, you may go to an accountant at the beginning of each year to help you sort through a grocery bag full of tax forms, receipts, and statements from *last* year. What is indecipherable to you is taken and transformed into an easy-to-understand standardized form, known of course as an income tax return. That is the magic done daily by accountants. Now, for a corporation, if the size of the grocery bag is magnified by 100, you get the same thing. There are more numbers, the rules are more complex, and the final report more detailed, but the idea is the same. Accountants do a wonderful job of creating concise reports detailing the financial performance of a past period.

Finance, conversely, is primarily a *forward-focused* discipline. Our job, as previously detailed, is to facilitate firm growth and transform this growth into shareholder wealth. Suppose the firm is trying to appeal to new shareholders. While the shareholders are undoubtedly interested in the financial performance of the firm last year, they are much more interested in the expected financial performance next year. Thus, while it is undoubtedly a fact that accountants sometimes look forward and financiers sometimes look backwards, one of the primary differences between the two is the primary period of focus.

Another way of describing this difference piggybacks upon the first, but from a different perspective. Since accounting is past focused, the values they report are generally *static* in nature, implying of course that they do not change, absent of any adjustments garnered to be necessary. Finance on the other hand is a *dynamic* discipline, by necessity. When attempting to predict the future, the values found are virtually certain to be erroneous to some degree. As such, adjustment is generally necessary as new information becomes available.

So, the ultimate question is how accounting and finance work together and build upon each other. The two disciplines, although certainly different, are interlinked and somewhat inextricably related. Finance generally starts by examining previous accounting statements. Then, financial information is developed based upon conclusions drawn from previous accounting statements before new accounting statements are again used in the financial planning process. Finally, once the financial decisions have been made, accounting tools are used to evaluate the success or failure of those decisions.

2.2 Income Statement

The most common and oft-used financial statement is the **income statement**, which is a fairly simple notion on the surface. It begins with revenues, or all raw cash inflows, the firm generated over a period of time. Then, once all costs associated

Table 2.1 Income statement for Firm ABC

ABC Corp.	
Income statement for the year ending Dec. 31, 2012 (values in 000s)	
Sales	$89,000
Cost of goods sold	49,000
Depreciation	7,600
EBIT	32,400
Interest	2,500
Taxable income	29,900
Taxes (35 %)	10,465
Net income	19,435
Dividends	14,550
Addition to retained earnings	4,885

with those sales are removed, the so-called bottom line is obtained. This latter figure is most often labeled **net income**. Therefore, the income statement attempts to obtain a reasonable estimate of how much of the company's revenues were retained as income throughout the accounting period.

Consider Table 2.1 to illustrate a model of the basic income statement. While there are many forms it can take (and many are more complicated), we can accomplish our goals with this simplified version. **Sales** is a slightly more specific title for revenues and is the sum of all cash inflows as a result of selling the firm's goods or services. **Cost of goods sold** (***COGS***) is a catchall to represent all direct costs that come about in the producing and selling of the firm's product(s). **Depreciation** will be considered in more depth later in this chapter, but for now the simple definition will suffice. Depreciation is the systematic retirement of the value of firm assets over time according to a predetermined schedule. As such, the company can "write-off" the depreciated value of assets each year and in doing so can reduce tax consequences. Once *COGS* and depreciation are removed, the first subtotal of real importance, **earnings before interest and taxes (*EBIT*)**, is obtained. Since the goal is to get only "earnings," the next step is to eliminate the interest and taxes portions.

Interest represents the amount of money the company has to pay in exchange for the right to maintain ownership of funds loaned to them. This will make considerably more sense as we move throughout the text, but it is likely that each of you already has a personal understanding of what it means to pay interest on a loan. Once this interest is excluded, we then have **taxable income**, which is a relatively important value since it determines the company's tax liability. The final step requires removing taxes to arrive at the **net income**. Notice the tax rate utilized in Table 2.1 is 35 %. We will discuss the reasoning behind this number in the next section.

Finally, notice that net income has been divided between two options: dividends and addition to retained earnings. The basic idea is that once a company makes money, they must then do something with it. This decision is actually more important than the amount of income itself. In our simplified textbook world,

Table 2.2 Corporate tax rates

Taxable income	Tax rate
\$0–\$50,000	15 %
50,001–75,000	25
75,001–100,000	34
100,001–335,000	39
335,001–10,000,000	34
10,000,001–15,000,000	35
15,000,001–18,333,333	38
> 18,333,333	35

there are only two options. One, they can give it to shareholders via **dividends**, which are simply monetary "gifts" awarded in exchange for investment in the company. The other option is to keep the money. If they do this, the money changes names, from net income to **retained earnings**. If you've been paying attention, your first thought may be to pay the entire amount (or at least the majority) to shareholders since our goal is to maximize their wealth and there seems no better way to do so than to write them a check. However, remember that to accomplish the goal of maximizing wealth, we must ensure long-term company success. In order to do this, the company must grow. In order to grow, the company needs money, and. . .well, you can see where that leads. As with most things, there has to be a balance between the two options.

2.2.1 *Taxes*

Before we move away from the income statement, two components need a closer examination. While taxes and depreciation are important for completely different reasons, understanding where the values of both come from is essential in making accurate capital budgeting decisions. Taxes are important because they represent a direct cash outflow from the firm. Current corporate tax rates are shown in Table 2.2. Notice the rates are not strictly increasing as the corporation makes more money. While this may seem odd from an individual's perspective, it does little good to wonder about where they came from. Rather, we just need to learn to use them. The bottom line is that a company has to pay whatever the rules dictate.

LOOK IT UP: Despite the above statement, the curious among you may want to know a bit more about where these rates come from and how they are calculated. You should be able to find this information in the Tax Reform Act of 1986 and the 1993 Omnibus Budget Reconciliation Act.

Unfortunately, calculating the tax liability is a bit more difficult than you may think. The best way to illustrate is with an example. Consider a firm with taxable income of $175,000. You may be inclined to just find the range in which $175,000 falls and multiply by the rate (39 %) to get a tax bill of $68,250. Unfortunately, that is incorrect. The tax bill is actually calculated as follows:

$$
\begin{aligned}
.15\ (50,000) &= \$7,500 \\
+.25\ (75,000-50,000) &= 6,250 \\
+.34\ (100,000-75,000) &= 8,500 \\
+.39\ (175,000-100,000) &= 29,250 \\
& \overline{\$51,500}
\end{aligned}
$$

As you can see, the tax bill has to be calculated in chunks. Therefore, it is a bit different than individual tax rates, which are specific to the tax bracket you fall into. Perhaps the most important thing to be concerned about is the difference between the average and the marginal tax rates. The **average tax rate** is the average tax payment made per dollar of taxable income. In other words, it spreads the tax paid evenly over each dollar of income over the period. On the other hand, the **marginal tax rate** is the rate you would have to pay on the *next* dollar of taxable income. It is an incremental tax rate and gives a much better idea of what future tax liabilities may be. To illustrate with our example, the average tax rate would be

$$
\begin{aligned}
\textbf{Average tax rate} &= \frac{51,500}{175,000} \\
&= 29.43\%
\end{aligned}
$$

This means each $1 of the $175,000 is taxed, on average, 29.43 cents. The marginal tax rate is easier to find. We need to do what we couldn't do when calculating the tax bill; locate the range in which the additional $1 of taxable income would fall and identify the corresponding tax rate. Therefore, in this case, the marginal tax rate is 39 %. Obviously the two rates are numerically different, so we need to take a close look at which one most matters.

In finance, probably the most important reason for examining corporate tax rates is the impact taxes have on capital budgeting decisions. The average tax rate is informative in that it tells us, on average, how much we *have* paid. However, it does little in terms of telling us what we *will* pay when we add additional taxable income. When we consider taking on new projects, it is likely that taxable income will increase. Thus, it is crucial we use the rate which will tell us the direct tax consequence of the additional income. This leads to the conclusion that we are most concerned with the marginal tax rate, which tells us how taxes will affect our future cash flows and, subsequently, the decision to accept or reject a project.

Luckily, there is one significant shortcut. Corporate tax rates are calculated based on a modified flat tax rate. This modified flat tax becomes a pure flat rate

Table 2.3 MACRS depreciation

	Property class		
Year	*3-year*	*5-year*	*7-year*
1	33.33	20.00	14.29
2	44.44	32.00	24.49
3	14.82	19.20	17.49
4	7.41	11.52	12.49
5		11.52	8.93
6		5.76	8.93
7			8.93
8			4.45

for the highest incomes. What all this means is that if a company has taxable income in excess of $18.33 million dollars, each dollar of that $18.33 million is taxed at a flat rate of 35 %. This is a function of the design of the corporate tax structure. For most examples we use in this text, we assume firms are already very large and therefore can apply the 35 % flat tax rate to future projects.

2.2.2 *Depreciation*

The last piece of the income statement that needs a bit more examination is depreciation. Much like taxes, the amount of depreciation is determined by a standardized schedule. Also much like taxes, there are a few shortcuts we need to be aware of. We will start by defining the **Modified Accelerated Cost Recovery System (MACRS)**. The Tax Reform Act of 1986 defined the specifics of MACRS, building upon the original accelerated cost recovery system instituted in 1981.

There are essentially two steps in the MACRS. The first is grouping assets into classes, effectively determining the expected life of the asset. Once that is done, each asset is depreciated by a certain percentage each year according to the MACRS schedule. At the end of the depreciation period, the assets are, on the books, worthless. There are several typical property classes for non-real estate properties, ranging from 3 years to 20 years. Table 2.3 shows the associated percentages of the first three classes of property.

LOOK IT UP: These figures are curious looking, aren't they? Wonder where they come from? Most people do. You can look it up and fill us all in. Try looking at the IRS website (www.irs.gov) and go from there. Or you could just check out the MACRS Wikipedia page. While you're at it, see if you can find out why a 5-year property is depreciated for 6 years.

Let's again illustrate with an example. Suppose your firm buys a computer that costs $15,000. Let's assume it will be classified as a 5-year property. Therefore, in the first year, the computer will be depreciated by 20 % of the initial asset value, or

$3,000. At the end of the first year, the computer will then have a book value of $12,000. We then repeat for the remaining 5 years. This results in a depreciation schedule of:

Year	Depreciation percentage	Depreciation amount	Ending book value
1	20.00 %	$3,000	$12,000
2	32.00	4,800	7,200
3	19.20	2,880	4,320
4	11.52	1,728	2,592
5	11.52	1,728	864
6	5.76	864	0

As you can see, the design of MACRS is such that at the end of the asset's life (as determined by its property class), it is fully depreciated. This means that some practical concerns, such as the true economic life (how long the asset can be used) and salvage value (how much it may be worth at the end of the depreciable life), are not considered.

The most important consideration for us in relation to depreciation is how it affects the tax bill. In order to see what is meant by this, we need to examine the differences between book and market asset values. The **book value** of any asset is the value recorded on period-ending accounting statements. This is a product of two things: historical cost and accumulated depreciation. The difference between the two can be crudely described as the net book value. The market value of that same asset is simpler in description, but more complicated in discovery. The **market value** is the true economic value of the asset and can be defined as the amount of money the asset could be sold for under current market conditions. An interesting note is that market values do not have to necessarily make sense to everyone. Just watch any episode of *Antique Roadshow* for evidence of this.

In finance, we are naturally concerned more about the market value of an asset than the book value. The book value is necessary for accounting purposes since, by design, accounting statements must be created under a disciplined structure, something not available with market values. On the other hand, market values are constantly changing and, more importantly, unknown in advance of the actual sale.

As mentioned, depreciation affects the tax bill. To see why, let's take it from the beginning. A very important result of depreciating an asset is getting a tax write-off. From the government's perspective, depreciation makes the assets at your disposal worth less, which is seen as an economic disadvantage. Therefore, the "reward" for this is a tax deduction. Sometimes, however, it is possible to over-depreciate the asset. How can you know that you've done this? If the asset can be sold on the market for more than the current book value, the asset has been over-depreciated. This doesn't mean anything has been done incorrectly since there is no way to know the market value until a buyer is actually found. However, there are ramifications if this should happen.

Revisiting the example from a few paragraphs ago, let's say, for the sake of argument, you sell the computer at the end of the third year for $5,000. The book value is only $4,320; therefore, it is being sold for more than it's worth on the books. The difference between the two is $680, which is the over-depreciated amount. The company has to pay taxes on that amount to make up for this "error." If the tax rate is 35 %, so the tax bill is $238.

Should the example have worked out differently, it is possible to have a tax savings. To prove this to yourself, make sure to get a tax savings of $92.40 if you sell the computer at the end of the fifth year for $600. Just keep the following in mind when doing problems related to depreciation: a market value greater than the book value results in a tax bill, but the opposite results in a tax savings.

The topic of depreciation is much more involved than can be covered in this text. There are many rules related to different types of assets. For example, nonresidential real property, such as an office building, is depreciated straight-line over 39 years. This is often important when considering projects, which is a major focus of this text. Residential property, such as condominiums, is depreciated over 27.5 years. Also, it may shock you to learn that land cannot be depreciated.

LOOK IT UP: Why can't land be depreciated? There must be some logical reason. Do you know why? Maybe you can get some extra credit!

2.3 The Balance Sheet

Anyone who has seen a **balance sheet** can quickly understand the meaning of the name. There are two sides and, well, they must balance. Each side must sum to an equal value. The variables on the left-hand side take many forms but are all some type of **asset**. An asset is anything the firm owns, likely in hopes of using it to generate revenue. It can be something tangible, such as a building or machine, or it can be intangible, such as a copyright or patent. Very generally speaking, assets are grouped into two categories based on asset life. While this is not set in stone, a good rule of thumb is that assets with a life of less than 1 year (current assets) are segmented from those with lives of more than 1 year (fixed assets). If these things don't sound familiar, review a basic accounting text before moving on.

There are two components on the other side (the right-hand side) of the balance sheet. The first is **liabilities**. A liability is essentially another name for debt obligations. It represents a contractual obligation to the firm's future cash flows. Like an asset, a liability can be short term (current liabilities) or long term (long-term debt), again usually loosely defined as less than or greater than 1 year. A short-term liability is one that has to be paid back by the firm in less than 1 year, while long-term debt represents a longer obligation.

The other category is common (or shareholder or owner's) **equity** and is perhaps most important due to its direct relationship to the goal of the firm. Equity represents the value of ownership, which again can come in several forms. For our simplistic example, we will also separate equity into two categories; however, these categories are not short versus long. Rather, it helps to understand the capital budgeting process by looking at equity as either internally generated or externally generated. The first of these two categories is generally referred to as retained earnings. Retained earnings represent the amount of firm money that was internally generated and kept. In other words, it represents the money the firm currently has that did not directly come from some outside source. Externally generated equity can take multiple forms, but most notably **common stock**. Common stock is a publicly available security that represents ownership in the firm. Preferred stock is also a source of externally generated equity but is a topic that will be discussed at length in a later chapter. Thus, for now, we will assume Firm ABC has no preferred equity.

The term additional paid in surplus is also sometimes found in this section of the balance sheet and refers to any additional amount paid in by investors in excess of the par value of the shares. The notion of a par value for common stock is largely antiquated but refers to the minimum amount the firms will accept for new issues of common stock. For example, if a firm agrees with its underwriter that shares will not be sold for less than $10 and they end up selling for $12, the $2 is additional surplus. As discussed in Chap. 1, most issues of common stock are completed with firm commitment underwritings, which makes the par value a mute issue. Therefore, we will assume that any additional surplus is also included under the umbrella of externally generated equity without need for distinction.

In short, the balance sheet of a firm can be summed up by the following statement: *a balance sheet is a snapshot of what the firm owns, owes, and the difference between the two*. To illustrate, consider the example in Table 2.4. Notice there are a few thus far unmentioned variables. Don't let that distract you from the basic form, which leads us to the balance sheet identity and can be succinctly described as follows:

$$Assets = Liabilities + Equity$$

There is a direct link between the balance sheet and the income statement that derives from the addition to retained earnings recording during the period in question. We see from Table 2.1 that the addition to retained earnings for 2012 was $4,885. From Table 2.4, we find the firm had retained earnings of $4,500 at the end of 2011. Therefore, the new retained earnings figure, assuming that none was removed, is $9,385. The remaining amount of equity needed to balance the sheet comes from the other equity category: externally generated.

2.4 Using Accounting Statements in Finance

This being a finance text, the focus must now turn to how accounting information can be used in finance. Accounting statements are extremely useful in identifying areas where financial planning will be most beneficial. The purpose of financial planning is to improve the firm in ways that are most advantageous to the

Table 2.4 Balance sheet for Firm ABC

ABC Corp.					
Balance sheet as of December 31, 2011 and 2012 (values in 000s)					
Assets			Liabilities		
	2011	2012		2011	2012
Current assets			Current liabilities		
Cash	9,300	7,800	A/P	6,500	9,000
A/R	2,600	3,500	N/P	8,200	4,500
Inventory	5,000	3,000	Total current	14,700	13,500
Total current	16,900	14,300	Long-term debt	7,800	14,000
Fixed assets	31,600	34,000	Total debt	22,500	27,500
Total assets	48,500	48,300			
			Equity		
				2011	2012
			Common stock	21,500	11,415
			Retained earnings	4,500	9,385
			Total equity	26,000	20,800
			Total debt and equity	48,500	48,300

shareholders. In many cases, this involves focusing on firm strengths and building upon them. In other cases, it involves identifying areas of weakness to focus on improvement. In each case, the paramount issue is the ability to identify the strength or weakness.

Think about yourself for a moment. We all have personal strengths and weaknesses and some of yours probably spring to mind at this moment. The question is how we define these things as strengths or weaknesses? For most people, the answer is that you do so *relatively*. For example, if you feel you have a strength in math, you probably believe so because you are better at math than most others. If you believe you have a weakness in public speaking, it is likely because most others seem to do it better than you.

The same is true of a firm. To identify what the firm excels at, as well as its shortcomings, we typically do so by comparison. Doing so requires transforming accounting statements into comparable forms. We need to be able to compare our firm to something else in order to see if we are better or worse in various aspects. This "something else" can take numerous forms, but three options come to mind. First, we would like to compare our current situation to our previous situation. It is generally a good thing to be better now than we were last year. Second, we can compare our firm to our competitors with whom we are directly competing for market share. Third, we can compare ourselves on a grander scale to our industry or sector. If our performance is trending in a positive direction and we compare favorably to our peers, we can confidently say things are moving in the right direction.

LOOK IT UP: How do you define an industry or sector? What makes a firm your competitor? Look up SIC and NAICS codes. What do these mean and how do they differ? As an exercise, what is Lowe's SIC and NAICS code? Who are their direct competitors?

However, there is a complication to this process. We use accounting statements to evaluate relative performance. However, accounting statements are largely firm and time specific and as such cannot be readily compared. Could you definitively conclude that you were better at math than your peers if you were taking a different test? Of course not. Likewise, if you have a net income of $25,000 and your competitor, who is a much bigger company, has net income of $300,000, what statements can you make regarding relative performance? We need to identify ways of creating an equal playing field, a standardized test if you will, only for firms instead of individuals.

2.5 Standardized Statements

When presented with accounting statements from both your firm and some comparison entity, one quick way of leveling the playing field is to standardize the statements. One way of doing this is to create a **common-size statement**. A common-size statement uses a base figure on each accounting statement to generate comparable values for both statements. The primary figure on an income statement is the sales figure, while total assets is typically used for balance sheets. To illustrate the process, consider Table 2.5, which again shows Firm ABC's income statement but this time in comparison to its competitor, Firm XYZ.

If we evaluate the raw values presented in the income statements, it could easily be concluded that Firm XYZ outperformed Firm ABC, and in some ways perhaps

Table 2.5 Standardized income statements for Firms ABC and XYZ

	Income statements		Common-size income statements	
	ABC	XYZ	ABC	XYZ
Sales	$89,000	$110,000	100.00 %	100.00 %
Cost of goods sold	49,000	67,000	55.06 %	60.91 %
Depreciation	7,600	6,700	8.54 %	6.09 %
EBIT	32,400	36,300	36.40 %	33.00 %
Interest	2,500	3,400	2.81 %	3.09 %
Taxable income	29,900	32,900	33.60 %	29.91 %
Taxes (35 %)	10,465	11,515	11.76 %	10.47 %
Net income	**19,435**	**21,385**	**21.84 %**	**19.44 %**
Dividends	14,550	15,400	16.35 %	14.00 %
Addition to retained earnings	4,885	5,985	5.49 %	5.44 %

they did. A larger sales figure is a desirable thing, all else equal. However, the goal is not to have the largest sales figure, but to maximize shareholder wealth. Making an additional dollar is useless if it costs too much to make. Firm XYZ does have larger *EBIT* and net income, both of which would indicate superiority. Also, from the shareholder's perspective, Firm XYZ pays out more in dividends than Firm ABC. However, the question remains whether the larger numbers are a result of larger sales figures or a more efficient operation in retaining the funds from sales. These questions cannot be answered from the raw figures.

The last two columns of Table 2.5 display the standardized figures, which are calculated by dividing each value by the sales amount. This allows us to accurately depict what happened to each average penny the firm made. For each dollar that Firm ABC brought in as sales, 55 % was used in the process of creating that sale. This, when compared to the 61 % for Firm XYZ, is a superior value. On average, ABC generated sales with less expense than XYZ. Further, for every dollar of sales, Firm ABC has a profit (net income) of nearly 22 cents, compared to less than 19.5 for Firm XYZ, which again suggests that Firm ABC was more efficient in retaining the money that came into the firm. In short, when put on a comparable level, Firm ABC outperformed Firm XYZ. An important note is that this does not suggest to ignore the differing levels of sales. A larger amount of sales and by extension a larger level of net income is desirable. But, it is even more desirable to efficiently retain sales as income.

2.6 Ratio Analysis

An alternative to standardized statements is a more involved process known as ratio analysis. One of the more extensively studied areas in both finance and accounting, ratio analysis is a massive topic that easily fills entire texts alone. Thus, our focus will not be a comprehensive, detailed analysis, but rather to obtain an overall understanding of why such an analysis is useful. **Ratio analysis** is a way of combining and comparing multiple pieces of financial information. The reason we would do so is to again create a comparable analysis between two entities, the subject group and the comparable group.

There are five categories of ratios, with numerous examples within each that we will discuss in time. However, the much more important issue is to consider why we want to complete ratio analysis. The five categories are as follows: (1) short-term solvency (liquidity) ratios, (2) long-term solvency (leverage) ratios, (3) asset utilization (turnover) ratios, (4) profitability ratios, and (5) market ratios. The ordering is not by coincidence. They are listed in this specific order so as to be consistent with the goal of the firm. Taken collectively, the first two categories can be referred to as *sustaining* categories. Remember that our job in finance is to plan for future growth, constantly attempting to make the firm better and more valuable. However, we cannot do that if we are not a firm that can sustain our current condition.

Short-term solvency simply refers to the firm's ability to pay their short-term bills without undue distress. Topics that fall into this category can be as simple as the ability to pay the power bill or to keep current on our short-term tab with suppliers. This is the first category of concern because if we find a problem in this area, there is little need to further proceed. It is relatively simple to draw analogies to your personal life. If you are having trouble paying the rent each month, you probably should not consider investing in a house that would cost more. The same is true of a firm. If a firm is struggling to meet its short-term obligations, then considering a large project for the future is likely a fruitless prospect.

Short-term solvency is sometimes referred to as **liquidity**, although they are not exactly the same thing. The easiest way to see the difference is to examine the counterarguments to each. If a firm is insolvent, they cannot currently pay their bills and have no avenue through which they can obtain cash to pay. If a firm is illiquid, they cannot pay their bills with the cash they currently have in a timely manner. It may be possible, however, for the firm to convert other assets to cash and then pay their bills. The term liquidity refers to the speed and ease with which an asset can be converted to cash, at a fair value. This seemingly simple notion is actually one of the more discussed topics in a firm.

Liquidity has both positive and negative connotations. On the positive side, the more liquid a firm is, the less likely they will have trouble paying their short-term bills. Therefore, *liquidity is valuable*. However, when searching for liquidity, one will most often find themselves in the category of current assets, most of which are relatively liquid. As an example, consider cash, which is the most liquid of all assets. Unfortunately, if you take a pile of cash and store it in a safe, moist-free environment for a large amount of time, it STILL is just the same amount of cash. In other words, cash, unless used, is unprofitable. And, when cash becomes used, it usually moves away from current assets and into fixed assets (via whatever the cash is spent on). Thus, we are stuck with a decision. We can stockpile current assets, such as cash, to fight against potential future financial distress, but we do so at the expense of profitability. Alternatively, we can use as much of our assets as possible in the effort to generate firm value, but do so at the risk of increasing the potential for financial distress. This balancing act is one of continuous concern for a firm. Opinions on holding cash differ drastically among firms. Some hold a great deal, while some hold almost none.

LOOK IT UP: The discussion of how much cash a firm should hold is an ongoing, highly debated issue. As an illustration, take some time to dig into the amount of cash that Apple has held over the last several years. (Hint: It's a lot.) As you read and research this, think about what a shareholder would like for a firm to do with the cash they hold. Would you like them to hold more of it or less of it? Getting back to Apple, something very important happened concerning shareholders and cash holdings on July 24, 2012. What was it?

Hopefully, the firm successfully dances this tightrope and will be able to essentially get a "pass" on the short-term solvency category, indicating short-term distress is not problematic. If so, we can move to the second category, **long-term solvency**, which simply measures the firm's ability to pay their long-term debt obligations. The term leverage is used as an alternative here, since the use of debt in a financial structure is often referred to as "leveraging" your money. An analogy here would be if you cannot make your current payment on your small house, you probably shouldn't buy a larger, more expensive house. Or, if the firm is struggling to meet its current debt obligations, considering funding a new project is perhaps a questionable proposition. Again, the hope is that the firm can again check this issue off the list of concern.

The reason the first two categories can be referred to as *sustaining* categories is that they measure the firm's performance in areas of the firm that are essential to current operations. The firm needs to reach certain levels within each category to sustain current levels of production, just as you need a certain level of income to maintain your current lifestyle. If you are successful in that pursuit, then you can proceed to try to improve your lifestyle, much as we can then proceed to improve the firm. Thus, we can then address the last three categories, which collectively present a path to follow in measuring the firm's ability to generate shareholder wealth. As such, we will refer to them as *progressing* categories.

The first of those three, the **asset utilization ratios**, are also known as turnover ratios since they measure the firm's ability to generate sales with their asset base. In short, they measure the firm's ability to get money in the door. The notion, naturally, is to get as much revenue into the firm as possible. However, while an excellent first step, the appropriate goal of the firm is not to maximize sales. In fact, as illustrated earlier with the common-size statements, obtaining sales is certainly not the same thing as obtaining profits and can often be misleading in measuring performance. Thus, the fourth category of ratios takes the next step in the process.

Profitability ratios measure the firm's ability to generate profits from sales. This takes into account the expenses used in the accumulation of sales, taxes, and interest expenses, as well as noncash issues such as depreciation. Ask yourself a question. Which do firms and shareholders care more about, sales or profits? Well, which do you care more about, your gross pay or your net pay? Naturally, the amount we get to keep or "bring home" is more important. It is impossible to spend money that you once had.

But wait! Shareholders do not truly care about profits either, because their wealth is not measured by firm profits. Profits are accounting values, or book values, which have only an indirect relationship with market values. What shareholders truly care about is the degree to which the firm's profits get transformed into market value, which leads to the final category of ratios, **market ratios**. The unique thing about this category is that they include values typically not found on accounting statements. These values are, unsurprisingly, market values such as shares outstanding and stock prices. Market ratios measure the firm's ability to generate market value with profits and, as such, present the most important conclusions pertaining to the goal of the firm. To review, Table 2.6 summarizes the ratio categories.

Table 2.6 Ratio categories

	Category	Purpose
Sustaining categories	Short-term solvency (liquidity) ratios	Measure the firm's short-run ability to pay their bills
	Long-term solvency (leverage) ratios	Measure the firms' long-run ability to pay their bills
Progressing categories	Asset utilization (turnover) ratios	Measure the firm's ability to generate sales with assets
	Profitability ratios	Measure the firm's ability to generate profits from sales
	Market ratios	Measure the firm's ability to generate market value from profits

2.6.1 *Short-Term Solvency Ratios*

Since this category of ratios measures the firm's ability to meet their short-term debt obligations, it makes sense that we would use short-term variables in calculation. Perhaps the most popular short-term solvency, or liquidity ratio, is the **current ratio**, which is calculated as

$$Current\ ratio = \frac{Current\,assets}{Current\,liabilities}$$

Since short-term liabilities generally represents a short-run contractual obligation of future cash flows, an overly small current ratio can create problems, since doing so would indicate a short-run deficiency in our ability to pay our short-term bills. In fact, a current ratio of less than one would indicate that debt outweighs assets in the short-run. Such a scenario is typically not ideal. The larger question would be *what value is a* good *value*? Unfortunately, that is a difficult question to answer. If we recall Firm ABC from earlier in the chapter, we can calculate their 2012 current ratio from Table 2.4:

$$\begin{aligned}\textbf{Current ratio} &= \frac{\mathbf{14,300}}{\mathbf{13,500}} \\ &= \mathbf{1.06\ times}\end{aligned}$$

The firm has \$1.06 in current assets for every \$1 in current liabilities, or, put differently, the firm can pay its short-term bills 1.06 times with short-term assets. In order to make any definitive statement on whether the firm should be pleased or disappointed with that number, comparisons to peer groups or past values would be necessary.

Another short-term solvency ratio that is often of importance is the **quick ratio**. The name is due to the fact that it relates short-term debt to short-term assets *that* *can be quickly converted to cash.* The ratio is designed to measure the relationship between short-term debt and *liquid* short-term assets. The current ratio assumes that all short-term assets are liquid, and most generally are. However, often there is a category of short-term assets that are relatively illiquid. For example, **inventory** may sometimes be liquid, but oftentimes is not, depending on the nature of the assets held in inventory. With this understanding, the quick ratio removes inventory from the total of current assets.

$$Quick\ ratio = \frac{Current\,assets - Inventory}{Current\,liabilities}$$

Since inventory for a traditional firm is rarely negative, the quick ratio is generally lower than the current ratio, and depending on the amount of inventory held, it could be considerably less. The intention of the quick ratio is to give a more accurate depiction of the firm's ability to pay their bills quickly without undue distress. The fact stands that often inventory cannot be converted to cash quickly and effectively, so converting it to cash and paying bills is an unlikely possibility. For Firm ABC, this works out to be

$$\begin{aligned}\textbf{Current ratio} &= \frac{\mathbf{14,300 - 3,000}}{\mathbf{13,500}}\\ &= \mathbf{.84\ times}\end{aligned}$$

An additional, or sometimes alternative, measure of the quick ratio could be computed by subtracting part of the firm's **accounts receivables (A/R)**. This value is included in current assets because it represents sales that were done on "credit" and should be repaid in relatively short order. However, in many cases, this repayment does not happen in short order, and it would be appropriate to omit the cash flows expected from repayment in liquidity analysis. The firm may choose to eliminate past-due A/R amounts from their liquidity ratios. An example would be

$$\frac{Current\,assets - Accounts\,receivables\,over\,90\,days\,old}{Current\,liabilities}$$

And, of course, sometimes it is appropriate for a firm to remove both past-due A/R and inventory from current assets. We can take this process one step further by examining the **cash ratio**. As the name implies, this ratio is concerned with only the amount of cash the firm has, again in relation to the firm's short-term debt obligations:

$$Cash\ ratio = \frac{Cash}{Current\,liabilities}$$

Firm ABC has a cash ratio of .58 times, indicating they can fund a bit more than half of their short-term debt with the cash they currently have available. The cash ratio is very restrictive in that it assumes only the most liquid of all assets are available for repayment of short-term debt. Naturally, if the firm's philosophy is to hold very little or no cash, the cash ratio is of little use to that firm. So, the idea is this. If the firm believes that all their current assets are liquid, then the appropriate measure of liquidity is the current ratio. If they feel that all assets are liquid except the inventory, the quick ratio is the appropriate measure. And, finally, if they feel that only the cash they hold should be used to finance short-term debt, the cash ratio is of most use.

2.6.2 Long-Term Solvency Ratios

We now turn our attention to long-term solvency. While the ability to repay short-term debt obligations is certainly important, from a financial standpoint, the ability to pay long-term debt obligation is perhaps even more important. And, naturally, the ability to repay both is the ultimate concern. In order to advance the firm, it is critical that we maintain the ability to obtain new financing, which would not happen if we fail to maintain our current financing. Would a bank give you a loan if you just defaulted on another one? Most likely not, and if so, it would be at a considerable cost. So, measuring the relationship between the firm's debt and asset levels is of considerable importance. The first three ratios in the long-term solvency category address this issue.

First, the **total debt ratio** is computed as follows:

$$Total\ debt\ ratio = \frac{Total\,debt}{Total\,assets}$$

and reports the relationship between total debt (short and long term) and total assets. For Firm ABC in 2012, this can be computed to be

$$\begin{aligned}\textbf{Total debt ratio} &= \frac{\mathbf{27,500}}{\mathbf{48,300}} \\ &= \mathbf{.57\ times}\end{aligned}$$

This implies the firm has \$.57 in debt for every \$1 in assets. However, it also means much more. From our understanding of the balance sheet identity, we know that if the firm has 57 % in debt, they must have 43 % in equity. This 57/43 split is the firm's current capital structure or the specific mixture of debt and equity the firm currently utilizes. Much later in the text, we will examine this notion, paying particular attention to whether this mixture is the best for the firm and whether any new financing should come from the same allocation of sources.

An alternative way of viewing this is to calculate the **debt-to-equity ratio**, which is fairly self-explanatory:

$$Debt\text{-}to\text{-}equity\ ratio = \frac{Total\,debt}{Total\,equity}$$

Firm ABC has 2012 total equity of $20,800, so their debt-to-equity ratio is 1.32 times. With a little mathematical finagling, we can again arrive at the capital structure of 57 % debt and 43 % equity.

The debt-to-equity ratio is of importance, particularly to shareholders, as it highlights the tradeoff the firm faces in asset allocation. The firm has a contractual obligation to the debtholders and an implied obligation to the equity holders. Thus, the relationship between the levels of these two is of paramount importance. If the debt-to equity ratio is greater than one, the firm has an allocation of debt in their capital structure in excess of 50 %. A ratio of less than one indicates the firm is weighted more towards equity.

A third measure of the relationship between debt, assets, and equity is the **equity multiplier**, calculated as

$$Equity\ multiplier = \frac{Total\,assets}{Total\,equity}$$

Before we calculate this ratio for Firm ABC, let's examine the relationship between the equity multiplier and the debt-to-equity ratio. Since assets must equal the summation of debt and equity, then

$$\begin{aligned} Equity\ multiplier &= \frac{Total\,debt + total\,equity}{Total\,equity} \\ &= \frac{Total\,debt}{Total\,equity} + \frac{Total\,equity}{Total\,equity} \end{aligned}$$

So,

$$Equity\ multiplier = Debt\text{-}to\text{-}equity\ ratio + 1$$

Thus, we know that the equity multiplier for Firm ABC must be 2.32 times, but that can easily be confirmed with a quick calculation. Also, we can again find the capital structure from this answer. In fact, it simply works out that if you divide 1 by the equity multiplier, the resulting answer is the weight of equity in the capital structure.

Since a primary concern of the firm is to measure the firm's ability to stay current on debt obligations, the **times interest earned ratio** is of particular importance. The period-by-period cost of debt is the interest expense of that debt, which is paid out of earnings before interest and taxes (*EBIT*). With this understanding, the ratio is calculated as follows:

$$Times\ interest\ earned = \frac{EBIT}{Interest}$$

Firm ABC has a times interest earned ratio of 12.96 for 2012, indicating they can pay their interest nearly 13 times with their earnings for the year. Whether this is a "good" number depends on comparison to past, competitors, and industry, but it at least appears the firm has an ability to maintain their current debt obligations, which is critical in moving forward with financial planning. An additional measure, of the same nature, includes acknowledging noncash expenses. Depreciation, although critical for the purpose of reconciling book and market values, does not require an actual cash payment or receipt, thus removing it from the amount available for interest payments may be misleading. Therefore, the **cash coverage ratio** is calculated as follows:

$$Cash\ coverage\ ratio = \frac{EBIT + Depreciation}{Interest}$$

Firm ABC has a cash coverage ratio of 16 times for 2012. The cash coverage ratio will always exceed the times interest earned ratio, provided the firm has some amount of depreciation.

2.6.3 Asset Utilization Ratios

We now arrive at the first of the *progressing* categories of ratios. The ability to pay debts both in the short and long run is a critical necessity for firm survival and sets the stage for progression. However, what we truly need is to effectively use our business plan to generate revenue that will turn into profit, which will in turn create shareholder wealth. We shall begin with the first step: the ability to get money into the firm from our business operations. Our operations are a product of our asset base. The aptly named asset utilization ratios are often called turnover ratios because they measure the ability of the firm to "turn over" their assets into revenue over and over again.

Total asset turnover is perhaps the most direct measure of this notion:

$$Total\ asset\ turnover = \frac{Sales}{Assets}$$

This ratio reports the amount of sales the firm receives per dollar of assets. A larger number is naturally desired. For Firm ABC, this is

$$\begin{aligned}\textbf{Total asset turnover} &= \frac{\textbf{89,000}}{\textbf{48,300}} \\ &= \textbf{1.84 times}\end{aligned}$$

Firm ABC generates $1.85 in sales for every $1 in assets. If this value compares favorably to those of Firm ABC's competitors or the industry at large, then it would suggest that ABC is doing an effective job of generating sales. If not, it provides an area where the firm should search for improvement.

Inventory turnover measures the number of times per period that the firm replaces their inventory. Since inventory is a large component of the expenses of creating sales, it typically falls into the cost of goods sold category. Thus, the more inventory used, the higher the cost of goods sold, but the sales level should also increase. It is helpful to imagine a firm that has a relatively set amount of inventory at any given time. In the simplest scenario, imagine a two-room business. In the front room, business takes place and customers buy the products. In the back room, inventory is stored, and anytime a piece of inventory is sold in the front room, it is replaced on the shelf in the back room. Inventory turnover is calculated as

$$Inventory\ turnover = \frac{Cost\ of\ goods\ sold}{Inventory}$$

In our example of Firm ABC, we can calculate the 2012 turnover to be

$$\begin{aligned}\textbf{Inventory turnover} &= \frac{\mathbf{49,000}}{\mathbf{3,000}}\\ &= \mathbf{16.33\ times}\end{aligned}$$

So, on average, each $1 worth of inventory gets replaced 16 times per year. Naturally, some pieces get replaced much more often and some may not be replaced at all during the period. A careful analysis would perhaps suggest certain items be replaced with those that have a shorter shelf life. Items that remain in inventory for an extended period represents money tied up in a profitless situation, which is naturally inconsistent with the goal of the firm.

A companion ratio is **days sales in inventory** and is designed to convert the inventory turnover ratio to a more readily understood interpretation:

$$Days\ sales\ in\ inventory = \frac{365}{Inventory\ turnover}$$

For any non-leap year, 365 is the number of days in the year, thus the resulting answer can be interpreted as the number of days an average $1 of inventory sits before being sold. For Firm ABC, this works out to be a little more than 22 days.

A very similar notion can be applied to receivables. Whereas the inventory turnover measure creates an analysis of the speed at which we are using a specific type of short-term asset to generate sales, the **receivables turnover** measures the speed at which we are recovering our short-term credit sales, which are typically classified as accounts receivable. For many firms this represents a large piece of their overall sales figures, and since sales are generally recognized at the point of sale, the amount of time between the sale and the receipt of the money is of high importance. The goal is to minimize this lag time, since the quicker the money is received, the quicker it can be used. Of course, interest charged to customers on past-due accounts negates some of this concern.

Receivables turnover and its companion ratio, **days sales in receivables**, are calculated as follows:

$$\begin{aligned} Receivables\ turnover &= \frac{Sales}{Accounts\,receivables} \\ Days\ sales\ in\ receivables &= \frac{365}{Receivables\ turnover} \end{aligned}$$

For Firm ABC, these values are 25.43 times and 14.35 days, respectively. While the definition for the receivables turnover is less intuitive, the days sales in receivables simply implies that it takes, on average, 14.35 days to recover each $1 of credit sales.

2.6.4 Profitability Ratios

Getting money into the firm is a great first step, but not the ultimate goal. In fact, obtaining revenues is a useless endeavor if they do not result in profits. If, for example, it costs $2 to produce $1 of sales, then the firm would be better off without that sale in the first place. Thus, we now turn our attention to ratios that focus on profits. The first is a widely used measure in many facets of finance. The **profit margin**, generally, can be calculated as

$$Profit\ margin = \frac{Net\ income}{Sales}$$

As such, we measure profit in relation to the sales from which profit is generated. This is often referred to as the net profit margin, since net income is net of all expenses that were incurred throughout the period. An alternative is measuring the *gross profit margin*, where *net income* is replaced with *sales – cost of goods sold*. Such a measure eliminates the expenses for depreciation, taxes, and interest, which may differ drastically among firms and, in a way, provides a cleaner comparison of profit performance. Also, a ratio known as *operating profit margin* is calculated by replacing *net income* with *EBIT*, which excludes taxes and interest.

For Firm ABC, the 2012 profit margin is 21.84 %, while the gross and operating profit margins are 44.94 % and 36.40 %, respectively. Firm ABC generated 21.84 cents in profit for every $1 in sales, while the numbers are naturally elevated when select expenses are removed. Notice that these ratios are measured in percentages, since they are generally thought of as *returns* on sales. While this is the standard convention, a note of caution regarding interpretation is important. These ratios are still accounting ratios measured using accounting data and, as such, cannot, and should not, be compared to market returns. For example, if you ever hear someone say, "this firm had a profit margin of 14 % and the market only made 10 % last year, so this firm did better," you may feel free to correct them post-haste.

Return on assets and **return on equity** are two other widely used profitability ratios. They are calculated in a similar and straightforward manner:

$$Return\ on\ assets = \frac{Net\ income}{Assets}$$

$$Return\ on\ equity = \frac{Net\ income}{Equity}$$

For Firm ABC, these are calculated as follows:

$$\textbf{Return on assets} = \frac{\mathbf{19,435}}{\mathbf{48,300}} = \mathbf{40.24\%}$$

$$\textbf{Return on equity} = \frac{\mathbf{19,435}}{\mathbf{20,800}} = \mathbf{93.44\%}$$

Firm ABC generates 40 cents in profit for every dollar in assets and 93 cents for every dollar in equity. Since the return on equity removes the debt obligation of the firm, it will always be higher than return on assets, provided the firm has a positive amount of debt. Note that for each of these, the alternatives in calculating profit (gross profit or operating profit) mentioned earlier in the section can also be used as the numerator value.

2.6.5 *Market Ratios*

Generating revenues is a great thing and generating profits is even better. However, as a shareholder in a publicly traded company, the major concern is neither, because quite simply, neither have any direct impact on the shareholders' bank accounts. A shareholder's wealth is determined not by revenues or profits, but by stock prices. So, the primary concern is in measuring how the firm's performance is reflected in the firm's stock price. We can measure this in a variety of ways, but most notably with the **price-to-earnings (P/E)** ratio:

$$Price\text{-}to\text{-}earnings\ ratio = \frac{Price\ per\ share}{Earnings\ per\ share}$$

Notice that this ratio, for the first time in our discussion, includes a value that cannot be found on either the income statement or the balance sheet. The price per share is market value and, as such, changes whenever the market dictates that it should. As discussed at the opening of the chapter, accounting statements cannot be based upon fluctuating values. The **earnings per share (EPS)** is an accounting ratio, calculated as *net income/number of shares outstanding*. The EPS is a very important number in the world of investments, as it is typically referred to when *earnings estimates* or *earnings statements* are released or when firms are said to *beat* or *fail to beat earnings estimates*. The number of shares outstanding can fluctuate for a firm as they can issue more or buy some back. However, the numbers will change much less frequently than the price and can often go long periods of time without changing at all.

For the sake of completion, let's assume that Firm ABC has 3,000 shares outstanding and each share is currently selling for $35. If so, then Firm ABC has an EPS of $6.48, which results in a P/E ratio of 5.40. An interpretation of this value would be that Firm ABC converts each dollar of earnings into $5.40 of market value. If, as with Firm ABC, the denominator is calculated using the past 12 months of earnings, then P/E ratio is referred to as a *trailing P/E*. If, instead, the calculation uses estimates of earnings over the next 12 months, it is referred to as a *forward P/E*. In the latter case, the earnings are typically obtained from an average of analysts' estimates of the firm's future earnings.

LOOK IT UP: These analysts' estimates are an indispensable source of information for investors. Analysts are paid professionals whose job is to evaluate a firm and report estimates of important financial numbers, such as stock prices or earnings. Such estimates can be widely obtained. As a relevant exercise, find at least three websites that report earnings estimates for Facebook next year. What value would you use as the denominator in calculating Facebook's forward P/E?

The P/E ratio has become such a fixture in investment strategy that it is often used to classify assets. For example, you have likely heard of a "growth" or "value" stock. The P/E ratio is one way of making such statements regarding an asset. An asset with a high P/E ratio has a high price in relation to earnings, suggesting the asset base has room to *grow* to catch up to the price. Alternatively, of course, the price could be inflated and the stock relatively overvalued. A stock with a low P/E has a low price in relation to earnings, which suggests purchase of such an asset is a good deal, or a good *value*.

The P/E ratio is just one of a larger group of ratios that are collectively known as **price ratios** and are widely used in investment analysis to theoretically valuating a firm's stock. Other commonly used examples include the *price-to-sales ratio* and the *price-to-cash flow ratio*. The price-to-sales ratio is calculated in the expected manner, as is the price-to cash flow ratio, although a thorough discussion of cash flow has not yet occurred in this text.

A second market ratio that serves largely the same purpose is the **market-to-book ratio**. As the name implies, the ratio examines the relationship between the firm's market value and the firm's book value on a per share basis:

$$\textit{Market-to-book ratio} = \frac{\textit{Price per share}}{\textit{Book value per share}}$$

Recall the market value of an asset is simply the amount that someone is willing to pay; thus, for a publicly traded security, the market value is the same as the price. The book value per share is computed by dividing total equity by the number of shares outstanding. Firm ABC has a 2012 market-to-book ratio of

$$\begin{aligned}\textbf{Market-to-book ratio} &= \frac{\mathbf{35.00}}{\mathbf{20,800/3,000}}\\ &= \mathbf{5.05\ times}\end{aligned}$$

For every \$1 in book value, Firm ABC generates \$5.05 in market value. As with everything else, conversion to a higher market value is always preferred.

2.6.6 *Dividend Ratios*

A final group of ratios deals with the choice of profit dispersion. From earlier in this chapter, you may recall that net income can only go to one of two places. The firm may choose to keep it and invest back into firm operations. Or, alternatively, they may choose to pay it out to shareholders. In most cases, the final choice is a mixture of both, and for that reason, examining ratios that measure the firm's chosen profit allocation is an appropriate extension to the five primary categories.

The **dividend payout ratio** is calculated as

$$\textit{Dividend payout ratio} = \frac{\textit{Dividend per share}}{\textit{Earnings per share}}$$

Another way of examining this would be done on an aggregate basis, by simply dividing the total amount of dividends paid by the net income. Either way, the resulting answer for Firm ABC is 75 %, indicating the firm paid out three-quarters of their profits in dividends. Naturally, this indicates they *retained* the other 25 %, a finding which can be formalized with the **retention ratio**:

$$\textit{Retention ratio} = \frac{\textit{Addition to retained earnings}}{\textit{Net income}}$$

Another often used dividend ratio is referred to as the **dividend yield**. Unlike the payout ratio, the yield examines the relationship between the dividend paid and the market price:

$$Dividend\ yield = \frac{Dividend\ per\ share}{Price\ per\ share}$$

Shareholders care a great deal about this value because it represents a portion of their return on investment. The denominator is the current cost of securing position in the firm, while the numerator is the current dividend "reward" for owning the securities. For example, should someone examine Firm ABC's current positions, they would note that an investment of \$35 would generate an annual return of \$4.85 from dividends. Of course, what really matters is not the dividend paid last year, but rather the one that will be paid next year.

2.6.7 DuPont Identity

In finance, we are constantly trying to identify solutions to issues that are holding the firm back. Ratio analysis helps do *half* of this, by aiding in the identification of potential problem areas. Unfortunately, finding problems is less of a concern than finding solutions to those problems. For example, the return on equity (*ROE*) is an important ratio since it most directly relates firm performance to shareholder interest. Suppose at the end of a given year, you are reviewing the ratio analysis just computed and notice the *ROE* is lower than in previous years and also lags behind your competitors and the industry. The conclusion drawn is that something is wrong. From the base *ROE* equation, all that can be concluded is either that net income is too low or that equity is too high. The first is the most likely scenario, although it is certainly possible that your capital structure needs to be realigned in some way.

So, what do you do? Do you call a meeting and tell your superiors that the problem is your profits were too low last year? Of course not, because you would immediately get the follow-up question of *why* this happened. Back in the 1920s, the DuPont Corporation found a solution to this scenario by introducing **ratio decomposition**. The process begins with the *ROE* formula:

$$Return\ on\ equity = \frac{Net\ income}{Equity}$$

The first step is to simply multiply by *assets*/*assets*, which of course changes nothing quantitatively:

Table 2.7 Summary of financial ratio equations

Ratio	Equation	Ratio	Equation
Short-term solvency ratios		Asset utilization ratios	
Current ratio	$\frac{Current\,assets}{Current\,liabilities}$	Total asset turnover	$\frac{Sales}{Assets}$
Quick ratio	$\frac{Current\,assets - inventory}{Current\,liabilities}$	Inventory turnover	$\frac{Cost\,of\,goods\,sold}{Inventory}$
Cash ratio	$\frac{Cash}{Current\,liabilities}$	Days sales in inventory	$\frac{365}{Inventory\,turnover}$
Long-term solvency ratios		Receivables turnover	$\frac{Sales}{Account\,receivables}$
Total debt ratio	$\frac{Total\,debt}{Total\,assets}$	Days sales in receivables	$\frac{365}{Receivables\,turnover}$
Debt-to-equity ratio	$\frac{Total\,debt}{Total\,equity}$	Profitability ratios	
Equity multiplier	$\frac{Total\,assets}{Total\,equity}$	Profit margin	$\frac{Net\,income}{Sales}$
Times interest earned	$\frac{EBIT}{Interest}$	Return on assets	$\frac{Net\,income}{Assets}$
Cash coverage ratio	$\frac{EBIT + depreciation}{Interest}$	Return on equity	$\frac{Net\,income}{Equity}$
Market ratios		Dividend ratios	
Price-to-earnings ratio	$\frac{Price\,per\,share}{Earnings\,per\,share}$	Dividend payout ratio	$\frac{Dividend\,per\,share}{Earnings\,per\,share}$
Market-to-book ratio	$\frac{Price\,per\,share}{Book\,value\,per\,share}$	Retention ratio	$\frac{Addition\,to\,ret.earnings}{Net\,income}$
		Dividend yield	$\frac{Dividend\,per\,share}{Price\,per\,share}$

$$Return\ on\ equity = \frac{Net\ income}{Equity} * \frac{Assets}{Assets}$$

Then, simply cross multiply to obtain

$$Return\ on\ Equity = \underbrace{\frac{Net\ Income}{Assets}}_{ROA} * \underbrace{\frac{Assets}{Equity}}_{EM}$$

Notice this simple process has decomposed the subject ratio into two other ratios, the return on assets (*ROA*) and the equity multiplier (EM). If the *ROE* is too low, it must be because either the *ROA* is too low or the capital structure needs to be adjusted. However, we can still go further in this analysis by again multiplying by one, which this time takes the form of *sales/sales*:

$$Return\ on\ equity = \frac{Sales}{Sales} * \frac{Net\ income}{Assets} * \frac{Assets}{Equity}$$

Again, cross multiplying results in

$$Return\ on\ Equity = \underbrace{\frac{Sales}{Assets}}_{TATO} * \underbrace{\frac{Net\ Income}{Sales}}_{PM} * \underbrace{\frac{Assets}{Equity}}_{EM}$$

So, the *ROE* depends upon three things: (1) the total asset turnover (TATO), (2) the profit margin (PM), and (3) the equity multiplier (EM). If it is deemed to be too low, then the reason must lie somewhere in those three categories. More to the point, recall that TATO is that a measure of asset use efficiency. If this is deemed to be the culprit, the conclusion is the firm simply isn't getting enough revenues into the company. Potential solutions could include price discounts, better advertising and promotion, or perhaps putting more desirable products on the shelves.

The profit margin is a measure of profitability. If it is deemed to be the culprit, the problem isn't necessarily in getting the money into the firm, but rather the rate in which it is retained. Potential solutions could perhaps lie in changes in the purchasing process, better training for employees, or identifying lower cost suppliers. Finally, if both of these values seem to be relatively on par with competitors and/or the industry, the issue must lie with the firm's chosen capital structure. The equity multiplier is a measure of the relationship between a firm's assets, equity, and, as an extension, debt.

2.6.8 Growth Rates

There is one final issue that warrants address before we move beyond financial statement analysis. Since the primary motivation of the firm is shareholder wealth maximization and this generally requires an attitude that facilitates firm growth, the expected growth rate is of obvious importance. While there are many ways of estimating a firm's growth rate, there are two that can be addressed readily alongside the materials in this chapter. The first, known as the **internal growth rate**, provides an estimate of how fast the firm can expect to grow when provided no external financing. Put differently, it is the rate the firm can expect to maintain if they only use the benefits from their business activities as a source of capital. With such an estimate, the possibility of external debt or equity financing is not considered, and the increase in assets is exactly offset by the increase in retained earnings:

$$Internal\ growth\ rate = \frac{ROA * b}{1 - (ROA * b)}$$

In the above equation, b refers to the retention ratio. If you think of it for a moment, the formula makes sense. ROA is the return on current assets, as calculated from the most recent financial statements. Thus, it is what the firm has shown to return from activities using the current asset base. The retention ratio, on other hand, represents *new money* that will be added, in some way, to the asset base of the firm. Thus, when you multiply the rate earned on existing assets with the ratio of new assets, the result is a growth rate that can be obtained including those new assets. The denominator of the ratio is a result of the assumption that we are using period-*ending* asset levels to calculate ROA. If, instead, you are using beginning of period levels, the dominator is removed from the equation.

The internal growth rate is a very restrictive measure of growth, since it allows the firm to have no outside "help" in financing projects. The second rate, the **sustainable growth rate**, is slightly less restrictive and is defined by a set of two characteristics:

1. The firm does not wish to issue new equity.
2. The firm wishes to maintain a constant debt-to-equity ratio.

The first characteristic is self-explanatory and has a strong basis. There are many reasons the firm would not wish to issue new equity, not the least of which is the large cost associated with doing so. The second characteristic is not the same as the internal growth rate because it doesn't require the firm to take *no* new debt or equity issuances. Rather, it says that as the firm increases their equity through retained earnings, they are willing to also add debt as long as the ratio between the two is maintained. Another way to put it is that the sustainable growth rate is the maximum rate at which the firm is expected to grow without an increase in financial leverage. They are, however, willing to take on debt in proportion to their increase in equity. Doing so allows the asset base to grow at a faster rate, which should also allow the firm to grow at a faster rate.

The formula for the sustainable growth rate is

$$Sustainable\ growth\ rate = \frac{ROE * b}{1 - (ROE * b)}$$

You can quickly see the only difference in the formulas is the inclusion of the return on equity instead of the return on assets. Since the *ROE* will always be greater than the *ROA* for any positive debt-level firm, the notion that the sustainable growth rate will be larger than the internal growth rate is confirmed. Again, the inclusion of the denominator is only appropriate when using ending of period accounting values, but that will be the customary assumption throughout the text. For Firm ABC, the growth rates can be calculated as follows:

$$\begin{aligned}\textbf{Internal growth rate} &= \frac{\mathbf{.4024 * .2514}}{\mathbf{1-(.4024 * .2514)}} \\ &= \mathbf{11.25\%} \\ \textbf{Sustainable growth rate} &= \frac{\mathbf{.9344 * .2514}}{\mathbf{1-(.9344 * .2514)}} \\ &= \mathbf{30.70\%}\end{aligned}$$

IN THE REAL WORLD

Dubarb Freeman always sat at his desk to have lunch. March 8, 2011, was no exception. While he could certainly afford to dine out and even had developed a certain level of fondness for the younger members of his team, he still felt most comfortable amid his stacks of papers. Tyler and Lilly had repeatedly attempted to lure him into one of the more spacious offices in the executive suite, but Freeman had steadfastly refused, choosing to remain lost in the back corridor of the junior employees' office space. That way he could be within easy shouting distance of all four of his team.

The team was less than thrilled by his loyalty.

Lunch for today was a fried egg and tomato sandwich with a side of potato salad, both lovingly prepared by Freeman's long-suffering wife. He was just finishing up when there was solid knock on his door.

"Come on in," Freeman mumbled as he gulped the last bit of his sandwich, leaving a small stream of tomato juice running down his chin. He quickly wiped it with the nearest thing to his left hand, which happened to be a neatly printed copy of last quarter's income statement.

"Uhm, hello, sorry to interrupt," came a cavernously deep voice that accompanied a mountain of a man into the tiny office space. Coleman Turner would have made an excellent exhibit for preschool teachers on square day. He carried broad shoulders as wide as the doorway with a block of cement perched squarely on top. He even wore square-rimmed glasses to further the look. It appeared as though he had traded his neck in for biceps. In short, Coleman did not look the part of a typecast accountant, but in reality, he was a top-notch numbers man.

Upon not receiving a response from Freeman, he ventured a half step further into the den of reckless organization. Each precipitously placed stack of papers

was exactly where it was supposed to be, since it was being used to hold up the neighboring stack. The Dubarb Freeman filing system. To Coleman, it was borderline unbearable. He defined his life by organization, which made him a perfect fit for his job.

"I'm a little early for the, uh, the meeting," he said and pointed at the tomato-stained paper in Freeman's hand. "We're supposed to go over the statements."

Freeman looked down and realized his dubious choice of napkin. He quickly placed the stained sheet on the nearest stack.

"Yes, yes, of course," he said. "I'll be right with you."

Like everything else, Freeman's actions undersold his attention to detail. He had studied the financial statements at length and was very much prepared for the meeting.

"I found a couple of things I thought would be good to talk about," Coleman said. His voice rumbled out of his throat like thunder, even though he had learned long ago to muffle it as much as possible.

"Yeah, yeah, absolutely," Freeman said, knowing he likely had many of the same thoughts. He craned his neck to direct his yell over Coleman's massive left shoulder.

"My office, please!" he bellowed. Moments later, Jane stuck her head in the door and inadvertently flinched when noticing Coleman. Marilyn arrived next and wedged herself in next to the big man. Stewart's head popped up over her shoulder. Brandon took the longest, taking a full ten seconds to arrive at the door. He was draining the last of his to-go cup of coffee.

"What's going on?" he said, speaking for the group.

"Coleman is here to go over those financials," Freeman said, "What say we take it to the conference room?"

Everyone breathed a sigh of relief. No one wanted to be the one that knocked over the first domino in Freeman's complex matrix of chaos.

Over the next 30 min, the small group discussed the previous quarter's statements, going into detail of the areas in which they had found improvement. Naturally, they also discussed areas where the firm was most struggling. Then, discussion turned to a longer time frame.

"Tyler and Lilly have been talking about making a large-scale financial commitment to improving the firm," Freeman announced, rather suddenly. This certainly caused his team to take notice. The young owners had taken a conservative approach to investment throughout the young public life of the firm. Even Coleman seemed excited. His left tricep twitched.

"Over the three-plus years since we've gone public, we have been working hard on getting the company in order, and we have, if I may say so myself, done a pretty good job. In fact, we've done about all we can with the infrastructure the firm currently has in place. Tyler and Lilly understand this and feel it is time to make an aggressive financial commitment to increasing firm value. And it is our job to figure out where that financial commitment would be best served. To that end, I propose we pull the annual statements for 2009 and 2010 and do some analysis."

"If I may," Coleman interjected, "I actually already have those numbers available. Marilyn and I were talking about this the other day and thought they may come in handy."

Jane, Stewart, and Brandon looked questioningly at Marilyn, who suddenly found a spot on the conference table fascinating. Coleman appeared oblivious to the extra attention as he held up a flash drive.

"They're right here," he announced.

Moments later, the overhead screen was filled with simplified versions of Hack Back's 2009 and 2010 income statements and balance sheets.

Hack Back, Inc.

Income statement for years ending December 31, 2009 and 2010

	2009	*2010*
Sales	*$327,890,500*	*$402,456,525*
Cost of goods sold	*244,606,313*	*327,599,611*
Depreciation	*37,435,864*	*41,385,900*
EBIT	*45,848,323*	*33,471,014*
Interest	*1,743,800*	*2,015,435*
Taxable income	*44,104,523*	*31,455,579*
Taxes (35%)	*15,436,583*	*11,009,453*
Net income	*28,667,940*	*20,446,126*
Dividends	*2,400,000*	*5,040,000*
Addition to retained earnings	*26,267,940*	*15,406,126*

Hack Back, Inc.

Balance sheet as of December 31, 2009 and 2010

Assets			*Liabilities*		
	2009	*2010*		*2009*	*2010*
Current assets			*Current liabilities*	*$20,435,135*	*$27,349,500*
Cash	*$37,970,869*	*$51,581,987*	*Long-term debt*	*28,197,000*	*30,125,346*
A/R	*17,976,050*	*19,341,907*	*Total debt*	*48,632,135*	*57,474,846*
Inventory	*102,987,500*	*140,891,891*			
Total	*158,934,419*	*211,815,785*	*Equity*		
				2009	*2010*
Fixed assets	*147,505,203*	*118,872,674*	*Common stock*	*223,200,000*	*223,200,000*
Total assets	*$306,439,622*	*$330,688,459*	*Retained earnings*	*34,607,487*	*50,013,613*
			Total equity	*257,807,487*	*273,213,613*
			Total debt and equity	*$306,439,622*	*$330,688,459*

"So, then we ran the standard ratio panel on it," Coleman said, as Marilyn nodded in agreement. "And here are the results of that."

A few moments later a new set of numbers flashed on the screen, divided into categories. Marilyn had recovered sufficiently to discuss the data being shown.

"You'll notice that we ran both years, along with peer analysis. We identified our closest competitors as Bubba's Golf Equipment, Inc., and PLC Golf, Inc.

Bubba's is a bigger company than ours in terms of market cap, while PLC is a bit smaller. We also included values for each ratio calculated from an industry composite index. This should give us a great idea of where we stand."

	HBCK2009	*HBCK2010*	*Bubba's*	*PLC Golf*	*Industry*
		Liquidity ratios			
Current ratio	7.7775	7.7448	6.4903	8.7606	6.5939
Quick ratio	2.7378	2.5932	3.9926	5.9055	4.3331
Cash ratio	1.8581	1.8860	2.6144	2.3602	2.7562
		Leverage ratios			
Total debt ratio	0.1587	0.1738	0.2781	0.1647	0.2355
Debt-to-equity ratio	0.1886	0.2104	0.3852	0.1971	0.3081
Equity multiplier	1.1886	1.2104	1.3852	1.1971	1.3081
Times interest earned	26.2922	16.6073	8.4221	7.7680	6.7602
Cash coverage ratio	47.7602	37.1418	14.7962	10.3281	10.7135
		Turnover ratios			
Total asset turnover	1.0700	1.2170	0.8670	0.9506	0.6935
Inventory turnover	2.3751	2.3252	3.4154	2.7560	3.1175
Days sales in inventory	153.6773	156.9768	106.8674	132.4365	117.0826
Receivables turnover	18.2404	20.8075	9.6945	4.0449	7.3414
Days sales in rec	20.0105	17.5418	37.6502	90.2374	49.7180
		Profitability ratios			
Profit margin	0.0874	0.0508	0.1179	0.1922	0.1367
Gross profit margin	0.2540	0.1860	0.3615	0.4513	0.3912
Operating profit margin	0.1398	0.0832	0.2058	0.3394	0.2468
Return on assets	0.0936	0.0618	0.1022	0.1827	0.0948
Return on equity	0.1112	0.0748	0.1416	0.2188	0.1240
		Market ratios			
Earnings per share	4.7780	3.4077	7.7002	6.0780	5.5826
Price-to-earnings	9.9875	19.0510	11.4283	8.3909	14.6884
Market-to-book	1.1106	1.4257	1.6177	1.8356	1.8218
		Dividend ratios			
Payout ratio	0.0837	0.2465	0.2279	0.5820	0.2962
Retention ratio	0.9163	0.7535	0.7721	0.4180	0.7038
Dividend yield	0.0084	0.0129	0.0199	0.0694	0.0202

After allowing a few moments to absorb the information, Freeman cleared his throat and offered a suggestion.

"What say we take them one category at a time," he said, settling deeper into his chair, "starting with the liquidity ratios."

It had become sort of an informal understanding that Brandon would begin discussions of this type, since he had no issue with leaping blindly. It was a task he knew he was suited for, so he didn't mind being the designated guinea pig. The others subconsciously angled towards him.

"I see nothing wrong with our ability to meet our short-term debt obligations," he said. "If you notice, our current ratio is on par with our competitors and the industry."

"Yes," Jane said, pointing at the screen, "but let's be careful. Look at the quick ratio. We trail the pack considerably there."

"And what is the difference between the two?" Freeman prompted.

"Inventory," Coleman boomed, the single word rattling around the walls.

"That's right," Freeman said, "and that is a number on our books that has been bothering me for a while. If you notice, we carry a lot of inventory."

"Do we know why?" Brandon asked.

Freeman knew the answer all too well, but was going to make them work for it.

"We have to in order to keep our business," he said cryptically. The others sat with furrowed brows thinking about the statement, until Coleman cleared his throat.

"If I may," he said in his softest loud voice. "I think I know what you mean, Mr. Freeman. I do all the billing for our distance deliveries, which we have been doing a lot lately. Our product isn't the easiest to ship so it takes time and money to get it to their destination. We keep a large reserve of inventory so that we can meet demand on all these distance orders."

"He's right," Freeman said, stabbing a finger in his direction. "And what is more, I personally know that we missed some earlier orders due to insufficient inventory. It takes too long to make the merchandise we sell, so we have to keep it in stock so as to get the deliveries to their destination in time."

"So, we can't make it when the orders come," Stewart said with a nod of understanding.

"Not given our current infrastructure," Freeman agreed with a shake of his rumpled head, "and along with the fact that a large portion of our demand is spread across the USA."

"You know," Jane said thoughtfully, "that also makes sense with something else I notice in these numbers. On average it takes us more than a month longer to move a piece of inventory than our benchmarks." She glanced at Freeman. "I get what you are saying about it being necessary, but that is a lot of money tied up in inventory for a long time."

"Which also drains our cash resources," Stewart added, "and makes us riskier and more susceptible to financial distress."

"This all suggests to me," Marilyn spoke up, "that we need to think about a way of more efficiently producing our merchandise and then more efficiently getting it to the customer." The sentiment was unmistakably Marilyn. It was her typical inclination to search for a broad fix as soon as possible. She was a more of a "bigger picture" thinker than the others.

"Well, let's get back to the point at hand for a moment before we go there," Freeman gently urged. "Although we clearly see the issue with excess inventory, can we now look at the long-term solvency?"

Around the room, five heads nodded. Only one spoke.

"I don't see a problem in that area," Coleman said, beginning to feel more a part of the group. "But that is a primarily a product of our low debt levels. Our ability to pay our interest is really not in doubt at the current time."

"Agreed. So we can move on," Freeman said. "You all know that the turnover measures are indicators of the demand for our products. Tell me your thoughts in that area."

"Aside from the inventory issue we have already discussed, they also look pretty good," Stewart said. "Our total asset turnover is higher than our competitors and the industry. Our receivables seem to be turning over very well also."

"It seems to me the problem is not in getting money, but rather in keeping it once we get it." Brandon said. "Our sales figure is up by more than 20 % over 2009, which is amazing. But, our net income is lower. *That is an odd, and bad, scenario."*

Stewart was nodding. "Look at our profitability ratios," he said. "Our profit margin is currently less than half that of the industry. We only keep a nickel on the dollar."

"And what's more," Marilyn said, "is that the problem seems to be largely the expenses of those sales. The operating profit margin is abysmal as well."

"Even worse," Jane added, "is our return on equity. It also considerably lags our benchmark measures."

"You are all making excellent, and worrisome, points," Freeman said encouragingly, which was hard for him to pull off. "And we can drive them home by also adding that not only are these numbers unflattering, but they seem to be getting worse. If you compare 2010 to 2009, we see a discouraging trend."

He paused and held up an open palm to emphasize the next point.

"But," he said emphatically, "you are all well aware that this discouraging news has, for some reason, not resulted in a negative market reaction. In fact, we had a wonderful year during 2010, with our stock price going from less than fifty dollars to nearly sixty-five."

Freeman again paused to let the group mull over the details.

"So," Brandon said slowly rolling his thoughts out of his mouth as they formed, "we had a great market year, despite the negative numbers in relation to peers and a troublesome trend within our own ratios.... What does that tell us?"

Jane answered first.

"I think it means that the market is viewing our stock as a profitable future investment, but that we are going to very soon have to earn that trust."

"Very good," Freeman encouraged, "carry on."

"Well, the reason I say that is because of the market ratios, particularly the P/E ratio. In 2009, it was well below industry average, but last year it shot up by more than 100 %, mostly as a product of the increase in stock price. Now we are above our competitors and the industry. This creates a scenario where we are viewed as a riskier security, since our price is high in relation to our earnings. Risk encourages investment but of course also encourages fickle investors. If we fail to continue to deliver both internally and externally, we will lose shareholders. And when we lose shareholders, we will lose value, which goes against everything we want to do. It's a vicious cycle."

"I agree with her," Marilyn added. "And if we continue to follow a pattern of eating our sales with expenses before they become profits, it will happen sooner rather than later."

"It seems to me," Stewart spoke up again, "that the way to solve this is to try to fix the issues we have brought up so that future statements can more favorably reflect the financial health of the firm."

"Good, good," Dubarb said, slightly impatient to get to the final point. "Who would like to summarize?"

"I will," Brandon offered, holding up his hand and ticking off points. "First, we need to work on a way of reducing money held in excess inventory, but we need to do so in a way that doesn't harm sales. This, in part, would require us to find a way to access our out-of-region customer base. Second, we need to work on more efficiently taking advantage of our demand. The turnover figures indicate that we have products that are marketable and in demand. But we have to work on generating profits from that demand."

"And third, we need to work on a way of reassuring shareholders that our stock price is not artificially inflated to an unsustainable level."

"That's a good assessment," Freeman said approvingly. "Now, let me add a few proprietary details that I am privy to."

This got everyone's attention. It was rare that Freeman let go of secrets.

"First, I can put numbers to the qualitative statements made regarding our customer base. Three years ago, over 90 % of our sales were within 300 miles of where we sit, with only the occasional large warehouse order from another region. Over the past twelve months, however, nearly 40 % of our sales have come from areas outside of that radius."

Everyone's eyebrows seemed to rise in unison.

"And, the marketing department is putting the final touches on a national advertising campaign, which will feature our two new spokespersons: Natalie Fulton and Shane Logan."

Everyone's mouths made the effort to get as far from their eyebrows as possible. Natalie Fulton and Shane Logan were professional golfers on the LPGA and PGA tours, respectively. Both had won multiple times over the past year and had huge followings. The fact that Hack Back had signed them to endorsement deals was a huge step forward in getting the Hack Back name into mainstream golf.

Freeman pretended he didn't notice their reactions and continued.

"So, we have no reason to believe the out-of-region demand will slow down in the near future. There is just no way we can continue to efficiently ship the goods to all over creation."

"So what's the proposal?" Marilyn asked, unable to hold her tongue any more.

"Well," Freeman paused for the dramatic, "with your agreement, I am going to propose to Tyler, Lilly, and the board that we begin analysis on a project that would result in two new production plants being placed at geographically

advantageous areas within the country. To do so will be a large undertaking, easily the largest that we have done. But, I personally feel it is time to move, since our market presence is starting to build along with our demand. If we wait too long, it will be too late to capture the market share that is currently there for the taking."

His words rang true to those in the small audience and their agreement was implied by eager nods of consent.

"So," Freeman continued, "you know your roles. Marilyn and Stewart," he turned in their direction, "you are assigned the arduous task of identifying potential projects and coming up with expected cash flows from those projects. I'm sure Coleman will assist you in the accounting aspect of the job."

Coleman eagerly nodded, and Marilyn failed to hide her smile. Freeman then turned to Jane and Brandon.

"And you two are assigned the task of identifying the best way to fund the projects that we decide are best."

Freeman then turned to address the entire crowd again.

"Naturally, we will also continue to work together as well when an issue arises. I want all of us to know what is happening at all times. This is an important time for Hack Back, and I want to make sure we do everything the correct way."

ALTERNATE ENDINGS

1. ***Assume that instead of ratio analysis, Anna and Coleman had completed common-size income statements for Hack Back, Bubba's, PLC, and the industry composite (the statements are presented in an appendix). Pretend you are either Marilyn or Coleman and make a report to Dubarb Freeman solely from the common-size statements. What is your advice? Does it differ?***
2. ***Suppose Coleman and Marilyn had completed the basic DuPont Identity as a way of furthering their arguments. How would that look? Does it support the contention that profitability is the primary issue with Hack Back?***
3. ***Insert the following statement somewhere in the dialogue above:***

   "Okay," said Dubarb, "now let's talk about the dividend ratios. What do they add to this discussion? Also, what is your recommendation on the percentages we are paying out? Given our needs, should we increase or decrease the payout ratio?"

   It is your turn to play author. Insert the dialogue you feel necessary to respond to this, using the characters you wish to respond.

Concept Questions

1. **Finance versus accounting** You have a friend that is a rising junior in college and is in the process of making a tough decision. She has narrowed her choice for major to either accounting or finance and knows that, with either one, she wants to work in a large corporation. She comes to you for advice. What are the

differences in the jobs she would be doing? What are the similarities? How should she go about deciding which one she wants?

2. **Income statement** Discuss the form and function of the typical income statement. Why is it important for a firm?
3. **Dividends versus retained earnings** Hank from the board of directors has issued a proposal that the firm start paying 98 % of their profits in dividends. "There's no better way to keep shareholders happy!" he exclaims. How do you respond?
4. **Corporate taxes** Julie is getting ready to file both her personal and corporate tax returns. She is confused because the tax rates seem to work differently. Explain to Julie what is going on with corporate taxes that differ from individual taxes.
5. **Corporate tax rates** Company XYZ is proposing a new multimillion dollar project that is expected to generate revenues for the next 10 years. They are using the average tax rate from last year in their estimations. What is the potential problem with doing this? What should they use?
6. **Market versus book values** Your company has a large machine that originally cost \$100,000. They just sold it for \$20,000 and actually got a tax reward for doing so. How could they have received a tax benefit from a cash inflow?
7. **Balance sheet** Discuss the form and function of the balance sheet. Why is it important for a firm?
8. **Using accounting statements** Your neighbor across the office just made the statement, "I don't understand how accounting statements help in finance at all. Accounting tells us what has happened and finance is concerned with what will happen." What is he missing?
9. **Peer analysis** How do you determine if values on accounting statements are "good" or "bad." Discuss the difficulties of doing so, along with potential solutions to those difficulties.
10. **Standardized statements** You are trying to explain standardized statements to your friend, who is an avid golfer. He doesn't understand, so you try it in his language. "Standardizing your statements is like handicaps in golfing. It puts everyone on a level playing field," you say. He still doesn't get it. "What do you mean?" he asks. Go ahead; explain the analogy to him.
11. **Ratio analysis** Discuss the five categories of ratio analysis, detailing the role they play in determining the financial well-being of the firm.
12. **DuPont identity** Explain the difference between the DuPont Identity and a standard ratio. What does the DuPont allow that the standard ratio does not?
13. **Growth rates** Internal and sustainable growth rates measure the firm's expected growth rate, with restrictions. Discuss those restrictions and how you can draw similarities between the way they are calculated and your personal financial decisions.

Problems

1. **Income statement** Fill in the blanks in the following income statements.

Income statement for the year ending Dec. 31, 2012	
Sales	1,369,534
Cost of goods sold	
Depreciation	146,897
EBIT	
Interest	86,389
Taxable income	
Taxes (35 %)	
Net income	**456,897**
Dividends	129,485
Addition to retained earnings	

2. **Net income** During 2012, Patrick's Dog Salon, Inc., had total sales of $430,000 and costs were 59 % of sales. They also had interest expense of $5,300 and depreciation of $3,400. What is the firm's net income if their tax rate is 35 %?
3. **Retained earnings** In the preceding problem, if Patrick pays out $15,000 in dividends, what is the addition to retained earnings?
4. **EPS and DPS** Using the two problems above, suppose Patrick has 34,000 shares outstanding. What is the earnings per share (EPS)? What is the dividend paid per share?
5. **Income statement** Last year, Billy's Boat Barn had net income of $1,285,000 and paid out dividends of $482,000. This year, Billy plans to implement a new project that will increase income by 15 %. If he desires to maintain a constant payout policy, how much does Billy expect to add to retained earnings this year?
6. **Taxes** Iam's Security, LLC, generated taxable income of $483,000 last year. What is her tax bill? What is her average tax rate? What is her marginal tax rate?
7. **Depreciation** Benefield's Matchmaking Company just bought a new computer network designed to match customer compatibilities electronically. The machine cost $87,000 and is classified as a 5-year property. What is the ending book value in year four?
8. **Market and book values** In the preceding problem, suppose Benefield sold the machine for $18,000 at the end of the fifth year. What are the tax ramifications? Is it a tax bill or tax savings?
9. **Balance sheet** As of the end of 2012, Summerville Paving, Inc., had current assets of $86,000, current liabilities of $45,000, long-term debt of $340,000, and total shareholder equity of 294,000. What is the amount of fixed assets?
10. **Market and book values** Exactly 3 years ago, you bought a van for your firm at a cost of $37,000. The van falls within a 5-year property class. Today, a competitor came to you and offered to buy the van. However, if you sold it to her, you would have a tax bill of $2,665.60. If your tax rate is 35 %, what was the price your competitor offered for the van?

11. **Profitability ratios** Holly's Fish Farm, Inc., has a current ratio of 2.1 times. In addition, she has total assets of $571,000 and total debt of $214,000. Holly's *ROE* is 18.7 %. What is her net income?
12. **Profitability ratios** Billy's Sheet Factory had taxable income of $20 million last year. In addition, they have total assets of $36 million and a tax rate of 35 %. What is Billy's return on assets?
13. **Long-term solvency ratios** If the firm has an equity multiplier of 1.85 times, what is the firm's existing capital structure?
14. **DuPont identity** Nanny's Doll Emporium has a profit margin of 11 %, total asset turnover of .8 times, and return on equity of 16.3 %. What percentage of the firm's capital structure is debt?
15. **DuPont identity** The firm's net income is $59,423, total assets is $458,008, total sales is $380,083, and debt-to-equity ratio is 2.81 times. What is the firm's *ROE*?
16. **Internal growth rate** Your firm had net income of $590,000 last year. The firm has debt of $2.4 million and equity of $1.8 million. The firm paid a dividend per share of $.05 for each of their five million shares of stock last year. What is the firm's internal growth rate?
17. **Sustainable growth rate** Mac and Lindsey's Doughnut Shop, Inc., had a taxable income of $1,152,546 and a tax rate of 35 %. They have 500,000 shares outstanding and have a dividend per share (DPS) of $.51. They have a *ROE* of 21.74 %. What is the firm's sustainable growth rate?
18. **Standardized statements** Create common-size income statements and balance sheets for Gennifer's Basket Shop, whose 2012 statements are below.

Gennifer's Basket Shop, Inc.	
Income statement for the year ending Dec. 31, 2012	
Sales	85,432
COGS	24,810
Depreciation	1,050
EBIT	59,572
Interest	11,211
Taxable income	48,361
Taxes (35%)	16,926
Net income	31,435
Dividends	21,976
Add to retained earnings	9,459

Gennifer's Basket Shop, Inc.			
Balance sheet as of December 31, 2012			
Assets		**Liabilities**	
Current assets		Current liabilities	
Cash	28,517	A/P	18,371
A/R	11,500	N/P	18,800
Inventory	5,320	Total current	37,171
Total current	45,337		
		Long-term debt	24,111
Fixed assets	50,333	Total debt	61,282
Total assets	95,670		
		Equity	
		Common stock	22,604
		Retained earnings	11,784
		Total equity	34,388
		Total liabilities and owners equity	95,670

19. **Ratio analysis** Complete a ratio panel on Gennifer's Basket Shop, Inc., using all ratios included in Table 2.7. Gennifer has 5,000 shares outstanding, each selling at $24 per share.
20. **Ratio analysis** Gennifer's Basket Shop has two primary competitors, Bob's Weave Shop and Harriet's Container Station. The ratios for each of those firms are presented below. Based upon your work in the preceding question, provide Gennifer with some guidance regarding areas of strengths and weaknesses.

	Bob's Weave Shop	Harriet's Container Station
	Liquidity ratios	
Current ratio	2.9631	2.9450
Quick ratio	2.6736	2.2764
Cash ratio	2.0476	0.3668
	Leverage ratios	
Total debt ratio	0.2853	0.2912
Debt-to-equity ratio	0.3992	0.4109
Equity multiplier	1.3992	1.4109
Times interest earned	6.1581	13.9828
Cash coverage ratio	7.1440	22.5984
	Turnover ratios	
Total asset turnover	0.9280	0.6336
Inventory turnover	13.7858	2.3274
Days sales in inventory	26.4765	156.8298
Receivables turnover	13.3419	1.6906
Days sales in rec.	27.3574	215.9039
	Profitability ratios	
Profit margin	0.2049	0.1934
Gross profit margin	0.5220	0.5180
Operating profit margin	0.4500	0.3205
Return on assets	0.1901	0.1226
Return on equity	0.2660	0.1729

(continued)

	Bob's Weave Shop	Harriet's Container Station
	Market ratios	
Earnings per share	5.1100	6.0700
Price-to-earnings	7.0360	6.8500
Market-to-book	6.3500	5.3400
	Dividend ratios	
Payout ratio	0.6991	0.7699
Retention ratio	0.3009	0.2301

Chapter 3
Cash Flow: Easy Come, Easy Go

Chapter 1 introduced the two major financial decisions that go into helping the firm grow and increase shareholder wealth. In Chap. 2, we learned how to use financial statement analysis to aid in making financial decisions. A primary goal of that process was to identify areas of opportunity, where a potential project would be most beneficial. Once that identification is complete, the next step involves closely examining the expected cash flows of those potential projects. This is the first step in capital budgeting, or the process of choosing projects in which we will invest company funds. The discussion will begin with an overview of cash flows in general, before moving into calculating them for the firm at large. Finally, we will address the process of calculating cash flows for a single project.

3.1 Introducing Cash Flows

Before starting with any calculations, we must first briefly discuss exactly what we mean by the term **cash flow**. The key is the "flow" component. Cash flow is the amount of money *flowing* in and out of the firm. When the inflows and outflows are combined together, we get the **net cash flow**, which is a primary variable used in making capital budgeting decisions. Again, we can use the bucket of water analogy from Chap. 1 to illustrate the concept. I bet you never knew there was such financial intuition in a bucket of water.

Imagine for a moment we have a stationary water bucket containing a certain level of water. That water level could represent a firm's net income as of last quarter. It is static in nature and will not change until a new quarter is concluded, and the water level is adjusted to the new income level. Now, instead of a stationary object, imagine that there is a stream of water flowing into the bucket. That stream of water represents cash *inflows* and is money that is coming into the firm as a result of asset utilization. Unfortunately, at the same time, you must imagine that there is a hole in the bottom of the bucket and that water is continuously streaming out as well. Naturally, this represents cash *outflows*.

M.K. Pyles, *Applied Corporate Finance: Questions, Problems and Making Decisions in the Real World*, Springer Texts in Business and Economics,
DOI 10.1007/978-1-4614-9173-6_3, © Springer Science+Business Media New York 2014

These come about as a result of expenses during the course of asset utilization. Thus, the end result should bring to mind a fountain, where water (cash) is constantly moving about.

Knowing the amount of money available at any point in time is of paramount importance in finance, a discipline that we have already discussed as being one of present and future focus. In addition, cash flow lends itself nicely to the philosophy that underlies finance, which is rooted in maximizing the benefits from the movement of firm money. Money flows in and money flows out and the specifics of this action are the crux of corporate finance. Thus, while the sales or net income figures are certainly valuable tools to use in corporate finance, cash flow is much more so.

3.2 Cash Flow Identity

The **cash flow identity** is very similar to the balance sheet identity, but you are likely much less familiar with this concept. The identity is as follows:

$$\textit{Cash flow from assets} = \textit{Cash flow to creditors} + \textit{Cash flow to shareholders}$$

Two things should automatically jump out. First, it looks a great deal like the balance sheet identity in that it contains the same three components. Second, the three terms now have movement attached to them. The second point is naturally the most important as it largely sums up the difference between the two identities. The balance sheet identity is rooted in static figures, whereas finance is concerned with monetary movements related to these figures. On the left-hand side of the cash flow identity is **cash flow from assets** (***CFFA***). The important distinction that must be drawn in relation to the balance sheet identity is that we are now trying to examine what the firm *does* with their asset base, not just the size of that base.

Consider an extreme example of a firm that has $1 million worth of assets, but has not produced or sold a single product or service over the past year. While it is certainly noteworthy that the firm has a significant asset base, the fact that it is not producing cash is much more so. Thus, cash flow *from* assets is designed to capture the money that flowed into the firm over the period in question. Money flows *from* assets and *to* the firm. This naturally is the specific manifestation of the water stream flowing into the bucket. Any firm would generally desire this to be a positive number, although a negative value is certainly possible. Usually this negative value would be unwelcomed by the firm, but there are instances where the firm's strategy could result in a negative *CFFA*, at least for a limited period of time. The upcoming text will discuss these possibilities as part of the discussion of the components of *CFFA*.

The right-hand side of the cash flow identity follows the design of the left. The balance sheet combines the firm's levels of debt and equity, which effectively indicates that every dollar of assets must have been in some way a result of creditors' loans or shareholders' investment. The cash flow identity is analogous to this in that the right-hand side must account for every dollar that flows into the firm by recognizing that it must then flow to either creditors or shareholders. Notice the change in direction of the monetary flows; dollars are now flowing *away* from the firm and *to* either creditors or shareholders. This is akin to the holes in the bottom of the firm's cash flow bucket.

3.2.1 Operating Cash Flow

CFFA is actually comprised of three underlying factors. The first of these is the most obvious and is most commonly known as **operating cash flow** (***OCF***). *OCF* results from the aggregation of day-to-day selling of assets the firm produces. Creating financial data from accounting values is slightly more complicated than just using those values as given, unfortunately. It becomes necessary to adjust certain accounting values to make use of them in a financial framework. While there are many ways to calculate *OCF*, we will focus our discussion on the following equation:

$$OCF = EBIT + Depreciation - Taxes$$

LOOK IT UP: As it says, there are various ways to find *OCF*. Try looking up a few, specifically the bottom-up, the top-down, and the tax shield approach. Do they all give you the same answer?

OCF is very similar in nature to net income, meaning the desire is to calculate revenues minus costs. However, the aim is to calculate the value from a financial perspective rather than an accounting perspective. Generally speaking, the objective is to produce a number that accurately reflects the number of dollars that flowed into the firm. This value would omit two very important pieces of the typical income statement. The first is depreciation. As covered in Chap. 2, depreciation is a necessity in accounting to adjust historical book values to more timely values in subsequent period-ending statements. However, when depreciation occurs, it does not directly result in cash moving. As such, the value inserted in standard income statements is classified as a **noncash expense** and should not be included in *OCF*.

The other necessary omission is dissimilar in that it most definitely results in money being moved. Interest expenses represent the firm's payment during the period to lending institutions to which they owe money. This does not fall under the umbrella of a noncash expense since real money must be shifted from the firm to the lender. The reason for omission is due to the direction of movement and the entity to which the money flows. *OCF* is designed to capture net income related specifically to the firm's sales of products or services. Interest does not fall under

Table 3.1 Income statement for XYZ Corporation

XYZ Corporation	
Income statement for the year ending Dec. 31, 2012 (values in 000s)	
Sales	374,534
Cost of goods sold	204,271
Depreciation	14,897
EBIT	155,366
Interest	14,389
Taxable income	140,977
Taxes (35 %)	49,342
Net income	91,635
Dividends	47,696
Addition to retained earnings	43,939

Table 3.2 Balance sheet for XYZ Corporation

XYZ Corp.					
Balance sheet as of December 31, 2011 and 2012 (values in 000s)					
Assets			Liabilities		
	2011	2012		2011	2012
Current			Current		
Cash	22,454	24,341	A/P	31,970	28,699
A/R	11,335	14,960	N/P	37,603	45,435
Inventory	45,980	50,123	Total current	69,573	74,134
Total current	79,769	89,424	Long term	105,343	104,797
Fixed assets	242,381	279,825	Total debt	174,916	178,931
Total assets	**322,150**	**369,249**	Equity		
				2011	2012
			Common stock	135,335	127,980
			Retained earnings	11,899	62,338
			Total equity	147,234	190,318
			Total debt and equity	**322,150**	**369,249**

this description, but rather falls on the right-hand side of the cash flow identity. It will be covered in due time a bit later in the chapter.

Back to the *OCF* equation, by starting with *EBIT*, we can begin with a number that is already net of costs of goods sold and depreciation, but has not yet removed interest or taxes. Since the objective is to remove depreciation as a noncash expense, we have to negate what was done on the income statement and add depreciation. By starting with *EBIT*, we need not deal with interest since it has not yet been addressed. However, taxes must be a consideration for the same reason that depreciation isn't; money indeed changes hands since a check must be cut to the government for the tax bill. Therefore, the tax amount must be subtracted. This series of actions results in the end equation. As an example to aid our discussion of cash flow, consider a fictitious firm XYZ, whose accounting statements are presented in Tables 3.1 and 3.2.

Using the information in Table 3.1, we can calculate *OCF* for XYZ Corporation as

$$\mathbf{155,366 + 14,897 - 49,342 = \$120,921}$$

3.2.2 Net Capital Spending

The second piece of *CFFA* is **net capital spending (*NCS*)**. While *OCF* is a product of a continuous series of day-to-day actions, *NCS* is generally a less frequent but longer-term concern. Specifically, it measures long-term investments in fixed assets made by the company. Mathematically, *NCS* is calculated as follows:

$$NCS = Ending\ net\ fixed\ assets - Beginning\ net\ fixed\ assets + Depreciation$$

The term fixed assets is another way of describing long-term assets. The "net" part means that the buying (increases) and selling (decreases) of long-term assets have already been combined into the end value on the balance sheet. Therefore, the difference between the ending and beginning values for this variable represents spending on net fixed assets throughout the year. It is worthwhile to note that there is no such thing as a beginning of the period accounting statement. So, in order to find both a beginning and an ending value for a specific period of time, we must have 2 years of statements, as we do for Firm XYZ in Table 3.2.

Depreciation is added back in for much the same reason as it was with *OCF*. Depreciable assets are generally fixed assets; thus, the adjustment is appropriate. The purpose, once again, is to calculate the number of dollars that flowed into and out of the firm as a result of purchases or sales of fixed assets. Depreciation serves to deflate the ending value and, if not accounted for, could result in a downward bias in the difference between the ending and beginning values. *NCS* can easily be positive or negative, where positive represents a greater value in purchases than sales throughout the period and negative represents the opposite.

For XYZ, this value is

$$\mathbf{279,825 - 242,381 + 14,897 = \$52,341}$$

3.2.3 Change in Net Working Capital

Finally, the last piece imbedded in *CFFA* is change in **net working capital (Δ*NWC*)**. **Net working capital (*NWC*)** is the difference between current assets and current liabilities at any period in time and measures the firm's operating liquidity, as evidenced by the relative levels of the firm's short-term assets and liabilities. Recall from Chap. 2 that liquidity is a subject of considerable concern for a firm due to the trade-off between security and profitability. In practice, liquidity is a broad concern, touching on any financial obligation the firm may have in the short and/or long run. **Operating liquidity** refers to the relationship between short-term assets and short-term liabilities, which are primary components of the firm's day-to-day operating processes. *NWC* is the prime example of this relationship. It is very similar to the current ratio, also covered in Chap. 2, except it examines the difference between current assets and current liabilities rather than the quotient.

Should the firm have a high *NWC*, this would suggest a high level of operating liquidity, as the firm has a large short-term asset base in relation to their short-term liability base. Such a value would also suggest that the firm has little concerns about interruptions to operations due to a shortage of liquidity. Of course, it could also mean the firm is not maximizing production, since the assets could potentially be used to increase the operating level of the firm. Contrarily, a low *NWC* level would suggest a low level of operating liquidity. In the relative extreme, if the firm has a negative *NWC*, this would imply the firm has more short-term bills than short-term assets. Such a situation is typically not ideal.

The change in *NWC* is the difference in operating liquidity from one period to the next, again calculated from two consecutive period-ending balance sheets. The numerical value can easily be a positive or negative number, depending on the circumstances. A positive change in *NWC* would indicate the firm either increased their level of current assets more than current liabilities or they decreased their level of current liabilities more than current assets. A negative change would necessarily require the opposite in each relative situation. The equation for ΔNWC is

$$\begin{aligned}\Delta NWC &= \textit{Ending net working capital} - \textit{Beginning net working capital} \\ &= (\textit{Ending current assets} - \textit{Ending current liabilities}) \\ &\quad - (\textit{Beginning current assets} - \textit{Beginning current liabilities})\end{aligned}$$

Therefore, for XYZ, this value is

$$\mathbf{(89,424 - 74,134) - (79,769 - 69,573) = \$5,094}$$

Before moving to the right-hand side of the identity, the three pieces of the left-hand side need to be put together. *OCF* is the primary cash flow variable from firm operations and one that typically needs to be positive. As mentioned, the other two (*NCS* and ΔNWC) can be either positive or negative. More importantly, if either (or both) is positive, that actually means the firm is *spending* money, either on fixed assets or on increasing operating liquidity. Spent money is money flowing away from the firm and, as such, decreases the *CFFA*. In fact, it is possible that the increase in spending on either or both areas would be so large as to overcome the *OCF*. The end result in such a situation would be a negative *CFFA*. While not ideal over a long period of time, such a finding could be a result of the firm aggressively investing in projects to benefit the firm in future periods. There will be a great deal of discussion of this type in the second phase of this chapter.

Together, we have the following relationship:

$$CFFA = OCF - NCS - \Delta NWC$$

For XYZ, this works out to

$$\mathbf{120,921 - 52,341 - 5,094 = 63,486}$$

3.2.4 Cash Flow to Creditors

Luckily, the right-hand side of the cash flow identity is simpler than the left. In fact, each of the two values has only one equation. **Cash flow to creditors (*CFTC*)** is the money that goes to pay those who have loaned money to the firm. These could be private (e.g., bank) loans or public loans. There are two basic ways that money can flow from the corporation to the lenders, or vice versa. The first is direct and is the already spoken of interest amount from the income statement. Interest is simply the contractual payment to the lender that allows the borrower to retain the balance of borrowed funds for the upcoming period. Then the cycle repeats each period. The second type of cash flow between the firm and creditors is the change to the total amount of debt outstanding. A corporation can either take on more debt or they can pay off debt already obtained. In sum, the equation is as follows:

$$\begin{aligned} CFTC &= Interest - (Net\ new\ borrowing) \\ &= Interest - (Ending\ long - Term\ debt - Beginning\ long - Term\ debt) \end{aligned}$$

CFTC can be either positive or negative depending upon the second component. In a nonfinancial firm, interest paid is typically a positive number. However, *net new borrowing* can be either positive or negative. A positive number means the firm borrowed more than they paid off during the period, while a negative number means they paid off more than they borrowed. Remember that interest payments alone do not reduce the outstanding balance, so the firm would have to pay any excess directly to reducing the balance. There will be much more on loans in Chap. 4.

In the case of XYZ, this value is

$$\mathbf{14,389 - (104,797 - 105,343) = \$14,935}$$

3.2.5 Cash Flow to Shareholders

The final piece of the identity is **cash flow to shareholders (*CFTS*)**. This takes much the same form as *CFTC* in that there is a direct cash flow that is easily identified and another that is more indirect. The equation is

$$\begin{aligned} CFTS &= Dividends - (Net\ new\ equity\ raised) \\ &= Dividends - [(Ending\ total\ equity - Beginning\ total\ equity) \\ &\quad - Addition\ to\ retained\ earnings] \end{aligned}$$

We've already briefly discussed dividends paid by a corporation and how they provide a source of cash flow to shareholders. *Net new equity raised* is a bit more complicated. Each of the four words is important, but the key is *raised*. Subtracting beginning equity from ending equity is instinctual. This provides the additional total equity the firm acquired during the course of the year. This isn't the value we are really concerned with, however. The concern is to identify the number of dollars that flowed from the firm to shareholders. A portion of the change in total equity did not leave or enter the firm, but instead was reinvesting internally. Naturally, this portion is the addition to retained earnings from the income statement.

For XYZ Corporation, *CFTS* is

$$\mathbf{47,696 - [(190,318 - 147,234) - 43,939] = \$48,551}$$

3.2.6 Balancing Act

Now comes the moment of truth. If everything has been done correctly, the two sides should balance. This is more than just mathematical trickery, however. At the risk of redundancy, remember that every dollar that comes in must go somewhere. This is simply how finance works. We try to follow the flow of funds from beginning to end and from that attempt to find ways to maximize the returns generated from that stream of cash flows.

For firm XYZ, we have computed each component:

$$CFFA = CFTC + CFTS$$
$$\mathbf{63,486 = 14,935 + 48,551}$$
$$\mathbf{63,486 = 63,486}$$

Thank goodness it worked. That would have been embarrassing!

IN THE REAL WORLD

Once the decision was made to actively increase their production capacity by building two additional plants, the entire finance team started working overtime to gather much needed information. On a Tuesday morning in mid-June, Marilyn and Coleman were working late to identify suitable geographical locations for the plants. They had convened in Coleman's office, which resembled a government-sanctioned experimental laboratory.

His large desk was covered in spotless glass, while the wooden furniture was a light shade of blonde. Everything was in its proper place, including the owner, who sat comfortably in his desk chair, which was roughly the size of a smart car. Marilyn was lounging much less comfortably in one of his straight-backed, un-cushioned visitor's chairs. They had just finished a conference call with the mayor of Landrum, Iowa, who said the town would be more than delighted to have Hack Back build a plant in his grand city. What could he do to help? Anything they needed....

"Well, it's a possibility," Coleman said with a sigh, "but I'm not sold."

"Yeah, we'll see," Marilyn agreed absently. "They all sound like ads on a dating site. Apparently every city is the equivalent of tall, dark, and handsome."

"Where's Stewart?" Coleman asked, smiling in amusement at her analogy.

"Doing the same thing we are," Marilyn said, rolling her neck to relieve the building stress. "This is a lot of work that I personally didn't see coming. The process of identifying a location is just the first step and it's becoming a nightmare."

Coleman nodded sympathetically. The groundwork to such a project was larger than any of them had ever anticipated. Everyone was determined to make the best decision possible, and they were leaving no stone unturned in the process. They had begun with the assumption that one plant should be in the Midwest and the other in the Southeast. But, of course, both areas are very large, so they had already spent a lot of time in narrowing down the list of possibilities. This included taking a close look at demand patterns by creating a detailed demand chart based upon historical client orders.

Using that, Marilyn and Stewart had attempted to pinpoint areas that would be as centrally located as possible. From there, the options had been narrowed substantially by looking at certain zoning restrictions, property availability, and employee potential. Local and state tax laws were a large concern as well. Data was gathered from many sources, and the collection process was tedious, but the end result was an isolated area of approximately 200 square miles in both geographical sections where building a production plant would be most advantageous. Then, following a suggestion by Dubarb Freeman, they started canvassing the major construction companies in each location to get estimates on costs. Requests were sent to approximately twenty architectural design firms in each area for estimates of building costs based upon the outlined parameters.

They were now in the process of analyzing all of that data and talking to political officials and community leaders to gauge interest in having Hack Back set up a shop there. As Marilyn had alluded, most had been uninhibitedly excited about the prospect of hundreds of jobs and potentially millions in tax revenues, but there had been a few that were uninterested in the increased traffic the plant would bring to their area. And some had even been honest enough to share the shortcomings of their location. It had been a fruitful process, but Marilyn and Stewart were absolutely exhausted and Jane and Brandon were working too hard on their own assignments to help. So, Marilyn had called in Coleman as reinforcement. Working with Marilyn wasn't a hard sell for the big man, and he willingly set his own work aside for the afternoon. But the afternoon had now bled into evening, and he was feeling like getting out of the office for the day.

"So, where are we in the process?" he prodded Marilyn, who looked to be in danger of falling asleep in the chair.

"Well, we are nearly ready to begin putting some numbers into the models," she replied wearily. "And then we can come up with expected cash flows."

"Then the end is in sight, isn't it?" Marilyn looked up to see a rare smile on Coleman's face.

"For tonight it is," she responded as she rose from her seat. "I'm beat."

As she started for the door, Coleman said, "Too beat for Mexican?"

Marilyn turned with a quizzical expression.
Coleman shrugged and said, "It's fajita night."
He didn't wait for an answer as he grabbed his coat.

3.3 Projects and Cash Flow

Now that we have a general understanding of cash flows, we need to work on getting a handle on how to estimate them for a specific project. As discussed in length in Chaps. 1 and 2, a large part of the purpose of corporate finance is to find areas in which the firm can expand and add value. Thus, while calculating cash flows for the entire firm is certainly a significant concern, it is also imperative to understand how to apply this knowledge to specific projects the firm may wish to undertake. This section of the text deals with this issue in considerable detail.

Whether on a firm or project basis, cash flows that are predicted for the future period are known as **expected cash flows**. In finance we often find ourselves looking forward, which creates considerable problems, many of which must be dealt with in later chapters. In fact, individuals who cannot deal with being wrong from time to time will find that finance is probably not the career for them. When predicting things that are *expected* to happen in the future, being wrong to some degree is a near certainty. Thus, our job is to not be *too* wrong so as to minimize the potential to reduce firm value.

3.3.1 Relevant Cash Flows

In order to best examine the expected cash flows, most projects go through a process called **stand-alone analysis**. During this, each project must be treated as a "mini-firm" that is proposed to exist exogenously but still within the firm as a whole. In other words, we pretend the rest of the firm doesn't exist and analyze only details pertaining to that individual investment opportunity. The difficult aspect of this is identifying cash flows that are relevant. A **relevant cash flow** can be defined as a change in the firm's overall future cash flows that comes about as a direct consequence of the decision to take on a specific project. Perhaps more clearly, if a cash flow, whether positive or negative, would occur regardless of whether the project was implemented or not, it is irrelevant. By omitting any irrelevant cash flow, we can create a much cleaner laboratory for examining the true value of the project.

Examples of difficulties in categorizing cash flows as relevant include sunk costs and opportunity costs. The former is irrelevant, while the latter is relevant. **Sunk costs** are considered irrelevant to the project because they represent monetary obligations that have already been paid or the liability to pay has already been incurred. Thus, the firm is liable for the cash flow regardless of the decision to accept the project or not. Consider a firm that is considering buying a dump truck, which for the sake of simplicity, we will assume is the entirety of the project.

Since the truck is used, the firm hires a local mechanic to give it an inspection prior to purchase. After the mechanic completes the inspection, the firm is provided a bill for $200 for the inspection. The $200 is a sunk cost because no matter what the firm decides to do about buying the dump truck, the mechanic expects to be paid. At this point it is irrelevant to the project decision because the liability to pay has no relation to the decision to accept the project.

On the other hand, **opportunity costs** are certainly relevant. Consider a razor company who is currently selling a mass amount of three-bladed razors but are considering a project that would produce four-bladed razors. The appeal is apparent, as the market suggests that more blades are better. However, the firm needs to be cognizant of the fact that a significant portion of the sales of four-bladed razors would have been sales of the old three-bladed razor anyway. For example, the firm projects sales of the four-bladed razor to be 25,000 units but somehow expects that 10,000 of those sales would have been sales for the existing three-bladed razor. A strong argument could be made that only 15,000 of the units could be considered in the project analysis. Regardless of the final decision on how to handle the opportunity cost of a potential new project, it is certainly relevant to the analysis.

3.3.2 Pro Forma Statements

Once all the relevant cash flows have been identified, they must then be combined in some organized way. When the most accurate base on which to build projections is needed, we lean on accounting tools. Thus, the first step in finding expected cash flows is to create **pro forma statements** for each project. Such a statement is very similar to typical financial statements but is a derivative of projected or estimated values. Naturally, these are subject to error, but the objective is to minimize those errors by using the most accurate estimates possible.

The problem, or shortcoming, of the statements is that each of the values included must to be estimated to some degree. Easily the most important of these is the sales variable, and because of this, considerable care must be put into coming up with the most accurate estimate possible. Following the sales estimate, the next step is to deduct all the various costs, which also have to be estimated. Generally, this is done with some type of technique, using the sales figure as a guide. For the sake of illustration, let's say a firm is considering a project that revolves around producing and selling a fictional product known as jidbits. Suppose the firm believes they can sell $2,670 worth of jidbits during the year. Of this, they feel that the costs of goods sold would be roughly 50 %. The project would include assets that would be depreciated by $580 during the year. Given this data, Table 3.3 presents a pro forma income statement for the jidbit project.

From this, we estimate the project will generate $491 in net income for the firm. Notice interest is not included in this analysis. The firm has not yet decided how to fund the project, so the amount of interest is unknown. Later versions of the pro forma statement may indeed include interest estimations, but that will not

Table 3.3 Project pro forma income statement

Jidbit project	
Pro forma statement (values in 000s)	
Sales	\$2,670
COGS	1,335
Depreciation	580
EBIT	755
Taxes (35 %)	264
Net income	\$491

occur until funding options have been analyzed. Interest is another example of an irrelevant cash flow, due to its placement on the cash flow identity. Being on the right-hand side, it is an example of where cash is used, not where it comes from. Rounding out the pro forma statement are estimates of depreciation for the project's depreciable asset(s) during the year and taxes, as calculated by the standard 35 % of taxable income (which is the same as *EBIT* in the absence of interest).

The above example is absent any indicators of time period, leading to the assumption that it is a 1-year project. Should this not be the case and there are multiple future years in which the project must be evaluated, it gets a bit trickier. Each year of the project has the potential to produce a different pro forma income statement. Each period would have projected sales, the corresponding level of costs, that year's depreciation (as determined by the depreciation policy), and the resulting tax bill. The necessity of creating a statement for each year is the worst-case scenario in terms of the amount of work that must be done. In many cases, for the sake of simplicity, the sales forecast is assumed to be the same for each year of the project, and costs often follow suit. If the project is property, such as buildings, then the depreciation amount may also be the same each period. Therefore, it is entirely plausible that the base pro forma statement will be same for each year of the project. If so, things are greatly simplified.

3.3.3 Project Expected Cash Flows

For now we need to worry about only one side of the cash flow identity. Since we can't worry about where the money is going to go until we know how much we are going to get, the left-hand side is our only concern. Specifically, we are now trying to calculate the following:

$$Project\ CFFA = Project\ OCF - Project\ NCS - Project\ \Delta NWC$$

As you can see, the only new thing here is that we are now only looking at the project rather than the entire firm. The *CFFA* represents the total cash flow from the project. Keep in mind there are only two ways funds can flow: in or out. In most cases, project *OCF* represents cash inflows, whereas the *NCS* usually represent cash outflows. As discussed in the entire firm example earlier in the chapter, it is certainly possible for *NCS* to be negative; however, this would be unlikely for a proposed new project. It would be unusual to create a new project that decreases the firm's amount of fixed assets. However, unusual is not impossible and some cases may present this anti-intuitive finding. On a project level, the ΔNWC could be either positive or negative. The positive scenario is more likely as new projects are prone to increasing the risk of the overall firm and increased operating liquidity may be the firm's response to this increased risk. However, a project could also require a disproportionate increase in current liabilities, which could serve to decrease *NWC*.

In the jidbit example above, project *OCF* is calculating as:

$$\begin{aligned}\textbf{Project } \boldsymbol{OCF} &= \textbf{Project } \boldsymbol{EBIT} + \textbf{Project depreciation} - \textbf{Project taxes}\\ &= \mathbf{755 + 580 - 264}\\ &= \mathbf{\$1,071}\end{aligned}$$

The other two values combine to form the initial cash flows associated with a project. Specifically, project *NCS* and project ΔNWC added together provide the **net investment (*NINV*)** of the project. In layman's term, the *NINV* of a project is what it costs to get the project started. The fact that *NCS* and ΔNWC make up this value is logical if you think about it for a moment. Net capital spending includes the cost of physical structures, such as buildings or machinery, whereas changes in net working capital are changes in the short-term relationship between assets and liabilities. Although this is taking some liberties, *NCS* is basically the long-term cost associated with the project, while ΔNWC measures the short-term cost.

Therefore, we need additional information to calculate the *NINV* of the jidbit project. The process of calculating the expected initial cost of something has its own issues, but for the sake of brevity, we will skip most of that. With that in mind, let's say net capital spending has been estimated to be $3,000 and that net working capital has to initially increase by $850 in order for the project to get under way. For the sake of completeness, let's say that the $3,000 is the cost of a jidbit machine and the $850 is a required increase in inventory (leading to a disproportionate increase in CA) needed to generate the amount of jidbits demanded.

Therefore, the *NINV* for the jidbit project is

$$\begin{aligned}\boldsymbol{NINV} &= \textbf{Project } \boldsymbol{NCS} + \textbf{Project } \boldsymbol{\Delta NWC}\\ &= \mathbf{3,000 + 850}\\ &= \mathbf{\$3,850}\end{aligned}$$

There is an interesting detail that also needs to be addressed. Although both *NCS* and ΔNWC are components of *NINV*, they are different types of cash flows. To best see the difference, consider an unrelated example. Suppose you buy a car, which

Table 3.4 Expected cash flows

	Year					
	0	1	2	3	4	5
Operating cash flows		1,071	1,071	1,071	1,071	1,071
Net capital spending	−3,000					
Change in *NWC*	−850					850
Total project cash flows	−3,850	1,071	1,071	1,071	1,071	1,921

effectively becomes a personal "project" in which you've invested. The cost of that car is $25,000. Unfortunately, that is not the end of the costs. If you want to actually drive the car, you must buy gas, get insurance, and pay your taxes on it. Let's say that adds up to $2,500 per year. Thus, the total cost at time zero to get you and your car on the road is $27,500.

As long as you drive the car, you must maintain the $2,500 increase in your personal expenses. Now, fast forward 10 years until the end of the car's life. If you do not sell the car, the $25,000 is gone and will never be recovered. However, the $2,500 you spent each year on the necessary extras will effectively go away, which results in a decrease in your automotive expenditures of $2,500. This decrease in expenditures is effectively the same thing as a cash inflow to you. To draw the parallels, buying the car is similar to increasing your personal *NCS*, while the expenditures on gas, insurance, and taxes are similar to an increase in *NWC*. *NCS* is a one-time expense, and after you pay it, nothing else happens unless you decide to sell it. On the other hand, the ΔNWC is an ongoing expense, and at the end of the project, the change can cease to exist.

Therefore, it is likely the firm will recover at least some of the cost associated with increased *NWC* at the end of the project. If it's still not clear why, consider this. The firm was running at an acceptable level of *NWC* prior to the implementation of the project. The only exogenous event that occurred was the project itself. Therefore, it stands to reason that when the project is completed, the company can go back to where it was before it began. This is not generally the case with *NCS*. Physical assets such as buildings or machinery get used up, for lack of a better term, and therefore cannot typically be redeemed at historical value. In fact, the example we are using above assumes the fixed assets are completely "used up" and have zero market value. While this is the most extreme case, it does simplify things. If this is not the case, and the asset is determined to have remaining market value, we have to address the difference between the market and book value. Specifically, if the market value is greater than the book value, the resulting after-tax salvage value must be added to the cash flow for the final year of the project.

To extend the example a bit, let's now assume that the jidbit project is expected to run for 5 years and that each year's pro forma income statement is expected to be the same. If so, we are likely to see the stream of cash flows in Table 3.4.

This is a pretty straightforward project. Since sales are estimated to be constant throughout the 5 years, we don't have to worry about changing *OCF*. Note the time zero *NCS* and ΔNWC are given negative signs to clearly indicate they are cash *out*flows, despite the fact they are positive values. Since each period's pro forma statement is identical, then each period's *OCF* will follow suit. The only additional data is the recovery of the ΔNWC at the end of the project's life. This example assumes the entire increase can be recovered, although the amount of recovery is certainly specific to each project.

Table 3.4 summarizes the completion of the first major component of capital budgeting, calculating expected cash flows. To review, a three-step process is completed to get this accomplished. First, the firm must identify cash flows that are relevant to the project. Second, those relevant cash flows are used to create pro forma statements for each period of the project. And third, those pro forma statements are used to estimate the project's expected cash flows. While expected cash flows alone do not provide a clear picture of whether the project is acceptable, they are an indispensable piece of the process, and considerable care must be given to their estimation.

IN THE REAL WORLD

It had taken countless hours of work, but on August 12, 2011, Stewart and Marilyn were finally ready to give their presentation to Tyler and Lilly. After gathering everyone in the large conference room, they began by explaining the process through which they had just gone.

"We know roughly how many of each product is currently demanded." Stewart said after everyone was settled. "From that, we estimated future demand using trend analysis, incorporating seasonal variations, increased productivity potential, and the significantly larger market presence. We did this for each product and merged the results to find the total additional revenue that can be expected from the additional plants. The marketing department aided considerably in helping to gauge demand. And to be honest, we will be receiving large bills from statisticians that were called in for consultation."

He and Marilyn were at front and center of the conference room. Tyler and Lilly took the first two seats. Jane sat to Tyler's right, while Brandon sat on Lilly's left. Dubarb Freeman held court at the far end of the table, along with Coleman, who was there in case there were questions pertaining to the accounting statements. When a platoon of administrative assistants and various representatives from other areas were added to the mix, the room was full. Several lower-level employees were relegated to the standing room only at the back of the room. The table was littered with piles of reports detailing the data Marilyn and Stewart had compiled. They had assembled the primary findings in a PowerPoint presentation but had hard copies on hand in case a more extensive review was requested.

"We started just by trying to get a handle on the type of project we want to consider." Marilyn continued. She had dressed carefully for the day, wearing a conservative yet sophisticated black suit by St. John paired with Jimmy Choo heels. Stewart's off-the-rack dark gray suit seemed utilitarian next to her, but he didn't seem to mind.

"The largest issue Hack Back is currently facing is the lack of manufacturing facilities," Marilyn continued. "As Mr. Freeman has put forth, we need at least two more major facilities in order to cope with the excess demand we are now

experiencing. So, our goal is to identify the option that best balances cost efficiency with revenue production. And, of course, the end result should be to add value to the firm and its shareholders."

Stewart and Marilyn spent the next half hour detailing the process they went through in identifying potential locations and plant designs. They fielded a number of questions but in the end had everyone on the same page and ready to move on.

"When all is said and done," Stewart added, "we have obtained what we believe are reasonable estimates for the revenues, costs, and profits of the potential projects."

Marilyn reached over the computer console to fiddle with opening the presentation. "What you will see is that we have identified two distinctly different plant designs. There is a large push in the sporting goods industry to move to a more automated production process. The first plant design lends itself to this purpose. The proposal is a relatively small structure, which houses a more streamlined process that requires considerably less manual labor. Based upon our current production rates and, hopefully, improvement in them, we believe costs at those plants will be approximately 55 % of sales."

"That is considerably less than where we are as a firm now," Coleman commented, just barely loud enough to rattle the paintings on the wall.

"This is very true," Marilyn agreed. "Naturally, however, the machinery required at this plant will cost more than traditional plants and will need more regular maintenance. These 'high-tech' plants would remain up to date for fifteen years before basically needing complete renovation. Therefore, for the sake of argument, we are treating it as a fifteen-year project."

She paused to catch her breath before continuing.

"The extensive research that we described earlier has led us to the belief that each new plant would generate additional revenue of approximately $15.7 million per year. For both plants combined, that would be a projection of an increase of a bit less than 8 % over last year's firm-wide revenues. In addition to the added revenue, it should also allow our existing assets to more efficiently generate income, which we have identified as a current shortcoming."

Stewart spoke up. "Rather than look at differing levels of projected sales over numerous years, we chose to project each year's sales figure as constant. This is admittedly a restrictive assumption, but we feel it provides the cleanest up-front look. That way, we can also estimate the same level of costs for each year. We will, naturally, evaluate other specifications before making a final decision."

He nodded slightly to Marilyn, who took the queue and maneuvered the mouse for a moment. A slide appeared on the overhead projection screen.

High-tech plant projected income statement	
Sales	***15,700,000***
COGS	***8,635,000***
Depreciation	***384,615***
EBIT	***6,680,385***
Taxes	***2,338,135***
Net income	***4,342,250***

"So, you believe each plant will generate revenues of two hundred and thirty-five million and profit of over sixty-five million over the fifteen years?" Lilly asked, after punching buttons on a small calculator in front of her. She was strenuously opposed to doing math in her head.

"That's certainly one way to look at it, but there are a couple of caveats to that," Marilyn responded.

"Such as?"

"Let me take that, if I may," Freeman responded, standing and walking to the front of the room. Lilly and Tyler whirled in their seats to follow his movement. "The first thing we must do is look at cash flows rather than income figures, since I believe we all agree that what matters is how much money is actually expected to flow into and out of the firm as a result of taking on this project. Right?"

"I suppose so," Tyler said. Turning to Stewart and Marilyn, he asked, "so what are the cash flows?"

"Based upon the projected statement, it appears each high-tech plant would generate a bit over $4.7 million per year in operating cash flows," Stewart responded. "That can roughly be defined as the amount of money expected to flow into the firm as a result of the production and selling of products made in each plant.

"So now you're saying we would make over $70 million over the fifteen years?" Lilly said, again clicking away at her calculator.

"That brings about the other caveat," Freeman said, holding up an open palm to halt her train of thought. "These cash flows are coming at different times in the future. So we have to worry about that as well. Suffice it to say, however, this project is not worth $70 million in current value. And before you ask how much it's really worth, I don't know. We have to do a lot more work before we get to that. What you should be asking is how much it costs?"

"Okay, I'll bite," Tyler said. "How much does it cost?"

"Well, that's the other thing," Freeman again cautioned. "There are two ways of thinking of the costs of the project. Probably the more important is the ongoing cost associated with obtaining the capital we need to finance the projects. That is the hard part that I was just mentioning. We have to figure out how we are to obtain the funding and then think about the costs of that attainment."

He paused and held up both open palms to the room.

"But, that is likely not the cost you are referring to," he said, emphasizing the word "cost" with air quotations. "You are likely asking about the amount of money it would take to get the project up and running, in other words the initial costs. We call that the net investment."

"Okay, I will again bite," Tyler said again. "What is the net investment?"

This time, Freeman simply nodded to Marilyn, who then clicked to the next slide and pointed out details as she spoke.

"We estimate the land would cost around $3 million. The architectural firms that provide the estimates say the plant itself would cost around $12 million. The other equipment needed would add about another $3 million."

"So, all together it costs $18 million," Lilly stated.

"That is the estimate for net capital spending we are currently working with," Stewart stated.

"We're not quite done though," Freeman interjected. He still stood but was now leaning on the edge of the table with one trouser leg hiked up mid-calf. It was a pleasant view.

"We also estimate that we will be required to increase NWC by $5 million dollars in order to run this plant," he added. "We might get that back at the end, but nonetheless, we have to spend it throughout the project to maintain operations with an acceptable level of risk."

"Net working what?" Lilly questioned.

"We'll explain later," Freeman said, waving off her question. "For now, here's what we know. The initial total cost of the high-tech plant is approximated at $23 million. For the sake of making it simple for this presentation, for now we've assumed the cost of the plant and equipment can be depreciated as business property over 39 years. In actuality, each depreciable asset will have to be considered separately, according to their class. Thus, the depreciation estimates presented here are underestimating the amount of depreciation, at least up front. The land can't be depreciated at all, of course."

"Of course. I'm glad we're making it simple," Lilly said, not attempting to hide her sarcasm.

"You said there were two plant options," Tyler jumped in, deflecting Lilly's scorn.

"There were hundreds of options," Freeman responded unnecessarily, "but we've narrowed it down to two."

"Well, the other option is a more traditional setup," Stewart jumped in diplomatically. "The building will have to be larger, with more employees required to run it. However, the equipment will be considerably cheaper and will last longer. Since we are dealing with a project less dependent on technology, the materials will not have to be replaced as often. In fact, we feel the traditional plant will run for 20 years before becoming largely obsolete."

"We firmly believe both plants can meet demand, and both can generate the same revenue as a result. However, this option will do it a bit less efficiently, as evidenced by the pro forma statement. The annual costs are estimated at 65 % of sales."

He cast a glance in Coleman's direction before adding, "Which is still a lot lower than we are currently operating at, firm-wide."

Traditional plant projected income statement	
Sales	*15,700,000*
COGS	*10,205,000*
Depreciation	*256,410*
EBIT	*5,238,590*
Taxes	*1,833,507*
Net income	*3,405,083*

"Therefore, we expect operating cash flows of about $3.66 million each year," Marilyn added. "So cash inflows are expected to be less, but so too are costs. As mentioned, the machinery and other materials required in the traditional building are less expensive. The land will cost the same $3 million, but the plant and equipment will only be about $10 million in total. Also, we estimate net working capital has to increase by only approximately $3 million."

"So here you have it, kids," Freeman boomed. "Two plants we need built and two options for the type we can build. Marilyn, put those other slides up." Marilyn obliged and the group turned to see the summary.

	High-tech	*Traditional*
# of years	*15*	*20*
OCF (per yr.)	*4,726,865*	*3,661,494*
NCS	*18,000,000*	*13,000,000*
ΔNWC	*5,000,000*	*3,000,000*

"This is a brief summary, and this," she paused to move the presentation forward, "is a little better idea of what the cash flow schedule looks like."

High-tech plant			
	Year 0	*Years 1–14*	*Year 15*
Operating cash flows		*4,726,865*	*4,726,865*
Net capital spending	*−18,000,000*		
Change in NWC	*−5,000,000*		*5,000,000*
Total project cash flows	*−23,000,000*	*4,726,865*	*9,726,865*

Traditional plant			
	Year 0	*Years 1–19*	*Year 20*
Operating cash flows		*3,661,494*	*3,661,494*
Net capital spending	*−13,000,000*		
Change in NWC	*−3,000,000*		*3,000,000*
Total project cash flows	*−16,000,000*	*3,661,494*	*6,661,494*

"Now let me tell you a bit more about the assumptions we made here," Marilyn continued. "First of all, if we are going to build these things, we plan to use them forever. However, for now we are only looking at the 15- and 20-year projects because that's when we would have to think about serious overhaul. Such a serious overhaul would then be evaluated as a new project for Hack Back to consider.

We don't plan, at this time, to sell the plant or equipment, and that's the reason we don't have any NCS money coming back to us at the end. That may change if we decide to sell some stuff, but we won't deal with that now. You can also see that we are assuming that we get the entire change in NWC back at the end, which also may not happen, but it is the simplest scenario when examining a standalone project."

The room fell eerily silent as everyone tried to take in the immense amount of information given them. Assistants tried to look busy while doodling on their notepads and avoiding direct stares.

"This is a pretty big piece of the puzzle that has been put before you, but we have really just started," Freeman cautioned the owners. "We have to take those numbers and make sense of them on many levels."

He then straightened from this perch.

"Marilyn, Stewart, go back through whatever they need again."

With that, he zipped out of the room, leaving everyone watching the empty doorway.

"How does he always manage to get to say the most important stuff just before making a grand exit?" Stewart asked, without thinking. As the entire room chuckled, Stewart couldn't hide a slight blush.

"You'll get used to it," Tyler responded, with a wave of his hand. "Now let's go over these numbers again."

"Much more slowly, please" Lilly added. The assistants sighed silently as the bosses bent toward the table.

ALTERNATE ENDINGS

1. ***Help Stewart and Anna out. Suppose they didn't choose to make the easy assumption that all years have equal sales amounts. What happens then?***
   (a) ***Describe the various complications that arise and how they must be dealt with.***
   (b) ***As an example, instead of assuming sales were going to be the same each year, assume the extensive research Hack Back put into the pro formas indicating sales would increase by $325,000 each year, starting with the $15,700,000 for the first year. How does this change the projected net income and operating cash flow each year?***

   Warning: This requires quite a bit of work. Keep in mind that you must create income statements for each of the 15 and 20 years for the high-tech and traditional plants, respectively.

   A bit of advice: Use Excel!

2. ***Now, believe it or not, it actually can get worse. For example, what if we added the assumption that NWC was a direct function of the sales figure? The implicit assumption in the base problem (where sales are a constant $15.7 million each year) is that NWC is 31.85 % (5,000,000/15,700,000) of sales for the high-tech project. If we keep this as a constant percentage, it would make the extended example just above (#1) more difficult because as sales increase, NWC would have to increase as well. Why not add that to your spreadsheet and see what happens? Also, what about the assumption that the firm gets the entire increase in NWC back at the completion of the project? Discuss situations where that may or may not be a logical assumption, and consider the resulting implications if changes to the assumption need to be made.***

3. ***Suppose that the firm gets more specific in their treatment of depreciation. In the current problem, the firm is projecting to depreciate all depreciable assets as long-term physical property. However, that will not actually happen, as things such as computers or vehicles are shorter-lived assets. Discuss how this would change the analysis. Remember that a high-tech project will have a lot of computerized equipment that might be shorter lived. How might that effect the decision between the two?***
4. ***Speaking of depreciation, what happens to the remaining depreciation after the 15 and 20 years are up? More generally, what happens to the remaining depreciation anytime you have book value remaining following the completion of the use of the asset? What are your options?***
5. ***How about something else to think about? What would happen if Hack Back decided at the end of the project to sell off at least some of the assets they bought with the NCS? As a hint, the answer would be related to our discussion of the relationship between book values and market values.***
6. ***Suppose Tyler makes the following statement:***

   "It seems like this may be a lot of work for only an 8 % increase in revenues. Can you give me any more substantiation for why this project will significantly help Hack Back?"

   This is a very good (and popular) boss-type question. How do you answer it?
7. ***After the assertion of the need for additional NWC to fund the projects, Lilly asked another very good question:***

   "I don't get it. Where does that value come from mechanically? Do we buy more assets, reduce liabilities, or what? More importantly, why do we need to do these things?"

   The answer to this question requires you to have an understanding of the role of additional risk brought about by the new project and the firm's response to this increasing risk.
8. ***In a somewhat unrelated issue, complete Hack Back's cash flow identity. The financial statements can be found in either Chap. 2 or an appendix at the end of the text. What do the numbers tell you about Hack Back?***

Concept Questions

1. **Cash flows** Describe the difference between cash flows and income. Why are we most concerned with cash flows?
2. **Cash flow identity** Hariet from accounting has forgotten her finance classes from school and just said, "I don't understand what this cash flow identity is all about. Where are the assets, liabilities, and equity? They have to be in there somewhere." Explain to her that they are still in there and how they are used. Outline the differences (and similarities) in the two identities.

3. **Cash flow identity** Is it possible for any (or all) of the three pieces of the cash flow identity to have negative values? For all that can, create a basic scenario that would explain the negative value.
4. **Cash flow identity** Your boss just burst into your cubicle, sweating profusely and screaming that the firm's cash flow from assets is negative for last year. "We're going under, we're going under!" he screams. How do you calm him down?
5. **Incremental cash flows** Consider the following cash flows: sunk costs, opportunity costs, and interest expense. Should these cash flows be considered as relevant to the project?
6. **Project net capital spending and change in *NWC*** Is it possible for an accepted project to require a decrease in net capital spending or net working capital? If so, what does that mean for the company?
7. **Project expected cash flows** You have been asked to obtain estimates of cash flows for a massive project the company is considering. Your head spins. Where do you start? On what number is everything else based?
8. **Project expected cash flows** "I just don't get it," your study-mate sighs, "I'm getting a positive number for net capital spending, but you're saying that it is really an outflow for the project? That doesn't make sense." Explain it to him again.
9. **Project expected cash flows** Your neighbor and good ole boy, Bo Duke, doesn't understand why you don't consider the right-hand side of the cash flow identity in estimated project expected cash flows. Explain it to him, real slow and easy.
10. **Depreciation, taxes, and interest** How does depreciation affect project expected cash flows? How do taxes affect project expected cash flows? How does interest affect project expected cash flows?

Problems

1. **Operating cash flow** Your firm has total sales of $1,200. Costs are $715 and depreciation is $145. The tax rate is 35 %. The firm does not have interest expenses. What is the operating cash flow?
2. **Change in *NWC*** Gil's Barrel Company has cash flow from assets of $162,489. Last year, they bought $334,489 worth of new long-term assets, while selling off $217,555. In addition, the firm had *EBIT* of $458,600, interest expense of $23,000, and depreciation of $24,500. Their tax rate is 35 %. This year, *NWC* is $168,700. What must *NWC* have been last year?
3. **Change in *NWC*** Suppose a firm had current assets of $13,500,000 and current liabilities of $6,590,000 in 2011. In 2012, the firm had current liabilities of $5,480,000. If the firm's change in *NWC* is 1,287,500, what are the firm's 2012 current assets?
4. **Net capital spending** A firm's cash flow from assets is −34,562. During the year, they added $78,000 in *NWC*. The firm had *EBIT* of $156,700, depreciation

of $26,425, and interest of $8,779. The firm also had a tax rate of 35 %. What is the firm's net capital spending during the year?

5. **Cash flow to creditors** At the beginning of the year, long-term debt of a firm is $280 and total debt is $340. At the end of the year, long-term debt is $260 and total debt is $350. The interest paid is $30. What is the amount of the cash flow to creditors?
6. **Cash flow from assets** Jill's Grape Vineyard, Inc., had net income last year of $126,555 from $358,000 of sales. They paid interest of $23,000 and depreciation of $9,500. The firm increased their fixed assets by $47,000 during the year and decreased *NWC* by $18,544. What is Jill's cash flow from assets (*CFFA*)? The firm's tax rate is 35 %.
7. **Cash flow from assets** You have calculated your cash flow from assets to be $8,800. Suppose you have net capital spending of $14,000 and a decrease in *NWC* of $2,000. You have *EBIT* of $25,500 and interest expenses of $4,600. The tax rate is 35 %. What is your depreciation expense?
8. **Cash flow** Suppose you are given the following information for Stone's Masonry Service.

	2011	2012
Sales	50,500	62,000
COGS	32,000	34,800
Depreciation	6,500	10,000
Interest	2,000	3,000
Dividends	5,500	6,000
Current assets	80,000	88,000
Fixed assets	120,000	136,000
Current liabilities	38,000	47,000
Long-term debt	78,000	84,000
Tax rate	35 %	35 %

(a) Create the income statement for 2011 and 2012.
(b) Create the balance sheet for both 2011 and 2012.
(c) What is operating cash flow for 2012?
(d) What is net capital spending for 2012?
(e) What is change in net working capital for 2012?
(f) What is cash flow from assets for 2012?
(g) What is cash flow to creditors for 2012?
(h) What is cash flow to shareholders for 2012?

9. **Project expected cash flows** Suppose you are considering a 7-year project with the following annual pro forma statement.

Firm XYZ	
Pro forma statement	
Sales	3,410
COGS	1,207
Depreciation	469
EBIT	1,734
Taxes	607
Net income	1,127

   In addition, the project is going to require net capital spending of 10,000 and an increase in *NWC* of 2,400:

   (a) What is the project *NINV*?
   (b) What is the project operating cash flow?
   (c) What is the expected total cash flow for each of the 7 years?
   (d) How would your answer to b and c above change if the sales were projected to increase by 5 % in each successive year following the first?
   (e) Suppose the project has a salvage value of $2,000 at the end of the project? How does this change the expected total cash flow?

10. **Project expected cash flows** Suppose Scotty's Exotic Pets, LLC, is considering a project that has a life of 4 years and total *NINV* of $450,000. During the first year, the company has estimated sales to be $125,000, a value they feel will increase by 10 % in each of the remaining 3 years. Based on their estimates, they feel *COGS* will be roughly 45 % of sales each year. Assume that the total amount of *NCS*, which is $380,000, will be depreciated as a 3-year property class:

   (a) What is the net income for each of the 4 years?
   (b) What is the operating cash flow for each of the 4 years?
   (c) What is the total project cash flow for each of the 4 years?

Chapter 4
The Right Frame of Time

The most important concept in all of finance is the time value of money. As a discipline primarily concerned with defining and calculating values, obtaining consistent, time-relevant estimates is critical. All aspect of corporate finance requires understanding and incorporating the time value of money principles. In the preceding chapter, we made note of the fact that cash flows often occur at different times, and those of most concern are expected to occur at some future time. However, financial decisions are typically made in the current time frame. Thus, the values of those future cash flows need to be adjusted to reflect the differential time periods. This is not to say, however, there aren't many instances where we want to know what a stream of cash flows will be worth at some point in the future as well. Therefore, we need to closely examine each of these options. There are three basic types of cash flows that comprise the study of time value of money: (1) single cash flows, (2) multiple unequal cash flows, and (3) multiple equal cash flows. We will address each of these, in turn, throughout this chapter.

4.1 Introducing the Time Value of Money

There are many ways to define the **time value of money (TVOM)**, but they all are based upon the same notion. According to the TVOM, *a dollar received today is worth more than a dollar received at any time in the future*. In other words, receiving an amount of money earlier rather than later is always preferred. Why is this? The answer comes in the form of a single word: **interest**. When an individual or a firm has money in their possession, they can choose to invest the funds. When doing so, they can earn interest. Interest represents the amount of additional money you can earn by saving some original amount, which is known as the **principal**. In case there is any confusion, this is the same interest that is mentioned in Chaps. 2 and 3. The difference is in the perspective. In the previous chapters, we were evaluating issues from the firm's perspective as a borrower, where interest is a debt that must be paid. Now, we are examining the lender's

M.K. Pyles, *Applied Corporate Finance: Questions, Problems and Making Decisions in the Real World*, Springer Texts in Business and Economics,
DOI 10.1007/978-1-4614-9173-6_4,

Table 4.1 Simple versus compound interest

	End balance		
Year	Simple interest	Compound interest	Difference
1	$110	$110.00	$0.00
2	120	121.00	1.00
3	130	133.10	3.10

perspective, which is analogous to investing. When one loans money with accompanying interest rates, they are essentially investing in the borrower.

Financial institutions pay savers for the right to hold onto their money over a period of time. The amount paid represents interest and is determined by the interest rate quoted on the investment. In its simplest form, interest is free money you "earn" as a reward for saving instead of spending. The institutions are willing to pay interest because they can then use the invested money to further their operations.

Therefore, the concept of earning interest is a driving force behind what happens in all of finance. There are two basic types, although one dominates the other, both in this text and in the real world. We'll start with the one you rarely encounter, known as **simple interest**. With simple interest, interest is earned only on the principal amount each period. To illustrate, consider an example. Let's suppose you deposit $100 in an account that pays 10 %, simple interest. You earn 10 % of $100 each year, which is simply $10 per annum. Therefore, at the end of the first year, the account balance would be $110. Likewise, at the end of year two, you would have $120, and the pattern continues. The point is that you earn a constant amount each and every year you hold the investment.

LOOK IT UP: See if you can find an example of a real-world account that pays simple interest. You may want to look at certificates of deposit (CDs).

The other type of interest is called **compound interest**. Compound interest is much more powerful than simple because interest is earned on both the original principal *and* the previously earned interest. To see how important this is, let's use the same example of depositing $100 in an account that earns 10 % interest. However, let's now assume the interest rate is *compounded* annually. Table 4.1 illustrates the difference in the two types of rates.

During the first year, there is no difference between earning simple and compound interest. However, that quickly changes. During the second year of compound interest, you still earn the $10 on the principal. However, you also earn interest on the interest previously earned. Take a second to chew on that last sentence. During the second year, you earn an additional $1 because you also earn 10 % on the $10 of interest you earned during year one. You earn free money on the free money you've already earned. Thus is the power of compound interest.

So, over the course of 2 years, compound interest earns an additional $1 relative to simple interest. That doesn't sound like much, but let's keep going. During the

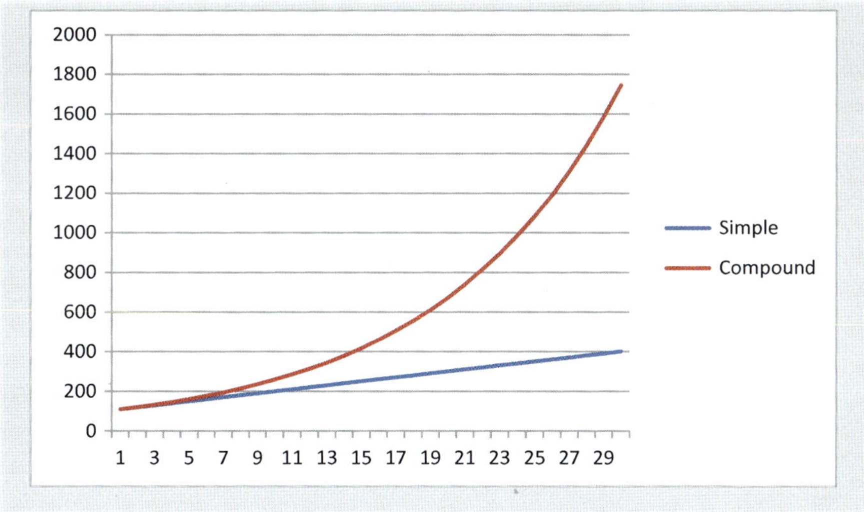

Fig. 4.1 Simple versus compound interest

third year, you earn the same \$10 on the principal, but now you also earn an additional \$2.10 on previously accumulated interest of \$21. Therefore, the total difference between the two accounts at the end of 3 years is \$3.10. The most important aspect of this is noticing the difference between the two account balances is increasing. This will happen each year the accounts continue. An account earning compound interest will grow faster than an account earning simple interest. In fact, it will grow considerably faster. To prove this, if we continued the above example for 30 years, the account with simple interest would be worth \$400, while the account earning compound interest would be worth \$1,745. Figure 4.1 graphically displays the above discussion.

4.2 Single Cash Flows

4.2.1 Future Value of Lump Sum

As mentioned in the opening chapter, there are three basic types of cash flows. We will start with the simplest, a **lump sum**. A lump sum is a single cash flow that occurs either today or at some point in the future. These lump sums are the cornerstones of the TVOM, which makes fully understanding how to quantify their value of primary importance. We will save discussion of lump sums that occur in the future for a bit and start with the single cash flow that occurs today. We are often interested in what this amount would be worth sometime in the future. This is called the **future value (*FV*)** of that lump sum.

Before we move on, a small caveat needs to be addressed. You will notice as we move throughout the text that, when addressing cash flows, the cash flow will be said to occur at the end of a given period. This is for simplicity as cash flows obviously do not have to occur at the end of a period. They can occur at the beginning, the middle, or any other time. However, by assuming they occur at the end of each period, we can keep the math relatively simple because each compounding cycle encompasses an entire period, rather than some fraction.

The equation is fairly straightforward and can be derived using the example in the previous section. The *FV* of the \$100 dollars at the end of the first period is worth

$$\mathbf{100 + (.10^{*}100) = \$110}$$

This is equivalent to

$$\mathbf{100\ \ (1.10) = \$110}$$

Continuing with this, the *FV* at the end of time two is

$$\mathbf{100^{*}\ (1.10)(1.10) = 100\ \ (1.10)^{2} = \$121}$$

Generalizing this notion, the *FV* of lump sum formula is

$$FV = PV(1 + r)^{t}$$

You may be a bit confused by the inclusion of *PV* in this equation. You are correct in thinking this stands for **present value**, but it also stands for principal value. The present value of any amount is simply the amount at time zero, or the original deposit put into an account. The $(1 + r)^{t}$ part of the equation is known as the future value interest factor (FVIF). The rate r is the interest rate per period and t is the number of periods. Note that for now, both of these variables are annual. In other words, r is the interest rate per year and t is the number of years. However, this will change shortly as we start to relax the critical restriction that cash flows (and interest accumulation) can only occur once per year.

Most of these things are best learned with an example or two, so let’s start there. Suppose you have \$5,000 given to you by your grandparents when you turn 18. Assume this amount is invested in a mutual fund earning 6 % per year over the next 4 years. How much would this be worth at the end of those 4 years?

Solving each TVOM problem, no matter how simple or difficult, should involve three steps. The first is deciding which equation to use. This is easy for now as we have only discussed one equation. Therefore, we can move to the second step, which is inserting the numerical values into the equation. In the example, this can be done as follows:

$$\boldsymbol{FV} = \mathbf{5,000(1.06)^{4}}$$

The last step is to complete the calculation:

$$\mathbf{5,000(1.06)^4 = \$6,312.38}$$

When we are finding the future value of something, given an original (or present) value, this is called **compounding**. This brings to light a couple of things of note. First, *the FV is always higher than the PV*. This should make sense given a positive rate of interest over a positive period of time. Therefore, the ending value must be greater than the beginning. If you find differently, then either you have done something wrong or you are dealing with a situation where you can have a negative rate of return (such as a stock market investment). We will discuss the latter situation in a future chapter, so for now the former is the only possible solution. Another point of note is *the higher the interest rate, the higher the FV*. Again, if you think about this, it should be intuitive. The meaning of the word *compound* says it all. Finance aside, to compound anything means to "add to," or to "make bigger." Therefore, if you add a larger amount each time (via a higher interest rate), you should expect a larger ending value. The same is true for the time period. The more times you add something, the larger the ending value.

To prove it to yourself, try the same problem above only varying the inputs. First, replace the 6 % interest rate with 8 %. You should get an answer of \$6,802.45. Second, if you replace the four years with five, you should get \$6,691.13 as *FV*. These directional relationships will always exist and are TVOM "Truths." We will add to the list as we move throughout this chapter.

TECH HELP 4.1 Future Value of Lump Sum

The following steps will allow you to perform the same calculations with the TI BA II Plus financial calculator. First, a little word to the wise. The calculator is only as smart as the person using it. If you tell it to do the wrong thing, it will give you the wrong answer. Make sure you understand the motivations first and you will save yourself considerable headaches.

There are a couple of things you need to check before starting to punch buttons. First, always tell the calculator how many compounding periods there are per year. While that may not make a lot of sense yet, it will in a few pages. At this point, we are assuming everything is happening once per year, or annually. Thus, you need to set your calculator accordingly:

Step 1: [2ND] [I/Y] (P/Y)
Step 2: 1
Step 3: [Enter] [2ND] [CPT] (Quit)

You also need to make sure all previous TVOM calculations have been erased. Thus,

(continued)

(continued)

Step 4: [2ND] [FV] (CLR TVM)

Now, you can begin to solve the problem. We will illustrate with the same example used in this section. First, input the known quantities:

Step 5: 5,000[+/-] [PV]
Step 6: 6 [I/Y]
Step 7: 4 [N]

Once this is done, you simply need to tell the calculator what you want it to solve for:

Step 8: [CPT] [FV]

The answer is then given to you as \$6,312.38, which is reassuringly the same as found earlier. You may wonder why we input the present values as a negative number. This is simply because the calculator needs the distinction between future and present values. Should you have put it in as a positive number, the answer would have been \$-6,312.38. As long as it doesn't confuse you, for this problem it doesn't matter. However, it will later, so it would probably be a good idea to get in the habit of always putting the present value in as a negative.

4.2.2 *Present Value of a Lump Sum*

We now turn to the other side of the issue (and the equation). The present value (*PV*) of a lump sum is what a future cash flow is actually worth at time zero, otherwise known as "right now" or "today." In finance, we must often make decisions in current time, but based upon cash flows expected in the future. The good news is that you don't have to remember a new equation, but rather just learn to rearrange the one just used. Therefore, to solve for the present value (*PV*) of some single future cash flow (*FV*), we use the following specification:

$$PV = \frac{FV}{(1+r)^t} = FV\frac{1}{(1+r)^t}$$

The $1/(1 + r)^t$ is known as the present value interest factor (PVIF) and is simply 1 divided by the FVIF. To illustrate the equation, consider another example. Suppose your great-uncle Bennie passes away and leaves you \$10,000. However, he refuses to allow you to have it until you graduate college, which is still three long years away. If the interest rate is 8 %, what is that really worth to you today? Recall the three steps. We now have two options for equations, or specifications of an equation, to use, so we must identify which answers the question. In this instance, we know we are looking for a *PV* because it we are looking for what the cash flow is worth *today*. Therefore, we insert the actual numerical values and solve

$$\frac{\mathbf{10,000}}{(\mathbf{1.08})^3} = \mathbf{\$7,938.32}$$

First, we see the *PV* is lower than the *FV*, which is comforting because it, at a minimum, *looks* correct. This is important because the solution to any TVOM problem, large or small, needs to be given what will be termed the "look right test." If it doesn't look right, it isn't right. In this case an answer larger than the *FV* amount of $10,000 would look incorrect. Let's take a moment and think about why our calculated answer looks correct. A way of looking at this is to imagine two monetary choices. You can either be handed $7,938.32 right now, or you can be promised $10,000 in exactly three years. You should be indifferent between these two options. If you get the lower amount today, you can invest it at the applicable rate of 8 % and get the larger amount the hard way. The difference of a bit more than $2,000 represents the interest that you can earn over the three years. Also, it represents the opportunity cost given up due to the time delay in receipt of the funds.

We need to introduce a new term: **discounting**. In all *PV* problems, we are discounting future cash flows to get them in current terms. The word *discount* is the antithesis of the word *compound*. Whereas compounding means "add to," discounting means "take away." Just think about when you go to a department store and buy something at a discounted rate. That naturally means it is less expensive than it was originally. Each time a cash flow is discounted, it becomes smaller. This leads fairly straightforwardly to the fact that a higher interest rate will lead to a lower *PV*. This is akin to saying that the shirt you bought at that department store was sold at 20 % off instead of 10 % off. The higher discount rate would result in a lower price at the cash register.

Likewise, a longer time period results in a lower *PV* because each time period that passes results in making the future value smaller more times. Again, the end result will be a lower *PV*. You don't have to take my word for it. In the example of uncle Bernie's gift, make sure that if you replace the 8 % with 10 %, you get $7,513.15 and if you replace the three years with four, you get $7,350.30.

Adding this to the relations for future value gives us the following "TVOM Truths" for lump sums:

1. $FV > PV$
2. $\uparrow r = \uparrow FV = \downarrow PV$
3. $\uparrow t = \uparrow FV = \downarrow PV$

TECH HELP 4.2 Present Value of Lump Sum

Since we've already set the calculator to annual compounding, we can skip Steps 1–3 from the previous TECH HELP box. Also, since you need to get into

(continued)

(continued)

the habit of clearing the TVOM values before beginning, go ahead and complete Step 4. Then, we simply follow the pattern of inputting the known values:

Step 1: 10,000 [FV]
Step 2: 8 [I/Y]
Step 3: 3 [N]

Then, solve for the variable in question:

Step 4: [CPT] [PV]

The answer given by the calculator is $-7,938.32, which is of course equivalent to what we found the old-fashioned way.

4.2.3 More Than Annual Compounding

Finding the *PV* or *FV* of a single amount is reasonably straightforward. However, we have intrinsically imposed a couple of important restrictions on our calculations to this point. Unfortunately, with restrictions also come unrealistic solutions. Therefore, we need to work on relaxing a couple of those restrictions. In this section, we start by taking a closer look at the interest rate. Thus far, the interest rate has been assumed to be compounded annually over annual time periods. However, that is not always the case. In fact, interest rates are most often compounded more than once per year. While it is a bit complicated, generally the more often you compound, the more money you will earn. This is good if you are saving money, but not if you are borrowing. However, that is an exogenous issue (see the "LOOK IT UP" box nearby). For now, we need to see what this changes in the calculations.

We need to first introduce the **annual percentage rate (*APR*)**. The *APR* is the rate that is quoted, or stated, on most investments. In other words, if you borrow money at a bank, the rate you will be quoted is the *APR*. For this reason, we will also use the *APR* as our primary rate of interest. When the interest rate is compounded more often than annually, the *APR* is equal to the interest rate per period multiplied by the number of periods per year. If we allow m to stand for the number of compounding periods per year and retain r as being the interest rate per period, we have the following:

$$APR = r^{*}m$$

To be consistent with previous calculations, the rate we really need in the equation is r, the interest rate per period. Therefore, rearranging a bit, we get

$$r = \frac{APR}{m}$$

LOOK IT UP: For those of you who have loans, whether it be for a car, house, or anything else, this box is very important. The rate you are quoted on these personal "investments" is indeed an *APR*. However, that is not the rate you will actually pay. The rate you will pay is known as an effective annual return (EAR) and takes into account interest rate compounding. See if you can find the equation for the EAR. What does the equation imply for the relationship between the values of EAR and *APR*?

As an extension to this, you may find it interesting that if you are saving money at a financial institution, the rate you are quoted is generally something called an annual percentage yield (APY) instead of the *APR*. Why do you think they do this? Well, it probably has a lot to do with your answer to the last sentence in the preceding paragraph.

With annual compounding, $m = 1$ mathematically. In such cases, r equals the *APR*. Now, however, we need to see what must happen when m is greater than 1. The same is true of the time variable. Make note that the t notation was defined as the number of time periods, which need not be the number of years. If we now allow y to represent the number of years of the investment, we can redefine t as

$$t = m^* y$$

Putting all of this together results in the following general equation for the *FV* of a lump sum:

$$FV = PV\left(1 + \frac{APR}{m}\right)^{m^* y}$$

And, likewise, the general form of the *PV* of a lump sum:

$$PV = \frac{FV}{\left(1 + \frac{APR}{m}\right)^{m^* y}}$$

It is important to understand these are not new equations, but rather just less restrictive forms of those previously examined. To illustrate, let's reuse the same examples from the prior sections, only assuming monthly compounding instead of annual. This would make $m = 12$. First, the *FV* example:

$$\begin{aligned} \boldsymbol{FV} &= \mathbf{5,000}\left(\mathbf{1}+\frac{\mathbf{.06}}{\mathbf{12}}\right)^{\mathbf{12^*4}} \\ &= \mathbf{\$6,352.45} \end{aligned}$$

Notice this value is larger than it was with annual compounding. This will always be the case, as you are getting more interest due to the frequency of compounding. Remember the value of compound interest lies in the fact that previously accrued interest can earn additional interest. In the case of more frequent compounding, this phenomenon is even more pronounced. Consider the example of semiannual compounding. While the *APR* is the same regardless of compounding cycle, 6-month compounding periods allows for interest earned during the first 6 months to then earn additional interest during the second 6 months of the year. Specifically consider \$700 invested at a rate of 10 %, compounded semiannually. Following the equation just above, this would be worth \$771.75 at the end of one year. In comparison, had the *APR* been compounded annually, the ending account balance would be \$770. So, how do we account for the extra \$1.75? The answer can be derived from a close look at the interest accumulation. At the end of the first 6 months, the account would be worth

$$\begin{aligned} \boldsymbol{FV} &= \mathbf{700}\left(\mathbf{1}+\frac{\mathbf{.10}}{\mathbf{2}}\right)^{\mathbf{2^*.5}} \\ &= \mathbf{\$735} \end{aligned}$$

This \$35 of interest earned during this first 6 months can then start earning its own interest, which demonstrates the effect of compounding:

$$\begin{aligned} \boldsymbol{FV} &= \mathbf{35}\left(\mathbf{1}+\frac{\mathbf{.10}}{\mathbf{2}}\right)^{\mathbf{2^*.5}} \\ &= \mathbf{\$36.75} \\ \textbf{Interest} &: \mathbf{\$36.75 - \$35.00 = \$1.75} \end{aligned}$$

While almost no one would get excited about the prospect of earning an additional \$1.75, rest assured the differentials get significantly larger as time periods lengthen, compounding cycles become more frequent, and investment amounts become larger. In fact, the difference in ending balances been annual and monthly compounding of \$50,000 over a period of twenty years at a rate of 10 % is in excess of \$30,000. It would be worth the time to check that for yourself.

Now, consider the previous *PV* example of \$10,000 to be received in three years with an 8 % *APR*. If the compounding is monthly instead of annually, we have the following:

$$\begin{aligned} \boldsymbol{PV} &= \frac{\mathbf{10,000}}{\left(\mathbf{1}+\frac{\mathbf{.08}}{\mathbf{12}}\right)^{\mathbf{12^*3}}} \\ &= \mathbf{\$7,872.55} \end{aligned}$$

Recall the annual compounded *PV* was \$7,938.32. This relation will always exist. A larger number of compounding periods per year will decrease the present value. This time, more frequent compounding means you are discounting more often each year. Therefore, the end value solution will be smaller. If we add these two relations to those already discussed, we have the following completed list of TVOM Truths. It would be a wise decision to understand these and dedicate to memory. Also, do not forget to apply them when evaluating solutions with the "look right test."

1. $FV > PV$
2. $\uparrow \mathrm{r} = \uparrow FV = \downarrow PV$
3. $\uparrow \mathrm{t} = \uparrow FV = \downarrow PV$
4. $\uparrow \mathrm{m} = \uparrow FV = \downarrow PV$

LOOK IT UP: There is another option for compounding frequency that is of considerable use in theoretical applications. If you take the compounding frequency to the extreme, it is continuous. Take a few minutes to look up continuous compounding. What do the equations look like in this regard? In what circumstances would such compounding be applicable?

TECH HELP 4.3 More Frequent Compounding

Now, here's where the financial calculator can really help. It can automatically adjust for the compounding period assuming you have it properly set up. Thus, before you ever begin a problem, you need to complete the following steps for more than annual compounding:

Step 1: [2ND] [I/Y] (P/Y)
Step 2: 12 (if monthly compounding)
Step 3: [ENTER] [2ND] [CPT] (Quit)

Once this is done, just repeat the same steps from the previous TECH HELP boxes. Try it for yourself and see if you can get the correct answers when the compounding cycle is monthly rather than annually. Be careful to check the set compounding period prior to each problem since the calculator will remain in the last setting until changed.

4.2.4 Solving for Rates and Time Periods

As with most things, sometimes the most interesting information is hidden in TVOM problems. There are many instances when solving for *FV* and *PV* is not the primary concern. There are four primary components to the lump sum equations, and any one can be solved for given the other three. This naturally leaves the open question of how to calculate *APRs* and time periods, given all other relevant information. To obtain the formulas to solve for these new variables of concern, we can rearrange either the *FV* or *PV* lump sum equations. Either way, the *APR* can be found with the following:

$$APR = m\left[\left(\frac{FV}{PV}\right)^{\frac{1}{m^{*}y}} - 1\right]$$

Suppose you currently have $7,500 in your investment account and you want to turn that into a car in ten years. You expect the car to cost $15,000 at that time. What *APR* compounded monthly would you have to earn to get to your goal?

$$\begin{aligned} \mathbf{APR} &= \mathbf{12}\left[\left(\frac{\mathbf{15,000}}{\mathbf{7,500}}\right)^{\frac{\mathbf{1}}{\mathbf{12^{*}10}}} \mathbf{-1}\right] \\ &= \mathbf{6.95\,\%} \end{aligned}$$

The good news about solving for both the interest rate and time period is that you can always check your work by plugging in the answer. In this case, the 6.95 % would be confirmed as the appropriate rate of return, with some small error due to rounding. Solving for the time period is a complicated a bit by the fact that it is an exponent. However, with a bit of mathematical maneuvering, we can arrive at the following:

$$y = \frac{1}{m}\left[\frac{\ln\left(\frac{FV}{PV}\right)}{\ln\left(1 + \frac{APR}{m}\right)}\right]$$

Consider another real-life example that most people encounter at some point. Suppose you currently have $200,000 in your retirement account and want to retire with $1,000,000. Assuming you put no more into the fund and that it can grow at an *APR* of 8 %, compounded monthly, how many years will it take to get to your goal?

$$\begin{aligned} \mathbf{y} &= \frac{\mathbf{1}}{\mathbf{12}}\left[\frac{\mathbf{ln}\left(\frac{\mathbf{1,000,000}}{\mathbf{200,000}}\right)}{\mathbf{ln}\left(\mathbf{1+}\frac{\mathbf{.08}}{\mathbf{12}}\right)}\right] \\ &= \mathbf{20.18\ years} \end{aligned}$$

A quick check will confirm that this is the correct answer. Such calculations are a bit burdensome, but this process can be significantly streamlined by using a financial calculator. This is detailed in a nearby TECH HELP box. Regardless of how the problems get solved, calculating rates and time periods is a very relevant issue and should be given the same attention as solving for future or present values.

TECH HELP 4.4 Solving for *APR* and Time for Lump Sums

Again, this is a valuable application of the financial calculator. On the BA II Plus, each of the four primary variables has a button. Thus, to solve for any one of them, you first input the known variables for the other three and then ask the machine to calculate the unknown.

To replicate the problem solving for *APR* in this section, first set the calculator to monthly compounding and clear the TVOM fields. Then, input the three known variables:

Step 1: 15,000 [FV]
Step 2: 7,500 [+|-] [PV]
Step 3: 10 [2ND] [N] (xP/Y) [N]

All that is left is to ask the calculator to compute the *APR*:

Step 4: [CPT] [I/Y]

This should provide the same 6.95 %. Follow through by also replicating the retirement problem in this section as well.

4.3 Multiple Cash Flows

4.3.1 Future Value of Multiple Cash Flows

In the real world of corporate finance, cash flows seldom occur only once. Therefore, we need to know how to handle multiple cash flows and the resulting present or future value. We will begin by examining the general formulas for both present and future values of multiple cash flows, starting again with the future value:

$$FV = \sum_{t=1}^{T} CF_t(1+r)^t$$

As you may notice, there are a lot of similarities in calculating the *FV* of multiple cash flows and lump sums. The process involves calculating the future value of each cash flow separately and then simply combining those future values. Consider the following example to illustrate. Suppose you have just given birth to a bumbling baby boy (more difficult for you gentlemen to imagine, but do your best). You realize babies cost quite a bit so you start investing in a fund for his future. You invest $4,000 at the end of the first year, $3,000 at the end of the second, and

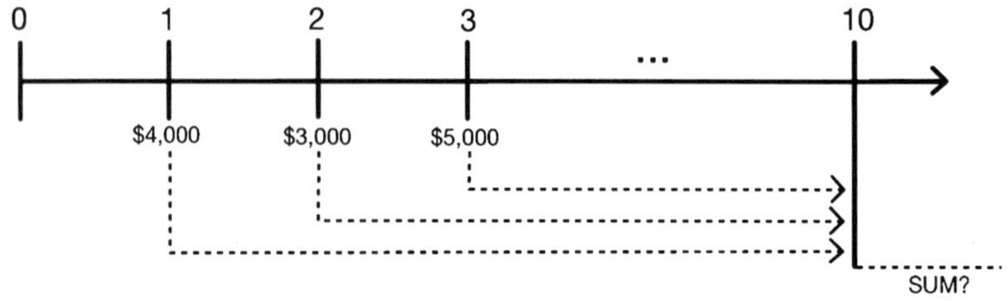

Fig. 4.2 Future value of multiple cash flows

$5,000 at the end of the third year. If you invest these amounts at a rate of 6 %, compounded annually, what will it be worth at the end of ten years?

When doing problems of this nature, it is best to draw a picture (Fig. 4.2) of the cash flow stream before you do the math. This helps visualize the time periods and reduce errors in calculating time periods, which is probably the area of most difficulty.

As can be seen by examining the time line, to calculate the FV, you need to literally count the number of compounding periods. Then calculate the FV of each of the three lump sums separately before summing the future values. Thus, the problem becomes

$$\boldsymbol{FV = 4000(1.06)^9 + 3,000(1.06)^8 + 5,000(1.06)^7}$$
$$\boldsymbol{FV = \$19,057.61}$$

Notice the answer is greater than the sum of the individual payments, which should always be the case.

4.3.2 *Present Value of Multiple Cash Flows*

If you have been halfheartedly reading until now thinking all this stuff was roughly the same level of importance, *stop*! This section is probably the most important you will read and should be considered with care, and probably more than once. The equation that is about to be put forward will be used several times throughout the remainder of the text because it does one very, very important thing; assign a current value to any asset. This is of utmost importance in finance as our decisions hinge on the correct valuation of assets. Even with the power to do all this, the equation isn't overly intimidating:

$$PV = \sum_{t=1}^{T} \frac{CF_t}{(1+r)^t}$$

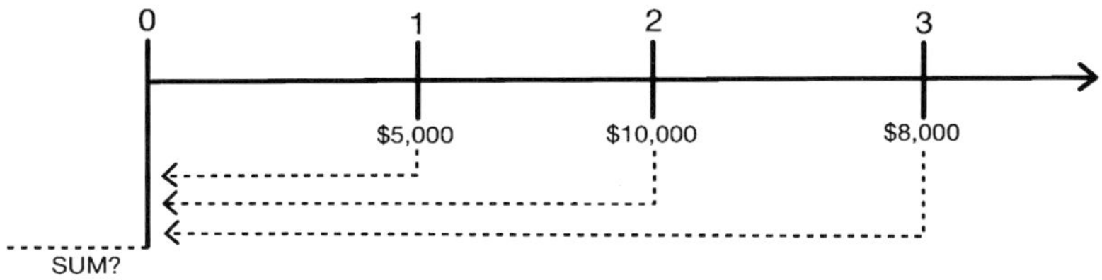

Fig. 4.3 Present value of multiple cash flows

This equation can accommodate any number of cash flows of any numerical value that occur at any point in the future. Given the applicable interest rate and the appropriate discount period, the equation will provide the time zero value of anything. Now is as good a time as any to introduce a mantra that you should store in permanent memory: *the current value of anything should be equal to the summation of its discounted future cash flows.* Obviously, numbers within the equation (the interest rate or cash flows themselves) can be incorrect as they are simply estimates of future values, but given this notable restriction, the process itself is without error.

Again, let's illustrate it with an example. Suppose you have been injured on your job and have been awarded a workman's comp settlement. The settlement will be paid in the following manner: $5,000 at the end of year one, $10,000 at the end of year two, and $8,000 at the end of year three. Again, given an interest rate of 6 %, what is this stream of payments really worth in today's money? We can set up the problem as in Fig. 4.3.

In one way, it is easier to calculate the present value of multiple cash flows than future values. The time period of concern with present value is nearly always time zero. Thus, counting the time periods for discounting each cash flow is relatively straightforward. If a cash flow is expected to occur four years from now, it should be discounted four years to get to current time. On the other hand, the future value is much more open in that the ending time period can be any future period. Solving the problem above can be done as

$$\begin{aligned} \boldsymbol{PV} &= \frac{\mathbf{5,000}}{(\mathbf{1.06})^1} + \frac{\mathbf{10,000}}{(\mathbf{1.06})^2} + \frac{\mathbf{8,000}}{(\mathbf{1.06})^3} \\ &= \mathbf{\$20,333.90} \end{aligned}$$

Again, we have an important relation between the raw figures and *PV*. The *PV* is always going to be less than the sum of the raw figures. This is a reflection of the basic concept of the time value of money. So, now we have covered four of the six options for TVOM calculations: *PV* and *FV* of both lump sums and multiple unequal cash flows. The only remaining option is multiple *equal* cash flows.

TECH HELP 4.5 Multiple Cash Flows

The good news is that, just like the equations, all we really need to do is calculate the present value of each lump sum and then add them together. There are two ways to do this. The obvious is to do each separately on the calculator and write them down. When this is finished, the values can then be summed. The other option is to let the calculator keep track of them for you.

This second scenario is a bit more complicated. First, as always, set the calculator to the appropriate compounding cycle (annually in this case) and clear the previous TVOM values. Then, you can begin with the future value problem from this section:

Step 1: 6 [I/Y]
Step 2: 4,000 [+|-] [*PV*]
Step 3: 9 [N]
Step 4: [CPT] [*FV*]
Step 5: [STO] 1 (stores the value)
Step 6: 3,000 [+|-] [*PV*]
Step 7: 8 [N]
Step 8: [CPT] [*FV*]
Step 9: [STO] [+] 1 (adds this value to the stored values and restores)
Step 10: 5,000 [+|-] [*PV*]
Step 11: 7 [N]
Step 12: [CPT] [*FV*]
Step 13: [STO] [+] 1
Step 14: [RCL] 1 (recalls the stored values)

At each step, compute the individual future value, store it, and then move on to the next one. Once you've completed the next one, you add it to the previously stored value, and the calculator automatically replaces the stored value with the cumulative total. You continue this pattern until you have completed all cash flows and then recall the last stored number. This should give you the correct answer of $19,057.61. The present value works much the same way, only with [*FV*] everywhere [*PV*] is, and vice versa. Make sure you can do both types of problems.

4.3.3 Future Value of an Annuity

The process described in the previous two sections allows us to find the present or future value for *any* stream of cash flows. That needs to be made clear. Whatever the timing or level of the cash flows, the systematic, one-cash-flow-at-a-time, approach will provide the correct answer when used correctly. However, in a corporate setting, we often find cash flow streams that go for an extensive period of time. Suppose, for example, that we are trying to find the present value of 35 cash flows received at different times in the future. Finding the *PV* of each would eventually get to the answer, but would be a tedious process. Luckily, there are certain situations where simplification is possible. Thus, let's define an annuity.

Strictly speaking, **an ordinary (or deferred) annuity** is one such that:

1. All cash flows are of an equal amount.
2. All cash flows occur at regular intervals.
3. All cash flows occur at the end of each period.
4. The cash flow period and the compounding cycle must coincide.

LOOK IT UP: Another type of annuity is called an annuity due. See if you can find out how it differs from an ordinary annuity. While you're at it, see if you can discover how this difference affects the calculations below.

Therefore, if we have a stream of cash flows that meets all four criteria, we then have an annuity, which effectively allows a shortcut. We will start with the formula for the *FV* of an annuity (*FVA*), which looks like this:

$$FVA = C\left[\frac{(1+r)^t - 1}{r}\right]$$

Breaking down the formula a bit, the part in brackets is known as the future value interest factor of an annuity (FVIFA), which you may notice includes the future value interest factor (FVIF) discussed earlier in this chapter. The C represents the annuity amount, or the amount of each equal cash flow. The reasoning behind this notation will become clearer in the next chapter.

This equation can be used to solve the following type of problem: suppose you are to receive payment of \$300 at the end of each of the next eight years as a result of an insurance settlement. The applicable interest rate is 8 %. What will this stream of cash flows be worth at the end of the eight years?

Inserting the numbers into the equation, we have the following:

$$\begin{aligned} \boldsymbol{FVA} &= \mathbf{300}\left[\frac{\mathbf{(1.08)^8 - 1}}{\mathbf{.08}}\right] \\ \boldsymbol{FVA} &= \mathbf{\$3,190.99} \end{aligned}$$

The *FVA* is greater than the sum of the raw values (\$300 × 8 = \$2,400), which is as it should be and consistent with the Truths of the TVOM. For good practice, do the problem using the formula in Sect. 4.3.1 to ensure they provide the same answer. The point, of course, is that either works, but the annuity formula can save considerable time and effort.

4.3.4 Present Value of an Annuity

At long last, we are near the end of our TVOM journey. The last piece of the puzzle is to find the present value of multiple equal cash flows. The equation is a bit more complex than the *FVA*, but still much easier than doing each cash flow separately:

$$PVA = C\left[\frac{1 - \frac{1}{(1+r)^t}}{r}\right]$$

Again, the part in brackets has a name; the present value interest factor of an annuity (PVIFA) and C is again the cash flow amount. As usual, let's consider an example. Suppose you have survived a divorce settlement and have been awarded \$15,000 at the end of each of the next fifteen years. If the interest rate is 8 %, what is the settlement worth to you today?

$$\boldsymbol{PVA = 15,000\left[\frac{1 - \frac{1}{(1.08)^{15}}}{.08}\right]}$$

$$\boldsymbol{PVA = \$128,392.18}$$

Not to beat a long-dead horse, but you should again notice the *PVA* is lower than the sum of the raw amounts (\$150,000). Also, you should still check to ensure this gives you the same answer as the equation presented in Sect. 4.3.2.

4.3.5 Multiple Cash Flows with More Frequent Compounding

It often becomes necessary to incorporate more than annual compounding into the multiple cash flow formulas in much the same way as with the lump sums. Luckily, it works the same way, but does require a bit more care. As with the lump sums, m represents the number of compounding periods per year.

If the cash flows are of unequal amounts, the formulas that must be used when dealing with more than annual compounding are

$$FV = \sum_{t=1}^{T} CF_t\left(1 + \frac{APR}{m}\right)^{m^* y}$$

and

$$PV = \sum_{t=1}^{T} \frac{CF_t}{\left(1 + \frac{APR}{m}\right)^{m^*y}}$$

If the cash flows meet the criteria to be an annuity, the formulas are also a bit uglier, but the pattern of adjustment should be familiar. Each r and t must be replaced with the more flexible APR/m and m^*y, respectively:

$$FVA = C\left[\frac{\left(1 + \frac{APR}{m}\right)^{m^*y} - 1}{\frac{APR}{m}}\right]$$

$$PVA = C\left[\frac{1 - \frac{1}{\left(1+\frac{APR}{m}\right)^{m^*y}}}{\frac{APR}{m}}\right]$$

Remember these are not new equations, but rather alternative specifications of the previous ones. There are three things to keep in mind:

1. The cash flow used must be the amount of money that comes each individual time period. For the annuity, this means that C must be the amount that is received m times per year.
2. The interest rate must be the interest rate per compounding period (APR/m).
3. The number of time periods (t) must be the number of compounding periods per year multiplied by the number of years (m^*y).

For the sake of completeness, let's use these generalized equations to reproduce the examples in Sects. 4.3.3 and 4.3.4, only assuming the cash flows are split into months instead of years. The compounding cycle must do so as well. This produces the following answers:

$$\boldsymbol{FVA = 25\left[\frac{\left(1 + \frac{.08}{12}\right)^{8^*12} - 1}{\frac{.08}{12}}\right]}$$

$$\boldsymbol{FVA = 3,346.71}$$

and

$$\boldsymbol{PVA = 1,250\left[\frac{1 - \frac{1}{\left(1+\frac{.08}{12}\right)^{15^*12}}}{\frac{.08}{12}}\right]}$$

$$\boldsymbol{PVA = 130,800.74}$$

4.3.6 Solving for Rates, Payment, and Time

As you may imagine, solving for variables other than present or future value when dealing with multiple cash flows is considerably more difficult than with lump sums. In fact, some are nearly impossible. Solving for any of the three variables (payments, time periods, and interest rates) of multiple unequal cash flows is incredibly burdensome due to the numerous possible answers to the same question. In fact, in most cases, the problems cannot be solved via closed-form equations.

The same is true of annuities, with one major exception. Solving for the annuity payment itself is one of the fundamental interests in TVOM. Numerous examples of questions involving this issue are readily apparent. For example, consider the following. If you want to retire in twenty years, and think you can obtain a 7 % *APR* during those twenty years, what monthly payment must you invest to obtain a retirement account balance of $500,000 at the end of the period?

$$\mathbf{500,000} = \mathbf{C}\left[\frac{\left(\mathbf{1}+\frac{.07}{12}\right)^{20^{*}12}-\mathbf{1}}{\frac{.07}{12}}\right]$$

The unknown variable is the payment (C), which can be solved to be $959.83. This is but one realistic example of solving for the payment with the annuity formulas. Others come in the form of present value and will be detailed later in this chapter.

Unfortunately, for or all other instances of solving for rates, payments, or time periods with multiple cash flows, one must resort to the old-fashioned trial and error. You try a value and get an answer. You then examine the "error" from the "trial" and adjust your input. Eventually, you can get to the point that the error is minimized to an acceptable level. Luckily, technology has greatly aided in this process. TECH HELP boxes 4.6 and 4.7 detail the process for allowing financial calculators and Excel to help out in solving for these variables.

TECH HELP 4.6 Annuities

The only real addition, both to the equation and on the calculator, is the introduction of a constant payment. This, naturally, is the primary determinant of the value of an annuity and, as such, warrants its own special button on the calculator. The most important thing to remember is that the process is much the same with annuities as with lump sums. An annuity is nothing more than the same lump sum amount that keeps occurring over a period of time. The point is, don't start looking for an [*FVA*] or [*PVA*] button, as they don't exist and are unneeded. To illustrate, consider the example in Sect. 4.3.3:

Step 1: 300 [+|-] [PMT]
Step 2: 8 [I/Y]
Step 3: 8 [N]
Step 4: [CPT] [*FV*]

You should be given the answer of $3,190.99. The PMT key just tells the calculator that the cash flow is going to occur more than once. The answer should be the same as those found when using the equation. If you want to find the present value of an annuity, you simply replace Step 4 with [CPT] [*PV*].

(continued)

(continued)

It is also relatively straightforward to solve for payments, interest rates, or time periods for annuities. In each instance, the last step would be instructing the calculator to solve for the unknown variable. In the preceding steps, all known variables (including the *PVA* or *FVA*) would be input in the machine.

Finally, if you want to calculate the present or future value of an annuity with more than annual compounding, the calculator must simply be set to the appropriate compounding cycle before beginning the problem.

TECH HELP 4.7 TVOM in Excel

In Excel, there are five relevant formulas when considering the time value of money and annuities in particular. They are "=pv(. . .)," "=fv(. . .)," "=rate (. . .)," "=nper(. . .)," and "=pmt(. . .)." These allow you to calculate the *PVA*, *FVA*, *APR*, number of time periods, and C, respectively. Consider an example of an annuity that makes annual payments of $4,000 for twenty years at an *APR* of 5 %, compounded monthly. The following screenshot displays the calculations of each of the variables referenced above.

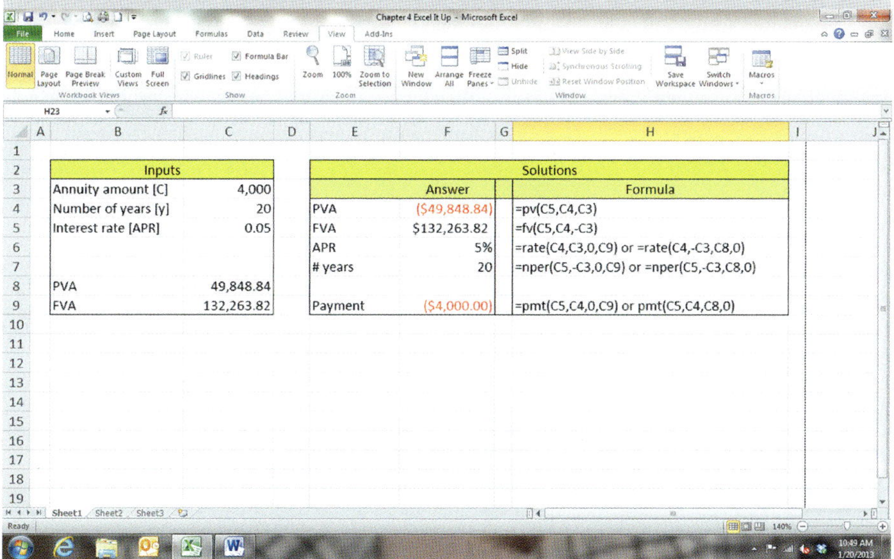

Inputs	
Annuity amount [C]	4,000
Number of years [y]	20
Interest rate [APR]	0.05
PVA	49,848.84
FVA	132,263.82

Solutions	Answer	Formula
PVA	($49,848.84)	=pv(C5,C4,C3)
FVA	$132,263.82	=fv(C5,C4,-C3)
APR	5%	=rate(C4,C3,0,C9) or =rate(C4,-C3,C8,0)
# years	20	=nper(C5,-C3,0,C9) or =nper(C5,-C3,C8,0)
Payment	($4,000.00)	=pmt(C5,C4,0,C9) or pmt(C5,C4,C8,0)

Note that in the cases of *APR*, time periods, and payments, calculations can be made on both a future and present value basis, depending on the specific question.

IN THE REAL WORLD

It was raining as Lilly and Tyler emerged from a squat brick building late on Friday afternoon, August 19, 2011. Holding legal pads over their heads, they ran towards the waiting car and jumped in just as the rain intensified. Neither was particularly happy with having spent much of the day in a classroom listening to a boring professor with suspenders and bifocals drone on and on while scribbling numbers and formulas on an old chalkboard. The rain was the perfect ending to an otherwise useless day, at least in their current view. Lilly, as always, began the protest.

"Why on earth did we have to go through that?" Lilly said angrily to the gentleman driving the car.

"Because you needed it lads," Dubarb Freeman said, turning in his seat to look at them. Feeling rather proud of his ability to not laugh at their soaked-rat appearance, he continued. "You have to understand the time value of money before we can talk about running this corporation. You'd be amazed at the number of executives that haven't the foggiest of understandings of basic financial principals. I figured you needed a refresher."

"While I certainly can tell you some things," he continued, "Herb can cover much more ground with the time than I can. Did you take notes?"

"Kinda," Tyler said, holding up his drenched legal pad, covered with equations scribbled in running ink.

"Well, I guess we can classify that as 'trying,'" Freeman said with a shake of his head. He turned around and started the car. "Come on then, we have a lot of work to do."

As they drove back to the office, he quizzed them on what they had learned. The private cram review course in the time value of money was naturally his idea, and Herb Robinson had been more than willing to provide instruction, for a nominal fee of course. Hack Back's owners had been more than a little reluctant to go back to school, but he had managed to convince them by regaling them with horror stories of miscalculated cash flows due to inadequate basic knowledge. Sure, most had been purely fictional, but there were a few real ones in there as well. At the end of it all, the two young executives had relented to the day of lecture.

"What I don't understand is why the team didn't do this instead of us," Lilly said. "Isn't that their job?"

"Oh, don't you worry. First of all, they have all been educated on the subject before. And second, they are all getting the full-blown review. Herb has spent all week with them while you two have been off at that leadership conference."

He lowered his voice before muttering, "Whatever that means."

His passengers pretended to not hear. They were too tired to argue.

"Exactly how much are we paying this fellow to teach them stuff they already know?" Tyler asked.

"We worked out a good deal. Don't worry about it."

"Besides, it's a sunk cost anyway, right Dube?" Lilly said, tilting her head so that her check pressed against the rain-cooled class. Freeman jerked his head up in surprise at the memory retention. Lilly just smiled out into the rain.

"We'll meet first thing Monday morning to discuss the projects more in-depth and where we need to go from here," Freeman said as they pulled into the office parking lot.

"All right," Tyler said dejectedly. He and Lilly got out of the car and shuffled to their own vehicles as Freeman watched. He hit the lock on the door of his 1995 Toyota Corolla and walked back towards the building. There was still daylight to burn and he had some financials to look over....

Monday morning brought sunshine and a much happier mood for the two young Hack Back executives. They met in the conference room with Freeman and the other four members of the finance department. Freshly baked donuts were passed around, laptops were warmly humming, and work was set to begin.

"Let's look back at the expected cash flows we generated for each of the two project options," Stewart began. Marilyn clicked a button and the summary of the two projects flashed on the overhead screen.

High-tech plant			
	Year 0	*Years 1–14*	*Year 15*
Operating cash flows		*4,726,865*	*4,726,865*
Net capital spending	*−18,000,000*		
Change in NWC	*−5,000,000*		*5,000,000*
Total project cash flows	*−23,000,000*	*4,726,865*	*9,726,865*
Traditional plant			
	Year 0	*Years 1–19*	*Year 20*
Operating cash flows		*3,661,494*	*3,661,494*
Net capital spending	*−13,000,000*		
Change in NWC	*−3,000,000*		*3,000,000*
Total project cash flows	*−16,000,000*	*3,661,494*	*6,661,494*

"As we said the last time we were discussing this, all we really have here is a start," she said. "We need to take those cash flows and adjust them for valuation purposes."

"Adjust them how?" Lilly asked.

"Wait, we know this Lilly," Tyler broke in, "We have to find the present value of each of them."

"Right," she responded, gazing at a spot on the wall as she tried to remember. "Dr. Robinson said we have to get everything in 'today's money'. He kept repeating that silly phrase."

"So you would remember it." Freeman broke in. "What we need to do is discount the cash flows back to see what they would be worth today."

Marilyn went to the computer console in front of the room to display their presentation on the screen. While she did this, Stewart handed out typed sheets of paper with calculations. Brandon pulled a well-used Texas Instruments BA II Plus financial calculator from his computer bag. Jane preferred to do time value of money calculations in Excel, so she had an open spreadsheet.

"We started simple," Stewart said as he moved around the table, "by assuming each cash flow will come in its entirety at the end of its respective year. We also assume the applicable interest rate is 7 %. The first table before you displays each cash flow in both raw and discounted form for the high-tech plant design."

Year	High-tech Expected CF	High-tech Disc. CF	% Deterioration
1	4,726,865	4,417,631	6.54
2	4,726,865	4,128,627	12.66
3	4,726,865	3,858,530	18.37
4	4,726,865	3,606,103	23.71
5	4,726,865	3,370,189	28.70
6	4,726,865	3,149,710	33.37
7	4,726,865	2,943,654	37.73
8	4,726,865	2,751,078	41.80
9	4,726,865	2,571,101	45.61
10	4,726,865	2,402,898	49.17
11	4,726,865	2,245,700	52.49
12	4,726,865	2,098,785	55.60
13	4,726,865	1,961,481	58.50
14	4,726,865	1,833,160	61.22
15	9,726,865	3,525,464	63.76

"In addition," Marilyn added, "the last column displays the percentage of deterioration from the raw expected cash flow to the discounted cash flow."

"See here, kids?" Freeman said, standing to point to the chart. "This is the issue with waiting for cash flows. There is an opportunity cost of waiting. If we invest in these plants, we are tying up our funds in the hope that we will receive a profit in our returns. The problem is that we have to wait on those returns and waiting has an expense, for the simple reason that we can't use the money until we get it."

"So, we may have to forego other investments during the 'wait' period?" Tyler asked thoughtfully.

"Absolutely," Freeman nodded so hard his chin seemed to bounce off his chest, "but there is also an issue of risk. Not only can we not use the money on other potential projects, but we also don't have it for liquidity issues should the firm experience tough financial times."

"And, are you saying that, in order to account for these issues, we need to discount the cash flows by some rate that is reflective of these costs?" Lilly pondered, mostly to herself.

"Yes, that is a large component of the time value of money," Marilyn said while leaning on the console. "If you look at the deterioration column, it is obvious that waiting has costs and it gets larger as the distance to receipt increases."

"To the point that we are losing nearly two-thirds of the expected cash flow?" Lilly asked, pointing at the last rows of the table.

"It's certainly possible," Freeman said, "and you need to know that. You must accept these projects will cripple the firm's available future cash flow to a degree and that cost has to be accounted for. Which is why we are here today..."

With that, he gestured at Marilyn to continue and retook his seat. Marilyn moved to the next slide and nodded at Stewart to carry on.

"So, given this understanding and the fact that we are assuming, in this first run, the expected flow amounts are consistent for the first fourteen years, we can treat those cash flows as an annuity. The last year then is discounted as a lump sum. The math works out to be number one on your handouts and," he pointed at the screen, "up there":

$$PVA = 4{,}726{,}865\left[\frac{1-\frac{1}{(1.07)^{14}}}{.07}\right]+\frac{9{,}726{,}865}{(1.07)^{15}}$$

$$= \$44{,}864{,}110$$

"So, let me see if I have this straight," Lilly said. "This project is going to bring in less than \$45 million dollars? That's a lot less than we had originally talked about."

"Especially since," Tyler added, "if I understand this correctly, the initial costs of the project do not get discounted, as they occur at time zero. Right? So, we are now comparing a smaller value for inflow to the same value of initial outflow."

"Yes, very good, Tyler," Freeman said, "I told you that understanding the time value of money was important."

"I had no idea it was THAT important," Lilly responded. "What does the other project look like?"

"Well, applying the same ideas, we have the following," Marilyn said, as she pointed out the second calculation on the sheet:

$$PVA = 3{,}661{,}494\left[\frac{1-\frac{1}{(1.07)^{19}}}{.07}\right]+\frac{6{,}661{,}494}{(1.07)^{20}}$$

$$= \$39{,}565{,}177$$

"Well, that doesn't look nearly as good either," Tyler said.

"I'm sorry," Lilly said, shaking her head, "but I still don't understand what these numbers really mean. I just don't quite have my head wrapped around the fact that we are going to be making," she paused and flipped through her legal pad until she found what she was looking for, "seventy million on the high-tech plant. Now you're telling me we'll only make less than forty-five. I just don't quite see how sixteen million dollars disappears just because time passes. Isn't the seventy million the number that flows into our bank account by the end of it all?"

Freeman tented his fingers in front of pursed lips for a long moment, before abruptly sitting up.

"Let's look at it from the other side," he said.

4.4 Loans

Loans play a vital role in life, both individually and in a business setting. We will learn as we progress through this text that a firm will likely find themselves seeking capital via the debt market. Knowing this, along with the fact that you will likely experience debt on a personal level at some point as well, suggests that we take a close look at the structure of loans, particularly from the borrower's perspective. There are many types of loans, but the basic details can be summed up by looking at three basic designs.

4.4.1 Pure Discount Loans

The first type is known as a **pure discount loan**. If you define the loan as having a distinct beginning at time 0 (when the money flows from the lender to the borrower) and a distinct ending at time T (when the money flows back to the lender from the borrower), it would take the pictorial form as in Fig. 4.4:

The picture sums up a pure discount loan in its entirety. There is no interest payment made throughout the time period. You just borrow an amount, hold it for the period, and then pay it back. Suffice it to say, as a borrower this loan would be a rare find in your personal life, outside of perhaps from a generous family member. Pure discount securities do exist, however, and in spades. We will learn about the specific nature of these in the debt chapter later on. It is worth a

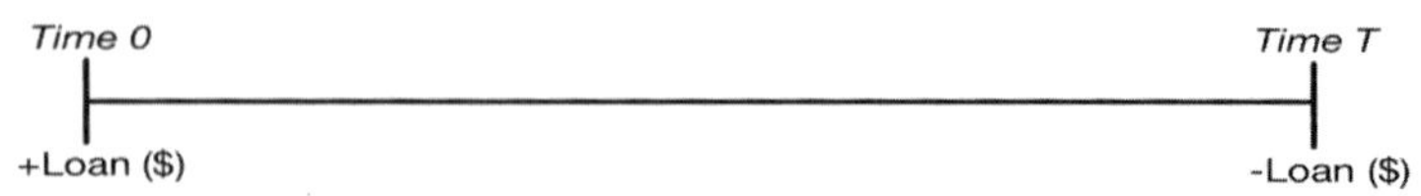

Fig. 4.4 Pure discount loan

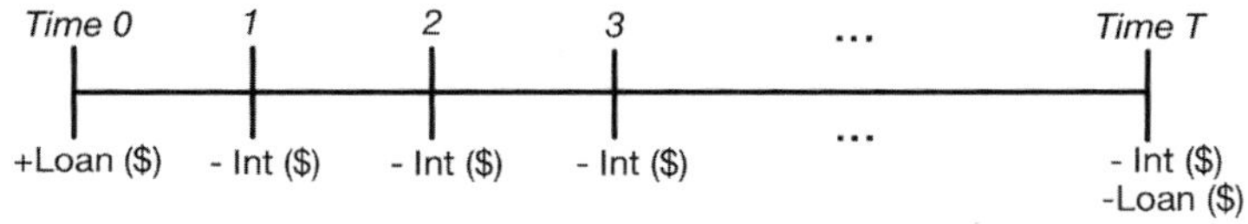

Fig. 4.5 Interest-only loan

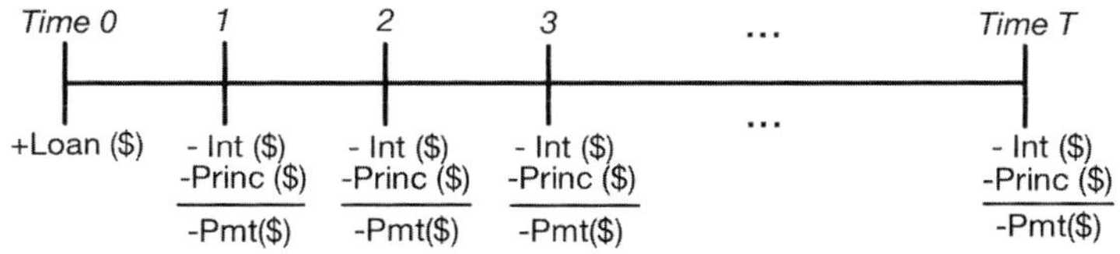

Fig. 4.6 Amortized loan

note here, however, to make clear one important point. Just because these loans do not *pay* interest doesn't mean they don't have interest. Rather than the interest being paid over time, the interest is captured in the difference between the amount borrowed at time 0 and the amount repaid at time T. The latter will be more than the former and the difference represents the interest on the loan. For example, suppose your father loans you $1,000 today but expects you to pay $1,500 back in five years. The $500 difference is the interest on the loan, captured in one lump sum amount at the end.

Now, let's consider a couple of loan types you are more likely to personally encounter. A second type of loan is called an **interest-only loan.** As the name implies, these loans do have a direct interest component to be paid throughout the life of the loan. Interest-only loans can be displayed as in Fig. 4.5.

The -Int ($) represents the amount of interest paid each period. Notice that you still owe the entire amount of the loan at the end. The interest payment is akin to paying "rent" on the money you've borrowed. It is your way of paying the lender for the right to hold onto the funds for one more period, but does nothing to change the amount of the outstanding loan balance.

The final type of loan differs in that you must still pay the "rent," but you also systematically reduce the loan balance over the life of the loan. This type of loan is easily most popular and can be depicted as in Fig. 4.6.

This is known as an **amortized loan**. As you can see, for each period, the payment made consists of both interest and payments to principal. As an average consumer, you likely do not make the distinction as they are bundled together in the bill you receive every month. Calculating this total payment is a very important application of the formulas covered earlier in this chapter. Consider an example of a house that costs $250,000. Your bank offers you a thirty-year loan at an *APR* of 8 %, compounded monthly. This provides a very good opportunity to remind ourselves of which TVOM equation to use. Assuming the rate is fixed at 8 % for the duration of the loan, we know there will certainly be more than one payment and these payments will be the same amount each period. Thus, we are dealing with an annuity situation. In addition, the rate is compounded monthly. The only remaining question is whether we are dealing with a present or future value situation. We can answer that by asking a simple question: when do we want the money? Today, of course! That is when we want to buy the house. So, we need to solve the following problem:

$$\mathbf{250,000 = C\left[\frac{1-\frac{1}{\left(1+\frac{.08}{12}\right)^{30^{*}12}}}{\frac{.08}{12}}\right]}$$

The unknown variable is the annuity amount, which in this application is the monthly loan payment. Solving for C results in an answer of \$1,834.41. In order for this house to be truly yours, you must make 360 payments of this amount, which roughly adds up to \$660,388. While that may indeed be a shocking number, such is the price of doing business with debt. The difference between the total amount paid and the purchase price represents the cost of the loan, or the interest paid to the bank. In this case, your \$250,000 house costs well more than double the purchase price, and this amount still excludes additional costs, such as taxes or insurance, which are also typically included in payments.

Let's look back for a moment at interest-only loans. This type of loan is also popular in the real world, particularly as a vehicle for investment assets. The benefit of buying the property with an interest-only loan is that the payment amount is much lower, since you do not pay down the principal. Thus, the payment is simply the interest amount each month, computed as the interest rate per period (.08/12 = .0066667), multiplied by the loan amount. Thus,

$$\mathbf{.0066667^{*}250,000 = \$1,666.68}$$

The problem with this is that you can pay the rate for thirty years, each month, and still owe the \$250,000 at the end. In short, this is probably not the loan type that you would choose if you want to eventually own the property. If you just want a relatively brief investment period, however, it does keep the payments down to a more manageable level until you can sell the property (hopefully at a profit).

LOOK IT UP: In actuality, most loans that are called interest-only loans aren't designed exactly in this fashion. Most are hybrid-type loans that are

(continued)

Table 4.2 Amortization schedule

Month	Beginning balance	Payment	Interest	To principal	Ending balance
1	250,000.00	1,834.4114	1,666.67	167.74	249,832.26
2	249,832.26	1,834.4114	1,665.55	168.86	249,663.39
3	249,663.39	1,834.4114	1,664.42	169.99	249,493.40
.	.	.	.	.	.
.	.	.	.	.	.
359	3,632.46	1,834.4114	24.22	1,810.20	1,822.26
360	1,822.26	1,834.4114	12.15	1,822.26	0.00

(continued)

interest only for a period of time and then convert to the amortized variety. Take a look around the web and see how that works and think about why people may wish to take this type of loan. You may want to focus on the difference in the total amount of interest paid in the different scenarios.

Now, getting back to the desire to actually *own* the property for which you've taken the loan, notice in Fig. 4.6 that the final time period in an amortized loan is missing the *-$Loan*. This indicates you don't have to pay the loan amount back at the time period. Why? The answer is simple; you have already done so. We can illustrate how by introducing the **amortization schedule**, depicted for our example in Table 4.2.

The table above omits the majority of time periods since there is a natural page limit on books of this sort. However, the first three and last two periods should provide the information needed. The amount of each payment that goes to interest each period is calculated as we described with the interest-only loan. However, in this case, each period has a different beginning balance. This results in the amount that gets paid to interest each period decrease. Think if it this way; you are paying the bank "rent" on the money that you owe them. As you slowly pay it off (the "to principal" amount), you are holding onto less of their money, and they will respond by charging you less "rent." In fact, as you can see, early in the loan, the proportion of your payment that goes to interest is quite large, resulting in the proportion that goes to principal being relatively low. It actually can get a bit depressing. Do this example in Excel for yourself and confirm that after making payments for ten years (10 * 12 * *$1,834.41* = *$220,129*), you still owe over $219,000 on your $250,000 loan.

Don't fear however, if you stick with it, the tide will turn in your favor. This can be seen in Table 4.2, as the final two periods have a very small portion of the payment going to interest, as by that time you are holding onto a small fraction of the original loan. In fact, confirm by looking at the total example that you pay off more than 60 % of the loan during just the final ten years. The end result is the most rewarding, as the ending balance for the last period is $0, indicating you no longer owe the bank anything and the asset is yours.

LOOK IT UP: All of the examples throughout this text assume the interest rates are fixed. An alternative is something called a variable rate. This type of rate, as the name implies, can change throughout the term of the loan. See if you can look up how these rates work and the implications they have for the borrower.

IN THE REAL WORLD

"You understand loans, right?" Freeman said to Lilly.

"Sure, you borrow money and pay it back," she responded, "plus interest of course."

"That's it!" he responded, a bit too aggressively. He pointed an index finger and stood. "The money you borrow isn't free, is it?"

"Sure."

"So, if you borrow, say, 200 grand for a house..."

"200 grand. Come on Dube."

"What?" Freeman was genuinely puzzled. His house had cost less than half that, twenty five years ago. Lilly just gave him a sad look. The rest of the audience settled in to watch the exchange.

"Okay, okay, let's just make it an example you will definitely understand. Let's say that you borrow the entire amount to finance these projects." He waved a hand at the stapled sheets lying on the table. "Not that we want to, but let's just pretend, shall we?"

No one spoke in disagreement. Freeman jerked his chair out and sat, flipping a sheet of paper as he did so. He reached into the inner pocket of his jacket and retrieved a thirty cent Bic pen.

"So, for example let's say that you borrow the entire amount of the start-up costs for the high-tech plant. That's twenty-three million per plant. Let's say that you get it all at a rate of 7 % for the fifteen years, compounded monthly. So, what is that monthly payment?"

Lilly angled her head to the left and stared annoyingly at Freeman, who shifted his gaze to Tyler, who responded with a full body shrug.

"It's $206,731 per plant," Jane said, barely beating out her fellow competitors in a calculator contest.

"Wow, so that's what a Kardashian mortgage feels like," Marilyn said. The room ignored her.

"Now, take that number and multiply it by the number of payments."

"$37,211,491," Brandon shouted. Stewart began to look uneasy for not contributing.

"So, I think I see where this is going," Tyler spoke up. "You're saying that once we pay to fund the project, it costs a lot more than the twenty-three million."

"$37,211,491," Brandon repeated unnecessarily.

"Yes," Freeman said, cutting his gaze in Brandon's direction.

"And that this is just another way of looking at it," Lilly said, light dawning in her eyes. "We have to be able to compare apples to apples and whether we talk about discounting the future cash flows or the cost of financing fees, we are acknowledging the fact that waiting for returns will be expensive."

The entire finance staff nodded in sync in her direction.

"That's it," Brandon spoke for the group.

"Wait," Tyler said, sitting up at bit straighter. "So, we get it. But, in all of this, you are just telling us bits and pieces. Let's cut to the chase then. Which project is better and when can be break ground?"

"Whoa, hold on there a minute," Freeman boomed. "We aren't anywhere near making that decision."

"Why," Lilly asked, "I thought we just took these discounted numbers and compare to the costs."

"Well, yes that is ALL we have to do," Freeman responded, saying "all" with exaggerated emphasis. "However, you are overlooking one major, major thing,"

"What's that?" Tyler asked.

"The discount rate," Freeman said, pointing at the screen. "That's the most important variable in this whole thing, and those calculations we just did are based upon 7 %, which we simply made up. It may be more or less than 7 %, but we really can't do anything until we figure that out."

"Which means," Jane spoke up with more than her normal level of assertiveness, "that it's now time for Brandon and I to earn our money. It's our job to figure out how to pay for these projects and once we discover that, we have to determine how much it's going to cost us. Then we can use that information to find the appropriate discount factor."

"And only then can we make any decisions regarding the best project," Freeman said with finality.

The room sat in silence until Tyler cleared his throat.

"Well, I guess you'd better do that then," he said. "Meeting adjourned."

<u>*ALTERNATE ENDINGS*</u>

1. *Suppose Tyler and Lilly are stubborn and refuse to get educated on the basics of time value of money, instead leaving it for the finance team. It is their job, after all. Would that be okay? Why or why not?*
2. *Suppose, instead of using 7 % as an example, they instead used 8 %? How would this change the present value of the future cash flows? What if they used 6 %? Suppose you are in the meeting when Tyler and Lilly are shown these values. Write the dialogue you would use to discuss the differing values and*

the underlying reasons for the differences. It would be a good idea to finish by using this to reiterate why the process that Brandon and Jane are about to undergo is so important. Explain why these relations exist.

3. ***Let's continue with the alternative endings from chapter three, specifically numbers 1–4. How do these alternatives (both individually and collectively) change the overall picture in regard to the benefits and costs of the projects? Do they it increase or decrease the likelihood of accepting the projects? You may begin by using the 7 % figure to come up with values.***
4. ***Suppose Lilly said,***

   "I still don't get it. Suppose you owe me five hundred dollars and give it to me a hundred dollars each year for five years. If I stand still for five years and collect my hundred bucks, I will have five hundred dollars at the end. Which is just the same as if you went ahead and gave me the five hundred right now. I just have to wait for it, which would be unpleasant, but I still see the same amount of money. I guess what I'm asking is, why does 'time' have value?"

   What is she missing? Choose a character and have them answer her question and convince her that time does indeed have value. In what instance would she be correct that time doesn't matter? What would the individual receiving the money have to do to make this happen?

Concept Questions

1. **Time value of money** Explain why this concept is so important in business. What are the potential pitfalls you may encounter if you fail to correctly account for the time value of money?
2. **Simple versus compound interest** Briefly discuss the differences between simple and compound interest. How do these differences affect both the present and future values of cash flows?
3. **Compounding versus discounting** What is the difference between compounding cash flows and discounting cash flows? Give an example of when you would use each.
4. **Lump sums and interest rates** What is the relationship between interest rate changes and present values? What about future values? Why do these relationships exist?
5. **Lump sums and time periods** What is the relationship between time periods and present values? What about future values? Why do these relationships exist?
6. **Annual percentage rate** What is the *APR*? How is it calculated, and what is its influence on present and future values?
7. **EAR and *APR*** Discuss the difference between the effective annual return (EAR) and the annual percentage rate (*APR*). Discuss the advantages and disadvantages of both rates and possible situations where each would be appropriate.

8. **More frequent compounding** What is the relationship between the number of compounding periods per year and present values? What about future values? Why do these relationships exist?
9. **Ordinary annuity** What are the four characteristics of an ordinary annuity? Give two real-life examples of an annuity.
10. **Annuities, interest rates, and time periods** Discuss the relationships between the interest rate and the present and future value of annuities. What about the relationship between time periods and the present and future value of annuities? Be sure to explain why these relationships exist.
11. **Interest rates** Suppose you have $1,000 to invest and are considering two alternative options. Option 1 has an *APR* of 10 %, compounded quarterly, while option two has an *APR* of 12 %, compounding annually. What is your thought process in deciding between the two? Why is it not as easy a question as it first appears? How could you definitively distinguish between the two?
12. **Annuities and lump sums** What is the difference between investing $120 at the end of the year and investing $10 at the end of each month of that same year?
13. **Loan types** What are the basic characteristics of the three loan types: pure discount, interest-only, and amortized loans. How do they differ? In what instances would you expect to see each of these?

Problems

1. **Future value** Suppose you have $5,000 to invest. If you invest it in an account earning 5.5 % annually over the next ten years, what will it be worth at the end of those ten years?
2. **Present value** If you are to receive a lump sum payment of $1,430 in eight years, what is it worth today? Suppose the *APR* is 14 %, compounded annually?
3. **Present value** You are to receive $13,900. You will receive it at the end of twenty three years from now. If the *APR* is 6 %, compounding monthly, what is the present value of the lump sum?
4. **Future value** Suppose you have $3,598 and want to invest it at 8 %, compounded quarterly. How much money would you have at the end of twenty five years?
5. **Future value** You just found a wallet laying on the ground outside of the Business School. Being a selfish and immoral person, you keep the $300 you find inside. However, being knowledgeable of the time value of money, you invest it with your bookie, who gives you 5 % interest, compounded semiannually for ten years. What will it be worth?
6. **Present value** Suppose you just received an inheritance of $25,000, but you can't get it until you're 21. Assume you are now only thirteen years old. If the

interest rate is 4.5 % *APR*, compounded monthly, what is that inheritance worth to you today?

7. **Future value** You recently won a drawing at work with a grand prize of $1,000. Being wise in the ways of finance, upon winning you immediately invest it in one of those online savings accounts that pays 3.8 %, compounded monthly. Assuming you don't put any more in or take any more out, what would the account balance be fifteen years from now?
8. **Present value** You have just bought an Andrew Luck rookie card. Assume you can jump in your time machine and see that he will turn out to be the greatest quarterback to ever play the game. As such, that card will be worth $5,000 in fifty years. Assuming the rate of interest is 6 %, compounded annually, what is it really worth to you now?
9. **Time period** You're a boating enthusiast. You have recently found the vessel of your dreams, a 20-foot, 500 horsepower piece of nautical delight. However, it costs $55,000 and as of now you only have $5,000. On your way home you see a sign on your local bank that guarantees a 5.5 % *APR*, annually on investments. If you put your $5,000 in today, how long would it take to get to your goal of $55,000?
10. **Time period** On your tenth birthday, you received $100, which you invested at a 4.5 % interest rate, compounded annually. That investment is now worth $3,000. How old are you now?
11. **Interest rate** Your savings account has doubled in the past thirteen years. You put one payment of $10,000 in at time 0. What annual interest rate have you earned?
12. **Interest rate** You have identified your dream home. Unfortunately, it costs $350,000, and you currently have a grand total of $78,000. What interest rate must an account give you in order to have the total amount needed in ten years?
13. ***PV* of unequal cash flows** You decide to become a professional gambler. You estimate that you can make $20,000 next year betting on sports. You then figure you will be better at it, so you estimate you will make $30,000 at the end of the second year and $35,000 at the end of the third year. What is the present value of this stream of income if the interest rate is 6.5 %, annually?
14. ***PV* of unequal cash flows** Suppose you have an incentive deal worked out with your father. For every year you survive college with an acceptable GPA, you get compensated. Since the classes get harder, the compensation goes up each year. You have just finished your freshman year, so you have three more years. When you successfully complete your sophomore year (at the end of year 1), you will receive $500, while at the end of your junior year (the second year), you will receive $1,000. Finally, at the end of your senior year, you will receive $1,500. What is the present value of this stream of payments if the interest rate is 6 %, compounded monthly?
15. ***FV* of unequal cash flows** You expect to receive cash flows of $12,000 at the end of year 1, $8,000 at the end of year 2, $4,500 at the end of year

3, and \$7,800 at the end of year 4. What will this be worth at the end of fifteen years from now?

16. **Annuities** You plan to invest \$15,000 at the end of each of the next twelve years into an account earning 6.4 % compounded annually. How much will it be worth at the end of those twelve years?
17. **Present value** You and your husband (wife) just had a nasty divorce. You, being the bread winner in the family, have to pay support to him (her) for the next fifteen years. You haggle out a price of \$3,000 to be paid at the end of every month. How much is this costing you in today's dollars, if the applicable interest rate is 5 %?
18. **Annuities** You just signed a loan agreement on a boat. You will pay \$867 each month for the next ten years. What was the purchase price of the boat if the *APR* is 8.5 %, compounded monthly?
19. **Annuities and time** You want to quit your day job and become a day trader. However, knowing the risk of doing so, you want to have a nest egg first. Your goal is to have \$100,000 in an investment account before you can quit your job. If you put \$600 a month into an account earning 9.5 % *APR*, compounded monthly, how long will it take to get to your goal?
20. **Annuities and rates** Your grandpa is a great guy and is willing to give you \$50,000 today to pay off some student loan. But he wants to be repaid \$200 each month for the next thirty years. What *APR* is he charging you?
21. **Interest-only loans** Suppose you buy a condo as an investment property. You buy it with a thirty-year interest-only loan with a rate of 5 %, compounded monthly. The condo costs \$215,000, and you finance the entire amount. Exactly three years later, you sell the condo for \$234,000. Including interest expenses, what was your profit or loss on the investment?
22. **Amortized loans** You want to buy a house with a price tag of \$277,777. You pay 10 % down and borrow the rest on an amortized loan at a rate of 6 %, compounded monthly, for thirty years. After 6 months of payments, how much do you owe on the loan?
23. **Loans types** Suppose you want to buy a \$200,000 home on a hybrid loan. For the first five years, the loan will be an interest-only loan, and then it will turn into an amortized loan. If the applicable *APR* is 8.4 %, compounded monthly, and the total time period is thirty years, how much would you pay in total (interest plus principal) for the home?
24. **Future value** Suppose you've just gotten a job that has an annual salary of \$105,000. You are also promised a 3 % raise in each of the following three years. However, you were fortunate to be born filthy rich so you don't need to use the money. You instead invest it in an account that pays 12 %, compounded annually. What would your account be worth at the end of five years?
25. **Present value** Mary Lee Tucker has just turned 17. Her boyfriend, Scotty, decided to have a party for her. The party was thrown in Scotty's parent's basement with their full knowledge and consent. Although there were many minors involved, alcohol flowed freely. On her way home, Mary Lee ran a

stop sign and got blindsided by a Volvo. Although she walked away from the accident unharmed, her parents were furious that Scotty's parents had allowed underage drinking in their own house. In response, Mary Lee's parents sued Mike's parents for $100,000, citing negligence, to cover the expense of the totaled car, as well as the emotional distress they endured. The judge sided with Mary Lee's parents and awarded her the $100,000 settlement. However, the payment schedule is a bit odd. Mary Lee is to receive nothing until her 21st birthday, at which time she will receive $5,000 every 6 months for the next four years. At that point (her 25th birthday), she will begin to receive $2,500 every 6 months until the entire $100,000 settlement is met. Assuming that we expect a constant rate of 9 % *APR*, compounded semiannually over the entire time period, what is the settlement worth to Mary Lee today?

26. **Present value** Susie bets you $1,000 that she can run a mile in 5 min. You obviously don't believe her, so you agree to take on the bet. However, at the last minute, she informs you that she doesn't have the money right now, but promises to pay you in 6 months, when her student loans come in. If the *APR* is 10 %, compounded quarterly, how much would your winnings actually be worth now should you win the bet?
27. **Future value** Following up on the previous question, suppose that you realize that you're not exactly getting a fair deal. How much would you be willing to accept in 6 months in exchange for the bet? In other words, you agree to pay her $1,000 now if she wins, but if you win, she has to pay you _____ in 6 months.
28. **Annuity amount** Suppose your goal is to have $200,000 at the end of ten years in order to buy a home. If you invest in an account that earns an interest rate of 6.7 %, compounded monthly, how much must you invest each month?
29. **Annuity amount** You just bought a car that costs $19,000. You finance it over the next five years, at a rate of 5.5 %, compounded monthly. How much is your monthly payment?
30. **Present value** Suppose you were just hired at a prestigious sales company. You have two options for your salary. You can get paid either on a commission basis or on a straight salary basis. If you choose to get paid on a commission basis, you only get paid once a year, in a lump sum payment at the end of the year. If you choose the straight salary, you get paid $5,000 at the end of every month. You are very confident that, should you choose the commission option, you can earn commission of $70,000 per year. You, being wise in the ways of finance, decide to get the one that is worth the most to you now. Which option would you choose? How much value have you added by choosing this method? Assume an *APR* of 9 %, compounded monthly.
31. **Future value** You have just started a side business making erasers for pencils. Your goal is to make enough to buy the house you desire on the lake. The house costs $200,000 and you want to buy it ten years from now. You think you can make a profit of $18,000 the first year. After that, you believe that the revenues can grow by 10 % each year for the remaining

nine years. Assuming you deposit every penny of profit in an account earning 6.8 %, compounded annually, will you have enough to buy the house at the end of ten years? If so, how much will you have left over? If not, how much are you lacking?

32. **Loans** You want to buy a farm that costs $650,000. You plan to finance over the next thirty years. You are considering two options. Option A is that you use savings of $25,000 as a down payment on the loan. If you do so, you can obtain a fixed rate loan at a rate of 5.5 %, compounded monthly. Option B is that you finance the entire amount at a rate of 6.1 %, compounded monthly. What is the difference in the total amount paid for the farm with the two options?

Chapter 5
Capital Structure: Borrow It!

We now take our first step in explaining capital structure. As outlined in Chap. 1, this is essentially a fancy way of categorizing the specific mixture of debt and equity a firm chooses to finance firm operations. One should view capital structure in two ways. First, we need to examine the firm's *existing* capital structure. Doing so is the specific objective of the next two chapters of this text. However, the real issue regarding capital structure is identifying the firm's *ideal* mixture of debt and equity to use in financing the firm's projects. This latter notion is critical in understanding corporate finance and will be covered in detail much later in our journey. In this chapter, we will start with the debt side of the firm's existing capital structure.

5.1 Private and Public Debt

There are many types of debt. More specifically, there are many types of debt *instruments*, but all fall within two very broad categories. The first, and one you are likely most familiar with, is **private debt**. Examples of this were discussed when looking at loan types in the previous chapter. For the average person, private debt is a part of their financial lives and is relatively well understood. The other category of debt is likely less familiar but is just as important (if not more so) in corporate finance. This category can be generally described as **public debt**. Both public and private debt represent contractual obligations between two financial parties: a borrower and a lender. The difference is in the identity of the lenders. It is helpful to think of private debt as a one-to-one transaction, where one borrower enters a contract with one lender. The lender is generally a financial institution, such as a bank. Conversely, public debt is more of a one-to-many transaction. There is still generally one borrower, but now there are many potential lenders. In fact, you could be one yourself!

M.K. Pyles, *Applied Corporate Finance: Questions, Problems and Making Decisions in the Real World*, Springer Texts in Business and Economics,
DOI 10.1007/978-1-4614-9173-6_5, © Springer Science+Business Media New York 2014

LOOK IT UP: The truth is that private debt is not always a one-to-one transaction. In fact, when corporations borrow money, there are often many lenders in one transaction. Such a situation is referred to as a syndicated loan. See what information you can dig up about these syndicated loans and how they work.

Public debt is essentially an open call for funds issued by a large firm to the investing public. A public debt offering is a contract between the borrower and anyone who has money they wish to "invest" in the company. The term *invest* is appropriate in that once the loan is tendered, it can then be resold via public debt markets in much the same way as stock via public equity markets. If this is a new concept for you, just think of public debt as another way for individuals to invest in a particular company. Debt does not represent ownership in a corporation as equities do, but it is still a financial asset of the firm that you may buy in hopes of generating a profit on your investment.

So, to sum, there are several differences between public and private debts. The first is the number of potential lenders. Second, the identity of the lender for private debt is typically a financial institution, while the lender for public loans is anyone in the investing public. Third, while private debt issues are sometimes bought and sold by lending institutions, public issues are traded as readily as common stock. A fourth, and perhaps most important, difference is that public debt issues tend to be substantially larger than private issues. For this reason, most large corporations generally turn to public debt when a large amount of money is needed—to fund a project, for example. Therefore, we will discuss private debt only peripherally from this point forward and will instead focus our attention on public debt for the remainder of the text.

5.2 Introducing Coupon Bonds

Public debt can be called many things, but we will cut through some of the confusion by just focusing on what we will call *bonds*. To start, a **bond** can be defined as a financial device through which a corporation (or government) borrows money from individuals, generally on a long-term basis. It is important to understand both sides of the bond market. From the firm's perspective, this is a loan and is categorized by a series of lenders. However, from the public's perspective, lenders are also investors and investors rarely give up money without the belief they will be rewarded. In exchange for the money loaned, the lender/investor receives two things: (1) coupon payments and (2) repayment of face value. The **face value** is the amount of money an investor loans the firm and is also often called the par or maturity value. The repayment of face value is simply an even exchange of the borrowed amount, albeit at different times. The **coupon payments** are specific types of interest payments made by the borrower (the firm) to the lender (the investor). The amount of the payment is determined by the **coupon rate**, which is typically a fixed interest rate. This rate specifies the amount of interest paid relative to the amount of the loan that is still outstanding.

This brings up a second point. When the firm makes these coupon payments, all of the payment goes to interest, meaning none goes to pay off the principal. Thus, the amount of the loan still to be repaid is simply the face value at all times. The coupon rate specifies the percentage of the face value the firm must pay each year. This cash flow stream may sound familiar, as the basic form that a bond takes is that of an **interest-only loan**.

5.2.1 The Bond Issuance Process

While, strictly speaking, there are several ways a company can issue bonds, the most popular by far is through an underwriter. In fact, the process is much the same as the underwriting process for stocks. The company first partners with an investment banker with whom they negotiate a price to be paid for the bonds. This price is based upon the required rate of return on the bond, which is, in turn, based upon many factors, including current market conditions and the creditworthiness of the issuing firm. In addition to the negotiated public selling price, the issuing firm must pay a spread to the underwriter, again in much the same fashion as with public stock issues.

For any bond issue of substantial size, the lead underwriter creates an underwriting syndicate to share the risk of the investment. Once the contract between the issuer and all the underwriters has been finalized, it then becomes each underwriter's responsibility to sell the percentage of the issue for which they are responsible. Any public issue has to be accompanied by the appropriate approval of the SEC, again similar to that of stock issues.

The bonds are then sold to the public, either to individual investors or, more likely, in large blocks to institutional investors. After that, the individual bonds can be bought and sold much like equity. As a general rule, corporate bonds are less risky than stocks. There are many reasons for this, but the primary one is that bonds have a defined series of future cash flows, which makes for more confident valuation than stock, whose future cash flows are never fully known in advance. Therefore, there is more volatility in equities due to this uncertainty. The risk among individual bonds depends on several factors, many of which we will now discuss.

LOOK IT UP: The process briefly described above relates to public bonds offered by corporations. In the case of government bonds, things go a bit differently. See if you can identify the underwriting process typically used for government bond issuances. As a clue, it is not the first time we have brought up the idea (see Chap. 1).

5.2.2 *Characteristics of Coupon Bonds*

When a firm issues bonds, they must create a bond **indenture** to be distributed to each lender upon purchase of the bond. Therefore, at the beginning of a bond's life, you are essentially trading money for a piece of paper. That piece of paper is crucial, however, because it is the loan's legal contract. So, it is important to understand what is inside that document.

The first things you should see, much as you would in a standard loan for a house or car, are the basic details of the loan. For example, the face value of the bond will be there, along with the number of bonds issued. The face value is the same for all bonds in an issue and is actually fairly standardized at $1,000 per bond. Therefore, if the firm needs $10 million, they would issue 10,000 bonds.

The length of the bond will also be detailed in the early stages of the indenture. The life of a bond can be anywhere from 1 to 100 years, but for practical purposes bonds with lives over 30 years are rare. Also, very short-term bonds (less than 1 year in length) fall under a different classification known as money market instruments. While certainly a worthy topic from an investment standpoint, in corporate finance we are primarily concerned about planning for the long run. The payment frequency of the bond is also very important, and there are really only two options. Coupon payments are usually made either once or twice a year, with twice being by far the most common.

There are many other things that may show up in a bond indenture. Many contracts contain a call provision, meaning they can be redeemed prior to expiration date. In other words, after an agreed-upon period of time, the company can decide they no longer want to make interest payments and therefore can pay back the debt. **Callable bonds** can benefit the issuing firm by reducing the overall cost of debt, but it can be good for the lender as well because the call price is often higher than the face value. A **sinking fund provision** is very similar to a call provision in that it could result in a firm's bonds not reaching maturity. These firms would set up a pool of money they will use at a later date to pay off part of the issuance prior to expiration. By paying off some of the debt obligation over time, the firm can reduce the financial hit when the bonds expire. Unlike the callable feature, there is generally a limit on the number of bonds a firm can buy back at the sinking fund price. Thus, from the investor's perspective, a bond with a sinking fund provision is less likely to be taken out of their portfolio than a callable bond. However, as a trade-off, the sinking fund price is usually lower than the call price.

Many debt issues have **security provisions** in the contract. While this is not a standard procedure, it is often required by riskier firms in order to entice investors. A security clause essentially outlines certain firm assets that will be liquidated should the firm not follow the rules. The proceeds from that liquidation will then be given to the bondholders. Bond contracts also often include **restrictive covenants**. These covenants can take many forms, among those cash flow requirements. In other words, a firm has to maintain a certain level of cash flow to avoid default. The same is often the case for various accounting ratios, such as the debt-to-equity

Table 5.1 Bond ratings

Moody's	S&P/Fitch	
Aaa	AAA	Investment Grade
Aa	AA	
A	A	
Baa	BBB	
Ba	BB	Speculative Grade
B	B	
Caa	CCC	
Ca	CC	
C	C	
-	D	

ratio or profit margin. It is also common to restrict the amount of dividends to common shareholders in order to ensure the balance of obligations between bondholders and shareholders is maintained.

This is not intended to be an exhaustive list of all things that can be included in a bond indenture, but it should provide a general idea. We now turn to, arguably, the most important bond characteristic: **bond ratings**. A basic assumption is that default is a very bad thing for a bond issuer (and the lender, naturally). Default can occur in a couple of ways. First, should a bond issuer fail to make coupon payments in full and on time, they are in default. Second, a firm can default by failing to adhere to the restrictive covenants. There are many reasons defaulting is a bad thing for the firm, starting with the fact they would have much more difficulty in obtaining future funding. And, even if they can secure this future funding, it would likely be at a higher cost.

Therefore, the probability of loan default is a very serious issue for both the borrower and lender of the loan. The probability of default is measured by bond ratings. In current times, bonds are rated by several rating agencies. However, there are three that stand out and are generally acknowledged to be the most reputable. Standard and Poor's (S&P) and Moody's have long been standard bearers in the agency world and still dominate the ratings market. However, Fitch ratings have been provided since the 1920s as well and have over the past couple of decades gained market share. S&P and Fitch use the same rating categories, while Moody's uses a different, but equivalent, reporting system (Table 5.1).

Ratings can be interpreted in much the same way as academic grades. The closer to the front of the alphabet, the better the rating. The better the rating, the lower the chance of default (or failing), which is another way of saying the bond is a safer investment. There are different degrees of the same base rating grade. Thus, an *AAA* rating is slightly better than an *AA* rating. In fact, *AAA* and *Aaa* are the highest ratings attainable for the respective agencies and represent the safest of all bond issues. These would be equivalent to individuals being awarded credit scores near the max of 850.

The ratings of *Baa* and *BBB* are important in that any rating on or above this level is known as **investment grade**. This represents relative safety in the investment and is commonly used to distinguish classes of bond ratings. Any rating below this level begins to have a significant level of risk attached, or a higher probability of default. Non-investment grade bonds are sometimes referred to as "speculative." Very low bond ratings are so-called **junk bonds**, which are exceedingly risky but also offer the possibility of an exceedingly high return.

There is a significant relation between the rating on a bond and the return on that bond. The lower the rating, the higher the risk, and there is a fundamental principle that then applies. *The higher the risk of the investment, the higher the expected return.* We will address this several times throughout the text and use it as a guiding principle throughout our discussions of various aspects of investing (primarily in Chap. 7). In this instance, it suggests that bonds rated highly will generally have lower expected returns than those with lower ratings. However, the most important word is *expected*. A lower rating may predict higher returns, but if the bond defaults, the higher return you expect will never be realized.

IN THE REAL WORLD

Shortly following Hack Back's IPO, the company had borrowed 12 million dollars in the form of 20-year bonds to fund the research and design of the new, more complicated products that were now in demand. This relatively modest amount of borrowing had helped Hack Back gain foothold in the public debt market. Jane and Brandon's first task in determining funding for the plant projects involved examining the potential to issue additional public debt.

September 21, 2011, was an unseasonably smoldering hot day. They had decided to brave the elements to have lunch at Louie's Diner. Louie's was a popular place due to very reasonable prices, decent service, and, most importantly, the proprietor himself. If there was ever a living testament to their product, Louie was it. He was nearly as tall lying down as standing up, and his ample girth was a testament to his own cooking. To current day, no matter how busy the diner was, Louie did all the cooking himself over a grease-stained griddle the size of Rhode Island. Louie was a conductor, the spatula his baton, as he masterfully juggled a dozen orders seamlessly. Everything was always cooked quickly and correctly by the maestro, and today was no exception. Jane and Brandon both had burgers with fat fries and a side of creamy coleslaw. They sat in a booth near the door and discussed work as they enjoyed their feast.

"Have you looked at this yet?" Jane asked. She was referring to the bond indenture in her hand. It had been thumbed through several times, clearly indicating that she had examined it. She was a sponge for information and had absorbed much of the material to memory. Brandon... well, not so much.

"Why don't you just give me the highlights?" he said. His job had been to contact the bond underwriters to gauge their receptiveness to issuing additional public debt. Hack Back hadn't decided if they wanted to yet, but the first step was

always to see if it was the possibility existed. No need testing the waters if the pond is dry.

"Well, the bonds were issued with a coupon rate of 8.62 %. That is a bit high considering that at the time standard market rates were relatively low. T-bond rates were in the low fours at the time of issuance."

Brandon wrinkled his nose in a grimace and the understanding of her words.

"And that's not the only evidence of taking a hit for being so young a business," Jane said, wiping a drop of ketchup from her chin.

"How so?" Brandon asked distractedly, his attention taken momentarily by Louie flipping three burgers at the same time. Show off.

"This contract has every investor perk in the business. There are four covenants."

"What are they?" Brandon said as he reached over with his non-burger hand to slide the thick document to his side of the table. He began to flip through. Jane sat back contentedly and sipped the last of her diet coke.

"Well, first we can't issue anything more than a 7 % dividend yield," she said. "That puts a limit on what we can do for the shareholders via *dividends."*

"Sure," Brandon responded, "but we aren't anywhere near that level yet. We also have to maintain operating cash flow of $40 million, which doesn't give us a ton of room for error. Also, we have to maintain a debt-to-equity ratio of less than 60 %. That last one shouldn't be a problem anytime soon."

He sat back and inhaled deeply. Then, slowly let it out as he thought.

"So, even though we seem to be fine in abiding by our agreements, it seems as though we gave the bondholders a lot of safety net," he said as he absently poked at the last of his burger. Finally, he gave into the temptation and shoved it in his mouth. A drop of mayo plopped onto his tray.

"If you'd read the whole thing, you'd understand why," a deep voice boomed from behind him. They looked up sharply to see that Dubarb Freeman had walked into the diner. He stood in the doorway and glanced around with an air of familiarity. Several regulars at the counter gave him a nod and Louie himself even risked a wave. Freeman stood next to the booth awkwardly for a moment before Brandon figured it out and slid over. The waitress immediately brought black coffee in a thick ceramic mug and placed it before him.

"Coffee break, sir?" Jane asked.

"Don't need a break to drink coffee," he responded. "I was just looking for you guys and you weren't in your office."

"Yeah, well it's lunchtime, Dube," Brandon said.

"I know that. How'd you think I found you here?" He responded, oblivious to why they felt that was important.

"Couldn't help but overhear you talking about the bonds. That's what I wanted to talk about anyway."

He paused to savor a deep gulp of his coffee before continuing.

"We had to give the shareholders something, kids. This was about three months after the IPO. How else would we convince people to give millions of

dollars to a company that just went public and had little to no capital reserves? So we gave them safeguards. You might note that people who know something about this type of thing recognized our shortcomings."

He took the contract from Brandon and flipped to near the end before handing it back to him. He had turned it to the rating report from Standard and Poor's. Freeman handed the paper to Brandon.

"We got a B?" Brandon questioned rhetorically as he read the report.

"Yes, and it was probably pretty fair at the time," Freeman responded. "The report is pretty accurate. We shouldn't and haven't had any problem keeping current on the payments, but we were far from a surefire thing from the investors' perspective. Not by any stretch."

"Then why issue them at all?" Jane asked.

"Several reasons," Freeman said, taking another sip before continuing. "One, we needed the money. Two, we needed the publicity to create a bit more investor interest. Our bonds, being relatively risky, were enticing to many speculative investors looking for a big winner. As big as you can get with bonds, anyway."

"But..." Brandon broke in.

"And most importantly in my opinion," Freeman carried on, holding up a hand to silence him, "we got a lot of information. We know what our rating is. Hopefully that will go up for any future issuances, but we can build upon what we know. We know how much it costs to go through the general process and we have further cemented our relationship with the investment bank. That will all become important when we need to issue more."

"I just saw that these are all callable," Jane said, reading another page of the indenture. She looked up. "That gives us a possible out."

"Thank you," Freeman replied with one of his half smiles. "It was the best we could do at the time. The real question now is whether we want to dip our toes in the debt pond again, and, if so, to what degree. That's what I wanted to talk to you about. But, we can discuss that when you get back."

He drained the last of his cup and waved off the waitress's offer of a refill.

"Get this for me?" he asked as he rose.

"Sure," Brandon said with a grin. "See you back at the office." His answer was to Freeman's back as he retreated out the door.

The two sat in silence for a moment before Jane spoke in her small voice.

"I think he just wanted a coffee break."

ALTERNATE ENDINGS

Suppose Hack Back had been issued a rating of A. How could that have changed the story above? What about a rating of C?

1. ***Imagine a scenario where Hack Back is in a position where they can call the bonds back. What would that mean to the firm, both good and bad? What about to the bondholders?***

5.3 Bond Valuation

5.3.1 *Bond Prices*

To continue our discussion of bonds in the context of capital structure, we turn to the second most important characteristic of any bond: the price. Recall from Chap. 4 the equation that can give the theoretical value of anything:

$$PV = \sum_{t=1}^{T} \frac{CF_t}{(1+r)^t}$$

An important note is that this equation tells you what the value *should* be. Put differently, if given known future cash flows and an accurate representation of the opportunity cost of foregoing those cash flows until you receive them, one can calculate the worth in today's dollars. The problem with reconciling this with current market values (the price tag) is that the future cash flows aren't always known and the discount factor is almost never perfectly predicted. In order to appropriately value any financial asset, we first must attempt to identify the future cash flows. With bonds, this is actually pretty straightforward since the only cash flows are the coupon payments and the repayment of face value. In the case of a coupon bond, neither of these need to be estimated since the coupon rate is fixed and the face value is known.

Once we take the present value of these future cash flows, the value of a normal coupon paying bond is

$$Value\ of\ bond = present\ value\ of\ coupon\ payments + present\ value\ of\ face\ value$$

Luckily, the equations for them are already familiar to us from Chap. 4. The coupons meet all the requirements of an annuity. All the coupon payments are the same since they are determined by a fixed coupon rate. Likewise, since the repayment of face value occurs only once, it can be treated as a lump sum. The equation for the price of a bond when these are put together is

$$P_B = C\left[\frac{1 - \frac{1}{(1+k)^t}}{k}\right] + \frac{Face}{(1+k)^t}$$

Notice a couple of things in this equation. First, we are now using different notation (k) for the interest rate. There's a large reason for this that you will have to wait until near the end of the book to completely understand. Another reason, however, is because the interest rate now has a name. In the last chapter it was just called an *APR*, which is appropriate when learning the tools, but not necessarily when applying those tools in corporate finance. Interest rates in the debt market are known as yields. Specifically, the k in the equation above is known as a **yield to**

maturity (YTM). In short, we switched the notation because there is value in signaling the movement from the world of learning the tool into the world of applying the tool to a specific situation.

The other thing that should make a bit more sense now is the reason for using C as the notation for the annuity amount in Chap. 4. One final note of importance pertains to the time variable. When valuing a bond, t is the number of periods *left until maturity*. In other words, it is unlikely this will be the same as the life of the bond. In fact, the only time this will happen is at the very beginning of the bond's life. To illustrate how the equation works, consider a 30-year bond with a coupon rate of 6 % and 15 years left until maturity. Suppose the bond has a current yield to maturity of 8 % and the standard face value of \$1,000. Given this, the current price of the bond is

$$\boldsymbol{P_B = 60\left[\frac{1-\frac{1}{(1.08)^{15}}}{.08}\right]+\frac{1,000}{(1.08)^{15}}}$$

$$\boldsymbol{P_B = \$828.81}$$

The current price is lower than the face value. This essentially tells us it is currently selling for less than the loan amount. When this happens, the bond is said to be selling at a discount or is a **discount bond**. More important than the name is what drives this result. A bond will sell for a discount any time the YTM is greater than the coupon rate, which makes sense if you think about it for a second. Focus on what each rate represents. The coupon rate is the rate of return you are truly earning on your investment. It is set in stone and cannot change. The YTM, on the other hand, is market driven and represents what the market has determined, through supply and demand, you *should* be earning.

Therefore, if the rate you should be earning is greater than the rate you are truly earning, the bond should be selling for less than its original loan amount. For the holder of the bond, this is a bad thing. Consider an analogy of potential jobs. Suppose current supply and demand dictates the current salary for paralegals to be \$50,000, but you are currently a typical paralegal making a salary of \$45,000. You would naturally consider this to be a less-than-optimal deal. The same is true for discount bonds. The market has determined that bonds with characteristics similar to the bond in question should demand a certain rate or return, but you are actually getting less than that value. Such negative realizations result in price decrease.

Naturally, this is not the only direction the rate can move. To illustrate the other option, let's repeat the example above, only with a current YTM of 5 %:

$$\boldsymbol{P_B = 60\left[\frac{1-\frac{1}{(1.05)^{15}}}{.05}\right]+\frac{1,000}{(1.05)^{15}}}$$

$$\boldsymbol{P_B = \$1,103.80}$$

As expected, now the bond is selling for more than $1,000. This will happen any time the coupon rate is greater than the YTM. In other words, you are earning a higher return than the market has determined you should currently earn. This is known as selling at a premium, or a **premium bond**. Finally, you should prove to yourself that if the YTM is equal to the coupon rate, the price will be equal to the face value. In this case, the market has determined the coupon rate is the appropriate rate of return. This is called selling at par, or a **par bond**. When the bond is first issued, they will sell at par, but then traditional market forces of supply and demand will influence the relationship between the CR and the YTM and, as an extension, how the price changes. Record these directional relationships to memory and you may prevent mistakes when completing calculations pertaining to bond prices and yields.

	Rates	Values
Premium bonds	CR > k	$P_B >$ face
Discount bonds	CR < k	$P_B <$ face
Par bonds	CR = k	$P_B =$ face

5.3.2 Bond Yields

If you read carefully in the previous section, you will note it states the price of the bond is the *second* most important issue. That may sound odd, but if so, you are likely thinking from the investor's standpoint, which is entirely logical since the vast majority of participants in bond markets do so from the investor's side. However, this is a corporate finance text, so we need to remember to look at things from the firm's perspective as well. And, in doing so, we can come to the realization that it's not the value of the debt that matters, but the cost of securing that debt. Remember the amount of the loan is simply an even trade. At time zero, it goes from the lender to the borrower; at time T (the end), it goes from the borrower to the lender.

So, if a firm borrows a million dollars, they must pay that amount back. That is a known fact, and whether the loan is worth $900,000 or $1.1 million during the time period is largely irrelevant from the firm's perspective. What does matter, of course, is the additional interest that must be paid to continue to hold onto the borrowed amount. This represents the profit to the lender/investor and the cost to the firm. And, when considering whether to take more or less debt, this is the primary variable of interest.

With any financial asset, *the price is driven by the interest rate*. This is a fact that needs to be carefully understood. The rate of return on the investment determines how we discount the future cash flows, which in turn allows calculation of the price. Your economics lessons were on target in suggesting that supply and demand of the marketplace determines how much you are willing to pay for the asset, but it does so a bit indirectly. If given a price, one can then derive the YTM, a process we now consider.

The problem with this mathematically is that the YTM shows up in more than one place in the equation. When this happens, there is no way to rearrange in order to solve for that variable. It is very similar to the issue we discussed when solving for the *APR* in any standard annuity problem, only complicated somewhat by the additional lump sum calculation. Just like in that situation, the only way to solve for it is trial and error. This is where those relations discussed in the previous sections come in very handy. They can provide a starting point.

Consider a bond that is currently selling at 103. First things first, you may notice the price seem a bit odd, and you may even think there is a typo since there is no dollar sign. The price is quoted as a percentage of face value, which is standard in the bond world. Therefore, a quote of 100 means the bond is a par value bond selling at exactly \$1,000. A quote of anything greater than 100 indicates a premium bond, while below 100 indicates a discount bond. In our case, the bond is selling for \$1,030. The coupon rate is 7 % and there are 10 years left until maturity. Therefore, we have the following setup:

$$\mathbf{\$1,030 = 70\left[\frac{1 - \frac{1}{(1+k)^{10}}}{k}\right] + \frac{1,000}{(1+k)^{10}}}$$

The first observation is that we are dealing with a premium bond, which means the YTM must be less than the coupon rate. So, let's start by "guessing" that *k* is equal to 6 %. Doing this results in

$$\boldsymbol{P_B = 70\left[\frac{1 - \frac{1}{(1.06)^{10}}}{.06}\right] + \frac{1,000}{(1.06)^{10}}}$$

$$\boldsymbol{P_B = \$1,073.60}$$

So, we know that *k* must be between 6 % and 7 %. We'll skip some of this here for the sake of conciseness, but you should check the following results.

k	P_B
6.25 %	\$1,054.55
6.50 %	\$1,035.94
6.60 %	\$1,028.62
6.58 %	\$1,030.08

Therefore, given enough time, we can manually *approximate* the YTM. Luckily, there is a faster way: to let technology take over. A financial calculator can find the YTM in the exact same fashion (trial and error) but much faster. See the "TECH HELP" box nearby for instruction on doing this.

5.3.3 Semiannual Payments

Coupon payments are not generally paid on an annual basis. While there are certainly bonds that follow this tradition, the majority of corporate bonds are paid semiannually, or every 6 months. While the overall equation doesn't change, it does require a bit of adjustment. There are three things to be careful of and all revolve around getting variables in the correct time frame. First, the coupon rate will always be given, as all rates are, in annual terms. Therefore, you have to work a bit harder to make sure the actual interest payment is in semiannual amounts.

Second, you have to make sure you have a semiannual discount rate. Therefore, the YTM must also be divided by two. And third, the number of time periods must be the number of semiannual time periods, not the number of years. Therefore, the equation for the price of a semiannual bond is as follows:

$$P_B = \frac{C}{2}\left[\frac{1-\frac{1}{\left(1+\frac{k}{2}\right)^{y*2}}}{\frac{k}{2}}\right] + \frac{Face}{\left(1+\frac{k}{2}\right)^{y*2}}$$

Consider a 30-year coupon paying bond with a coupon rate of 6 % and 15 years left until maturity. Suppose the bond has a current YTM of 8 %. If the coupons are paid semiannually, what is the current price?

Making the appropriate adjustments, we have

$$\begin{aligned} \mathbf{P_B} &= \mathbf{30}\left[\frac{\mathbf{1}-\frac{\mathbf{1}}{(\mathbf{1.04})^{\mathbf{30}}}}{\mathbf{.04}}\right] + \frac{\mathbf{1,000}}{(\mathbf{1.04})^{\mathbf{30}}} \\ &= \mathbf{\$827.08} \end{aligned}$$

5.3.4 Callable Bonds

As mentioned in Sect. 5.2.2, a large percentage of bonds are callable. In this instance, the investor must acknowledge the possibility that the bonds in which they have invested will not reach maturity. This is of particular interest if the bonds represent a large proportion of the individual's income. It would be quite disturbing to depend upon the steady stream of income that the bond provides, only to have it dry up as the firm recalls the loan. This is not dissimilar to individuals paying off their personal loans early, as virtually any loan allows. The motivation for the borrower is the same, to eliminate the interest payments for the remainder of the loan period.

From the investor's perspective, however, the value of the asset needs to be adjusted because the expected future cash flows are altered. The coupon rate will not change, but it is very possible the number of payments will be smaller. Also, the call price will replace the face value as the future lump sum amount, since that is what you would receive at the end. Generally, the call price is also quoted as a percentage of face value. So, for example, a bond may be callable in 8 years at 102. The 102 indicates that if the bond is called, you get $1,020 for a typical $1,000 face value.

Again consider the previous example of a 30-year semiannually paying coupon paying bond with a coupon rate of 6 % and 15 years left until maturity. Now, suppose we add the condition that the bond is callable in 10 years for 101. Also, notice there is a very important variable that is missing in this discussion. The YTM measures the yield *to maturity*, and if a bond is called, it simply will not reach maturity. As an investor in a callable bond, you should not automatically assume you will receive payments until maturity. Thus, in order to calculate the cost of a bond you feel will be called, a **yield to call (*YTC*)** should be used. The *YTC* is the return to be received between the time of purchase and the time until earliest call.

Thus, we can solve for one of two variables. First, we could use the *YTC* to solve for the theoretical price assuming the bond is called at earliest opportunity, but the benefit from doing so is limited. While the calculated theoretical price of a bond that will be called is different from the theoretical price of that same bond that will not be called, there is only one market price at any point in time. The bond market may intrinsically account for a bond being callable; however, the market does not report a price based upon assumptions the bond will be called. Thus, any concern over the theoretical price will have to be addressed by the investor by examining their expected stream of cash flows.

Perhaps a better use of this knowledge is calculating the *YTC* from the reported market price. Earlier, we assumed a YTM of 8 %, which resulting in a price of $827.08. Doing so for the above problem would result in

$$\$827.08 = 30\left[\frac{1-\frac{1}{(1+YTC)^{10*2}}}{YTC}\right] + \frac{1,010}{(1+YTC)^{10*2}}$$

$$YTC = 8.69\,\%$$

The higher yield (in relation to the YTM) should be consistent with prediction, given the same expected coupon payment amount over a shorter period of time and a higher face value at call time.

LOOK IT UP: If you have never bought a bond, you may be surprised to find the price you actually pay for the bond to differ from the quoted price. The reason behind this is the difference between the “clean” and “dirty” prices. Find the difference and think about how this would affect you as an investor.

TECH HELP 5.1 Bond Prices and Yields

Solving for Price

Let us do an example of a 9.5 % coupon bond with 17 years left until maturity and a current YTM of 8.1 %. The payments are made semiannually. Just as we learned in Chap. 4, the first thing to tell the calculator is how many compounding periods there are per year:

Step 1: [2ND] [I/Y] (P/Y)
Step 2: 2
Step 3: [Enter] [2ND] [CPT] (Quit)

You also need to make sure all previous TVOM calculations have been erased. Thus,

Step 4: [2ND] [*FV*] (CLR TVM)

Now, you can begin to solve the problem. First, input the known quantities:

Step 5: 17 [2ND] [N] (xP/Y) [N]
Step 6: 8.1 [I/Y]
Step 7: 47.5 [PMT]
Step 8: 1,000 [*FV*]
Once this is done, you simply need to tell the calculator what you want it to solve for:

Step 9: [CPT] [*PV*]

The answer is then given to you as $-1,128.03, which makes sense given the fact that the CR is considerably higher than the YTM. Feel free to confirm this by comparing to the answer obtained using the equation.

Solving for YTM

You can solve for the YTM in much the same way, as long as you have the current price. After clearing the TVM data, the inputs would then be as follows:

17 [2ND] [N] (xP/Y) [N]
47.5 [PMT]
1,000 [*FV*]
1,128.03 [+|-] [*PV*]

Then, to solve for the YTM,

[CPT] [I/Y]

Callable Bonds

When bonds are callable, we must be careful to adjust our inputs. For the sake of illustration, let's add a dimension to this problem. What if the bond were

(continued)

(continued)

callable in 10 years for 101? If we need to solve for the *YTC*, assuming it would be called at the earliest opportunity, the new inputs would be as follows:

10 [2ND] [N] (xP/Y) [N]
47.5 [PMT]
1,010 [FV]
1,128.03 [+|-] [PV]

Then, to solve for the *YTC*,

[CPT] [I/Y]

Make sure you can find the *YTC* to be 7.71 %.

5.4 Other Types of Bonds

5.4.1 Zero-Coupon Bonds

The straight coupon bond is not the only type of public debt asset. For example, a **zero-coupon bond** is one that (shock!) doesn't pay coupons. Generally, the math behind zero-coupon bonds is fairly straightforward. If a bond doesn't pay coupons, then C must be equal to 0. Therefore, the annuity section of the equation disappears, and we are left with a very simple conclusion: the value of a zero-coupon bond is simply the present value of the face amount:

$$P_{zc} = \frac{Face}{\left(1 + \frac{k_{zc}}{m}\right)^{y^{*}m}}$$

This naturally means, should we desire, that we can calculate the required return on a zero-coupon bond by the following:

$$k_{zc} = m\left[\left(\frac{Face}{P_{zc}}\right)^{\frac{1}{y^{*}m}} - 1\right]$$

You may recognize this as the equation used to find *APR* in a lump sum. This is again an example of a specific application of a generic principle. Zero-coupon bonds are often referred to as pure discount securities, since they are structured as pure discount loans (see Chap. 4). Therefore, the only two transactions that take place are the initial loan and then the repayment. At any time after issuance, an investor will buy the bond at a discounted rate, and the profit (interest) to the investor is the difference between that discounted value and the full repayment of the loan.

The equations above reference the number of compounding periods per year (m), but in reality zero-coupon bonds are always semiannually compounded, which means that $m = 2$. For example, a zero-coupon bond with face value of $1,000 may be bought for $600. The $400 difference represents the interest earned by the investor. If we add that the bond will mature in 12 years, the rate of return on the bond is equal to

$$\mathbf{k_{zc}} = \mathbf{2}\left[\left(\frac{\mathbf{1,000}}{\mathbf{600}}\right)^{\frac{\mathbf{1}}{\mathbf{2^*12}}} - \mathbf{1}\right]$$

$$\mathbf{k_{zc}} = \mathbf{4.30\%}$$

Zero-coupon bonds can be short or long-term and can come from a variety of sources, including local, state, and national governments, as well as corporations. It is interesting to note that the government (in the USA) sells millions of dollars' worth of bonds per year. This means, simply, that the government "borrows" vast amounts of money. At the time of this writing, the US government has over $12 trillion in outstanding public debt. This works out to be about $35,000 for every living person in America. Kind of fun to think about, huh?

LOOK IT UP: Want to know where the numbers on public debt come from? All the information you would ever want to see (and then some) can be found on a couple of websites: the Bureau of the Public Debt (http://www.publicdebt.treas.gov/) and Treasury Direct (http://www.treasurydirect.gov). Among the many interesting things in there, you can find out exactly (to the penny) how much debt the government has on a daily basis.

A large part of this massive amount of government borrowing comes in the form of zero-coupon bonds. In fact, by far the most active lender in the debt market is the US government. For the most part, **government bonds** have the same basic characteristics as any other bond, with one notable exception: they have significantly less risk. For example, the treasury bill is a short-term debt instrument that is widely acknowledged to be among the safest investments in the world. The chances of default on such an asset have historically been very nearly negligible. For this reason, the T-bill is used as a risk-free rate of return in many financial calculations.

LOOK IT UP: There are actually four types of securities issued by the US government for purchase by investors. Can you find their names? What distinguishes them from one another?

Government securities are generally taxable at the federal level, but not the state level. As an interesting note, even though zero-coupon bonds do not make interest payments, the *pseudo* interest accumulated during the year is taxable. Government securities can also be issued by state or local governments. In this case, the debt instruments are known as **municipal bonds**, because they are issued by a municipality. The advantage of these bonds is they are not taxed on a federal level. The offsetting disadvantage is that the yields are much lower. For example, consider a municipal bond with a yield of 3.8 % and a corporate bond with a yield of 4.9 %. Which is better? It's not as straightforward as it may seem since corporate bonds are taxed and municipals are not. To keep the numbers easy, let's assume a 30 % tax bracket. Therefore, the actual yield on the corporate bond is 4.9 (1−.3) = 3.43 %, which is *lower* than that on the municipal.

STRIPS (Separate Trading of Registered Interest and Principal Securities) are another very notable type of government bonds. In fact, the numerical example early in this section is likely an example of a STRIP security. This is perhaps the best use of an acronym in finance. STRIPS originate as government bonds or notes. However, when they hit the market, investment bankers or brokerage firms "tear" the bond into "strips." This allows each separate cash flow from the bond to be bought and sold as an individual asset. Thus, for example, a bond with 20 coupon payments and one face value payment can be converted to 21 separate debt securities.

The benefits of STRIPS as financial instruments are as much theoretical as practical. Prior to the implementation of STRIPS in the mid-1980s, identification of a risk-free asset with maturity of longer than 6 months was practically impossible due to the fact that treasury bills are short-term assets. However, once strippable treasury bonds are split into their individual cash flows, each cash flow effectively becomes a risk-free asset alone. Thus, STRIPS can have maturities up to 30 years in length and provide representation of risk-free assets for long-term analysis.

LOOK IT UP: A primary benefit of long-term risk-free assets is that it makes it possible to calculate the relationship between time and yield on pure discount, default-free assets. Graphically, this relationship is known as the term structure of interest rates. Why is this such an important part of the debt market? What are some theoretical explanations for the shape of the term structure? While you are at it, also look up the yield curve. What is the difference between the two?

5.4.2 Convertible Bonds

There is a certain type of bond that bridges the gap between the two possible sources of funding: debt and equity. By now, you should understand that bonds of any type represent debt. However, convertible bonds give the shareholder the option of converting a debt instrument (i.e., the **convertible bond**) into a predetermined number of pieces of equity (i.e., the firm's stock). As with almost everything, there is a trade-off potential investors must be aware of with convertible bonds.

The option to convert to equity (and therefore benefit from an increase in the firm's stock price) is valuable. Therefore, conversion from debt to equity, while benefiting the shareholder, is not necessarily beneficial to the company. To balance this, convertible bonds often have a lower yield, or return, than other types of bonds. Thus, if the stock price does not appreciate to the level that it is beneficial to convert to shares, the bondholder is stuck with an asset that has a lower relative return.

LOOK IT UP: Each and every example in this chapter assumes bonds pay coupons (interest payments) based upon a fixed rate of interest. There are examples, however, where this is not the case. In fact, the government issues bonds that have variable rates of interest as dictated by inflation. What are they called? How do they work and how could they be useful?

IN THE REAL WORLD

When Brandon and Jane got back to the office, they found Freeman waiting for them in the conference room. They quickly assembled their paperwork and joined him.

"So, we need to figure out whether we want to add more debt?" Brandon said, just as a way of getting the conversation started.

"And if we do, what type?" Jane added, cautiously sitting in the chair next to Freeman.

"We thought," Brandon said, "that it would make sense to take a deeper look at our current debt and go from there. That's what we've been doing for the last several days."

"That is an excellent idea," Dubarb said. "So, what's the current price of our bonds?"

There was a moment of silence before both began pecking at their computers sitting in front of them.

"You've already looked at the current price, haven't you?" Freeman asked, although the answer was obvious.

"Well, to be honest," Brandon said, "I didn't think it really mattered, since that debt is already set in stone and there's nothing we can do about it. I mean, we know the interest rate."

"Well, that's true," Freeman responded amicably, "but, as we said earlier, there is information in our current debt that we can use to plan for future debt."

He then pushed himself back from the table and threw his legs up, crossing his bare ankles where socks should have been. Freeman was a staunch opponent of anything cloth on his feet. Jane and Brandon looked on in confusion, as he took the Wall Street Journal from behind him and settled his reading classes over his bulbous nose. After several uncomfortable moments, he looked over the glasses at the two youngsters.

"I'll wait while you look it up," he said.

They responded in completely different ways. Brandon multitasked by simultaneously working the mouse on his laptop and scrolling through his iPad and iPhone with blindingly fast finger flicks. Jane simply sat back and stared at the wall, her eyes boring a hole through it as her mind raced.

Freeman settled back to his paper and hummed "Wabash Cannonball" to himself. Exactly 4 minutes later, Brandon huffed and sat back.

"I still think that I'm right on this. We have already talked about the bond rating, the terms of the bonds, and everything else about the contract. But, that is all old information and, sure, it gives us an idea of what the new debt could look like, but we have to start all over. There's nothing current in this data."

His words pushed Jane's brain over the finish line. She started shaking her head before he had finished speaking.

"That's not true," she said. She bent over her computer and tapped several buttons in rapid motion. Then, she grabbed a HMDI cord lying on the table and snapped it into her machine. A clone of her screen popped up on the wall. Displayed on it was Hack Back's bond quote from Yahoo! Finance.

Issuer	*Price*	*Coupon (%)*	*Maturity*	*YTM(%)*	*Rating*	*Callable*
Hack Back, Inc.	*94.89*	*8.62 %*	*1-Mar-2028*	*9.23 %*	*B*	*Yes*

"So, our bonds are selling at a discount," Brandon said.

"Yeah, but…," Jane started to respond, but Dube cut her off. He had hired Brandon because of his excellent communication skills and commonsense approach to problem solving. He had hired Jane due to her incredible intellectual capacities. It was important to let each of their strengths help the other.

"Think about why that is," he said, pointedly to Brandon.

"Because the price is less than $1,000."

"Yes, yes, I know," Freeman said, "but that's not the important part."

Jane couldn't hold it anymore and the words burst out. "Because the current YTM is higher than the coupon rate."

The light bulb went off behind Brandon's eyes. He sat up straight in his chair.

"And that variable is NOT old information, is it?"

"There it is." Freeman said. "That is the important part. We need that number. If you look at that data on the screen, the only two that ever change are the price and the yield. And the price is just a byproduct of the yield."

"The market determines, through investor supply and demand, what the investors currently require as a return to buy the bond," Jane said.

"And that number is the current estimate for what new bonds would cost us," Brandon added.

Freeman spoke up to say, "as long as the characteristics of the issue are similar."

They all paused a moment before Brandon summed up what they were thinking.

"So, that is our estimated cost of debt right now."

"Our estimated cost of public debt, at least," Jane nodded in affirmative.

They again paused for a moment.

"Good," Freeman said. "You are both correct. The current YTM is calculated based upon the current price of the bond, which is determined by market forces. Simply put, that is the rate that the investing body as a whole has determined they currently require to purchase our bonds."

"I'm not sure I understand," a new voice said from the doorway. Tyler leaned casually against the doorframe, looking in on the three.

"Ah, there you are," Freeman said. "It's about doggone time. I've been waiting on you all day."

"First thing Dube, no one says 'doggone' anymore," Tyler said with an amused grin. "And second, I came looking for you earlier and was told you were having a coffee break at Louie's."

Freeman made sure he didn't look towards Brandon or Jane.

"And, it's still only 1:00," Tyler continued. "But, nonetheless, what can I do for you?"

"I wanted to go over your talking points before the board meeting tomorrow. But first, what don't you understand?"

Tyler stepped in and looked at the bond information on the screen.

"I heard you say this YTM number here is our cost of debt," he said. "But when we write checks each six months, it's not based upon that number, but rather the interest rate in the contract. This number. . .." He pointed at the coupon rate.

"Let me explain," said Brandon, moving into his comfort zone. "We are working on moving the company forward with this new project. And when we do so, if we use debt to finance at least part of it, we are in no way guaranteed the same interest rate as on the old debt. The market has changed and we have changed. It's kinda the same idea as assuming the rate you got on your last mortgage is the same as you would get on the new mortgage."

"Yeah," Tyler muttered, "I guess that wouldn't make sense."

After an additional moment of reflection, he shrugged slightly and said, "Well, carry on then." He started away and then turned back. "How are you going on the projects?"

"Working on it," Brandon said, "we're starting to get a good handle on the debt side. We'll start next week on the equity side."

"What's wrong with today?" Freeman interrupted. "The day is still very young and we're done here."

With that, he stormed out of the room, leaving Jane and Brandon to shake their heads.

Tyler took a moment to flash a sympathy smile. He then turned to follow Freeman down the hall.

ALTERNATE ENDINGS

1. ***Discuss what would happen if the firm believes bonds they would issue are now less risky. As a result, their credit rating increases. What do you think this means for the firm's required rate of return on public debt? Can you describe why?***
2. ***The discussion implicitly assumes the bonds will not be called. How would the story change if Hack Back had the option of calling some or all of the bonds?***
3. ***The scenario played out above assumes the firm's YTM increased since the bonds were issued. How do we know it increased? Consider the alternative. What could have hypothetically made the bond yields decrease? What would that have meant for the firm and their future investments?***
4. ***Suppose Brandon had answered Tyler's question about the current YTM as follows:***

   "Think about it from the bondholders' perspective. If they buy a bond today, the market says they should be getting a payment of $46.15 each six months. Instead, they are only getting a payment of $43.10 each six months. The trade-off is that they pay less than face value for the bond, knowing they will receive full face value at maturity. Dividing the $6.10 annual difference by the face value gives you the percentage difference between the YTM and the CR. So, from our perspective the YTM is the current cost of any new bond debt, since any new issuances would have to have the adjustment build into the coupon rate instead of the price."

   Tyler scratches his head and says, "What?"

It's your job to further explain it to him, including the calculations.

Concept Questions

1. **Public debt** Discuss the similarities and differences between private and public debts. What are the advantages of public debt relative to private debt? What are the disadvantages?
2. **Bond investment** As an investor, what is the appeal of investing in bonds? What are the cash flows that you can look forward to in the future?
3. **Bond underwriting** Compare and contrast the processes of going public in the equity markets and debt markets.
4. **Bond types** Structurally speaking, what is a coupon paying bond? What type of loan? Answer by drawing comparisons between coupon bonds and personal loans.
5. **Bond indenture** Discuss the following features that may be included in a bond contract: (1) call provision, (2) sinking fund provision, (3) security clause, and (4) restrictive covenants. For each, be sure to detail the potential benefit or cost to the borrower and/or the lender.
6. **Bond ratings** What are the benefits of bond ratings? How do they affect both the issuing firm and the investor?

7. **YTM and CR** Define both the yield to maturity and the coupon rate. What do each tell the investor and the issuing firm? How does the relationship between the two interact with the price of the bond?
8. **Government bonds** How do government bonds differ from corporate bonds. Why would an investor be interested?
9. **STRIPS** What is a STRIPS bond? How is it created and what purpose does it serve?
10. **Rates and prices** What is the relationship between rates and prices? Why is this, both in a mathematical and practical sense? Which variable is the driving force behind the other?

Problems

1. **Bond price** What is the current price of a 25-year, 8 % coupon bond that has a required return of 8.26 %, 12 years left until maturity, and makes annual payments?
2. **Bond price** Consider 30-year bonds that pay semiannual coupons and have 7 years left until maturity. If you bought the bonds, you would receive a coupon payment of $49.43 each 6 months. The bonds have a YTM of 7.45 % and face value of $1,000. What is the current price?
3. **Bond price** What is the price of an 18-year coupon bond that has been outstanding for the past 10 years, if the current YTM is 12.43 % and the coupon rate is 10.4 %, paid semiannually?
4. **Bond costs** Judy's Makeup Shop, Inc., just issued 20-year bonds that pay coupons of 5.89 % on a face value of $1,000. How much is it going to cost Judy, in total throughout the life of the bond to pay for each bond, including all interest expenses?
5. **Coupon rates** Suppose you have a 25-year coupon semiannual paying bond selling for $895.68. The bond is currently selling at a yield of 8.5 % and has 16 years left until maturity. What is the coupon rate?
6. **Bond income** Your grandma is searching for some investments that will generate a stream of income in her elderly years. She needs $16,000 to cover her living expenses. Her advisor has just used her funds to invest in 200 corporate bonds that have face values of $1,000. 100 of these bonds have coupon rates of 7.4 % and YTM of 8.1 %, while the other 100 have coupon rates of 6.9 % and YTM of 8.1 %. Will grandma have enough money to live on?
7. **Bond maturity** Suppose you have a bond with a current selling price of $1,123.26. It is a 30-year bond currently selling at 7.06 %. If the coupon rate is 8.6 % paid semiannually, how many years are left until maturity?
8. **Bond yields** Consider a coupon bond that is currently selling for $897.07. If the bond pays a coupon rate of 7.1 % and has 18 years left until maturity, what is the current YTM on these bonds?
9. **Bond yields** Consider a 30-year bond that was issued 14 years ago. The bond is callable in 5 years at 104. Currently, it is selling at $976.39. The coupon rate is

8.10 %, the face value is $1,000, and coupons are paid semiannually. What is the YTM on this bond?

10. **Bond yields** In the above (#9), what is the *YTC* on the bond?
11. **Zero-coupon bonds** You want to buy zero-coupon bonds with face value of $1,000 and 14 years left until maturity. The bonds have a YTM of 4.33 %, compounded semiannually. What is the current price?
12. **Zero-coupon bonds** You have just purchased a debt security that has no coupon payments and expires in 8 years. The security has a face value of $800 and currently sells for $524.98. What is the annual return?
13. **Clean and dirty prices** Consider a bond that is currently quoted at 102.5. The bond pays a 6 % coupon, semiannually. You bought this bond one-fourth of the way through a coupon cycle. How much would you pay for this bond? In other words, what is the "dirty" price?
14. **STRIPS** What is the YTM on a coupon STRIPS that will mature in 15 years. The parent bond pays a semiannual coupon based upon a coupon rate of 8.6 % and face value of $1,000. The 15-year coupon STRIP is currently selling for $28.73.
15. **STRIPS** Consider an issuance of government bonds that have 20 years until maturity. The bond pays semiannual coupons based upon a CR of 5.2 % and face value of $1,000. Suppose the bonds get "STRIPped" and you want to buy 10 of the coupon strips that mature 10 years from now and 10 of the coupon strips that mature 8 years from now. If the YTM on the 10-year STRIPS is 4.5 % and the YTM on the 8-year STRIPS is 4.1 %, how much would you have to pay in total for these securities?
16. **Bond prices** You buy 30 STRIPs that have 12 years left until maturity and a required return of 7.43 %. In addition, you buy twelve 5 % coupon bonds that have 10 years left until maturity and yield 6.3 %. Both have face value of $1,000 and are compounded semiannually. How much did this cost you?
17. **Callable bonds** Consider a bond that is callable at 102. If the current *YTC* is 7.4 %, the CR is 6.9 %, and the bond has 14 years left until earliest call. If you believe the bond is going to be called at earliest opportunity, what is the value of this bond to you today?
18. **Callable bond yields** Consider Bond XYZ, which is currently priced at $986.76 and is callable in 2 years at 102. It pays a coupon rate of 7.54 % in semiannual coupons. It will expire in 4 years and has face value of $1,000. What is the bond's current *YTC*?
19. **Bond portfolios** Exactly 3 years ago, you started a portfolio. The portfolio was made up of 12 coupon bonds and 14 zero-coupon bonds:

    - The coupon bonds have a coupon rate of 6.69 %, paid semiannually. When you bought them, they had 15 years left until maturity and sold at YTM of 7.11 %. The coupon bonds have a face value of $1,000.
    - The zero-coupon bonds also have a face value of $1,000 and were issued originally as 30-year bonds 13 years ago (from today, so 10 years before you bought them). When you bought them, they had YTM of 4.32 %.

Today:

- The YTM on the coupon bonds is 6.32 %.
- The YTM on the zero-coupon bonds is 4.21 %.

How much money did you make (or lose) on your portfolio? In other words, how much higher (or lower) is your portfolio value today than 3 years ago when you bought them?

20. **Bond portfolio yield** Suppose you have just created a bond portfolio made up of 3 bond holdings. You bought 100 corporate bonds that have coupon rates of 7.4 %, compounded semiannually, with 14 years left until maturity. You bought 50 government coupon bonds that have coupon rates of 4.1 % and are compounded semiannually with 21 years left until maturity. You bought 150 zero-coupon government bonds that have 5 years left until maturity. All three bonds have face value of $1,000.

    Your purchase prices on the bonds are (1) corporate bonds ($1,078.35), (2) government coupon bonds ($976.34), and (3) zero-coupon bonds ($776.55). What is your portfolio YTM?

Chapter 6
Capital Structure: Sell It Off!

In this chapter, we will examine the other primary component of capital structure. Most individuals understand the basic idea of stocks and stock markets, and for good reason. Equity markets are not just the focus of financial professionals. The idea that individual investors can own a piece of a publicly traded firm is probably the most important concept in investments as it allows firms to have a direct influence on individual wealth. In this chapter, we will cover the characteristics of equity, learn how to theoretically value stock, and most importantly, discuss equity from the company's perspective.

6.1 Public and Private Equity

We will follow the same basic pattern as with the previous chapter by beginning as broadly as possible and then work on isolating details. We first need to understand the difference between private and public equity. Also, we need to define **equity** in the context of capital structure. From the firm's perspective, equity can be internally or externally generated. Internally generated equity is derived from the firm's operations and is the proportion of the firm's income they retain as earnings (hence, retained earnings). Externally generated equity represents ownership in the firm, evidenced by shares of stock that are "sold" to investors. The investors exchange the stock for ownership in the firm. The firm is then free to use the proceeds from the sale of the stock in firm activities, and the shareholders would benefit as a by-product of any stock price increase. Likewise, they would suffer from any price decrease.

A firm's equity can come from a variety of sources, but for our purpose, we are most concerned with equity obtained from individual investors. Recall the balance sheet identity. *Assets* represent the total value of the firm's possessions, while *liabilities* represent the total amount of firm's debt obligations. Thus, *equity* represents the remaining value in the firm once liabilities have been paid. Equity is also often referred to as owner's equity. When the owners are shareholders, the equity

M.K. Pyles, *Applied Corporate Finance: Questions, Problems and Making Decisions in the Real World*, Springer Texts in Business and Economics,
DOI 10.1007/978-1-4614-9173-6_6,

interest is known as shareholders' equity. Shareholders' equity can then take two forms, private and public. **Private equity** strictly means any financial interest that cannot be publicly traded. Also, private equity cannot be raised via any public markets you are likely familiar with.

As with the debt side of capital structure, private equity is not the major concern, at least as a primary source of funding. Rather, we are most often concerned with **public equity**, which is raised and then traded on public markets. It is raised, most usually, via an IPO, a concept discussed in Chap. 1. Therefore, we don't need to cover the procedural issues of that process again. Instead, we want to focus on the resulting influences on the value of the firm and shareholder interests. We will begin by discussing how to value common stock.

6.2 Valuation of Common Stock

There is more than one type of public equity; however, by far the most popular is common stock. **Common stock**, sold in shares, represents a proportional piece of the firm. Unlike debt, owning equity does not represent a contractual right to the firm's future cash flows. Rather, individuals purchase shares of stock in the respective firm with the *belief* that their investment will be rewarded. Thus, the risk taken with equity is far above that with debt.

Once again, recall from Chap. 4 that the current value of anything should be represented by the following general equation:

$$PV = \sum_{t=1}^{T} \frac{CF_t}{(1+r)^t}$$

In order to value common stock, we have to identify the relevant cash flows for this specific type of financial asset. Note there are two basic forms of cash flows: a regular systematic payment throughout the life of the investment and a one-time payment at the end of the investment. When dealing with public debt, these became: (1) coupon payments and (2) face repayment. The good news is that common stock has the two same basic types of cash flows, just with different names and somewhat different characteristics. Instead of coupon payments, we now have to consider **dividends**. And instead of face repayment, we now have the future stock price. Once the numerical values of the cash flows are identified, the valuation process is the same. Unfortunately, there are a few things about common stock that make this process more difficult than with bonds.

First, none of the cash flows are known in advance. Coupon payments are dictated by a contract (the bond indenture) and will never stop or change in value. This is not true for dividends, however. Dividends are not rights of the shareholder. In other words, they are not required. Instead, they are usually known as good-faith tokens given to the investors by the firm to encourage them to maintain their ownership in the firm, or to perhaps even increase it. On a related note, the presence of dividend payments is an enticement for potential future investors. The problem, for valuation purposes, is that a company does not have to pay dividends, and even if they do, they can be changed (or eliminated) at any time. The same issue is true of the future stock price. Unless one has a particularly reliable crystal ball, the amount of money one would receive for selling their common stock in the future is far from certain.

The second problem is that the life of the investment is, at least potentially, forever. Again, in comparison to bonds, which have a clearly defined life, common stock never has to be redeemed. We have already discussed in the opening chapter the difference between ownership and control of a publicly traded firm. This separation allows the company to exist long after the original owners have passed away. The life of the share of stock, or the piece of ownership, can go on indefinitely. Thus, should we be able to identify the future value of the dividends, we still cannot discount them because we don't know the future time period at which to begin discounting.

A third problem is the discount factor, which will eventually be shown to be the most important variable in the equity valuation process. With bonds, there are only a relatively small number of types, defined by a few variables, such as maturity, coupon rate, and default probability. Thus, in order to estimate a required rate of return, one simply has to look at bonds currently trading that match those criteria. The required rate is very similar on all bonds that meet this set of criteria. Unfortunately, it is virtually impossible to do the same with equity. There is no maturity value, no stationary interest rate to determine payments, and no justifiable way to measure default.

So, with these three rather handcuffing issues, we can make one conclusion. *Unless we make some assumptions, we're stuck.* It's not a fulfilling conclusion. We understand that when assumptions are made, the answers they provide are only as reliable as the accuracy of the assumptions. In the bond equation, the only variable in question was the YTM. In the equity world, we have many more moving pieces; in fact, all of the pieces are moving. On that note, I bet you can't wait to get started.

Let's start by identifying some notation we will use throughout this process. Let's assume:

P_0 = The current price of a share of common stock
P_t = The price of a share of common stock at the end of any time t in the future
D_0 = The dividend paid at the end of the most recent period; the current dividend
D_1 = The dividend expected to be paid at the end of the next period
D_t = The dividend expected to be paid at the end of period t
g = The firm's growth rate (both in dividends and capital gains)
k = The firm's required rate of return on common stock

We are most often concerned with the current price, since most of the decisions we make are made in the present. Now, a word for the wise. The most important understanding you should attempt to master is the distinction between D_0 and D_1.

Understanding whether you are given an existing dividend or an expected future dividend will determine how you proceed with the problem. The current dividend (D_0) is known, as it is the most recent dividend paid. The expected dividend is very different in that is not yet a known certainty. However, from the investor's standpoint, where the purpose of this exercise is to think about the potential gains to be received, the expected dividend is certainly of importance.

6.3 Dividends

It has been noted that a firm has no obligation to issue a dividend of any type. However, the decision of doing so, and to what degree, is of utmost importance to any firm, particularly ones that are publicly traded. Thus, we will devote some time to briefly discuss dividends in more detail. Dividends are payments made to shareholders out of retained or current earnings. If payments are made from some other source, they are referred to as *distributions*, rather than dividends. Cash dividends can come in four types: (1) regular, (2) extra, (3) special, or (4) liquidating. Most are issued as regular dividends four times a year, at some point in each quarter. An extra or special dividend is one the company has issued with the indication the shareholders are not expected to view this as a recurrent cash flow. Special dividends, in particular, are used for unique and rare events and should not be expected to happen again. Liquidating dividends indicate that at least part of the firm has been liquidated, or sold off, and the proceeds are being passed through to the shareholders.

There are two primary questions that have plagued both researchers and investors for decades. First, simply put, *do dividends matter*? This question has an easy answer. Yes, they matter. They matter, if for no other reason than they represent the movement of cash and that always matters. As investors, we care about when and to what degree we are going to receive rewards for investing. Dividends represent a large part of that reward, and as such investors care a great deal. In order to understand how dividends influence an investment, let's create an example. You own 100 shares of Billy's Bean Barn, Incorporated. The board of directors declares on May 1 that the firm will pay a dividend of $.25 on May 25. May 1 then becomes the **declaration date,** and May 25 will be the **date of payment**. There are two other dates of concerns, as well. First is the **date of record**. On this day, the firm will accumulate a list of shareholders who are to receive dividends. However, the final date of importance, the **ex-dividend date**, will determine who exactly is on that list. It is possible to buy the stock just prior to the date of record and miss out on the dividend check due to delays of reporting. For our example, suppose the record date is Monday, May 15. The ex-dividend date is two business days prior to the record date, so May 13 in our example. As long as you buy the stock before this date, you will receive the dividend. If you buy on or after, you will not.

For this reason, there is considerable attention paid to whether stocks are bought *cum-dividend* or *ex-dividend*. That sounds much better than "with" or "without" dividend. In actuality, market forces make the decision largely mute. If you think about it, when a company pays dividends, that automatically reduces the amount of money the firm has for operations. In other words, they can't both give it away and keep it. The market realizes this and generally corrects the stock price downward on the ex-dividend date. In our example, suppose that 1 second before market closes on May 12, you buy the stock for $35. You will then be on record (ignoring any delay in reporting) and be eligible to receive the dividend on May 25. If instead, you buy the stock 1 second after the market opens on May 13 (the ex-dividend date), the stock price will likely have decreased roughly by the after-tax dividend amount, which would be approximately $34.84 if you assume a 35 % tax rate.

The second question of concern is much tougher to answer than the first. *Does dividend policy matter?* Dividend policy does not refer to the actual mechanical action of paying dividends, but rather the decision process of whether to pay dividends and, if so, how much and when. One could argue that firms should invest the cash into the firm itself up front and then, when the cash flows have had opportunity to generate profit, pay out dividends to the shareholders. This would allow the money to *work* for the company before giving it to the shareholders. However, from a purely mechanical standpoint, it makes little difference when the firm issues the dividends. The most straightforward example of this argument is called **homemade dividends**. This simply refers to the investor's ability to immediately reinvest the dividends received into the firm. Thus, even though the firm has paid out the dividend, it comes right back to them. In fact, many well-known firms offer built-in homemade dividend policies, known as automatic dividend reinvestment plans. There will be more discussion of this notion in Chap. 7. Such plans help make the argument for the notion that dividend policy is irrelevant.

However, there are several "real-world" reasons to counter this argument. Among the most notable include taxes, flotation costs, and dividend restrictions. Perhaps the most important proponent for the importance of dividend policy is generally known as the **information content of dividends**. Shareholders are largely creatures of expectation, and once dividends are paid, firms are very reluctant to disappoint the shareholders by failing to fulfill the expectation of again receiving the dividend. In fact, any change in the expected dividend is generally met with a large market reaction. If the dividend turns out to be larger than expected, this is a very positive signal to the market. If a dividend gets cut, it is a negative signal to the market. As such, managers are very reluctant to reduce dividends unless absolutely necessary and are very reluctant to increase dividends unless they are convinced they can sustain the higher dividend. To put it succinctly, the information content argues that dividend policy matters simply because investors believe it foreshadows the firm's financial future and, in turn, the investment potential of the stock.

LOOK IT UP: Cash dividends are not the only way to give the shareholders a reward for investment. Other options are stock repurchases and stock dividends. What are the pros and cons of each from both the investor's and firm's perspective? While you are digging around, see if you can define a stock split and what it means for the firm and investors?

IN THE REAL WORLD

Way back on a Friday evening in April 2009, Tyler and Lilly were having a late dinner with one of their largest clients Eli Eldridge, CEO of Winnie's World of Golf, was a short, stooping fellow with a pointy nose and a balding head. In fact, he drew a startling resemblance to Mr. Weatherbee of Archie comic fame. He had named his chain of golf warehouses in the memory of his mother, Winnifred, who hadn't swung a golf club in her life. And who wasn't dead yet. Eli thought it was a better story the other way.

After starting with a single store on the end of strip mall in his native Texas, Eldridge had ridden shrewd business decisions to massive expansion. His business strategy was to bring golf to the masses, and he did so by mass purchases, which allowed him to work out excellent deals with suppliers, like Hack Back. He passed on these savings to his customer base, and as such, his stores became increasingly popular for the average golfer. His comedic appearance was surpassed only by his quick wit and magnetic personality. Both Tyler and Lilly were big fans, both personally and professionally, and made a special attempt to meet him any time they found themselves in the same area.

In this situation, the evening was a celebration of the largest contract to date between the two companies. Winnie's had just opened two large warehouses in Pennsylvania, their first exposure in the northeastern area. Each store included a section of Hack Back merchandise.

The relationship had begun in the fledgling days of a then-private Hack Back, following a chance encounter with Lilly at a merchandising conference. Using her wily charms on the aging gentlemen worked wonders, and soon Eli was a close advisor to the youngsters.

During the after-dinner cocktail, talk finally turned to business.

"How's the shop, kids?" Eli had begun calling Hack Back a "shop" back when that was all it was and refused to change the description.

"Oh, it's a never-ending roller coaster," Lilly responded, taking a sip from her chocolate martini, "but we're buckled in."

"At the risk of sounding boastful, we think we are on pace to have a record sales quarter," Tyler added.

Eli slyly glanced over the top of his tumbler of bourbon and water, light on the water. "I notice you were careful to not say record 'profits'," he said, receiving a sheepish glance in return. "Trouble with the numbers, lads?"

"Oh, we're working on it," Tyler said with a sigh. "We're trying to expand our production and need to improve the distribution process, but it's a tough fix."

"Yes, it always is, isn't it?" Eli responded.

"Any advice?" Lilly asked, draining her martini and signaling the waiter for another.

"Oh, there's never any real answer to this type of thing. Speaking as someone who knows all about expansion, it's tough when you are strugglin' just to keep up with the status quo."

Then he added a probing thought.

"However, if it's money you need, you should start by trying to please the people you've already convinced."

"What do you mean?" Tyler responded curiously, the statement having garnered his full attention.

"Your shareholders, of course," Eli said matter-of-factly. "Now, kids, I don't mean to stick my spoon in your stew..."

"That's disgusting," Lilly muttered.

"Please, Eli," Tyler said, ignoring Lilly, "you would know more than anyone about this type of thing and we would value your opinion."

Eli was not the type who had to be asked for his opinion twice.

"Okay, here it is. You are at a very important time in the progression of your company. Those who have invested in your firm have done so based on potential, not necessarily results. They have hopes of owning a relatively valuable piece of equity for a relatively low price. The problem with that is if you don't satisfy them along the way, they will jump ship before you have a chance to realize that potential. Now, if one person skips out, no problem. But, suppose a buddy follows him. And another, and another, and... well you get the point. Pretty soon, your promising little shop has lost its sponsors. Your main job is to make sure you keep those investors you already have, and keep them happy. If you do so, not only will they maintain their equity positions, but they will likely increase their position. And then, if they're still happy, you arrive at the most magical moment of all..."

"Which is...?" Lilly prompted, while taking a bite out of an olive.

Eli displayed his sly grin, took a sip of bourbon, and left Tyler and Lilly to suffer through an indeterminable pause.

"They tell their friends," he finally said. "Their friends take their advice and buy some of your little shop. Those friends tell their friends, and BAM!" He accompanied the last word with a slap on the table, causing Lilly to jump backwards and Tyler to spill his scotch on his tie.

"What was that?" Lilly exclaimed.

"That, young lady, was the sound of your company stock price shooting through the roof."

"Well, I would argue that was a bit too demonstrative," Tyler said, dabbing his tie with a napkin, "but the point is made."

"So what do we do?" Lilly jumped in. "That is a whole lot of fruit baskets to send out."

"I don't think that would be very useful," Eli responded with a smile, "but perhaps you could just give them some money and they could buy their own."

"You're talking about a dividend?" Tyler queried thoughtfully.

"Yes, a dividend. Money, dinero, mula, whatever you want to call it," Eli said, waving his nondrinking arm at Tyler. "That's what keeps people interested."

"Can we afford it?" Lilly asked Tyler, "I always thought that only well-established firms issue dividends."

"It doesn't have to be a large dividend," Eli interrupted. "It's not the quantity that is important, really. It's the signal. You paying a dividend is a signal of health, and more importantly, the future outlook."

"If you would kindly permit an old man a last bit of advice," Eli added. A bit of alcohol always tended to make his dialogue go back in time. "The amount of the dividend is probably less important than the consistency with which it is paid. So, I wouldn't stretch my budget if I were you. You need to leave room to run your company, of course. And, you also need to leave room to increase the dividend in the future. Your shareholders will want to see that, too."

The two young executives became quiet as they pondered the thought.

Tyler finally voiced his thoughts out loud. "Of course, the board would have to agree with all this... Not to mention Dube..."

"I don't think they would disagree with the logic," Lilly said. "As long as we have a solid foundation for our arguments. We should get some of the finance folks to do some research to get things started."

Eli spent another moment staring at his younger companions, running the scenarios through their heads. After a long pause, he drained his cup, wiped his mouth with his napkin, and stood.

"Well, I'm going to call it a night," he said. "Think about it kids. It would make us shareholders very happy."

He walked away, leaving Lilly and Tyler staring at his back.

"'Us' shareholders?" Lilly repeated.

"So," Tyler said slowing, taking a sip of the scotch, "it appears that not only did he just stick us with the tab, but I think he also just convinced us to write him a check every three months. Remind me again who sells to whom."

...

The proposal, spurred by Eli Eldridge, was met with surprising acceptance by Freeman. He agreed that a dividend may serve to hold shareholder interest long enough to get Hack Back operating on a higher level. After extensive discussions involving the entire finance department, they decided to propose a modest $.20 dividend per share to the board. After lengthy deliberation, the board of directors issued the resolution.

A few months later, in August of 2009, Hack Back declared their first divided.

ALTERNATE ENDINGS

1. *Suppose Tyler and Lilly decided to ignore Eli's suggestion of paying a dividend. What ramifications could this have for their firm, particularly when it comes to issuing future stock and paying for future projects? Alternatively, what are the potential negative ramifications of following his advice and paying a dividend?*

2. ***Suppose Eli had said:***

   "I think the best way to reward the shareholders is to issue a share buyback. Yup, I think you should do a share repurchase of 500,000 shares of stock."

   How would this work and how would it change the firm going forward? Does it make sense to do this? What are the strengths and weaknesses of the Eli's argument?
3. ***What about if Eli had said:***

   Don't you kids think it is time for a stock split?

   Do you think this makes sense to do at this stage? Why or why not? How would this influence the firm (and investors) going forward?
4. ***Suppose Hack Back completely ignored Eli's advice about being conservative on the dividend amount and issued the maximum allowable dividend. Unfortunately, Tyler and Lilly know they cannot maintain the dividend. What are the potential pitfalls of doing this?***

6.4 Pricing Models

We can begin the valuation process by looking at an example of a one-period stock. In other words, think about buying the stock today with the plan of selling it 1 year later. In this case, the equation for the theoretical value of this stock at time zero is

$$P_0 = \frac{D_1}{(1+k)} + \frac{P_1}{(1+k)}$$

In this most simple of situations, we assume we have a dividend payment at the end of the first year. As a note, even though dividend payments usually made quarterly, for simplicity, we assume all four quarters are lumped together. At the end of 1 year, there is a price attached to the share of common stock, which represents the "face" value of the equity. Discounting both cash flows by one period by the appropriate discount factor should approximate the current value. Now, suppose that instead of a one-period stock, we have two periods. The current price would then be

$$P_0 = \frac{D_1}{(1+k)} + \frac{D_2}{(1+k)^2} + \frac{P_2}{(1+k)^2}$$

Extending this, since the time period of a share of common stock is potentially forever, we can then generalize this idea to get the following:

$$\begin{aligned} P_0 &= \frac{D_1}{(1+k)} + \frac{D_2}{(1+k)^2} + \frac{D_3}{(1+k)^3} + \ldots + \frac{D_T}{(1+k)^T} + \frac{P_T}{(1+k)^T} \\ &= \sum_{t=1}^{T} \frac{D_t}{(1+k)^t} + \frac{P_T}{(1+k)^T} \end{aligned}$$

There's good news and bad news. Good news first, the last factor in the equation is actually theoretically irrelevant to valuation due to the fact that the time period is infinite. Thus, T (which represents the final time period) can be infinity. As T approaches infinity,

$$\frac{P_T}{(1+k)^T} \to 0$$

and we are left with

$$\begin{aligned} P_0 &= \frac{D_1}{(1+k)} + \frac{D_2}{(1+k)^2} + \frac{D_3}{(1+k)^3} + \ldots + \frac{D_T}{(1+k)^T} \\ &= \sum_{t=1}^{T} \frac{D_t}{(1+k)^t} \end{aligned}$$

Simply put, the theoretical current value of a share of stock is equal to the present value of all future dividend payments.

Now, for the bad news. We are *still* stuck because we still do not know any of the dividend payments in advance. Thus, we must come back to the need for some type of assumption regarding future dividends. While this can be accomplished in numerous ways, the most popular involve assumptions of **growth rates**. In the following, we will discuss two distinct possibilities that have relevancy in the world of equity valuation.

6.4.1 Zero Growth

The first assumption we will examine is zero growth. Since in this case the dividends never grow nor diminish, we have no need for time period distinctions. Thus,

$$D_0 = D_1 = D_2 = D_3 = \ldots = D$$

and the above equation simplifies to

$$\begin{aligned} P_0 &= \frac{D}{(1+k)} + \frac{D}{(1+k)^2} + \frac{D}{(1+k)^3} + \ldots + \frac{D}{(1+k)^T} \\ &= \sum_{t=1}^{T} \frac{D}{(1+k)^t} \end{aligned}$$

Essentially, we no longer have any need for the individual distinctions in dividend payments because they are all the same. This is a prime example of a stream of cash flows known as a **perpetuity**, which has a natural definition. A perpetuity is an annuity that continues *perpetually*. Since the D is a constant in each time period, it can be pulled out of the summation, leaving

$$P_0 = D\sum_{t=1}^{T} \frac{1}{(1+k)^t}$$

Again recalling that the T can go to infinity, this then represents a constant multiplied by an infinite sum. This infinite sum actually converges to simply $1/k$. If this is hard to believe, you can try it for yourself in Excel. You won't need to go to infinity to see the convergence taking place. Thus, the price of a share of common stock that has zero growth is

$$P_{zerogrowth} = D/k$$

There is a very important example of zero growth stocks in the investment world. **Preferred stock** is a type of equity, but it is very different than common stock. Preferred stock generally has a stated face value, very similar to that of bonds. In addition, most have a set dividend payout, which is again very similar to debt in that it indicates a known and unchanging stream of future cash flows to the investor. An example would be a 5 %, $20 preferred share of stock. This would indicate the firm will pay $1 per year per share to the holders of this stock. The term preferred stock is based upon the fact that the holders have preference in receiving dividends. This indicates that *if* dividends are paid, they go to preferred holders first.

Dividends on preferred stock do not have to be paid, so they are unlike interest payments in that regard. For some preferred stock issues, if dividend payments are missed, they are **cumulative**, meaning the missed payments add up and the entire amount must be paid before the common shareholders can receive a dividend. Other issues are **noncumulative**, which means the dividends can be deferred forever. While this may not thrill the holders, it highlights a crucial detail to examine before purchase.

6.4.2 Constant Growth

While the assumption of zero growth has definite purpose in the public equity world, it does raise a bit of an issue in relation to the goal of the firm. The purpose of finance is to maximize shareholder wealth, which for a publicly traded firm means maximizing the share price. Therefore, the problem with zero growth is that it conflicts with stock price appreciation. So, we come to a second possible growth rate assumption: that the firm grows at a constant rate. While still restrictive, this one is more reasonable, given our previous discussions concerning the necessity to grow. In doing so, we are then able to utilize the basic time value of money equations from Chap. 4. Specifically, given a current dividend (D_0), we can calculate the next dividend (D_1) as follows:

$$D_1 = D_0(1 + g)$$

Likewise, we can calculate the dividend two time periods from now as

$$D_2 = D_0(1 + g)^2$$

and the dividend during any future time period as

$$D_t = D_0(1 + g)^t$$

In fact, this assumption can allow us to find any dividend as long as we are given any other dividend. For example, if you are given a current dividend of \$.45 and a constant growth rate of 4 %, we can find the expected dividend 28 years from now by

$$\begin{aligned} \mathbf{D_{28}} &= \mathbf{D_0(1{+}g)^{28}} \\ &= \mathbf{.45(1.04)^{28}} = \mathbf{\$1.35} \end{aligned}$$

The most important result of this is that we can rewrite the value equation as

$$P_0 = \frac{D_0(1 + g)}{(1 + k)} + \frac{D_0(1 + g)^2}{(1 + k)^2} + \frac{D_0(1 + g)^3}{(1 + k)^3} + \ldots + \frac{D_0(1 + g)^T}{(1 + k)^T}$$

$$P_0 = \sum_{t=1}^{T} \frac{D_0(1 + g)^t}{(1 + k)^t}$$

where each dividend is a function of the current dividend. This is important because we now again have a common factor in each quotient, which can be factored out:

$$P_0 = D_0 \sum_{t=1}^{T} \frac{(1 + g)}{(1 + k)}$$

Again, this leaves an infinite sum. If we add the requirement that $k > g$, it also converges to a relatively simple closed-form solution of

$$\frac{1 + g}{k - g}$$

Putting it together results in a very elegant conclusion:

$$P_0 = \frac{D_0(1+g)}{k-g}$$

This is one of the most important equations in all of finance and is known by many names. Perhaps the most appropriate is the **Gordon Growth Model (GGM)**, named after Myron Gordon, who first published the finding in 1959. Other aliases of the model are the Constant Growth Model, the Dividend Growth Model, and the Dividend Discount Model, all for obvious reasons.

The simplicity of the equation does not deter from the usefulness. Of course, it is important to remember two basic assumptions which lend to the results. The first is, of course, that growth must be constant from the time period of concern until forever. It can *never* change after it begins. The second assumption was previously mentioned, but needs further explanation. The model requires that the discount rate of k be greater than the constant growth rate of g. Otherwise, the denominator is a negative value. Since neither a dividend nor a growth rate (in this context) can be negative, this would imply a negative stock price, which cannot happen.

The beauty of the GGM is the flexibility it allows. For example, if you are faced with an expected dividend instead of a current dividend, it becomes

$$P_0 = \frac{D_1}{k-g}$$

which is the exact same equation in theory, assuming the growth rates from time 0 to time 1 are the same as all growth rates beyond time 1.

There are also situations where estimating the expected price at some time in the future is of concern. Luckily, the GGM is flexible enough to accommodate this as well in the following form:

$$P_t = \frac{D_t(1+g)}{k-g} \quad \text{or} \quad \frac{D_{t+1}}{k-g}$$

Now, at long last, we can see how this works. Given all the buildup, you may actually be unimpressed by the difficulty in valuing common stock. In fact, it is mathematically easier than valuing bonds. Of course, the caveat is that no assumptions are required to value a bond. Consider Miranda's Pizza Shop, a publicly traded company that just paid a dividend of \$1.20. They estimate a constant growth rate of 5.5 % for the foreseeable future and estimate their required return on equity to be 7.4 %. What is the current stock price?

Since we are given D_0, we can set up the problem as follows:

$$\begin{aligned}\mathbf{P_0} &= \frac{\mathbf{1.20\,(1.055)}}{\mathbf{.074 - .055}} \\ &= \mathbf{\$66.63}\end{aligned}$$

Now, suppose we are asked to calculate the expected value of the stock at time four. We can set it up a couple of ways:

$$P_4 = \frac{D_4(1+g)}{k-g} \text{ or } \frac{D_5}{k-g}$$

The only issue is that we don't know either D_4 or D_5. However, that is easily remedied since we know that we can find any dividend as long as we are given any other dividend and a constant growth rate. Thus,

$$D_4 = D_0(1+g)^4 \text{ and } D_5 = D_0(1+g)^5$$

Thus,

$$\begin{aligned}\mathbf{D_4} &= \mathbf{1.20\,(1.055)^4} \text{ and } & \mathbf{D_5} &= \mathbf{1.20\,(1.055)^5}\\ &= \mathbf{\$1.49} & &= \mathbf{\$1.57}\end{aligned}$$

Now, we can put that back in the GGM (and not rounding the dividend values):

$$\begin{aligned}\mathbf{P_4} &= \frac{\mathbf{1.49\,(1{+}.055)}}{\mathbf{.074{-}.055}} \text{ and } & &\frac{\mathbf{1.57}}{\mathbf{.074{-}.055}}\\ &= \mathbf{\$82.54} & &= \mathbf{\$82.54}\end{aligned}$$

There is actually a simpler way of accomplishing the goal in this setting. If we know the current price and maintain the assumption of constant growth, we can actually just do the following:

$$\begin{aligned}\mathbf{P_4} &= \mathbf{P_0(1{+}g)^4}\\ &= \mathbf{66.63(1{+}.055)^4}\\ &= \mathbf{\$82.54}\end{aligned}$$

This is a reflection of the understanding that g doesn't just estimate the rate of dividend growth but also the rate of firm growth. Of course, this underlying assumption that dividends change at the same rate as firm value can be subject to scrutiny as well. Also remember that the \$66.63 is the theoretically derived value of the stock. The same problem could be computed using the current market value, which in all likelihood is different from the P_0 calculated theoretically.

6.4.3 *Multiple Growth Rates*

The constant growth model has distinct limitations, the most notable of those being the necessity of constant growth from *some point* until the end of time. However, that point doesn't necessarily have to be time zero, which has been the assumption until this point. In fact, you can use the constant growth formula as long as you assume the growth rate becomes constant at any point and then remains that way forever thereafter. In such cases, it just requires a bit more work and a more complete understanding of the time value of money.

As an example, consider a start-up firm that plans to pay dividends of \$.50 at the end of the first year. After that, in order to encourage investor demand, they plan to increase the dividend by 13 % in each of the following 3 years. After that time, they plan to have constant growth of 4 % in their dividend for the foreseeable future. The firm's required rate of return is 9 %. In this situation, we can use the constant growth model, only just as a piece of the solution rather than the whole solution. To find the current value of the stock in this particular firm, we have to revert to the basic equation to find the present value, which requires us to discount each and every cash flow separately. For clarity, we will assign a label of g_1 on the 13 % for the first 3 years and g_2 on the 4 % forever after. We are told the dividend at the end of time 1 is \$.50. Therefore, the dividend during the second time period is

$$\begin{aligned} \mathbf{D_2} &= \mathbf{D_1(1+g_1)} \\ &= \mathbf{.50\,(1.13)} \\ &= \mathbf{\$.57} \end{aligned}$$

The dividend for the third time period is

$$\begin{aligned} \mathbf{D_3} &= \mathbf{D_1(1+g_1)^2} \\ &= \mathbf{.50\,(1.13)^2} \\ &= \mathbf{\$.64} \end{aligned}$$

And the dividend for the fourth time period is

$$\begin{aligned} \mathbf{D_4} &= \mathbf{D_1(1+g_1)^3} \\ &= \mathbf{.50\,(1.13)^3} \\ &= \mathbf{\$.72} \end{aligned}$$

We now know the cash flows for the first four time periods. At this time, the growth rate is expected to remain constant forever. Thus, we can use the GGM. Specifically, we need to find the present value of all dividends from time five until forever, which we can get by finding P_4 with the GGM:

$$\begin{aligned} P_4 &= \frac{D_4(1+g_2)}{k-g_2} \\ &= \frac{\mathbf{.72\,(1.04)}}{\mathbf{.09-.04}} \\ &= \mathbf{\$15.01} \end{aligned}$$

Thus, the hard part is done. This \$15.01 is the present value of all dividends from time five until infinity. Note that this value is calculated without rounding throughout. We must be careful here. While it is the present value of all forthcoming dividends, it is the present value at the beginning of that stream of payments. So, including this, we now have all the cash flows, so the last remaining step is to find the present value. We shall use 9 % discount rate:

$$\mathbf{P_0} = \frac{\mathbf{.50}}{\mathbf{1.09}} + \frac{\mathbf{.57}}{\mathbf{(1.09)^2}} + \frac{\mathbf{.64}}{\mathbf{(1.09)^3}} + \frac{\mathbf{.74}}{\mathbf{(1.09)^4}} + \frac{\mathbf{15.01}}{\mathbf{(1.09)^4}}$$
$$= \mathbf{\$12.59}$$

Notice the last two values are both discounted four time periods. This will always be the case if you follow this process. The natural impulse is to discount the price by five time periods; however to do so would essentially skip a payment period. The bottom line is this. You can use the GGM to find the value of any stock as long as there is a point in the dividend stream where growth rate is assumed to become constant from that point until forever. You should be able to handle any situation that occurs before that time so long as you remember to calculate the dividends individually according to the applicable growth rate. If the growth rate never becomes constant forever thereafter, then there is no choice but to manually calculate the present value of each dividend forever. This should perhaps give reason to appreciate the value of assumptions, despite their limitations. The ending value found with the DGM that captures the *PV* of all remaining cash flows is also often referred to as the **terminal value**.

IN THE REAL WORLD

Hack Back continued to pay a dividend, maintaining the \$.20 per share for the last quarter of 2009 and then increasing it to \$.21 per share in each quarter of 2010. In 2011, they again increased the dividend by one penny, to \$.22 per share each quarter.

Dubarb Freeman requested a meeting with Tyler and Lilly early in the morning on October 3, 2011. Originally, it had been scheduled to include Jane and Brandon, but, unfortunately, they had been called away to deal with an issue regarding an erroneous news report pertaining to Hack Back's second quarter earnings. The article cast an unfavorable light on Hack Back's reported earnings, and all four members of the finance team had been sent to do damage control with the local and national media. It was the kind of thing Freeman abhorred, so he was all too happy to get back into the trenches and do some of the capital structure groundwork in their absence. Thus, the meeting began as scheduled.

"You know we could have just rescheduled this until they get back," Lilly said. They had decided, randomly, to meet in her office. Whereas Freeman's office was a disaster and Coleman's was immaculate, Lilly's fell somewhere in between. She was not naturally tidy and preferred to leave things in disorderly order. Unfortunately, she entertained many important clients and colleagues in her role with the firm, so the chaos has to be mitigated somewhat to maintain an air of

professionalism. It had taken a month for a team of interior designers to satisfy Lilly's "vision." The end result included walls of a deep pink, which she referred to as salmon, and gunmetal gray furniture that appeared to have been borrowed from the Starship Galaxy. The chairs were perched on an oval-shaped porcelain base with a thin metal pole, leading to a sharply angular seat and back. They were ergonomically engineered to reduce stress on the joints and encourage correct posture. Thus, they were the most uncomfortable chairs ever invented. Freeman was miserable.

"Nope, no need," he said, while attempting to cross his legs. The chair was too high, so his top leg simply slid down the other until he was forced to settle for an ankle cross instead. "We need to get cranking on this thing. I want a decision made this year so that one year from now we should have the two operable plants. That means we are on a tight schedule."

Tyler was handling the chair much better than Freeman, since his long lean frame lent itself to the setup. He brushed an invisible piece of dust from his trouser leg before speaking.

"I think we both agree," he said, "that time is of the essence, particularly given the new national advertising campaign. So, what is the purpose of this meeting?"

"We have to look at what paying a dividend means for our company," Freeman started.

"We know what it means, Dube," Tyler answered. "We've gone over all of this. It's been two years now. We've already paid a dividend nine times. The boards of directors agree that paying this dividend is our best shot at maintaining, and hopefully expanding, our equity base."

"And we know the financial obligation we're entering into and we're confident that we can meet it," Lilly added. "Besides, I was under the impression this meeting was about the plant project."

"It is," Freeman said. He couldn't take sitting any longer. He rose to his feet and began pacing in front of the picture window that made up the right-hand wall of Lilly's office.

"I'm not talking about the decision to issue a dividend. That's all water under the bridge, and I have already made it clear that I am in agreement with the decisions we have made. No, kids, believe it or not, I'm not here to caution you of ill-conceived ambition. Rather, we need to discuss the implications of dividend payments on our current issues, namely, deciding which project we want to undertake and, more to the point, how to pay for them."

"I'm afraid I don't see the connection," Lilly said.

"Get out your gizmos," Freeman said with a wag of his finger. After a moment of confusion, Tyler obeyed by slipping his iPhone from his pocket. Lilly sighed and then swirled slightly to bump her mouse. Her computer flashed to life.

"I've sent you an email outlining what the payment of dividends tells us about the price of the stock."

"We know what the price of the stock is, Dube," Tyler said. "I look at it every day. Several times each day." Despite his words, he automatically opened his

email and clicked on the inbox, which, as Freeman claimed, signaled he had one new message.

"I know, I know. But for now, I want you to pretend we don't know the price. Remember the little lesson Herb gave you on finding the theoretical value of something."

"Sure," Lilly answered, "we just have to find the present value of all future cash flows. Just like we did to value the plants."

"Yes, exactly," Freeman responded. "And as you recall, the present value you just described should be the amount that any rational person should be willing to pay for the asset. We now have to apply this same logic to the value of your firm, which to an investor is just another asset."

"So the dividends we are issuing are the expected cash flows from our stock?" Tyler queried.

"Yes," Freeman answered, "and more importantly, the dividends we have issued have created the expectation for all others."

"What about the cash flow the shareholder gets when they sell the stock?" Lilly asked.

"That is a very good question," Freeman responded, "but mostly from the investor side, not from ours. To us, all that really matters is that the stock is out there, and we have to pay dividends to whomever is holding the share at that time. So, what we are really concerned about is what the stream of dividend payments tell us about the value of each share of stock. In essence, this would tell us the value of the stock today to us."

He emphasized the last word by poking his chest with both index fingers.

"Okay, how do we do that?" Tyler interrupted. "We are up to paying a $.22 dividend each quarter now. What does that mean our stock is worth?"

"Well, that brings us to the email I told you about."

Lilly quickly turned back to the computer and clicked on the new message. The screen filled with calculations. Tyler did the same on his phone. The attachment was actually just a scanned copy of his handwritten notes.

"Why didn't you just write this when you got here?" Lilly asked, "Or better yet just make copies and bring to us?"

"Best I can tell, no one here can read anything unless it's on an electronic box of some kind."

Lilly cast a paralyzing look from the corner of her eyes, as she flicked the mouse to scroll down the screen.

"The first calculation is much as you just suggested," Freeman said in a rush. "If we assume that we are always going to pay the same dividend, then the calculation is pretty simple. A cash flow that never changes is called a perpetuity and is calculated by that first equation there."

Tyler scrolled down to the first calculation, which was simply

$$\begin{aligned} P_0 &= .88/.07 \\ &= \$12.57 \end{aligned}$$

"Notice that I've assumed we pay the $.22 every quarter of upcoming year. I've also assumed a discount rate of 7 %, which is coming from nowhere but my imagination."

"But isn't that important?" Lilly asked.

"Oh, absolutely," Freeman responded. "And we'll get to that in time. For now, let's finish this."

"Less than thirteen dollars?" Tyler said, looking over the top of his phone in disbelief. "Forgive me if I question your methods, Dube. Our stock is currently worth over fifty-seven dollars per share."

"It depends on how you define 'worth'," Freeman responded, "but to give the simplest answer, you are correct. It's technically worth whatever the current stock price is."

"Then, what is the point of doing this?" Lilly asked, starting to see the morning slipping away fruitlessly.

"Give me a minute," Dubarb said, waving her down.

"What's all this other stuff?" Tyler asked, indicating the rest of the message.

"That is a bit more realistic situation," Freeman said. "We just assumed zero growth in our dividends, which essentially says we don't expect our company to grow either. So, an interpretation is that if we don't expect our company to grow, then, yes, the firm is worth around thirteen dollars per share."

"Well, I don't think that's an assumption we want to make," Lilly said. "We certainly hope that we grow, and as we do, we can pay out more."

"You are very correct, young lady," Freeman responded. "We do indeed hope to grow. Thus, we need to make some assumption about what this future growth will look like. And the simplest assumption to start with is constant growth."

"So, we grow at a constant rate, what, every year?" Tyler asked, pointing at the new calculation:

$$P_0 = \frac{.88(1.05)}{.07 - .05}$$
$$= \$46.20$$

"That's right," Freeman answered. "I assumed a five percent growth rate each year. This is taking some liberties, but I think it is reasonable since it is roughly the average growth rate of our dividends thus far. That equation I'm using is called the Gordon Growth Model. It tells you the current price, assuming constant growth from now until the end of time."

"Well, that price looks a lot better," Lilly said. She paused and pulled up another screen on her phone... "But still too low, over ten dollars less than market value."

"Well, yes," Dube said, "but the price really isn't the point. In fact, calculating the theoretical price of our stock is almost a foolish endeavor, when as you've both pointed out, we can just look it up."

Lilly threw her hands up in exasperation, but Freeman cut her off before she could object.

"What we really need to focus on is what this tells us ***about shareholder expectations."***

"I assume that is what the rest of this stuff is about," Tyler said. Freeman was nodding before he finished.

"That's the most important part, son. Let's get to it."

ALTERNATE ENDINGS

1. ***The assumption of constant growth is a pretty stringent restriction. What if Mr. Freeman suggests the following instead:***

   I think we should increase our dividend rapidly over the next couple of years, kids. I propose we increase our current $.22 dividend by 15 % over the next three years and then maintain the constant growth of 5 % for the foreseeable future thereafter.

   Using this information, what is the current value of the stock given by the dividend growth model?
2. ***Suppose that after the calculation of zero growth value, Lilly says, "Why would anyone want to invest in a stock that doesn't have estimated growth? Does such a stock really exist?"***

   Answer her. Does it? Why would you, as an investor, consider such an investment? What about as a firm?

6.5 A Note on the Usefulness of the GGM

Some of you may be wondering about the practical application of such activities such as theoretically calculating the value of a firm's stock. Since it is relatively straightforward to look up the market value of any stock at any point in time, then why would we want to calculate what the price *should* be based upon a set of questionable assumptions? The answer, like most, depends upon the lens through which you are examining the question.

From the investor's perspective, such actions are completed with the design of identifying mispricing. Mispricing can be defined as a situation in which a current market price is inconsistent with the theoretical price as calculated from academic models. For example, suppose you have completed your GGM analysis and find Firm ABC to be theoretically valued at $50. But, then you see that it is actually only selling for $35 on the open market. This could signal a degree of mispricing that, theoretically, should be rectified via market supply and demand forces. After, all, if you can do the calculations and determine the stock is undervalued, eventually so too should a large number of other investors and the increased demand will force the stock price to increase to a more aligned level.

Should you have bought at $35 based upon your calculations, then you can benefit from this market "rebalancing." Of course, the other side of the coin is that the market doesn't *have* to correct itself. Or, the assumptions from which you made your underpriced assessment may be incorrect. There is no guarantee this process will result in any profits at all. Nonetheless, the appeal of identifying profitable investments is the primary reason that investors use valuation techniques, such as the GGM.

Of course, this does little to answer the question of why to include it in a corporate finance text, since the materials are presented from the firm's perspective. We could certainly make an argument that knowing the difference between the theoretical and market values of their firm is valuable information for the firm itself. However, the true value of theoretical valuation techniques, from the firm's perspective, is not in knowing the theoretical value. Rather, the true benefit lies in calculating the firm's required rate of return.

LOOK IT UP: The GGM is not, by far, the only model that is designed to calculate the theoretical price of share of stock. In fact, the GGM is just part of a larger group of valuation methods that can be categorized as "discounted cash flow" methodologies. Some examples are the free cash flow (FCF) or residual income (RI) models. Try looking them up and focusing on the similarities and differences relative to the GGM.

6.6 Required Return

The firm must be concerned with how movements in the stock price influence their **required return**. This notion is consistent with the idea that was presented in Chap. 5 with bonds. As with everything, market forces of supply and demand will determine whether stock prices increase or decrease. We can then use the DGM model (and others) to determine what the market-driven price infers about the firm's required return. Another way to define the required return is that it is the return investors expect on their investment. The firm needs to view it as *required*, since failure to reach that value could result in the investors being disappointed to the point they would sell their holdings.

As with most any equation, we can rearrange to solve for more than one variable. In the case of the constant growth model, we can solve for the required rate of return with the following:

$$k = \frac{D_0(1+g)}{P_{MKT}} + g \text{ or } \frac{D_1}{P_{MKT}} + g$$

Notice we are now using P_{MKT} instead of P_0. P_0 is the theoretical price based upon the assumptions of the dividend growth model, whereas the P_{MKT} is the actual market value today. Since the objective is to get an accurate reflection of the market's current view of the stock and the return investors require for investment, the use of the market value is appropriate. The current market price of a stock

(P_{MKT}) is always easy to find, particularly with today's technology. Thus, the only variable that must be estimated in this instance is the growth rate of the firm.

The two pieces of this equation have names, which makes remembering what they mean much easier. In fact, we've already talked about the first one, but from a different perspective. The first part is called the **dividend yield**. Back in Chap. 2, the dividend yield was calculated as the dividend just paid (as obtained from the existing income statement) divided by the current price. The current version tells us the *expected* cash payout to shareholders in relation to the price that same shareholder must pay for the share to which that dividend is attached. For an investor that is considering purchase of the stock, the expected dividend yield is likely more relevant.

The other piece is just the estimated growth rate, but it is also more. Thus far, we have focused on the growth rate as being the rate at which the dividend amount grows. However, the assumption of the model is that the firm grows at the same rate. Knowing this, another name for the growth rate is the **capital gains yield**. Capital gains represent the growth of the underlying asset's value, or on a practical level, the money you hope to make on the changing share price. Thus, by combining both the dividend and capital gains yields, one can identify the total required return shareholders require. Specifically, the dividend yield represents the amount of money (in percentage terms) that shareholders expect from dividends, while the capital gains yield represents the amount of money (again in percentage terms) that shareholders expect from price appreciation. From the firm's perspective, the word "expect" should be replaced with "require" because of the desire to keep their existing shareholders happy.

Let's again illustrate with the example of Miranda's Pizza Shop from earlier. Let's assume, however, that we know the stock price is \$65 and wish to find the implied required return. Recall that Miranda has just paid a dividend of \$1.20 and they estimate a constant growth rate of 5.5 %.

In this case, the required rate of return is

$$\begin{aligned}\mathbf{k} &= \frac{\mathbf{1.20\,(1.055)}}{\mathbf{65}} + \mathbf{.055} \\ &= \mathbf{7.45\,\%}\end{aligned}$$

This same process would work in the context of the multiple growth rates examples, but with the added complexity that it cannot be solved in a closed-form equation. Thus, you must either spend an inordinate amount of time on the problem or use modern technology as an aid.

IN THE REAL WORLD

They decided to take a little break before digging into what Freeman had deemed "the important part." In the interim, Brandon and Jane had returned from their assignment, assuring Freeman the situation had been resolved and a printed retraction would be in all media outlets tomorrow. Brandon said he had also sent

a tweet confirming the correction and had updated the firm's Facebook page. Freeman asked if he had also asked aliens to write it in the stars.

The meeting was again called to order. Jane quickly worked to get Freeman's email put up on the small projector screen in the corner of Lilly's office, so they could all see.

"If you recall," Freeman said, pointing at the computer screen, "the most important thing we looked at with the bonds was the current yield to maturity."

"Yeah, I remember," Lilly jumped in. "That was the important number because it is essentially what we should consider our current cost of debt."

"Yes, we did," Brandon said, "and now we need to do the same thing for equity to find the 'cost of equity'."

Always the cautious one, Jane interceded.

"We have to remember that there is much more guesswork in this process than there was in the debt world. But, now that we've paid a dividend, we can start hypothesizing what the shareholders are going to expect from us."

"By rearranging that equation?" Tyler asked, pointing at the screen.

"That's the beginning," Freeman said. "Look at what it tells you. The current stock price is... what?"

Tyler quickly pulled it up on his phone.

"Looks like it is currently going at $57.71," he said.

"Okay, then our cost of equity would look like....that," Freeman said. Jane had read his mind and, with Lilly's easy agreement, had taken her office seat. Jane had quickly altered Thompson's calculation to reflect the most up-to-date market price:

$$k = \frac{.88(1.05)}{57.71} + .05$$
$$= 6.60\%$$

"So, our cost of equity is 6.6 %?" Lilly questioned. "What exactly does that mean to me?"

"It means that supply and demand for our stock price currently indicates our shareholders expect a return of 6.6 % next year."

"Give me more, Dube," Tyler said. "Are you saying that we should increase the dividend growth rate?"

"No, no," Freeman said, putting the palms of his hands out in a "hold on" gesture. "Not necessarily. Think about it. An investor probably always expects an increase in the stock price. Therefore, the investor required return will always be theoretically higher than the dividend payout, so at any growth rate, we would always say it should be higher if we follow that logic."

"All it really means," Jane said, "is that through some combination of dividend payments and price appreciation, the shareholders are expecting a return of about 6.6 %."

"Forgive my ignorance," Tyler interjected, "but it seems like this is putting a lot of faith in a simple little equation that is based upon a dividend and a growth rate that we just made up."

"You're right," said Brandon, slipping seamlessly into salesman mode. "And we are very glad that you understand the limitations of what we've just shown you. You are actually correct in several ways. There are a lot of assumptions and a lot of unknowns about what we are doing. But there are also a few absolutes. First, the relationship between dividends, prices, and required returns is most definitely important."

"And this is the first step in examining that relationship for our stock," Dubarb interrupted.

Brandon jumped back in. "Right. And, we need to remember that anything that we use the funds received from equity for needs to generate at least a 6.6 % return, so the shareholders aren't disappointed with their investment."

"Is that true for new equity we may issue as well?" Lilly asked.

"Not necessarily," Freeman said. "There may be even a higher hurdle there. We will discuss that at a later date."

"I have another question," Tyler said. "How would we have figured out how much the shareholders want if we didn't pay dividends?"

"There are ways," Dubarb responded. "In fact, that is the next assignment for these lads." He tilted his head towards Brandon and Jane.

Lilly moved to open a drawer on her desk, pulling out several sheets of paper. She quickly found what she was looking for.

"We found the cost of debt to be 9.32 %," she said. "So does this mean we should just fund the project with equity?" Lilly asked. "It seems a lot cheaper."

"Not at all, lad," Freeman said. "We are nowhere near making that decision yet. This is just yet another piece of the puzzle. Just print this off and stick it in there with your other stuff. Eventually we'll have enough to start putting it all together."

He stood, indicating the end of the meeting. Brandon and Jane followed suit.

"In the meantime, you guys have a company to run," Freeman said.

Lilly did as instructed by printing out the scribbled notes from the email. She pounded the edges straight on the table and slid them into the drawer.

ALTERNATE ENDINGS

1. *Reconsider the alternative ending from the previous section, where Mr. Freeman suggests growth of 15 % for 3 years and then 5 % forever after. What is the estimated required return in that case?*
2. *What if the firm plans to grow at a rate of 8 % instead of 5 %? How does this change things? More generally, discuss the relationship between growth rates and required rates of return, focusing on the importance the level of dividend payment is to the cost of the firm's equity.*

6.7 Stock Exchanges

Once a firm has initially issued shares to the public (review Chap. 1), they then must decide on which exchange they want their shares listed. A **stock exchange** has the primary purpose of creating market liquidity, giving investors a vehicle through which they can buy or sell equity securities. Such trades are said to take place on the secondary market, which is where shares go once gone through the initial public offering process. There are many different financial markets and most of those are referred to as "stock" markets.

Stock exchanges occupy many different countries across six different continents and trade securities from all over the world. In fact, that is what makes the world of finance so amazing. With the current vast array of technological gizmos, you can literally trade any asset in the world from your desk (or your phone). The ease of asset trading brought about by the rise of the internet often masks the true process that occurs when you instigate a trade. Thus, we are going to go back in time for a few moments in order to catch everyone up.

6.7.1 The New York Stock Exchange

Until March 8, 2006, **the New York Stock Exchange** (NYSE) was a not-for-profit organization, which means its sole purpose was to serve as an intermediary. It was simply a place to meet and trade, and there was no money left over after the investing winners and losers were accounted for. That all changed when the NYSE Group, Inc. went public and became a for-profit firm. Now, the firm is known as NYSE Euronext, due to its merger with the electronic exchange Euronext in 2007. The exchange is by far the largest exchange in the world, with assets included on the exchange having market capitalization in excess of $14 trillion.

Prior to going public, the NYSE was comprised of "members," who bought "seats" on the exchange. These seats, at times, became very expensive. For example, seats sold for as high as $4 million dollars during the bubble period in the late 1990s. Going public changed this practice as well, however. Shareholders now own the exchange, and licenses for seats are now sold on an annual basis.

LOOK IT UP: The history of the NYSE is very interesting and plays a major role in the development of the financial system we now see. Dig around a little and see what you can find. Try to answer some important questions. Where is the NYSE? When did it start? What transformations have taken place over the past two centuries? Make a challenge to detail ten important dates in the history of the NYSE.

To illustrate the role of the NYSE as a marketplace for equity transactions, let's discuss the process that a trade would go through before the days of automated trading. Suppose the year is 1968 and you want to buy 1,000 shares of General Electric. You would pick up the phone and place a call. The person you call is likely a broker of some type, like Edward Jones (well, not actually him, but a representative). Generically, we shall call this an external broker, to signify that they operate outside of the exchange. A **broker** is a financial professional who brings buyers and sellers together, but does not maintain an inventory of assets. Conversely, a **dealer** maintains an inventory of assets and stands ready to buy or sell at any time.

Your external broker would then place a call to the NYSE, and the person most likely to answer would be a **commission broker**. Commission brokers execute buy and sell transactions. Upon receiving the order, she would likely take one of two courses of action. First, she may walk across the floor herself until she finds a particular **specialist** desk. A specialist is pretty much as the name implies in that he or she specializes in a small basket of stocks. Specialists are dealers in that, if need be, they can buy or sell stock from their own inventory. Their job is to collect all buy and sell orders for the small set of stocks and use the supply (sell orders) and demand (buy orders) to create the current price of the stock at any time. They do so by posting a bid and ask price for each asset. The **bid price** is the price at which the specialist will buy the stock, while the **ask price** is the price at which the specialist will sell the stock. This process has led to specialists often being known as *market makers*. For every stock that trades on the NYSE, there is a specialist through which every trade must pass. In 2009, to aid in maintaining a competitive edge, the specialist role was replaced with two classes of market makers. *Designed market makers* (DMMs) largely take over the actions of the traditional specialist, while *supplemental liquidity providers* (SLPs) perform the role in offices outside of the exchange.

The other, and more likely option, is the commission broker will be too busy to go find the specialist desk herself. In this situation, the commission broker will delegate the responsibility to a **floor broker**. Once either the commission broker or the floor broker gets to the specialist post in question, he or she begins the process of obtaining the best possible price to fulfill the order. There are two general ways this can happen. The preferred option is to work the order, which means identifying a counterpart that has the opposite order (a sell order). So, one floor broker walks around the post until they run into an acceptable offer from another broker, who is representing someone who wants to sell their position in the stock. Should an acceptable agreement not be reached "on the floor," the other option is to buy directly from (or sell directly to) the specialist. When this happens, the deal reached will typically be less optimal than if the brokers can get together on their own. Once the deal is agreed upon, the broker calls you back and lets you know that your trade has gone through and you are the proud owner of 1,000 shares of General Electric.

All right, so that was how it used to happen. As you can imagine, that process can become cumbersome. In fact, back in the day, it could take hours or more. That wasn't such a problem then because the volume of trading was a fraction of current amounts and prices were less volatile. Should a trade take hours today, it would create an insurmountable bottleneck in the system. Luckily, it doesn't take hours to make a trade. In fact, it takes seconds (at most).

So, fast-forward to today and say you want to again buy 1,000 shares of GE. Instead of picking up the phone, you would wake up your computer, probably sign into an online brokerage account, and click a few buttons. Then you press enter and away it goes. A second later, your trade is complete. What you probably haven't thought about is that during that second, roughly the same process is completed as described above. Specifically, your computer sends a message to the online brokerage's automated computers, which, in turn, sends it to the commission broker's computer. That computer, in turn, sends it to the specialist's computer. The specialist's computer then does the work of matching buy and sell orders and finds the best deal. That computer then sends an "order filled" message back to the commission broker's desk, then to the online broker's desk, and then to your laptop. And all of that takes up most of a second while you impatiently tap your fingers in frustration of slow technology.

LOOK IT UP: Over the past two decades, online brokerages have greatly changed the investing landscape. Look up some examples of the options available and see what you can find out about how they work. Talk about the differing cost structures of these online brokers and the more traditional "walk-in" brokers (like Edward Jones).

Today, most orders involving firms listed on the NYSE are completed by the **Universal Trading Platform**, which is the successor of the super display book system (SDBK), which in turn was the successor to the well-known SuperDOT (Designated Order Turnaround) system. In reality, since the mid-1970s, most trades have been electronically transmitted to the trading floor with these programs. Today, only the largest orders are still manually transacted in the method described above. The benefit of the increased technology is a drastically reduced time of transaction. For example, the Universal Trading Platform reduced the time of transaction to (at most) a few milliseconds. This compares very favorable to the excruciatingly slow time of 100 milliseconds that it used to take for the old SuperDOT system to operate.

An interesting side effect of the increased technology is that the **floor traders**, which were synonymous with trading on the NYSE, are being made obsolete. A once popular occupation, the razor thin margins that can be gained by being on the trading floor (as opposed to sitting in the comfort of an office) are being overwhelmed by the high costs of doing business. As such, floor traders are an endangered species.

LOOK IT UP: The rapid increase in electronic trading and, more importantly, the frequency with which trades could take place have given rise to a new brand of investment strategy. See what you can find about high-frequency trading (HFT) and focus a brief report on the impact this type of trading has on financial markets.

6.7.2 Nasdaq

This second largest exchange mentioned began in 1971 and was at the time a fresh approach to investing. Originally, the term "Nasdaq" stood for National Association of Securities Dealers Automated Quotations system. However, since that time, the market has grown to the point that the term has been given full-fledged "word" status. Nasdaq was created as a place where smaller, less known firms could trade and not be forced to meet the strict listing requirements of the NYSE or other large marketplaces. In recent years, particularly since the mid-1990s, Nasdaq has become known as the "high-tech" market due to the huge surge of dot-coms during that time period.

While there are many technology and small firms trading on Nasdaq, there are also many non-technology and very large firms that trade on the exchange. In fact, some of the largest firms in the world trade on Nasdaq. You may have heard of some little Nasdaq companies like Microsoft and Apple. In fact, in some ways, including volume traded, Nasdaq is larger than the NYSE.

There are two primary differences between the NYSE and Nasdaq. The first is most profound, particularly given our discussion of the trading process involved on the NYSE. *Nasdaq has no physical location.* There is no trading floor, no large building, and no central location where TV cameras can go and get a close-up view of the chaotic trading taking place. In fact, if forced to describe where Nasdaq is located, you may state that it is located in just about every pocket, backpack, and office; in short everywhere where there is an internet connection.

> LOOK IT UP: Nasdaq is actually made up of three smaller sub-exchanges. What are they? See if you can identify a few companies in each sub-exchange.

The second difference is that Nasdaq is a multiple market maker system, as opposed to the specialist system discussed earlier with the NYSE. There is no central clearing house, directed by a specialist. Instead, there are many people spread across the world that make the market. This is made possible, of course, due to the rapid increase in technology over the past twenty years or so. One such development was the **Electronic Communications Network (ECN)**, which allow individuals to effectively bypass the exchange buy and sell directly with each other. Today, a large percentage of trades, on all exchanges, are done through ECNs.

6.7.3 The Changing World of Stock Exchanges

We can end this discussion by making a curious statement. You may be currently reading one of the last rounds of texts that discuss the NYSE in the manner it has been discussed for over two centuries. The world of financial asset trading is becoming continuously more consolidated, and traditional methods, such as those used on the NYSE, are being usurped by more technologically savvy processes and companies. In December 2012, the NYSE Euronext was *sold* to an (insanely successful) upstart derivatives trading firm based in Atlanta named IntercontinentalExchange (ICE). The very near future of equity trading is complete electronic trading, a process that the world's second largest exchange saw coming well before the pack.

The NYSE is not alone in experiencing the rapidly changing landscape of financial asset exchanges. The wave of consolidation has also influenced Nasdaq in many ways. Now operating under Nasdaq OMX due to a purchase of Swedish-Finnish firm OMX in 2007, the firm made a serious attempt to purchase the NYSE. In fact, to continue the consolidation theme, Nasdaq OMX and ICE actually joined forces on a bid to buy the NYSE in 2011. The deal, however, was axed, due in large part to concerns the justice department held over too much consolidation of American equities.

All of this actually shields a larger truth; equities are relatively minor players in the world of tradable assets. While the size of the worldwide equity markets is mind-boggling at a value in excess of $50 trillion, debt markets are significantly larger. Larger still is the world of derivatives trading, where some estimates have worldwide market values in excess of a quadrillion. That's right, more than $1,000 trillion, which is about 20 times the size of the world economy. Such numbers are staggering and should provide some insight on why exchanges worldwide are focusing more and more attention on such assets. The equity world, though always important, is often being taken along for the ride.

LOOK IT UP: This is not an investments text, so the topic of derivatives will not be covered. However, those numbers above have to perk your interest. The two most popular derivative assets are options and futures contracts. See what they are and how they are used.

Concept Questions

1. **Equity** Define to someone who has never heard the notion exactly what equity is. Do so from both the firm and investor perspective.
2. **Public equity** What distinguishes public equity from private equity? Why would a firm want either, or both?
3. **Common stock** Your grandpa doesn't understand why anyone would want to invest in the stock market instead of just putting their money in the bank. Explain to him the benefits of investing in common stock. Make sure to detail the characteristics of the cash flows associated with common stock.
4. **Equity valuation** Why is equity valuation more difficult than bond valuation? Create an analogy to help explain to a beginner.

5. **Dividends** What is the difference between current dividends and expected dividends? When would you use each, and why?
6. **Preferred stock** Your investing buddy says to you, "Why not buy preferred stock? It says right in the name that we should *prefer* them over common stock." How do you respond?
7. **Gordon Growth Model** What is the mathematical basis underlying the dividend growth model? If the required return increases, does this increase or decrease the stock price?
8. **Gordon Growth Model** Show three ways the Gordon Growth Model can be used, from either firm's or investor's perspective.
9. **Required return** What are the two components to the required return on common stock? What do they mean for the firm? What about for the investor?
10. **Required return** What is the relationship between required returns and growth rates in the Gordon Growth Model?
11. **Dividends** Detail the four dates of concern dealing with dividend payments. From an investor's perspective, when would you have to buy to receive the dividend?
12. **Dividends** CEO Davidson knows the firm is falling into a financial black hole but refuses to reduce the dividend. Why is he being so stubborn? Is there any reason why he is correct in his stubbornness?
13. **Stock exchanges** Compare and contrast the NYSE and Nasdaq. How do they work, and what role do they play in the financial landscape?
14. **Stock exchanges** Your best friend, Betty, just burst into your apartment with the following proclamation. "I just saw the movie 'Wall Street,' and I was so blown away by all the action on the trading floor. That is what I definitely want to do with my career. I would love to have all that intense face-to-face interaction." You hate to burst her bubble, but you've gotta tell her... What do you say?

Problems

1. **Gordon Growth Model** A firm just paid a dividend of $1.45. If the growth rate is a constant 5.42 % and the required return is 6.4 %, what is the current price of a share of stock, according to the GGM?
2. **Gordon Growth Model** Suppose Scotty is expected to pay a dividend of $1.75 next year. If the required return is 5.47 % and the expected growth rate is 3.64 %, what is the expected price at time 6?
3. **Gordon Growth Model** The current price of share of common stock is $25.80. If the company expects perpetual growth of 3.6 % and has a required return of 8 %, what dividend could be expected at time 4?
4. **Common stock valuation** Suppose a firm is expected to pay a dividend of $1.25 in each of the next 4 years and then never pay a dividend again. If the firms required return is 5.4 %, at what price would you estimate the current value of this stock?
5. **Common stock valuation** Ned's Aquarium Hut, Inc., plans to pay a constant dividend of $.40 in each of the next 4 years. At that point, he plans to increase

the dividend at a constant rate of 6 % each year for the foreseeable future. If Ned's required rate of return is 8.4 %, what should the current price of a share of stock be?

6. **Required rate of return** Judy's Fabric Emporium has a capital gains yield of 6.1 %, is expected to pay dividends of $3.15, and has a current market price of $15.51. What is Judy's required return?
7. **Required rate of return** Suppose a firm has a current price of $43.53 and expect growth of 4 %. The firm expects constant growth of 5 % from this point forward. If the required rate of return on the equity is 8.75 %, what is the current dividend?
8. **Required rate of return** Henry's Hammer Shop, Inc., has common stock that is currently selling for $28.06. They just paid a dividend of $1.78 and expect to increase this amount by $.15 in each of the next 3 years. Following that, they plan growth of 3 % forever thereafter. What is the firm's required rate of return?
9. **Multiple growth rates** A share of common stock paid a dividend exactly 5 years ago of $1.85 and have increased this by $.18 each year until now. They are now planning on growth of 10 % for the next 3 years before a constant growth rate of 5 % is implemented for the rest of time. If the firm's required rate of return is 6.31 %, what should the current price of share of stock be?
10. **Multiple growth rates** Greta's Garden and Variety began issuing common stock 12 years ago. Eight years ago, Greta issued her first dividend at $.10 per share. For each year since then, she had increased the value of the dividend by 5 %. Today, after a meeting with her board of directors, she has decided some changes need to take place. Her firm is currently going through a growth spurt and needs all the funds it can manage just to run operations at a level that meets demand. Therefore, she has decided to not issue a dividend for the upcoming year, as well as the following 2 years (times two and three). After that, she is confident that she can afford to issue a dividend of $.20 at time four. She plans to increase this dividend by $.05 in each of the following 4 years thereafter. At that time, she thinks her cash flows will be adequate to produce a growth rate of 6 % for the foreseeable future. If her required rate of return is 8.54 %, what should be the current price of her stock?
11. **Multiple growth rates** Tyler's Doggie Park, Inc., was founded exactly 10 years ago. For the first 7 years, they paid no dividend, as they sought to increase their market share first. However, at that time (exactly 3 years ago), they issued a dividend of $3.00 per share and have increased that amount by 5 % since then. They plan for the next dividend to be 7 % higher than the current dividend. They then plan to continue this 7 % growth rate for the following 3 years thereafter. Then they plan to go back to a 5 % growth rate for the rest of time. Tyler has a required return of 11 %. What should be the current price of this stock?
12. **Common stock valuation** Suppose you have a firm that plans to pay a constant dividend of $.45 during each of the next 6 years and then never pay dividends again. At that time, the price will be $3.64. Given this, what is the current price of a share of stock if $k = 8.5\ \%$?

13. **Common stock valuation** Hattie's Hat Emporium just went public at a price of \$12.90 per share. They do not plan to pay a dividend for the next 3 years but then plan to pay a special one-time dividend of \$2.50 to reward their existing shareholders' loyalty at time 4. They then plan, beginning at time five, to pay a constant dividend of \$.30 for each of the following 5 years. Following that, they plan to increase the dividend by 3 % each year for the rest of time. The firm has a required rate of return of 7.3 %. What should be the current price of a share of stock?
14. **Multiple growth rates** Consider Firm ABC. They just paid a dividend of \$.23 per share. They plan to increase this by 12 % during each of the next 3 years. In addition, during the third time period, plans are in place to merge with another company. This merger will result in a one-time influx of cash to Firm ABC. They plan to disburse part of this cash as a one-time special dividend of \$4.00 per share, which will be issued in addition to the normal dividend at time three. Following that, the firm plans to continue to increase their dividends by 4 % per year forever after. As a further complication, the merger will increase the risk of the firm, which will be reflected in a higher required rate of return. Thus, for the next 2 years (starting at time 0), the firm will have a required return of 5.5 %. However, for time periods three and beyond, the firm will have a required return of 6.7 %. Given all this, what should be the current price of a share of ABC stock?
15. **Equity portfolios** Suppose you buy 180 shares of Stock A and 100 shares of Stock B. Stock A pays a constant dividend of \$.20 and will do so forever. They have a required rate of return of 7.42 %. Stock B just paid a dividend of \$.80. They expect this dividend to grow at a rate of 6 % for the rest of time. They have a required return of 11 %. How much should you have to spend in total?
16. **Equity portfolios** Suppose you are creating an investment portfolio. You have decided upon two assets:

    (a) Fifty shares of common stock in Firm A. The stock just paid a dividend of \$1.25. However, they do not plan to pay another dividend until year four (as they expand their company). That dividend will be 5 % greater than the current dividend. They then plan to increase the dividend by 8 % for the next 2 years (to gain back investors). Following that, the dividend will increase by 5 % for the rest of time. Firm A has a required return of 9.14 %.
    (b) Seventy-five shares of preferred stock in Firm B. The preferred stock is a 2 %, \$20 pfd stock. Firm B has a 5.81 % required return on preferred stock.

    What should be the total cost of your portfolio?
17. **Portfolio required return** Suppose you have a portfolio made up of 55 % common stock A and 45 % preferred stock B. The common stock is expected to pay a dividend of \$4.54 and is currently selling for \$67.23 per share. They expect a growth rate of 6 % for the foreseeable future. The preferred stock pays a dividend of 5 % based upon a face value of \$100 and is currently selling for \$23.54. What is your portfolio required return?

Chapter 7
The Rocky Marriage of Risk and Return

This chapter introduces a topic that is perhaps most valuable in the investments arena. However, this text has made a conscious effort to point out that financial assets must be viewed from multiple angles. Also, keep in mind that an investment can be any number of things, particularly in corporate finance. So, although we will focus on financial investments to illustrate the points of interest throughout the chapter, keep in mind the materials will readily apply to physical investments as well. Thus, it is of particular interest to understand how this material fits into the overall context of capital structure and capital budgeting. This chapter will be roughly divided into two concepts, both with the same end objective. The first examines a data-driven method of determining the relationship between risk and return. The second concept examines the risk/return relationship on a more theoretical basis.

7.1 Introduction to Risk and Return

We have a long history of data that we can use to examine the potential costs and benefits of any particular investment. These two sides of each investment are going to be the guiding force behind what we do in this chapter. The potential benefits are known as "returns," while the uncertainty surrounding these returns are generally referred to as "risks." It is imperative that we mathematically calculate (or estimate) the potential benefits and costs when considering any investment.

The good news is that the return (or benefit) side is fairly straightforward to examine. Put fairly simply, the return on an investment is the difference between the amount of money you have before the investment and the amount you have afterwards. Related calculations are relatively routine. Unfortunately, measuring risk is a much more subjective task. The reason will likely become clear if you think about the issues surrounding measuring how risky something is. While it is not an overwhelming task to discuss the risk of an investment in qualitative terms, it is

M.K. Pyles, *Applied Corporate Finance: Questions, Problems and Making Decisions in the Real World*, Springer Texts in Business and Economics,
DOI 10.1007/978-1-4614-9173-6_7,

quite another issue to quantitatively measure that same risk. In other words, how do you put a number on the level of risk of an investment?

To be forthright, it is actually impossible to "calculate" risk. Instead, risk must be proxied for in some way. As you will see, this turns out to be our biggest issue throughout the discussion of risk and return.

7.2 Historical Returns

A natural starting point is learning how to calculate the historical return of an asset. For the sake of simplicity, we will use common stock as our tool for exposition. However, the process applies to virtually any financial asset. Recall from Chap. 6, for any share of stock, cash flows can be earned from two sources: dividend payments and price appreciation. We used those two sources to calculate the value of a share of common stock in Chap. 6, but now we want to look at historical returns instead of current values. To put it another way, we want to say "this is how much money you *have* made on the stock in the past" instead of "here are the future cash flows you can *expect* in the future."

We are going to examine two ways of measuring returns. The first is in dollar amounts, while the other is in percentage form. Both have importance for investors and firms, and the discussion of which is *most* important depends on the context. Generally speaking, if the desire is to examine a specific situation, whether a specific project for a firm or a specific investment for the individual, dollar returns are very useful. They simply allow you to answer the following question: *How many more dollars do I now have as a result of my investment?* Percentage returns have the advantage of being comparable. They allow you to answer the following question: *How many more dollars do I have now, in relation to the amount I spent?* Therefore, whether you spend \$100 or \$1,000,000, you can make the decision of which was the better investment. Making a profit of \$50 on an investment of \$100 is a wonderful return, whereas a \$50 profit on a \$1,000,000 investment is nothing to get excited about.

7.2.1 Dollar Returns

The basic format for calculating a total dollar return is

$$TDR = \underbrace{[(Inc * \#Shares)]}_{\text{Income Component}} + \underbrace{[(P_E - P_B) * \#Shares]}_{\text{Capital Gains Component}}$$

where *Inc* represents the total income received throughout the entire investment period. This can take various forms, most notably either dividends (when investing in equity) or interest payments (when investing in debt). P_E and P_B represent the price of the security at the end of the investment period and the price at the beginning of the investment period, respectively. The period can be of any length, from seconds to decades. Just as we discussed in Chaps. 5 and 6, the two components of any investment are represented by the **income component** and the **capital gains component**. These are the two places one can expect to receive money from an investment. As a note, the income component will be either zero (e.g., for firms that do not pay dividends) or a positive number. Unfortunately, the same cannot be said for the capital gains component, which can be either positive or negative (or zero), as asset prices can either go up or down (or stay the same) during the investment period.

To illustrate with an example, consider the following. Suppose you bought 250 shares of Walmart Stock (ticker WMT) at the open of markets on January 2, 2009. At that time, the price was $55.98 per share. Now, let's say you held the stock for 3 years and sold it at the close of market on December 30, 2011 (December 31, 2011, was a Saturday). At that time, the stock was selling for $59.76. In addition, Walmart paid a dividend throughout the time period. During 2009, the dividend was $.273 per share each quarter. During 2010, it was $.303 per share each quarter. And during 2011, the company paid $.365 per share each quarter. Thus, the dollar return for the investment is

$$\begin{aligned}
&\textbf{Income component} && \Rightarrow [(.273 * 4) + (.303 * 4) + (.365 * 4)] * 250 = \$941 \\
&\textbf{Capital gains component} && \Rightarrow (59.76 - 55.98) * 250 = \$945 \\
&\textbf{Total dollar return} && = \$1{,}886
\end{aligned}$$

7.2.2 Percentage Returns

There are actually several ways of calculating percentage returns from an investment. First, there is a return associated with the income component of the cash flow. For example, with equity, the **dividend yield (*DY*)** is calculated as follows:

$$DY = \frac{D}{P_B}$$

You likely recognize this as an equation we dealt with in both Chaps. 2 and 6. The current use is more similar to the treatment in Chap. 2, as the dividend in the numerator is based upon a dividend payment that has already occurred. Inserting the values for the above example yields

$$\frac{\mathbf{3.764}}{\mathbf{55.98}} = \mathbf{.0672\ or\ 6.72\%}$$

This can be interpreted as "for every dollar you invested, you received 6.72 cents in dividends." This answer accounts for the dividend component of the cash flow stream. As a note, the same basic formula applies for any type of investment. For example, with a bond, the numerator would be the total amount of coupon payments received per bond over the life of the investment, and the denominator would again just be the beginning price of the bond.

The price appreciation portion of the total return is called, unsurprisingly, the **capital gains yield (*CGY*)**. The capital gains yield is calculated as

$$CGY = \frac{P_E - P_B}{P_B}$$

If you recall from Chap. 6, we define the growth rate as a capital gains yield because that is exactly what it was, a measurement of change in firm value over a period of time.

For our example, this turns out to be

$$\mathbf{\frac{59.76 - 55.98}{55.98} = .0675 \text{ or } 6.75\%}$$

and the interpretation is very similar to that for the dividend yield. In this case, for every dollar you invested, you received 6.75 cents in capital gains. So, now that we have calculated both the dividend yield and the capital gains yield, we can arrive at the number we really care about, the **total percentage return (*TPR*)**. As you can probably guess, the total percentage return is simply the sum of the dividend yield and the capital gains yield:

$$DY + CGY = TPR$$

For the example, this results in a total return of 13.47 %. For every dollar invested, we earned a total return of 13.47 cents. There is some good news associated with calculating percentage returns. Often, the *DY* and *CGY* are not of primary concern alone. Rather, the *TPR* is the number of most interest. There is a shortcut that can readily be derived from looking at the equations we have just discussed.

If we know

$$TPR = \frac{D}{P_B} + \frac{P_E - P_B}{P_B}$$

then we can see there is a common denominator. We can therefore combine into a single equation, which goes by the title of **holding period return (*HPR*)**:

$$HPR = \frac{P_E - P_B + D}{P_B}$$

Don't let this confuse you. The *TPR* and the *HPR* are the exact same equations and will give you the exact same answer. To prove it, using the *HPR* on our example yields the following:

$$\frac{59.76 - 55.98 + 3.764}{55.98} = 13.48\%$$

An interesting extension to all of this is in understanding how the dollar and percentage returns co-align. Notice that with the dollar return, it is crucial to account for the number of shares, while this is not the case with the percentage return. But, they ultimately tell us the same thing. We bought 250 shares at $55.98 per share, for a total investment of $13,995. We then calculated a dollar return of $1,886. Thus, at the end of the investment, we have $15,881.

So, we have a beginning and an ending value, only this time for our investment account instead of a single share of stock. Since the dollar return value has already accounted for the dividend payout, the return can be calculated as

$$\frac{15,881 - 13,995}{13,995} = 13.48\%$$

In addition, another way to calculate the percentage return is to simply take the dollar return and divide by the investment amount.

LOOK IT UP: One very popular place to look up historical stock price data is Yahoo! Finance. In fact, that's where those numbers above came from. If you go to their historical prices page for any firm, you will notice they give something called an "adjusted close" price in addition to the traditional close price. What is this? How and why is it calculated? Perhaps most importantly, how could it streamline what we did above?

7.2.3 Geometric Returns

The process in the previous section details how to calculate single returns over a period of any length. However, it is often important to think about a sequence of returns that collectively make up a period. Think of links in a chain. Each link represents a period return, such as months, weeks, or days. If you connect 12 monthly returns together, you have a stream of annual returns. Let's reconsider the Walmart example above as three one-year investments as opposed to a single 3-year investment. In a way, this distinction doesn't matter at all. In another way, it matters a great deal. In such a case, we need beginning and ending values for *each* period. Walmart was selling for $53.45 at the end of 2009. This becomes both the ending of the first time period and the beginning of the second. At the end of 2010, Walmart was selling for $53.93. Putting it all together, we can calculate the annual returns:

$$\boldsymbol{HPR_{09}}=\frac{\mathbf{53.45-55.98+(.273*4)}}{\mathbf{55.98}}=-\mathbf{2.57\%}$$

$$\boldsymbol{HPR_{10}}=\frac{\mathbf{53.93-53.45+(.303*4)}}{\mathbf{53.45}}=\mathbf{3.17\%}$$

$$\boldsymbol{HPR_{11}}=\frac{\mathbf{59.76-53.93+(.365*4)}}{\mathbf{53.93}}=\mathbf{13.52\%}$$

During the 3-year period, there was one poor year, one decent year, and one very good year. Now, let's revisit the question of "how much better off are you as a result of the investment?" We have already answered that, at least in one way. By investing, you would have made a dollar return of $1,886. You started with $13,995 and ended up with $15,881. However, there is another way of thinking about it, and it's based upon the basic time value of money calculations we learned in Chap. 4. If we start with a portfolio of $13,995 and earn a −2.57 % return for 1 year, then we would have a future value at the end of the time period of

$$\begin{aligned}\boldsymbol{FV_1} &= \mathbf{13,995\ (1+(-.0257))}\\ &= \mathbf{\$13,635}\end{aligned}$$

This amount would then be compounded by the return during the second time period:

$$\begin{aligned}\boldsymbol{FV_2} &= \mathbf{13,635\ (1+.0317)}\\ &= \mathbf{\$14,067}\end{aligned}$$

And, likewise for the third and final year:

$$\begin{aligned}\boldsymbol{FV_3} &= \mathbf{14,067\ (1+.1352)}\\ &= \mathbf{\$15,969}\end{aligned}$$

But, wait a second. That is a different number than we got before. So, which is it? At the end of the investment, do we have $15,881 or $15,969?

The answer is that *it depends*. The first value and the basic calculation of a dollar return does not account for **reinvestment**, or more specifically, reinvestment of the income received during the holding period. To obtain the second, larger number you reinvest the dividends received at the end of each year and therefore earn interest on that additional financial position as well. The first process is simply using **arithmetic returns**, while the second uses **geometric returns**.

The basic formula for a geometric cumulative holding period return (*GCR*) is

$$GCR = [(1+HPR_1)*(1+HPR_2)+(1+HPR_3)+\ldots+(1+HPR_T)]-1$$

For our example, this would be

$$\begin{aligned} \boldsymbol{GCR} &= [(\mathbf{1} - .\mathbf{0257}) * (\mathbf{1} + .\mathbf{0317}) * (\mathbf{1} + .\mathbf{1352})] - \mathbf{1} \\ &= \mathbf{14.11\%} \end{aligned}$$

This is again different from the *HPR* of 13.47 % calculated earlier. So, let's again ask the question at hand. Did you earn 13.47 % or 14.11 %?

Again, the assumption underlying geometric returns is that you can reinvest your profits in the same place in which you earned it in the first place. So, in our example, the 14.11 % return assumes that you can reinvest the capital gains returns and dividend returns in Walmart stock at the end of each year.

But, in reality, this may be a faulty assumption. On the capital gains side, the assumption is suitable, as maintaining a position as the price changes effectively allows you to start a new investment period any time you wish. As such, you can continue to gain rolling returns period by period as the stock price appreciates (or depreciates). Thus, for assets that pay no dividends, it makes no difference whether you consider *HPR*s or CGRs.

Dividends create another set of issues, however. You can, in some instances, reinvest the dividends you receive in the form of stock, but not always. Also, consider that this would usually mean investing in fractions of shares. For example, receiving dividends of \$.273 quarterly on each of your 250 shares would mean receiving dividends of \$273, which would equate to 4.84 new shares. An alternative scenario is that your received dividends can be put into some other interest earning account until you decide where to invest them. However, the rate on that investment in the interim would likely differ from the return of Walmart. Also complicating the issue is the fact that dividends are paid quarterly, which means we really need to think about reinvesting four times per year instead of once.

So, let's go back to the questions of which return is "correct." First, did you earn the *HPR* of 13.47 % or the CGR of 14.11 %? The answer depends on whether you can reinvest your dividends at the same return. Assuming you can, the two values can be reconciled with the following:

$$\textbf{Capital gains yield} = \frac{\mathbf{59.76 - 55.98}}{\mathbf{55.98}} = \mathbf{6.75\%}$$

$$\begin{aligned} \textbf{Dividend yield} &= \frac{(.\mathbf{273}*\mathbf{4})(\mathbf{1.0317})(\mathbf{1.1352}) + (.\mathbf{303}*\mathbf{4})(\mathbf{1.1352}) + (.\mathbf{365}*\mathbf{4})}{\mathbf{55.98}} \\ &= \mathbf{7.35\%} \end{aligned}$$

$$\textbf{Total return} = \mathbf{14.10\%}$$

Dividends received during the first year earn the returns for the succeeding 2 years, while the dividend received during the second year earns the return for the final year. The dividends received during the final year are unadjusted, as they are recognized at the end of the holding period. Collectively, the additional interest earned on the dividend payments make up the difference (within a rounding error of margin) between the two percentage returns.

We can also examine the difference between the two dollar returns ($15,881 vs. $15,969) by considering the entire investment of 250 shares:

$$\begin{aligned}
&\textbf{Dividends earned with interest} = \\
&\quad \textbf{First years dividends}: [\mathbf{250} * (\mathbf{.273} * \mathbf{4})] * (\mathbf{1.0317})(\mathbf{1.1352}) = \mathbf{\$320} \\
&\quad \textbf{Second years dividends}: [\mathbf{250} * (\mathbf{.303} * \mathbf{4})] * (\mathbf{1.1352}) = \mathbf{\$344} \\
&\quad \textbf{Third years dividends}: [\mathbf{250} * (\mathbf{.365} * \mathbf{4})] = \mathbf{\$365} \\
&\quad \textbf{Total} = \mathbf{\$1,029} \\
&\textbf{Interest earned on dividend reinvestment} = \\
&\qquad \mathbf{\$1,029} - \mathbf{\$941} = \mathbf{\$88} \leftrightarrow (\mathbf{15,969} - \mathbf{15,881})
\end{aligned}$$

LOOK IT UP: The notion of automatically reinvesting returns is not uncommon. In fact, many firms have enacted dividend reinvestment plans (DRIPS). See if you can find out exactly what these are and how they work.

Considerable attention is paid to calculating average returns, based upon a series of period returns. For example, if you have had an investment portfolio for the past 5 years, you would probably tell people that you earned an *average* of X percent. The number you would brag about would most likely be the arithmetic average return, which is calculated the same way you have been calculating averages for many years. For example, over the 3-year period of 2009–2011, Walmart's arithmetic average return is

$$\begin{aligned}
\boldsymbol{AAR} &= \frac{\mathbf{-2.57+3.17+13.52}}{\mathbf{3}} \\
&= \mathbf{4.71\%}
\end{aligned}$$

Again, however, if returns are reinvested, the geometric average return can be calculated as

$$GAR = [(1 + HPR_1) * (1 + HPR_2) + (1 + HPR_3) + \ldots + (1 + HPR_T)]^{1/T} - 1$$

For our example, this would be

$$\begin{aligned}
\boldsymbol{GAR} &= [(\mathbf{1} - \mathbf{.0257}) * (\mathbf{1} + \mathbf{.0317}) * (\mathbf{1} + \mathbf{.1352})]^{\mathbf{1/3}} - \mathbf{1} \\
&= \mathbf{4.50\%}
\end{aligned}$$

The geometric average is likely the more relevant value, particularly in the case of investments. The arithmetic average assumes that each period's return is independent of other period returns, which is not the case when investing. For example, if an investor loses money one year, they have less money at the beginning of the next year. This, of course affects the percentage return during that subsequent year.

The end result of all this is that calculating returns isn't quite as easy as you may have hoped.

7.3 Historical Risk

Now we turn to the more difficult side of the story and attempt to calculate the risk of an investment. This really involves asking two questions. The first is straightforward to both ask and answer.

Question: *Are my expectations correct?*

Answer: *Almost certainly not!*

We cannot predict the future. We can, and readily do, *guess* about what the future will hold, but short of the development of a reliable crystal ball, any numerical value that you predict for the future return of a firm is almost certainly going to turn out to be false. Thus, we can smoothly slide to the next question.

Question: *How wrong am I likely to be?*

Now, this question isn't as easy to answer. To understand what we want to do, let's move away from the world of finance for a moment. Consider a basketball team or, rather, two specific players on that team. Player A is slow and steady, averages 14 points a game, and is almost always right around that number. Player B also averages 14 points a game, but is anything but slow and steady. He can be a star with 30 points one night, a dud with 2 the next. Which of those players is most risky? The answer is quite obviously Player B, since what you are going to get from day to day is much less of a certainty.

Our goal, therefore, is to put this qualitative notion into quantitative form. How much riskier is Player B than Player A? Or, back into the world of finance, how much riskier is Stock A than B, or vice versa? We have an a priori expectation of each, which is usually their average historical performance, such as an average return of 10 % or an average of 14 points per game. But, as we discussed with the first question, we realize the chance of our expectation being exactly correct is very slim. Therefore, we start thinking about ways to measure how far our expectations are likely to deviate from reality. We draw conclusions of this sort by using **variance (σ^2)**, which is calculated as

$$\sigma_i^2 = \frac{\sum_{t=1}^{T} (r_{i,t} - \overline{r_i})^2}{N - 1}$$

where $\overline{r_i}$ represents the average historical return of asset i and $r_{i,t}$ represents the return of the stock i in time period t. Finally, N represents the number of time

Table 7.1 Historical returns for Stock XYZ

Year	*Return*
1	7.43 %
2	9.25
3	10.45
4	14.26
5	6.38
6	5.14
7	7.03
8	7.98
9	8.25
10	11.39

periods. To see how this works, let's examine historical return data on fictional Firm XYZ, as presented in Table 7.1.

We can calculate the average return to be 8.76 %. Then, we use this to calculate variance as follows:

$$\frac{(\mathbf{7.43-8.76})^2+(\mathbf{9.25-8.76})^2+\ldots+(\mathbf{11.29-8.76})^2}{\mathbf{10-1}}$$
$$=\mathbf{7.18\%^2}$$

Notice that the unit for the answer is percentage squared, which unfortunately is difficult to interpret or use. This leads to the introduction of an alternative measure of risk that is used much more often than variance. The **standard deviation (σ)** of an asset's returns is simply the square root of the variance:

$$\sigma_r = \sqrt{\sigma_r^2}$$

So, in this example,

$$\sqrt{\mathbf{7.18}} = \mathbf{2.68\%}$$

Thus, we now understand how to estimate both the historical return and risk on an investment, which is quite an accomplishment in itself. However, we can use this knowledge to demonstrate a valuable extension in the following section.

7.4 Confidence Intervals

Let's go back to the basketball player dilemma. Suppose you have pulled both players' game data for the past five seasons. In addition to the average of 14 points per game, you have now calculated the standard deviation for each. Player A has a standard deviation of two points, while Player B has a standard deviation of six points. First, this evidence confirms the anecdotal knowledge that Player B is riskier. But, what else does it tell us?

While the scope of this text precludes extensive discussion of the technical aspects of statistics, a brief discussion of a few notions is warranted here. The average return and the standard deviation represent what is formally known as the first two moments of any statistical distribution. A statistical distribution is just a fancy way of describing the stream of historical data from any financial asset. For us, this is simply referring to the return data that we have for any security, such as those reported in Table 7.1.

The first moment is the central moment around which everything else revolves. The second moment is a measure of the distribution around this central moment. Perhaps the most popular application of this is found in the **standard normal distribution**, often referred to as the "bell curve." Figure 7.1 illustrates this well-known figure.

This is useful because of an application known as **confidence intervals**. Confidence intervals are much as the name entails. Specifically, a confidence interval provides an estimated range that a certain percentage of observations in the distribution will fall. There are many options for this, but perhaps the most popular is the 95 % confidence interval. It is calculated as

$$95\%\ \mathrm{CI} \cong \overline{r} \pm 2\sigma$$

So, given the known average of 14 points per game, Player A would have a 95 % CI of 10–18. This indicates, as coach, you would expect him to score between 10 and 18 points in 95 % of your games. In other words, there is only a 2.5 % chance he will score less than 10 points and only a 2.5 % chance he will score more than 18 points. Using the same logic for Player B, you could expect anywhere from 2 to 26 points. Anywhere in that range could be considered "normal."

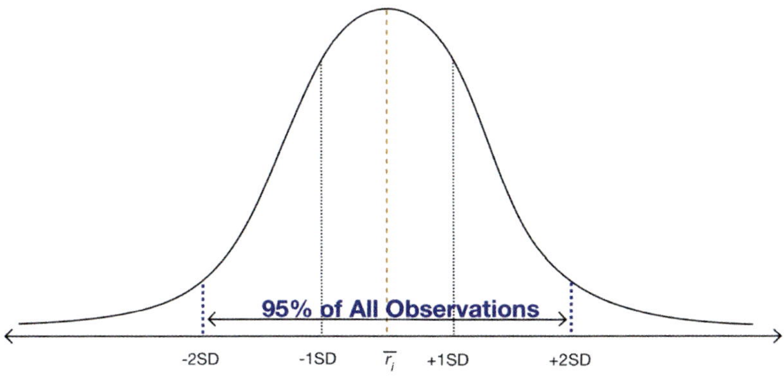

Fig. 7.1 Standard normal distribution

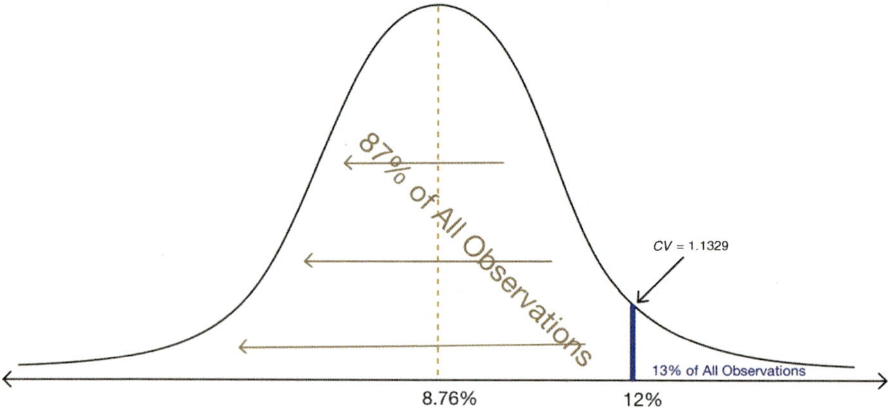

Fig. 7.2 Standard normal distribution example

The same thing is true in relation to financial assets. Given an average and standard deviation, one can tell within a range what the next return will be, to a degree of certainty. That degree is not restricted to 95 %, however. It can be any degree of certainly that you wish. In fact, even the 95 % CI as described above is not exactly accurate. If you notice the equation, there is an approximately equal sign. A two standard deviation range from the mean actually creates a 95.45 % confidence interval.

Perhaps a more direct application of this idea is to calculate the probability of being greater than or less than some specific number. For example, if we revisit the example from the previous section of Stock XYZ. We calculated the average return to be 8.76 % and the standard deviation to be 2.86 %. Given this, suppose we want to ask the question of what is the likelihood of having a return more than 12 % next year? We can do that by solving for the critical value (*CV*) as follows:

$$\begin{aligned} \bar{r}+(CV*\sigma) &= 12\% \\ 8.76+(CV*2.86) &= 12 \\ CV &= 1.1329 \end{aligned}$$

The next step is to convert this critical value to a probability, based upon a normal distribution. This can be done in a variety of ways, from probability tables to more modern techniques such as Excel. In whatever manner, the probability associated with the critical value of 1.1329 is approximately 87.14 %. Thus, there is a 12.86 % chance the return will exceed 12 %. Figure 7.2 visually describes this process.

Alternatively, we may want to examine the bottom of the range. For example, what is the probability of the return being less than 5 %?

$$\begin{aligned} \bar{r} - (CV * \sigma) &= 5\% \\ 8.76 - (CV * 2.86) &= 5 \\ CV &= 1.3147 \end{aligned}$$

If we carry this through, we find a 9.43 % chance the next return will be less than 5 %.

7.5 Relationship Between Risk and Return

Calculating historical risk and historical returns is the first step in finding our way to one of the fundamental truths in the world of finance. Here it is:

An investment with a higher level of risk will have a higher level of expected return.

The most important word in this sentence is *expected*. This means that a higher risk does not necessarily guarantee you will also get a higher *realized* return. Boy, do I wish it did. Of course, if it did, then there would be no use in writing this book. We would all just take insanely crazy risks and be rewarded abundantly. Unfortunately, the world doesn't work in this manner because there is, in fact, risk. An investment in risky assets will likely generate many periods of negative returns, some extremely so. However, there will also be many periods of extremely positive returns, and we expect the positive should override the negative.

So, once we've gained an understanding that risk comes with an expectation of reward, we need to address how to either obtain or avoid risk. There are a few absolutes that we can use to start this process:

1. *Equity is riskier than debt.*

This is particularly true for common stock in relation to coupon bonds. Perhaps the predominant reason for this is the lack of cash flow certainty associated with stocks relative to bonds. If you recall our discussion from previous chapters, the periodic cash flows from bonds (coupons) are constant, as is the payoff at expiration (Face). Neither of these things is true for the equivalent stock cash flow (dividends and stock prices). Uncertain payoffs equal more risk.

2. *Size matters.*

This is largely due to the differing levels of information about and resources available to the firms. Large firms are followed constantly by hoards of financial press and millions of investors. Thus, any informational deficiency that may result in an inefficient stock price will likely be ferreted out by these groups of people before it becomes conducive to a profitable trading strategy. Also, large firms are more immune to both peaks and values that accompany most business cycles. Thus, very similar to the argument made just above, large firms normally have the benefit of being able to estimate their future cash flows more accurately than smaller firms. Size, for equities in particular, is typically measured by market capitalization, defined as price per share multiplied by number of shares outstanding.

Table 7.2 Summary of asset types

Asset Class	Asset Type	
Small Stocks	Equity	
Medium Stocks	Equity	Expected
Large Stocks	Equity	Risk Return
Corporate Bonds	Debt	
Long-term Government Bonds	Debt	
Short-term Government Bonds	Debt	

In addition, from a percentage return perspective, there is a mechanical reason that small equities are more risky. Smaller firms typically have smaller stock prices. Thus, an equivalent numerical change results in a more dramatic percentage change. Consider Large Firm A selling for $50 and Small Firm B selling for $20. A $1 change in price would result in a 2 % change for Firm A, but a 5 % for Firm B. Given that most risk measurement is calculated based upon percentage returns, this also has the effect of confirming that size matters.

3. *Securities issued by the government are safer than securities issued by corporations.*

Naturally, this only applies to debt securities and is predominantly due to the lack of default risk associated with government securities. Governments are more immune to default than corporations, even high-quality corporations.

LOOK IT UP: You may recall all the hubbub about the government's debt credit rating being downgraded in 2011. See what details you can find about that situation. More importantly, why was this such a crucial decision?

4. *Time matters.*

Long-term securities, regardless of issuer, are riskier than short-term (all else equal) securities due to the fact that many things, both economically and financially, are more likely to change significantly in the long run than in the short run.

If we put all of this together, we can make a basic list of asset classes and rank them in terms of risk. Table 7.2 displays a summary.

Naturally, this is far from an exhaustive list of all assets that can be traded, but the intent is to facilitate an understanding of how risk gets rewarded. Luckily, we can be reassured in the fundamental truth by examining historical returns. In order to drive home the risk/reward relationship, let's compare and contrast two specific asset classes. A prime example of large stocks would be the S&P 500 stock index. An index is a basket of assets that are chosen to be representative of the entire marketplace. Thus, inclusion into the index requires a large market presence. So, while certainly not as risky as the smaller asset classes, they do represent the overall risk of the equity markets during a particular period of time.

Table 7.3 T-bills versus S&P 500

Year	Risk-free (3-month T-bill	S&P 500
1990	7.50 %	−3.10 %
1991	5.38	30.47
1992	3.43	7.62
1993	3.00	10.08
1994	4.25	1.32
1995	5.49	37.58
1996	5.01	22.96
1997	5.06	33.36
1998	4.78	28.58
1999	4.64	21.04
2000	5.82	−9.10
2001	3.40	−11.89
2002	1.61	−22.10
2003	1.01	28.68
2004	1.37	10.88
2005	3.15	4.91
2006	4.73	15.79
2007	4.36	5.49
2008	1.37	−37.00
2009	0.15	26.46
2010	0.14	15.06
2011	0.05	2.11
Average	3.44	9.96
Standard deviation	2.10	18.88

Source: T-bills: Board of Governors of the Federal Reserve System, www.federalreserve.gov. S&P 500: Standard and Poor's, www.standardandpoors.com

On the other hand, assets in the last category listed above (short-term government bonds) is also known as treasury bills, which were discussed in Chap. 5. Since these securities are essentially default-free, have short lives (less than 6 months), and known cash flows, they are as safe as any public financial asset. As such, the rate of return on treasury bills (or T-bills, for short) is often referred as a "risk-free" rate of return. Table 7.3 displays the annual returns for the S&P 500 market index and treasury bills from 1990 through 2011, along with averages and standard deviations of those returns.

The numbers appear consistent with expectation. The average market return is almost three times that of the risk-free rate of return. This is counterbalanced by a standard deviation that is nine times higher than the risk-free rate. So, in short, taking risk has been rewarded. Upon closer examination, notice the risk-free rate is never negative. This is consistent with expectation, since pure discount securities are priced in such a manner to ensure the purchase price is less than the face value.

Contrarily, the market had a negative return in nearly 20 % of the years, including very poor years in 2002 and 2008. Thus, had you remained invested throughout the time period, the increased risk would have paid off, but there would

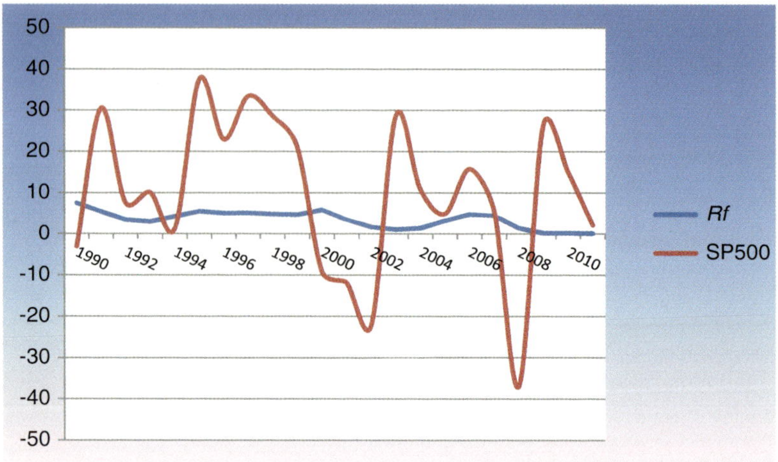

Fig. 7.3 S&P 500 versus T-bills

definitely have been some dark periods. Figure 7.3 compares the returns over the sample period. Notice the extreme highs and lows of the market in relation to the risk-free asset. Imagine the lines drawn are roller coasters. Riding the risk-free roller coaster is safe, if a bit boring, kind of like riding the roller coaster in kiddie land. The market, on the other hand, is the real deal, complete with steep climbs, dangerous drop-offs, and stomach-lurching changes in direction.

Finally, to see how this is manifest in actual earnings, Fig. 7.4 displays the results of a $100 invested into each asset type at the beginning of 1990. The theory of increasing returns from increasing risk is confirmed. Notice the trend line with the risk-free asset is much as would be expected, a slow and relatively steady increase. Over the 22 years, you more than double your money with essentially no risk of losing any. However, the market return would have allowed you to turn your $100 investment into $569, but in a far-from-steady manner. Notice the very large drops in value in 2002 and 2008. That, my friends, is risk.

Before moving on, there are a couple other items of note. First, if the risk-free asset is not rewarding risk, then what is it rewarding exactly? Put simply, it is rewarding the investor simply for patience—for saving instead of spending. However, over time things cost more, which is a phenomenon that we generally categorize as **inflation**. Thus, should an investor decide to invest rather than instantly spend, they run the risk of a price increase in the assets to be purchased, which would eat away significantly from their investment returns. For example, suppose you experience a rate of return of 5 % on a financial asset and the rate of inflation turns out to be 1.3 % for that period. In reality, you have only gained 3.7 % increase in purchasing power (the amount of stuff you can buy). Therefore, while there is a reward associated with both risk-free and risky assets, one must be careful to examine an inflation-adjusted measure.

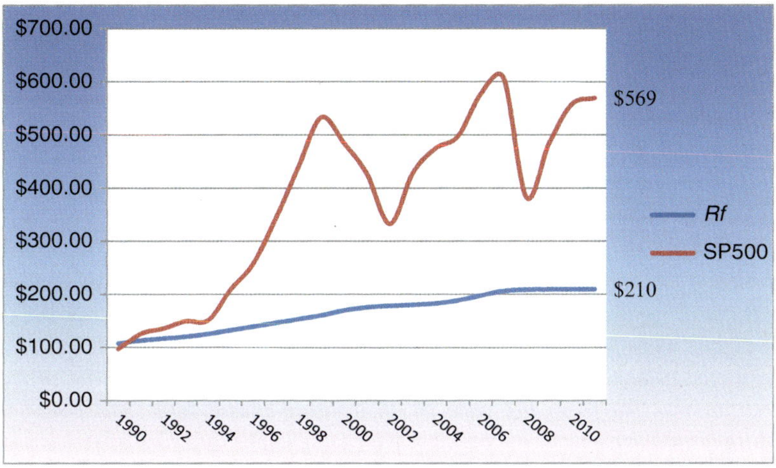

Fig. 7.4 Investment comparison: S&P 500 versus T-bill

> LOOK IT UP: This brings up an interesting extension to the example comparing the S&P 500 to the risk-free asset. Do some digging on exactly what is used to calculate inflation. Then find the annual rates of inflation and compare to the returns on the two asset classes. How much more in purchasing power would you have had with each, after factoring out inflation?

Finally, we need to briefly discuss the concept of a **risk premium**. We already know two things. The first is that we expect to be compensated for risk, while the second is that there exists an asset that is essentially risk-free. Thus, common reason dictates that a return on any risky asset equal to or less than the return on the risk-free rate should be interpreted as unacceptable by the investor. Otherwise, the investor is intrinsically saying they are willing to accept risk without compensation, which doesn't make sense to a rational investor. To correct for this, a number we are often concerned about instead of the raw return is the risk premium (RP), which is simply the difference between the raw return of asset i (r_i) and the risk-free return (r_f), or

$$RP = r_i - r_f$$

For example, using the average returns over the period of 1990–2011, the risk premium on the S&P500 is

$$\mathbf{9.96 - 3.44 = 6.52\%}$$

Thus, on average, investing in the risky market returns about 6.5 % more than investing in a risk-free debt instrument.

IN THE REAL WORLD

November 14, 2011, brought a rainy Monday evening to Clearwater, FL, but Eli Eldridge was cheering himself up by doing the two things he enjoyed most: drinking—a nicely aged double barreled bourbon on the rocks—and counting his money. As he took a gulp of the warm amber liquid, he rapidly pounded on his ancient counting machine. His eyesight was not what it used to be, so the thumb-sized buttons were welcomed. His movements were so familiar as to be automatic, and to a casual observer, it would appear he had little interest in the process.

But that was far from the case. With a much closer look, you could see the sparkling concentration in his beady little eyes and the thin line of sweat along his generous forehead. No, this was not just a casual time-wasting activity for Eli; it was his pride and joy. After several minutes of calculating, he stopped, pulled the paper trail from the calculator, and sat back in his chair.

"Ha," he proclaimed to the four walls surrounding him in his comfortable study. "That's my baby." His words reverberated around the oak panels and shelves filled with books. Eli had just finished calculating his portfolio returns. He did nothing in small measures, and investing was no exception. His motto was "nothing ventured, nothing to brag about."

Now that he had figured out the grand total, he turned his attention to specific securities. Eldridge struggled to get his relatively wide girth from his sitting position and was proud when he accomplished the task. He wobbled to a filing cabinet, drink in hand, and fumbled through a row of manila folders until he found the one he was looking for. Bringing it back to his desk, he tossed it on the surface before plopping himself into the leather chair. Lucky, he thought. The seat hadn't even had time to get cold.

He opened the folder so that the handwritten name along the top was clearly visible. In large block letters, Eli himself had printed "HACK BACK." The folder contained several sheets of paper. The first dozen or so were publicly available financial statements Eli had examined prior to investing. Behind those sheets was the trade confirmation from his online brokerage account for his purchase of 2,000 shares of common stock at a price of $48.14 on April 4, 2008.

The firm had gone public on December 14, 2007, for $40 a share. Eli had known the kids since the company was private and growing. He was pretty sure the company was going to do well due to the young owners' level heads and their unique products. However, he wanted to wait until the initial price surge had ebbed before buying.

Eldridge shifted to his computer, narrowly avoiding a pulled muscle while reaching over his glass. It took longer than it should, but he eventually pulled up Hack Back's most recent price quote. At close today, each share had been selling for $66.17. He glanced at the chart.

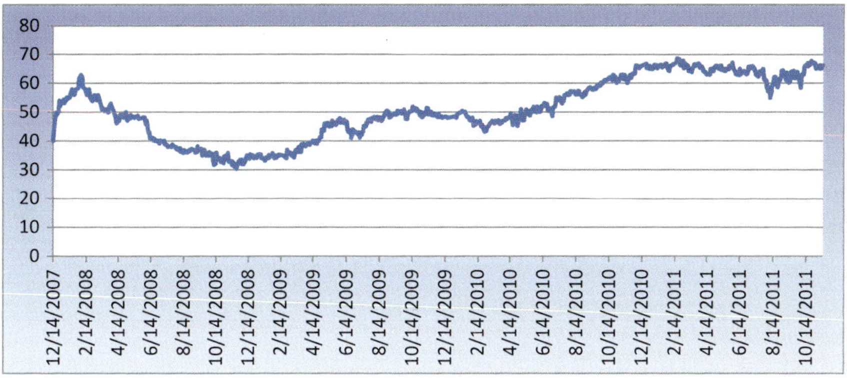

In Eli's view, this was the pattern of a fairly successful company over the time period. The price had increased from the IPO value of $40 to the low $60s in the few months following issuance. Following this initial rise, the company was like many others and had been caught up in the negative market conditions throughout 2008. The overall market had lost over 35 % during the year, and Hack Back had lost a bit less than 35 %. They had rebounded admirably, however. At market close on December 31, 2008, the stock had been selling for $35.48. One year later, the company had rebounded to nearly $48 per share. And, at the end of 2010, the stock price was almost $65, and it had maintained roughly that level since. The highest price thus far was on February 17, 2011, at $68.91.

Eli turned away from the computer screen and shuffled through some more papers in the folder. The last few sheets contained information on the dividend payments he had received for the last year and a half. He was very pleased that Tyler and Lilly had taken his suggestion and smugly reflected that he was partially responsible for the increase in stock price over the past year. Why, some may go so far as to say that he had insider information, which was frowned upon. Regardless, he wasn't overly worried about it. It's not like he **knew** ***they were going to issue a dividend.***

Eli licked the end of his pencil and then spit out the acidic taste of lead, idly wondering why he had just done that.

"Hhhmm," he said to himself, his brow furrowing in concentration. "I've gotten dividends of $.20 twice, $.21 four times, and $.22 three times." He looked up at his wall calendar, checking the date.

"Should be getting another check pretty soon, too," he said. Tucking his chin again, he scribbled his beginning and ending prices as well.

The way he saw it, he had made a total dollar return of

$$[((.20*2)+(.21*4)+(.22*3))*2{,}000] + [(66.17 - 48.04)*2{,}000] = \$40{,}060$$

which translated to a percentage return of

$$\frac{66.17 - 48.04 + 1.90}{48.04} = 41.69\%$$

"Well, how about them apples?" he muttered. "That works out to about 10 % a year, including the beast of a year that was oh-eight. I do believe I deserve a pat on the back for that pick."

He made the attempt to do so, but flexibility was not his strong suit, so he settled for a rewarding pat on the top of his shoulder.

Eli stood, stretched, and ambled across the room to partake in his third favorite activity, listening to classic country music. He fell deep into the comforting confines of his easy chair in the corner and then used his stereo remote to turn on the soothing sounds of Hank Williams, Sr.

"Oh, Hank," Eli mumbled, his eyes at half-mast, "don't you go crying in that beer."

ALTERNATE ENDINGS

1. ***Suppose that Eli had also bought 10 of Hack Back's bonds. He bought them on September 17, 2008. Remember the bonds pay a semiannual coupon based upon a coupon rate of 8.62 %. Assume that when he bought the bonds, they were selling at a YTM of 8.89 %. Also assume that on November 14, 2011, the YTM was 9.27 %. What is Eli's dollar return on the bond investment? What is his percentage return? Review the bond information in Chap. 5 if necessary.***
2. ***The calculations assume that Eli receives the dividend check and keeps it and also does not use the proceeds to buy additional shares. Suppose that Eli has an automatic reinvestment plan, whereas Eli's monthly returns were immediately reinvested in Hack Back's stock. As such, the geometric return is the important figure. If this is the case, how much money did Eli make on the investment? What is the geometric cumulative return on the investment? The complete daily returns are included in the appendix.***
3. ***Suppose that Eli had bought the stocks immediately at issuance, thus paying the $40 per share. However, during the downturn of 2008, he sold the entire position at market close on September 4. He then rebought the 2,000 shares on July 12, 2009. How would this change his return? Consider both dollar and percentage. Consider both holding period returns and geometric returns.***

7.6 Expected Returns

While the past is certainly interesting and provides meaningful information, what we really care about is our expectations for what the investment will do in the future. It is exceedingly simple to choose to invest in assets that made money last year. It is exceedingly difficult to choose assets that will make money *next* year. It is a tough chore to predict the future in any capacity, particularly with financial markets and securities whose values are derived largely from investor demand. In fact, there is no way we can predict anything about future returns or risks for

Table 7.4 Expected returns example

Year	GDP growth rate	Stock AAA return	Type
1	3.39	10.07	Normal
2	2.85	7.41	Normal
3	4.07	14.97	Expansion
4	2.51	6.07	Normal
5	3.74	6.16	Normal
6	4.46	8.76	Expansion
7	4.36	7.26	Expansion
8	4.83	17.08	Expansion
9	4.14	16.57	Expansion
10	1.08	−2.87	Contraction
11	1.81	4.97	Contraction
12	2.54	12.07	Normal
13	3.47	8.73	Normal
14	3.07	9.71	Normal
15	2.66	6.00	Normal
16	1.91	11.11	Contraction
17	−0.34	2.97	Contraction
18	−3.49	5.50	Contraction
19	3.03	5.91	Normal
20	1.50	−.96	Contraction

certain. Rather, we simply have to do our best to compute estimates that have a low probability of deviating drastically from reality.

So, we are essentially giving our best guesses of what is going to happen. However, instead of calling it a "guess," we call it an "expectation." Thus, we are concerned with **expected returns**, which require two components:

1. A historical basis
2. An expectation of the future

Of these, the first is perhaps more time consuming, but considerably less difficult to accurately measure. In fact, we have spent the first half of this chapter learning how to calculate historical returns. The second component is the wild card, as it depends upon individual's opinion of what the future financial world will look like. This is no easy matter, as you can imagine, as it requires consideration of both economic conditions (e.g., GDP, inflation, employment, consumer confidence) and financial conditions (e.g., interest rates, market returns). And this doesn't include other exogenous influences such as government intervention or other newsworthy events (political elections, wars, etc.) that can influence returns.

The typical theory of "the past will repeat itself" is put into play here. Any calculation of expected returns begins with calculating historical returns. Let's use a slightly larger example to illustrate the process from beginning to end. Consider fictional firm AAA, for which we have calculated annual returns for the past 20 years. In addition, suppose we have decided that we are going to use GDP growth rates as our measure to categorize the historical time periods into types.

Table 7.5 Summary returns in states of the economy

State	*Average return in state*	*Probability of state*
Expansion	12.93 %	30 %
Normal	8.01	50
Contraction	3.45	20

There is no definitive reason to use this measure over other options. The choice of categorization criteria is to the discretion of the individual or firm. Table 7.4 presents these fictional data.

For simplicity, we will assume there are only three options for categorizing market conditions: (1) expansion, (2) contraction, and (3) normal. In order to classify historical periods according to these terms, we first must define what we mean by that term. This is a two-step process. The first is identifying the categorizing variable (GDP growth in this example) and then segmenting the variable into ranges. For the sake of this example, let's assume that a growth rate in excess of 4 % would represent an expansionary period. A growth rate less than 2 % would represent a period of contraction. Anything in between would be, simply put, a normal period. Using these criteria, years 3, 6, 7, 8, and 9 are expansionary periods, and years 10, 11, 16, 17, 18, and 20 are contractionary periods.

From this, we can estimate the historical returns in each of the three types of economies. This is a relatively straightforward process that is accomplished by taking the historical average of the subperiods. The average return during good periods is almost 13 % but less than 4 % in poor periods. The average return during normal market conditions is right around 8 %. We can now turn to the second ingredient in finding the expected return, our expectation of the probability the state will occur next year. These should be based upon, at minimum, educated guesses, and there are more elaborate modeling techniques that can be employed. However, for the lack of these at the moment, we will simply argue that there is a 30 % chance of an expansionary economy next year. That is counterbalanced by a 20 % chance of a contraction. This leaves the remaining 50 % chance of a normal economy (Table 7.5).[1]

Notice the sum of the probabilities must equal one, reflective of the fact that these are, by assumption, the only three possibilities. Finally, once this is settled, we can get to the equation for calculating expected returns:

$$E[r_i] = \sum_{s=1}^{N} r_{i,s} P_s$$

where s represents all different possible states of economy. Thus, $r_{i,s}$ is the return of security i in state s and P_s is the probability of state s occurring. Notice that the only

[1] These figures in no way represent the opinions of the author or any affiliates. The author is in no way responsible for monetary losses as a result of investments based upon these values. Any monetary gain as a result of these values should be immediately remitted to the author's checking account.☺

Table 7.6 Mike Morgan's portfolio

Security (i)	*\$ Amount invested*	*Portfolio weight (w_i)*	*Security return ($E[r_i]$)*	*Security standard deviation (σ_i)*
A	\$9,000	.05	15.5 %	18.25 %
B	27,000	.15	8.74	11.58
C	45,000	.25	6.25	9.63
D	72,000	.40	5.19	10.25
E	27,000	.15	9.67	9.58

real difference between this equation and the traditional average historical return is that the values have proportional weights rather than equal. The influence of the state-specific return is directly proportional to the probability associated with it. For Firm AAA, the expected return is

$$E[r_{AAA}] = \underbrace{(.30 * 12.93)}_{\textbf{Part A}} + \underbrace{(.50 * 8.01)}_{\textbf{Part B}} + \underbrace{(.20 * 3.45)}_{\textbf{Part C}} = 8.57\%$$

Thus, our best expectation for Firm AAA's return next year is 8.57 %. Part A represents the portion of the expected return attributable to the possibility that the economy will be in an expansion next year. Parts B and C of the equation, likewise, are the portions attributable to the possibility that the economy will be in a normal or contraction economy, respectively.

7.7 Portfolios

Now that we know how to calculate both historical and future values for an individual security, we will move on to the logical next step: looking at more than one security at a time. Few individuals or companies invest in only one thing at a time, whether it is financial assets or any other use of funds. Rather, both entities are likely to invest in several different things simultaneously. There are many reasons to do so, but we will save discussion of the motivation for a latter section. Here, instead, we are going to assume the motivation is established, so we can concentrate on the resulting calculations.

The name for any investment that includes more than a single security is a **portfolio**. Thus, the goal in this section is to learn how to calculate **portfolio returns** and **portfolio risk**. Strictly speaking, it only takes any two securities to make a portfolio, although most portfolios include many more. We must introduce one new variable before beginning with the calculations. **Portfolio weights (w_i)** represent the percentage of your portfolio comprised of asset i. For example, if you have a total investment of \$50,000 and \$10,000 of that is invested in Stock ZZZ, the weight of ZZZ (w_{ZZZ}) is .20 or 20 %. Therefore, let's consider Mike Morgan, a retired circus clown, who currently has the portfolio in Table 7.6.

7.7.1 Portfolio Expected Returns

The equation for portfolio expected returns looks very much like the expected return on an individual security. The variables change, but it is still a weighted average formula:

$$E[r_p] = \sum_{i=1}^{N} E[r_i] * w_i$$

Plugging in the numbers for Mike, we find that he has a portfolio expected return of

$$\boldsymbol{E[r_p] = (.05 * 15.5) + (.15 * 8.74) + (.25 * 6.25) + (.40 * 5.19) + (.15 * 9.67)}$$
$$\boldsymbol{= 7.18\%}$$

Be careful not to get overly confident with the brevity of this section. Sure, the final equation is relatively painless and something that we have seen before. However, remember that each of the variables in the equation has to be calculated prior to implementing the formula. In other words, even though the final equation to calculate your expected return is relatively brief, creating Table 7.6 takes a considerable amount of time and effort.

7.7.2 Portfolio Risk

This is where it is possible to hit a snag in the process of calculating risks and returns. Calculating the standard deviation of a portfolio is not as straightforward as you would perhaps like it to be. The equation you would logically expect to see is the following:

$$E[\sigma_p] = w_i\sigma_i$$

However, *this is not correct*. To understand why, let's back up a bit. Anyone who has spent even a small amount of time watching, listening to, or learning about investments is likely aware of the mantra "diversify, diversify, diversify." **Diversification** can be defined as spreading your monetary investments across several securities in such a way to reduce the overall risk of monetary loss. Diversification works because of a statistical calculation known as **correlation**. Correlation refers to the co-movement between prices (and subsequently returns) of financial assets.

Correlation is measured with the **correlation coefficient** (ρ), a variable that can be any value from +1 to −1. A +1 correlation coefficient indicates *perfect positive correlation*, meaning the returns of the two assets move together at the same pace and in the same direction. In other words, if the price of Stock A increases by 1 %, the price of Stock B increases by 1 % as well. Contrarily, a −1 correlation coefficient indicates *perfect negative correlation*. The antithesis of a perfectly positive correlation, this indicates the two securities move at the same magnitude, but in opposite directions. So, if the price of Stock A increases by 1 %, the price of Stock B would *decrease* by exactly 1 %. The third, and far more likely, scenario is that the coefficient will fall somewhere between −1 and +1, which creates the beauty of diversification. Notice that this includes a coefficient of 0, which would indicate that the returns of the two securities have no relation whatsoever to each other. This is a situation that rarely occurs.

Correlation between assets A and B is calculated by the following:

$$\rho_{A,B} = \frac{cov(A,B)}{\sigma_A \sigma_B}$$

where *cov(A,B)* is the **covariance** between assets A and B. There is little difference in the fundamental ideas of covariance and correlation. Perhaps the easiest way to view the difference is to think of covariance as a more raw measurement of co-movement than correlation. Covariance measures how much the deviations of two variables match. Correlation extends this notion in that it is the covariance of standardized variables. Variables are standardized once they are made comparable by subtracting the mean and dividing by the standard deviation.

Covariance is calculated by the following:

$$cov(A,B) = \frac{\sum_{t=1}^{T} (r_{A,t} - \overline{r_A})(r_{B,t} - \overline{r_B})}{N-1}$$

where $r_{A,t}$ is the return of Asset *A* in historical time *t* and $r_{B,t}$ is the same for Asset B. Consider the following example for illustration purposes:

Year	*Stock A (%)*	*Stock B (%)*
1	11.45	7.34
2	6.34	2.02
3	14.23	5.11

The average return for Firm A is 10.67 %, and the average return for the Asset B is 4.82 %. Given this, we can calculate the standard deviations as 4.00 % and 2.67 %, respectively. Covariance would be calculated as follows:

$$\begin{aligned} \boldsymbol{cov(X,m)} &= \frac{(\mathbf{.78*2.52})+(\mathbf{-4.33*-2.80})+(\mathbf{3.56*.29})}{\mathbf{2}} \\ &= \mathbf{7.56\%} \end{aligned}$$

Using this, correlation between assets A and B is

Table 7.7 John Morgan's portfolio

Security (i)	*Portfolio weight (w_i)*	*Security standard deviation (σ_r)*
A	.60	4.00 %
B	.40	2.67

$$\rho_{\mathbf{ABC},m} = \frac{\mathbf{7.56}}{(\mathbf{4.00*2.67})} = \mathbf{.71}$$

As long as any two securities are anything other than perfectly positively or perfectly negatively correlated (and both cases are exceedingly rare), adding both to your portfolio will diversify your holdings. Let's take a little break from Mike's portfolio and consider his brother John. John is a simpleton who can only think about a couple of investments at a time, so he invests in the aforementioned assets A and B. Thus, he has the portfolio in Table 7.7.

The formula for the standard deviation of a two-asset portfolio is as follows:

$$\sigma_p = \sqrt{\underbrace{w_x^2\sigma_x^2}_{\text{Part A}} + \underbrace{w_y^2\sigma_y^2}_{\text{Part B}} + \underbrace{2w_x w_y \sigma_x \sigma_y \rho_{x,y}}_{\text{Part C}}}$$

where Part A can be roughly defined as the risk, within the portfolio, of Stock X alone; Part B, likewise, can be roughly defined as the risk of Stock Y alone; and Part C, on the other hand, is the risk of Stock X and Stock Y in relation to each other. Thus, the sum of those parts will give us the total risk of the portfolio. Then, the standard deviation of John's portfolio is

$$\sigma_p = \sqrt{\mathbf{.60^2*4.00^2+.40^2*2.67^2+2*.60*.40*4.00*2.67*.71}} = \mathbf{3.24\%}$$

Now, suppose for a moment that you invested in these assets sequentially instead of simultaneously. In such a case, we would ignore the correlation component. If we assume the input variables are unchanged, this would result in a weighted average standard deviation of 3.47 %. Therefore, the act of investing in both assets simultaneously actually has the effect of one's risk eating away at the risk of the other.

The problem with portfolio risk is that it gets really complicated in a hurry if you start to consider more than two securities. In fact, the general formula for portfolio standard deviation is

$$\sigma_p = \sqrt{\underbrace{\sum_{i=1}^{N} w_i^2\sigma_i^2}_{\textbf{\textit{Part A}}} + \underbrace{\sum_{i=1}^{N}\sum_{i\neq j}^{N} w_i w_j \sigma_i \sigma_j \rho_{i,j}}_{\textbf{\textit{Part B}}}}$$

where Part A represents the weight of each asset in the portfolio multiplied by the variance of each asset (so, for each asset in the portfolio, you would have a representative product) and Part B is the tricky part because correlation potentially exists between each pair of assets. If there are three assets, this means there are three correlations (AB, AC, BC), and each must be included in the equation. If there are ten assets, you would have 45 combinations of assets, which means Part B would be repeated 45 times. It goes without saying that you would get old very quickly. To illustrate, recall Mike Morgan's more complicated portfolio. To calculate the standard deviation of this portfolio, we first must obtain correlations between each pair of assets. Let's assume these are as follows:

Pair	Correlation coefficient
A,B	.4908
A,C	.5480
A,D	.6023
A,E	.5012
B,C	.3338
B,D	.7653
B,E	.3674
C,D	.7153
C,E	.6697
D,E	.5759

Note that actual calculation of these correlation coefficients would require the use of historical data and quite a bit of work. A nearby TECH HELP box takes you through the process in Excel, which is a far preferable method of doing complicated portfolio standard deviation problems. For Mike's portfolio, the standard deviation would be calculated to be 5.99 %. Brace yourself and accept the challenge of proving that to yourself.

TECH HELP 7.1 Portfolio Standard Deviation
Excel is a wonderful tool for viewing and analyzing financial data. Consider the example of two fictitious firms, Alpha and Omega, who have 5 years of historical returns, as shown in the screenshots below. In addition, assume that a portfolio is made up of 40 % Alpha and 60 % Omega. Given this information, the standard deviation of such a portfolio can be calculated in two ways. First, we can replicate the process above by using the equation. Or, alternatively, we can calculate returns for the portfolio during each period based upon chosen weights. As the screenshots indicate, you will get the same answer either way.

(continued)

TECH HELP 7.1 Portfolio Standard Deviation (continued)

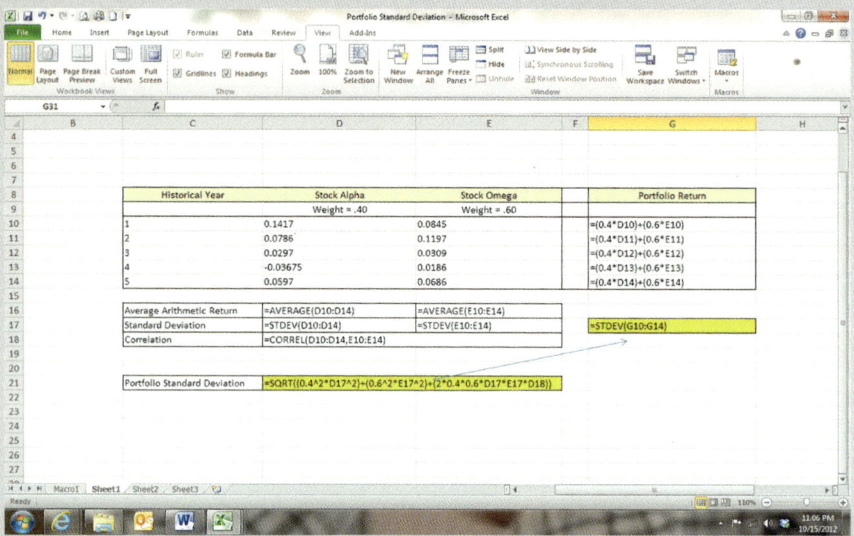

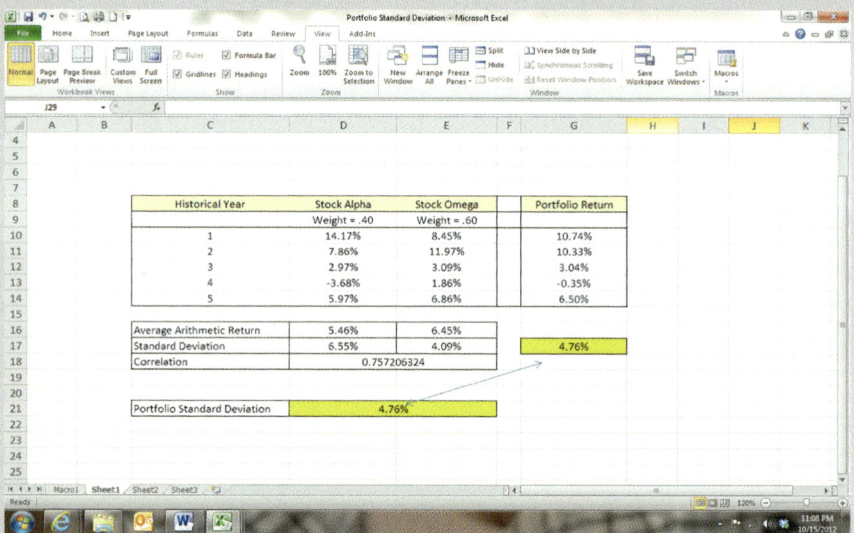

As a note, there is also an alternate way of doing this, by using matrix multiplication. This process is technically more complex but can accommodate a larger number of assets in an expedited manner.

7.8 Quantifying the Relationship Between Risk and Return

We're going to shift gears a bit in switching from purely mathematical exercises designed to quantitatively identify the relationship between risk and return to a more theoretical process. Throughout this section, we will aim to accomplish three basic goals:

1. Identify the risk that is most crucial in predicting the return on an investment.
2. Once defined, find a way to calculate this risk.
3. Identify an equation that will relate this risk to the return on the investment.

The ordering of these goals is important in understanding the foundations of the risk/return relationship. It bears mention again: *risk drives return*, not the other way. Thus, it is critical that we identify the appropriate level of risk as a first step in predicting returns. Historical standard deviation measures the total risk from a post hoc standpoint. However, when attempting to predict returns, total risk is usually not what matters most since a large part of historical risk is likely already factored into the price.

7.8.1 Systematic and Unsystematic Risk

In our never-ending desire to determine successful investment opportunities, we would ideally like to be able to perfectly predict the future. Unfortunately, that will never happen. Thus, the next best thing is to realize what we can and cannot predict with any measure of consistency and accuracy. We'll start with this:

$$\textit{Actual return} = \textit{expected return} + \textit{unexpected return}$$

That's a pretty simple statement, but it sums up an important notion. There is a part of return that we can reasonably predict, and in fact, we have already learned how to do this. We have examined how to calculate the expected return of a stock in depth, and it is largely based upon historical patterns. Expected return is driven by expected risk, and expected risk, in turn, comes from historical patterns. However, we are now acknowledging the other piece of the actual, or realized, return. The *unexpected* return can be either positive or negative, depending on whether the expected return overstates or understates the actual return. Unexpected returns must be driven by unexpected risk. So, what is this mystery variable?

The answer is derived from two potential sources. If there is a degree of risk that cannot be calculated based upon known historical risk factors, it must come from either **systematic** or **unsystematic risk**. Before we get into the definitions, it is important to note that each type of risk has multiple names, which are presented in Table 7.8.

Table 7.8 Systematic and unsystematic risk

Risk type	*Also known as*
Systematic risk	Market risk; non-diversifiable risk
Unsystematic risk	Firm-specific risk; diversifiable risk

To explain the difference, we will add one additional description of each type. It helps to think of systematic risk as *external* risk and unsystematic risk as *internal* risk. Systematic risk is the risk the firm has because it is part of a larger market. It is a small cog in a big machine and therefore has to accept that the market will change around it, and these changes will likely influence the firm's stock value. Thus, this is a risk that, to a large degree, is external of activities within the firm. The same can be said for an individual's investment account. It is possible to make the best decisions, based upon the best work and using the best available tools, and still lose money. Consider 2008 as an example. The market return was −37 %. As such, most people lost money, including many (I'm sure) that did a great job of working their own portfolios. It is a risk that is largely out of your control, but that must be accepted as part of the "game."

On the other hand, unsystematic risk is simply the risk that the firm (or investor) may make mistakes. Any firm runs the risk that there will be unforeseen issues in any aspect of their operations. This is particularly important for public firms. Thus, this type of risk is largely an internal issue and, as we will see momentarily, can be eliminated to any meaningful level with the appropriate investment behavior. The same is again true for an investor. Sure, some of the results you obtain (both good and bad) are derived because you are a piece of the larger market. However, it would be foolish to not realize that some of your results are also attributable to your individual decisions. This can be good or bad and that is the risk of being an imperfect human being.

Before we move any farther, let's take a look at where we stand in a simplified manner.

We know

$$\textit{Unexpected return} = \textit{systematic component} + \textit{unsystematic component}$$

Thus,

$$\begin{aligned}\textit{Actual return} = {} & \textit{expected return} + \textit{systematic component} \\ & + \textit{unsystematic component}\end{aligned}$$

Luckily, our progress is hastened by the fact that we are focused on theory, which means we can cast ourselves in a theoretically perfect world. This is an important consideration as we introduce a new idea, **the principle of diversification (POD)**. The POD says that spreading an investment across many assets can eliminate some part of risk, namely, the unsystematic risk portion. This shouldn't come as any shock, particularly if you paid attention to the last (thus far unmentioned) definitions of the two types of unexpected risk in Table 7.8. If you haven't, take a second and look back now.

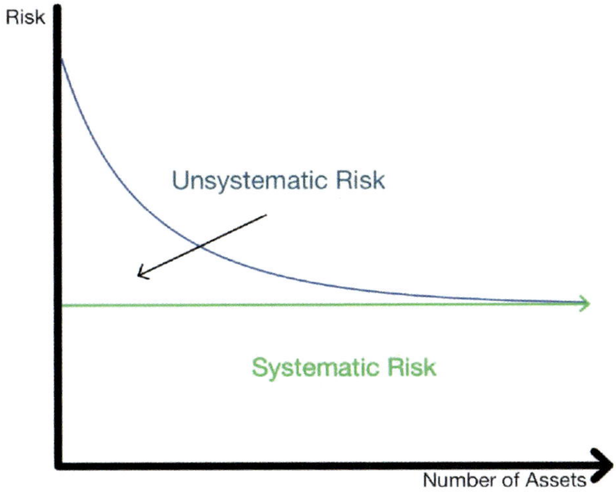

Fig. 7.5 The principle of diversification

Unsystematic risk is diversifiable, indicating that it can go away, while systematic risk is the opposite on both accounts. This is also consistent with our earlier discussion of risk reduction in portfolios via interacting correlations. If systematic risk is the risk you have because you are part of a much larger market, it would stand to reason that it couldn't be eliminated no matter how much you diversify. You could still not control the rest of the marketplace. However, the belief is that, if appropriately managed, a company can control the risk from within their own firm. Likewise, if an investor appropriately manages their portfolios, they can eliminate the risk they will occasionally make mistakes. In either case, the idea is the same: the negative unexpected return from some assets is offset by the positive unexpected returns from others. Over time, the two sides will average out, as long as you have enough pairs of assets, with differing levels of correlation. Figure 7.5 depicts the phenomenon just described.

In the theoretically perfect world, we can assume unsystematic risk is removed. After the simplification, we now know that there are only two components to the actual return on an investment: (1) the expected return and (2) some level of unexpected return as dictated by the systematic risk of the firm. Thus, the first part of our goal is accomplished as we now know what part of risk matters most in theoretically predicting the actual return. Now we can turn to the task of measuring it.

LOOK IT UP: This notion of complete diversification is a bit tougher than it perhaps sounds. Take a little bit of time to look up what it means to be completely diversified (i.e., to have no unsystematic risk) and the challenges of doing so. Can you answer the question of how many assets you need to hold to be completely diversified?

7.8.2 *Beta*

All firms are subject to systematic risk. There is a measure of market "surprise" in the sense that actual returns on the market are rarely the same as the expected return on the market. However, each firm is subjected to this market-wide surprise to a differing degree. The effect of market surprise is dramatic on firms that are very risky but relatively minimal on firms that are relatively safe. Thus, we need to identify a way of combining two elements: (1) the risk of the firm and (2) the risk in relation to the market's risk.

The monumentally important variable designed for this purpose is known as **beta**. Beta is a measure of systematic risk and, perhaps more clearly, indicates the price movement of the subject firm in relation to the movement of the market. Before we discuss the process of calculating beta, let's spend some time discussing what it means. Consider a completely made-up beta of .25.

Beta can be, theoretically, any value. There are two aspects involved in the interpretation. The first is direction. Thus, the *positive* value indicates that this particular stock moves in the same direction as the market. A negative value would predict that, as the market increased, the value of that stock would decrease. Negative beta values are rare, unless the financial asset is of a more sophisticated variety that is designed to move in the opposite direction of the market. The second (and more important) aspect of beta is the magnitude. A beta of .25 means that as the market increases by 1 %, this particular stock will increase by .25 %. Likewise, if the market decreases by 1 %, this stock will decrease by .25 %. An important note is that the magnitude of beta determines the risk level, not the sign.

> LOOK IT UP: An example of this sophisticated financial asset that moves against the market would be an inverse ETF. So, we have a three-part question. First, what is an ETF? Second, what is an inverse ETF? Third, why would you invest in either or both?

Beta can be calculated in a number of ways, including the following:

$$\beta_i = \rho_{i,m} * \frac{\sigma_i}{\sigma_m}$$

where $\rho_{i,m}$ is the correlation between asset i and the market (m) and σ_i and σ_m are the standard deviations of asset i and the market, respectively. We will illustrate with the example of Stock X, whose historical data is depicted in Table 7.9. The market returns for the same time period are also included.

Table 7.9 Actual returns

Year	*Stock X*	*Market*
1	21.50 %	16.86 %
2	6.50	8.50
3	7.90	12.87

Given the calculations for all three of the component variables have been covered earlier in the chapter, we'll leave the mechanics to each of you to figure out. The results are as follows:

$$\begin{aligned} \sigma_x &= 8.29\% \\ \sigma_m &= 4.18\% \\ \rho_{x,m} &= .89 \end{aligned}$$

We can use all the above to calculate beta for Stock X:

$$\begin{aligned} \boldsymbol{\beta}_{\mathbf{ABC}} &= .89 * \frac{8.29}{4.18} \\ &= 1.77 \end{aligned}$$

To conclude this section, there's something else you need to know when it comes to beta and measuring relative risk.

1. If $|\beta_i|$ is > 1 ▸ Stock $_i$ is more volatile than the market.
2. If $|\beta_i|$ is < 1 ▸ Stock $_i$ is less volatile than the market.

It can then be said that a stock that has a beta in excess of the market beta is a relatively risky stock, whereas a beta less than the market is relatively safe. Also, this implies the beta of the market is always 1. This should make sense, given the relative nature of the beta interpretation. Mathematically, it is also borne out since the covariance of any asset with itself ($cov(_{m,m})$) is the variance of that asset. The equation for beta then simplifies to

$$\beta_i = \frac{\sigma_m^2}{\sigma_i \sigma_m} * \frac{\sigma_i}{\sigma_m}$$

which, after cancelling out, equals 1.

TECH HELP 7.2 Using Excel to Calculate Beta
The calculation for beta of an asset (or collection of assets) can become relatively burdensome if given a large amount of data. Thus, while the calculations shown in the primary text will always work, it is also possible to shorten the process with a little technological help in the form of Excel. We

(continued)

TECH HELP 7.2 Using Excel to Calculate Beta (continued)

will use the three years of historical returns for Stock X and replicate the work done in the text. However, as you will soon see in an upcoming section, beta is actually nothing more than a slope coefficient of the market return's influence on Stock X's return. Thus, we can use the built-in Excel formula (=slope) to streamline the process. The screen capture below illustrates the process while also showing the Excel formulas for standard deviation, covariance, and correlation.

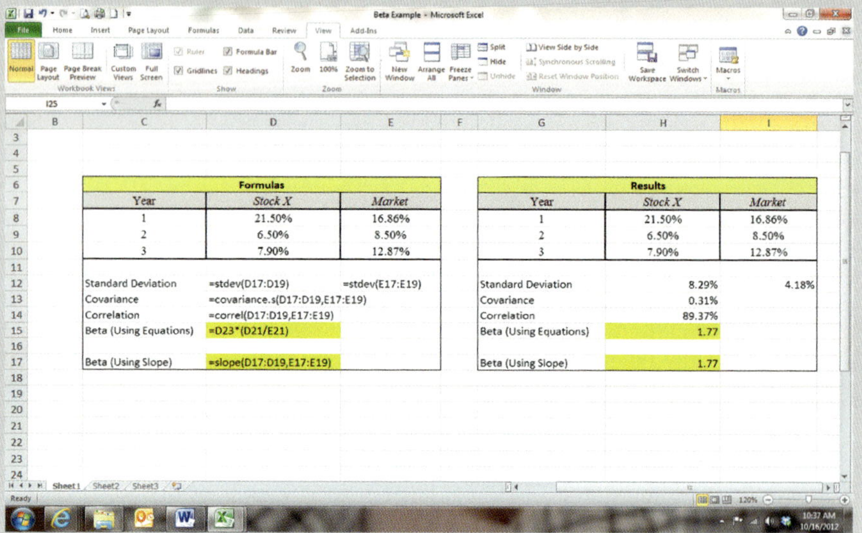

7.8.3 Portfolio Beta

Suppose you own more than one stock, which is the norm. In this case, the investor would be interested in knowing how their entire basket of stocks moves when the market moves. Thus, we need to create a weighted combination of our betas, in much the same way as we created a weighted combination of returns in an earlier section:

$$\beta_p = \sum_{i=1}^{N} w_i \beta_i$$

Let's illustrate with Mike's portfolio from earlier. In Table 7.10, we reproduce the weighting information (from Table 7.6) and add the beta for each security.

Table 7.10 Mike Morgan's portfolio

Security (i)	*Portfolio weight (w_i)*	*Beta*
A	.05	1.42
B	.15	1.05
C	.25	.45
D	.40	1.50
E	.15	.95

So, Mike's portfolio beta is

$$\begin{aligned}\boldsymbol{\beta p} &= (\mathbf{.05} * \mathbf{1.42}) + (\mathbf{.15} * \mathbf{1.05}) + (\mathbf{.25} * \mathbf{.45}) + (\mathbf{.40} * \mathbf{1.50}) + (\mathbf{.15} * \mathbf{.95}) \\ &= \mathbf{1.08}\end{aligned}$$

Thus, if the market increases by 1 %, the value of Mike's portfolio increases by slightly more, which indicates that Mike's basket of securities is a bit riskier than the average set of securities. As a result, Mike would expect a slightly higher than market average return, which leads nicely to the following topic.

7.8.4 The Security Market Line

We will now examine one of the most celebrated concepts you will encounter in your journey through finance. The **security market line (SML)** depicts a linear relationship between the risk of a security (or group of securities) and the return on that security (or group of securities). As such, it will allow us to address the third objective of quantifying the relationship between risk and reward. Notice that prior to this section, we have spent a lot of time calculating risk and return separately, but we haven't done anything with them simultaneously. The SML allows us to make this natural extension. Put simply, the SML is a line, and the equation we're looking for is the equation of that line. But alas, we're getting ahead of ourselves.

A good starting point is introducing the **reward-to-risk ratio (*RTR*)**, which is appropriately named. It is calculated by the following for any asset *i*:

$$RTR = \frac{E[r_i] - r_f}{\beta_i}$$

The risk-free rate (r_f) is generally assumed to be the annualized rate of the three-month treasury bill, as mentioned earlier. The numerator in the equation is, as the name implies, the expected reward for investing in asset *i*, as measured by the risk premium. Likewise, the denominator is the systematic risk of asset *i*, as measured by beta. Thus, the *RTR* ratio reports the additional reward expected per additional unit of risk.

To illustrate, let's revisit Stock X that we used earlier to calculate beta. In addition to the beta, which was calculated to be 1.77, assume we also know the

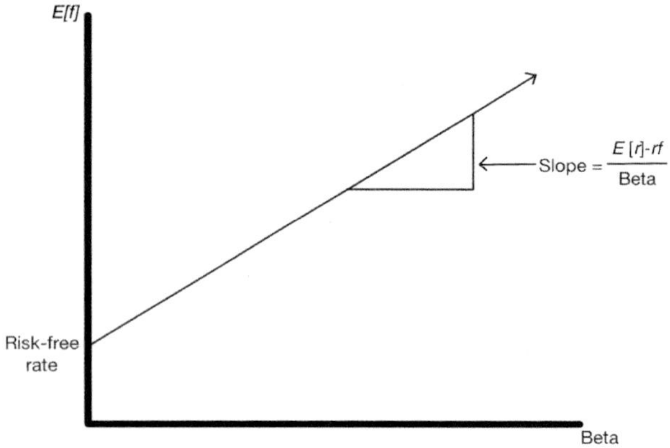

Fig. 7.6 Reward-to-risk ratio

expected return for this stock is 11.46 % and the current risk-free rate is 2.5 %. Combining this information, we have the following *RTR* ratio:

$$\frac{\mathbf{11.46 - 2.5}}{\mathbf{1.77}} = \mathbf{5.06\%}$$

This says that for every one unit increase in risk for Stock X, you would require a 5.06 % additional return. The primary reason the *RTR* ratio is so important is that it represents a slope. This can perhaps best be seen with a picture, as shown in Fig. 7.6.

If you venture back in the recesses of your mind, you may recall that to create a line, two basic components are required. The first is known as the y-intercept, which is the risk-free rate in this case. In other words, if you were willing to take zero risk (i.e., beta = 0), you would generate a return equal to the risk-free rate, by definition. The second component is the aforementioned slope. Dig a little deeper in your memory and you may recall the slope is equal to the "rise" over the "run." In other words, it's equal, graphically, to the vertical distance traveled divided by the horizontal distance traveled. You can now see, referring to the graph, how the *RTR* ratio does just that.

Now we come to a primary point of concern in this analysis. Suppose for a moment that there is a second line on the graph above, as depicted in Fig. 7.7. Think about this line being for some Security Y.

Notice that since both have the same intercept, Security X dominates Security Y at every level of risk. Put more specifically, Security X provides a higher level of return for the same amount of risk. Thus, any rational investor would never invest in Stock Y as they would not be compensated equally for taking risk. In a rational world, which we theoretically assume is the case, Security Y could never exist. And, if you consider for a moment the possibility of another line on the graph that is above X, you can see in that case Stock X could not exist. The same is true for any line on the graph that has a security line with the same intercept and a steeper slope.

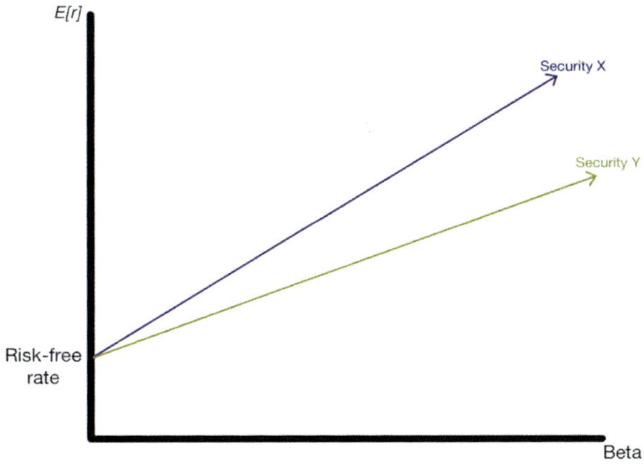

Fig. 7.7 Multiple security market lines

Thus, we arrive at a much needed conclusion. In expectation, the *RTR ratio must be the same for all securities in the market*. This doesn't mean that each firm has the same risk and return values, but rather, that each security must have the same ratio between the two variables. If one security has twice the risk as another, it must also have twice the expected return. This is true for any security, and by extension, it is also true for any combination of securities as well. Therefore, in theory all individual securities and all portfolios must fall on a line that has the same slope and the same y-intercept. In short, all securities must fall on a single line, summarily known as the security market line. Therefore, we can replace the multiple lines for securities X and Y with a single line, labeled as the SML, as in Fig. 7.8.

7.8.5 *The Capital Asset Pricing Model*

We are almost to our goal, which is to create an equation that relates the risk of an investment to the return on that investment. All we have to do is apply a larger scope to what we've just learned. Every asset and combination of assets in the market must, theoretically, have the same *RTR* ratio. This is true regardless of the size of the portfolio. Therefore, imagine a portfolio made up of every asset in the market. While this isn't very practical, it is theoretically possible. The fundamental result that the *RTR* must be the same applies in this extreme case as well. Therefore, the SML slope must be

$$\frac{E[r_m] - r_f}{\beta_m}$$

where $E[r_m]$ and β_m are the expected return and beta, respectively, of the market as a whole. This is beneficial because we know the beta of the market must always equal one. Thus, the slope of the SML simplifies to

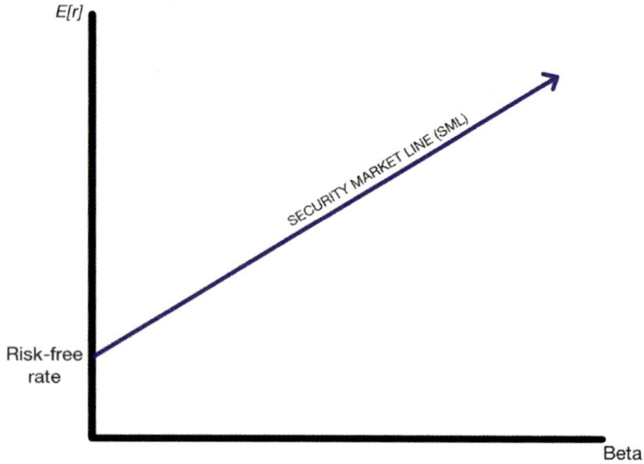

Fig. 7.8 The security market line

$$E[r_m] - r_f$$

Again, if you jump in the wayback machine, you may remember learning the equation of a line:

$$y = mx + b$$

where m represents the slope, b represents the y-intercept, and y (x) represents the variable measured along the vertical (horizontal) axis. So, it becomes pretty much paint by numbers at this point. We already know the slope and the y-intercept to be $E[r_m]$-r_f and r_f, respectively, and we can find the y and x axes from simply looking at the graph that we've been using. We are measuring the return ($E[r_i]$) on the vertical (or y) axis and risk (β_i) on the horizontal (or x) axis.

Thus, putting it all together

$$E[r_i] = r_f + (E[r_m] - r_f)\beta_i$$

Part A (↗ r_f) Part B (↑ $(E[r_m] - r_f)$) Part C (↖ β_i)

creates the well-known **capital asset pricing model (CAPM)**, which indicates that the expected return on an asset depends on three things. The first (Part A) is the risk-free rate, which is reflective of the pure time value of money. Very loosely speaking, the risk-free rate is designed to reflect increased costs over time so that you can invest in a security and maintain a relative wealth, even after accounting for issues such as inflationary concerns. The CAPM maintains that any risky security should have an expected return of at least this value.

The second piece (Part B) is called the **market risk premium** and is representative of the overall reward for bearing risk in the market. Notice that neither Part A or B is specifically related to the individual security being examined. In fact, the only variable on the right-hand side of the equation that is specific to asset i is the beta (Part C). This is the simple beauty of the equation. In a very straightforward way, it allows us to examine the relationship between a single input variable for risk and expected return. Let's go back to Firm X to illustrate how this equation works. Recall we calculated the beta to be 1.77 and were given the risk-free rate of 2.5 %. Let's also assume the expected return on the market is 10 %. Therefore, we can calculate the expected return to be

$$\begin{aligned} \boldsymbol{E[r_{\mathrm{ABC}}]} &= \mathbf{2.5 + (10 - 2.5) * 1.77} \\ &= \mathbf{15.78\%} \end{aligned}$$

LOOK IT UP: In practical application, how do you find an expected return on the market? The short answer is that there are many options. One is to use historical averages, while another is to use the expansion, normal, and contraction process just as with an individual stock. For either of these, the task then becomes identifying a "market" for which historical returns can be calculated. It is practically impossible to measure the return of the true market (of all traded assets), so one must turn to market indices. What are these? What are some popular examples?

This may seem a very high return to expect from a security that has an average return over the 3-year time period of less than 12 %. However, it is the volatility of the stock that creates the necessity of expecting a higher return. Some of this volatility would perhaps be mitigated if given a longer history of returns. Note that given any three of the variables in the CAPM, it is possible to calculate the fourth. So, even though we are most often concerned with the expected return, it is also likely you will encounter problems where you need to solve for the other pieces of the CAPM, such as beta. As a final thing to keep in mind, the CAPM also works with portfolios as opposed to individual assets, with the only changes being the "*i*"s being replaced with "*p*"s.

7.8.6 Fama-French Models

The CAPM is known as a single-factor model, which means that the level of systematic risk is the only determinant of returns. The risk-free rate is a control factor, held as a constant for each security or portfolio evaluated. Likewise, the expected return of the market does not vary based upon the asset(s) being evaluated. Since developed in the early 1960s, the CAPM has stood the test of time very well and has been documented to predict in excess of 70 % of the variation in stock prices. However, in the early 1990s, Eugene Fama and Kenneth French extended the CAPM by adding two more factors. They noted that two groups of securities have consistently generated higher levels of returns than average. These groups are (1) small securities and (2) "value" stocks. Small securities have returns that are generally higher than those of larger securities and value stocks typically outperform "growth" stocks. One way of defining value and growth is the **book-to-market (BM) ratio**, which is what the Fama-French model uses. You may recognize this as the reciprocal of the market-to-book ratio discussed in Chap. 2.

The BM is calculated as the book value of the firm divided by the market value of the firm. A high value indicates that the book value is high in relation to the market value, so you appear to be getting a good deal, or a "value." Contrarily, if the book value is relatively low in relation to the market value, then the firm has room to "grow." Historically, value stocks tend to outperform growth stocks. Thus, the Fama-French 3-Factor Model includes a factor to control for these two subcategories of securities. *SMB* (small minus big) is a factor that controls for the size effect. *HML* (high minus low) is a factor that controls for the value effect. The model takes the final form of

$$E[r_i] = r_f + \left(E[r_m] - r_f\right)\beta_{Sys} + (SMB)\beta_{SMB} + (HML)\beta_{HML}$$

Notice that the traditional beta is now just one of three beta estimates and the model takes the form of a traditional multivariate regression model, where each beta estimate is the influence on the securities from each factor. The Fama-French model has been shown to control for more than 90 % of security's stock prices movements, a considerable upgrade over the traditional CAPM.

LOOK IT UP: A full discussion of the Fama-French model takes considerably more space than can be allocated in this text. Luckily, Kenneth French provides an outstanding service by making the Fama-French factors available for free on his website (http://mba.tuck.dartmouth.edu/pages/faculty/ken.french/). Take a look around and see if you can see how the model works.

7.9 CAPM and the Cost of Equity

The discussion leading to the derivation of the CAPM focused primarily on the investor's perspective. However, the story has more than one character. The expected return to the individual is the return *required* by the individual in order to maintain a level of satisfaction in their ownership. Theoretically, the firm should view this value as an equivalent to their cost of equity. The last thing a firm wants to do is to lose their shareholders as orders to sell stock create supply in lieu of demand. And the market then views excess supply as a negative signal, which would cause the share price to decrease. This would create the opposite effect of maximizing shareholder wealth. If this sounds familiar, it should. It is largely the same as that in Chap. 6.

Thus, from the firm's perspective, the CAPM can be rewritten as

$$k = r_f + \left(E[r_m] - r_f\right) * \beta_{cs}$$

where β_{cs} is the beta of the firm's common stock and k is another estimate of the firm's cost of common stock.

IN THE REAL WORLD

December 14, 2011. Exactly 4 years since the IPO. It was a celebratory evening at Hack Back, particularly for the employees that had been there from the start. Everyone was in high spirits. Well, everyone except Dubarb Freeman.

"There's cake in the conference room, sir," Stewart said, his head sticking through the cracked door at the entrance of Freeman's office.

"Yeah, yeah, so I've been told. Several times." He looked up over the glasses that he had begun to wear at half-mast anytime he was reading. Currently, the topic that captured his attention was the performance of the firm's stock price. His desk was littered with stacks of papers, all printed out by one of the administrative staff. Freeman's printing demands were as well known as his distaste for modern technology. Tyler often joked they were going to put a limit on his copy code. So far, it was an idle threat.

Stewart shrugged and began to retreat, but was stopped by Freeman's voice.

"Let me run this by you."

Stewart, somewhat reluctantly, returned to sit in one of the client chairs. He took the sheet of paper offered to him.

"What's this?"

"Those are the calculations I've been working on." Sure enough, numbers were scribbled all over the sheet. Unfortunately, they were indecipherable.

"Is this in code?" Stewart said, only half-joking. He was rewarded with a scalding look of disapproval.

"Just write those," Dube pointed at the spiraling column of numbers in the margin of the sheet of paper, "up there."

The "up there" referred to an ancient whiteboard that was currently a dingy gray board due to the 27 layers of dry erase dust caked on.

Stewart knew better than to complain, so he did as instructed.

Date	*Price*	*Return*
12/14/2007	*$49.25*	
12/15/2008	*33.24*	*−32.52 %*
12/14/2009	*48.45*	*45.78*
12/14/2010	*66.15*	*36.53*
12/14/2011	*58.78*	*−11.15*

"What ya looking at?" Marilyn's voice first entered the room, followed by the scent of her perfume, for which she has become infamously known. Finally, her flaming red head bounced into the room. After looking for a moment, she answered her own question.

"Our stock prices, huh? What's the point of all this Dube?" She was the only one of her peers who was comfortable in calling her boss by his nickname. Or brave enough. Or dumb enough.

"Well, I figured the 4-year anniversary of this place was a good time to reflect a bit on where we've been, but more importantly, where we need to go."

He sat back and laced his fingers behind his head. Marilyn and Stewart looked at him curiously. It was not like Dubarb Freeman to "reflect."

"Well, let's see what we've got here then," Marilyn said, taking her customary approach of jumping right in. She grabbed a red marker off the holder and gently nudged Stewart out of the way.

"Grab a calculator," she ordered. Stewart obliged with his typical good humor.

"What for?" Jane said from the threshold. She had clearly gone the opposite way around the office space, since she already had a piece of cake, precariously perched atop a thin paper plate. A white plastic fork stuck out of her hand. Over the past year, Jane had managed to shed much of her natural reluctance to speak out. In fact, she was beginning to be looked to as more of a leader than one could ever have imagined when she was first hired. It was personal advancement that Jane was proud of and that had not escaped the attention of her bosses.

"Can you please find our average annual return?" Marilyn asked Stewart. He began punching buttons, but Jane's warp speed mind beat him to the punch.

"Nine point seven percent," she said, shoveling a piece of cake in her mouth at the same time. Stewart looked at her sideways, midway through punching buttons.

"Really?" he said.

"So, that's not bad," Marilyn commented, as she scribbled the figure on the board.

"No, not bad, but that's not the point," Dubarb said. He unlaced his hands from behind his head and sat forward.

"What's the point? And what are you all doing here? Party's down the hall." Brandon squeezed into the room and quickly appraised the situation.

"This actually has a lot to do with you right now, son," Dubarb said.

"Me?" Brandon said. "How's that?"

"You and Jane are working on how we should fund the new plant," he responded, "and a large part of that is figuring out the cost of common equity."

"I thought we had that figured out." The voice came from outside the crowded office door.

"And what is everyone doing in here?" added another voice, this one feminine.

One at a time, Lilly and Tyler stuck their heads in the door. They had learned by now that anything happening in this office needed their attention. The building was full of people celebrating the 4-year anniversary. And everyone except

Dubarb Freeman knew that it was okay to take a few hours off. Still, they couldn't help but wonder.

"I thought we figured out the cost of equity with the dividend growth thingy," Lilly said again. She was dressed for the occasion, wearing a tailored suit that cost more than some people's entire wardrobe. She usually didn't splurge on such excess, but, truth be told, she felt she deserved a little reward. Of course, that didn't stop her from very carefully sliding her cup hand past Brandon, who blocked most of the doorway. No need to spill wine on a $2,000 outfit.

"This must be that other way of looking at it he was talking about," Tyler said. Although slender, a quick mental calculation told Tyler he was safer in the hall. He settled for sticking his head through the crack over Jane's shoulder.

"Yep, this one gets more use than the DGM," Dubarb said, "because it is more flexible." The other four members had picked up on the process now. They quickly and amicably assigned tasks, aided by their ever-present iPhones.

"I'll get the market returns," Stewart said, "for the same time periods."

"I'll find the T-bill rate," Brandon said.

"I'll look up beta," Marilyn said.

"I'll calculate it, too," Jane said, "just to check."

Brandon's task was the easiest, so he finished first, but took a moment to stare at it.

"Looks like the current T-bill rate is almost... nothing. About twelve points." He scribbled .12 % on the board.

"Rough times," Tyler said, absently.

"Here are the market returns," Stewart said, taking the marker from Brandon's hand. He wrote on the board.

Year	*Mkt return*
12/14/2007–12/15/2008	*−40.83 %*
12/16/2008–12/14/2009	*28.27*
12/15/2009–12/14/2010	*11.44*
12/15/2010–12/14/2011	*−2.40*

"Alright, so given this...," Jane said, walking around behind Freeman's desk. "May I?"

Freeman quickly moved against the wall and let Jane have his seat. She pulled up an empty Excel sheet and copied the numbers written on the board into two columns. Then she quickly calculated the necessary variables.

"Alright," she said. "The standard deviation of our returns is 37.59 %, and the market's is 29.44 %. Correlation is .9340."

As she had been speaking, Stewart wrote the numbers on the board in the form of the equation for beta:

$$\beta = .9340 * \frac{37.59}{29.44}$$

Brandon had picked up the vacated calculator and quickly punched in the figures.

"So, our beta is 1.19," he said.

"That's what I get too," Jane said, looking up from her screen.

"It's also pretty close to what they're reporting for us as well," Marilyn said. She had been busy surfing around various financial websites looking at the reported beta figures.

"So, what do we do with that?" Tyler's voice floated into the room.

That was Freeman's signal.

"That tells us," he began, "that the market views us as slightly riskier than average. So, if they expect the market to generate a return of 5 %, they expect us to generate just a bit more than that. And, to remain invested in us, they need to get that return. Otherwise, they may jump ship."

"I get it," Lilly said, happy to be out of the tornado of numbers for the moment. "So we need to beat the market by 20 %, approximately, because to the investor, we are a 20 % riskier than the market."

"Close," Freeman said, "but investors also expect our return to include some adjustment for the risk-free rate, since they can get that without taking risk anyway."

"But that is next to nothing now," Lilly responded. "So we need to beat the market by a tiny bit more than a little bit."

The others grinned at her accurate qualitative reflection of the situation.

"Yep, that's about right," Freeman said. "Finish it up there, Stewart. Let's use about 10 % for the expected return on the market." Stewart obliged by writing on the last remaining corner of the board.

$$\begin{aligned} k_{cs} &= .12 + (10 - .12) * 1.19 \\ &= 11.88\% \end{aligned}$$

"So, eleven point nine percent," Brandon said. He held up the calculator for all to see.

"That's what the shareholders expect?" Tyler asked, to no one in general.

"That is a scientifically justifiable guess," Freeman said.

"If this wine hasn't jaded my memory to a large degree," Lilly said, "that is quite a bit larger than the estimate with the dividend method. Which is correct?"

Freeman shrugged before adding, "Both…neither. They are just estimates that add to the information we have available. One way or the other, we are trying to get a handle on what shareholders expect." He pointed at the number circled on the well-used board.

"This is one way of doing that."

"Well, if that is what they expect," Tyler said, "I guess that's what we'd better give them."

***

Meanwhile, at his mansion halfway across the country, Eli Eldridge was again reflecting on his own Hack Back calculations. Same chair, same Scotch. The music was now from the 1970s. Charlie Pride was crooning about kissing his angel good morning. Eli sighed contentedly.

"Almost twelve percent," he said to himself. His forehead puckered up, and he stared at the ceiling in thought.

"I think they'll do it," he mumbled. He reached over and took a yellow legal pad. He scribbled on a scrap sheet of paper.

HBCK – 1,000 more?

ALTERNATE ENDINGS

1. ***The calculations above use annual return figures and a very small sample size. Many beta calculations are done using monthly price data. Using the complete price file available in the appendix, calculate beta in this manner. How does this change things?***
2. ***Dubarb said to just assume a 10 % expected return on the market, presumably since that is roughly the average historical return on most large market indices. Suppose, however, that you want to be more careful than that and wish to calculate the expected return on the market based upon your expectation of the market conditions next year and categorized historical returns. You may start by assuming you believe the market next year has a 40 % chance of being expansionary, a 10 % chance of being contractionary, and a 50 % chance of being normal. Feel free, however, to also try whatever percentages that you wish. Define an expansionary market as one that has returns higher than 20 % and a contractionary economy as one that has returns less than 5 %. Use the S&P 500 as your market proxy. Given the dearth of historical annual periods, you may want to also examine doing this using monthly data.***
3. ***Suppose you wanted to extend the model and use the Fama-French model to predict Hack Back's return. Using the monthly factors from Ken French's website, what would you do? What are the barriers to completing this?***

Concept Questions

1. **Risk and return** What is the theoretical relationship between risk and return?
2. **Risk and return** Your best friend just said that she took a large risk last year and lost money. She is angry at you because she says you told her that higher risk equaled higher return. What is your response?
3. **Returns** Define both dollar returns and percentage returns. In what situations would you prefer one over the other?
4. **Returns** What are the two components of returns? Describe how each relates to the value of the asset. Also describe the two components from both the investor and firm perspective.

5. **Returns** Bob just calculated a return of 3.86 % last year on Asset A. However, Asset A's stock price decreased by $3 last year. So, what must have happened?
6. **Returns** Describe the differences between arithmetic and geometric returns. In what situation would you prefer to calculate one over the other?
7. **Risk** What is the difficulty in calculating risk? Describe the process through which one estimates the risk of an asset.
8. **Confidence intervals** What purpose does the confidence interval serve? How does it help extend the application of risk and reward?
9. **Assets and risk** You want a safe portfolio. Given that, should you invest primarily in equity or debt? Why? What makes the difference in relation to risk levels?
10. **Assets and risk** Are small assets riskier or safer than large, all else equal? Why?
11. **Assets and risk** Debt can be issued by corporations or governments. Which is riskier and why?
12. **Expected returns** What exactly is meant by expected return? What are the components to the expected return and how are they used in the calculation?
13. **Portfolios risk** What makes portfolio risk difficult to calculate? Why is it important to consider all correlation between pairs of assets?
14. **Correlation and diversification** You just started your retirement portfolio and went to your dad for advice. He said to simply, "diversify, diversify, diversify." What did he mean by that? Why would he say it?
15. **Unexpected risk** What is the difference between systematic and unsystematic risk?
16. **Diversification** Your finance professor just stated that if you diversify correctly, you can eliminate, over time, losses from your investment mistakes. Is that correct? What are the conditions for this statement to be correct?
17. **Beta** You have three assets, A, B, and C. The beta of Asset A is 1.35, the beta of Asset B is −.13, and the beta of Asset C is .77. Describe what should happen to each if the market goes up by 2 %. Which of the three is the riskiest? Which is safest?
18. **Security market line** What is the security market line? What is the slope? What is the y-intercept? Answer both in mathematical and definitional terms.
19. **Cost of equity** How does the CAPM help in estimating the cost of equity? Discuss the implications of the answer for both the firm and the investor.

Problems

1. **Dollar return** Suppose you bought 100 shares of Stock ABC at $105.65. Today, they are selling for $102.31. You received dividends of $.26 per quarter for each of the 5 years you have owned the stock. What is the dollar return on this investment?
2. **Holding period return** Suppose you bought 20 shares of Stock XYZ 10 years ago for $5.31. For the first 5 years, Stock XYZ did not pay any dividends. For

the remaining 5 years, they paid a dividend of \$.30 per share each quarter. If you sell today for \$10.31, what is the holding period return on this investment?

3. **Bond dollar return** You just sold 300 bonds that pay an annual coupon of \$76. When you bought them, exactly 3 years ago, they were selling at \$956.28. Today they are selling at \$854.24. How is your total dollar return on the investment?
4. **Physical asset percentage return** Suppose you paid \$30,000 for a work truck and have used it for 15 years. During each of those 15 years, the truck earned you a profit of \$2,000. Today you are selling it for \$10,000. What is your percentage return on the investment?
5. **Dollar return** Exactly three and a half years ago, you began your portfolio using \$10,000 given to you by your grandfather. You bought 40 shares of Stock A, which was selling at \$83.00. You also bought 500 shares of Stock B, selling at \$3.72. The rest of your portfolio was spent on Stock C, which was currently selling at \$4.00. Throughout the period, Stock A paid a \$.15 dividend per share each quarter, while Stock B paid a quarterly dividend of \$.20. Stock C paid no dividends. Today, the market values are \$78.50, \$4.51, and \$3.95 for Stocks A, B, and C, respectively. What was your dollar return on your portfolio?
6. **Holding period return** If the *HPR* on a stock throughout time t is 18.26 % and the beginning price is \$11.50, what is the ending price? Assume that \$2.10 in dividends was paid throughout time t.
7. **Holding period return** Suppose you entered into an investment 8 years ago. You just sold your entire position of 8,000 shares and have calculated you received a total dollar return of \$13,590. You sold the stock at \$18.52. In addition, you received a \$.13 dividend each quarter for the first 5 years. After that, you received a \$.18 dividend each quarter. At what price did you buy the stock?
8. **Holding period returns** 4 years ago, you bought 100 shares of Stock A at \$23.99 per share and 200 shares of Stock B at \$12.90 per share. During the first year, Stock A paid a dividend of \$.85 per share each quarter, and Stock B paid a dividend of \$.34 per share each quarter. Stock A continued to pay the same dividend each quarter through current time. Stock B increases their quarterly dividend by \$.05 each year (each quarter during each respective year pays the same dividend) as a policy. Today, Stock A is selling for \$25.78, while Stock B is selling at \$6.52. What is your *HPR* over the 4-year period?
9. **Geometric returns** Suppose a company has had returns over the past 4 years of 6 %, −8 %, 7.5 %, and −2.5 %, respectively. What is the geometric average return for this stock?
10. **Geometric cumulative returns** Over the past 4 years, Stock CCC had returns of 5.04 %, 16.14 %, −1.85 %, and 5.78 %. If you invested \$1,000 at the beginning of those 4 years and all returns can be automatically reinvested, how much do you have today?

11. **Historical standard deviation** The return on Stock A has been 3.45 %, -5.33 %, −6.43 %, and 2.84 % for the last 4 years, respectively. Given this, what is the historical standard deviation?
12. **Confidence intervals** Suppose a stock had returns of 10 %, −1 %, 8 %, −3 %, and 11 % over the past 5 years. What is the 95 % confidence interval?
13. **Confidence intervals** Suppose you have managed a mutual fund for the last 5 years, with returns of 15.4 %, 13.5 %, 18.4 %, 9.87 %, and 10.32 % in each of them. There is approximately a 2.5 % chance that you will have a return less than ______ over the next 6 year.
14. **Confidence intervals** Suppose you have average returns over the last 25 years of 15.65 %, while the variance of those returns is 17.98 %. Given this, what is the probability your return next year will be less than 10 %?
15. **Expected returns** Over the past 50 years, Stock AAA has an average return of 6.4 % during normal economies. The return is half this during recessionary years. Contrarily, the return is double this during boom years. You think there is a 40 % chance of a normal economy and an equal chance of a recession and a boom next year. If Stock AAA's stock price is $10 today, what do you think it will be next year?
16. **Expected returns** Over the past 25 years, the average return for Stock ABC has been 12.43 % per year. However, during booming economies, this return is 45 % higher. On the other hand, during recessionary economies, this return is 25 % lower than the average. If you believe there is an equal 25 % chance of both a recession and a booming economy next year, what is your expected return on Stock ABC?
17. **Portfolio returns** Suppose you have an expected return on the portfolio of 15.6 %. You are invested in only two stocks, A and B. The expected return on A is 18.55 %, and the expected return on B is 8.96 %. What percentage of your portfolio is invested in Stock A?
18. **Portfolio risk** Your portfolio is made up of 75 % Stock A and 25 % Stock B. Stock A has a variance of 31.36 %, while Stock B has a standard deviation of 6.25 %. The covariance between them is 6.8 %. What is your portfolio standard deviation?
19. **Portfolio risk** Consider a two-asset portfolio. Stock A has a standard deviation of 15 %, and Stock B has a standard deviation of 25 %. You own 14,000 share of Stock A, which is currently selling at $16.32. You own 8,000 shares of Stock B, which is currently selling at $31.08. If the correlation coefficient between the two is .69, what is the standard deviation of the portfolio?
20. **Portfolio risk** Consider the following historical returns for stocks R, S, and T.

Year	Stock R	Stock S	Stock T
1	14.34 %	15.46 %	11.35 %
2	11.35	13.35	10.99
3	8.42	6.45	−4.52 %
4	12.54	7.01	2.14 %

If you have weights of 45 % R, 25 % S, and 20 % T, what is your portfolio standard deviation?

21. **Beta** A stock has a beta of 1.43. If the current stock price is $18.02, what would you expect the price to be if the market goes up by 1.4 %?
22. **Beta** Suppose Firm VIP has a covariance of 84.87 % with the market. The standard deviation of the market is 22.90 % and the standard deviation of Firm VIP is 16.89 %. What is the beta of Firm VIP?
23. **Portfolio beta** Suppose you want a portfolio such that when the market goes up by 2 %, your portfolio goes up by 1.70 %. In addition, you only have 2 assets in your portfolio. Asset A has a beta of 1.25, while Asset B has a beta of .62. What is the weight of Asset B in your portfolio?
24. **Portfolio beta** Suppose you have a portfolio made up of 36.8 % Stock A, 25 % Stock B, and 38.2 % in a risk-free asset. The beta of Stock A is .60, while the beta of Stock B is 1.19. If the market goes down by 1.75 %, what happens to your portfolio?
25. **Portfolio beta** Suppose that over a given month, the market has increased from an index value of 887.76 to 1,023.32. During the same time period, your portfolio has increased from $13,400 to $17,211. What does this infer regarding the beta of your portfolio?
26. **Capital asset pricing model** Consider Stock X, which is 50 % riskier than the market. If the expected return on the market is 8.9 % and the current risk-free rate is 3.2 %, what is the expected return on Stock X?
27. **Holding period return** Exactly 6 years ago, you started your own investment portfolio. To do so, you bought 1,000 shares of common stock A, each selling at $12.97 per share. Common stock A paid a dividend of $.12 per quarter for the first year, $.15/quarter for the next year, $.28/quarter for the next year, and then $.30/quarter for each of the remaining years. You also bought 250 shares of preferred stock B, which is selling at $7.70 per share. The preferred stock is a 4 %, $50 preferred issuance. You also bought five treasury bills C, each selling at $565.97 and 10 coupon bonds D selling at $875.62 per bond. The coupon bonds have a 5.4 % coupon rate, a 6.3 % YTM, and 15 years left until maturity.

    Today, the prices are $10.86, $8.01, $754.86, and $866.97 for assets A, B, C, and D, respectively. What is the holding period return on your portfolio?
28. **Portfolio beta** You want to create a portfolio that is exactly 50 % as risky as the market. You want to create this portfolio from three assets: Stock A, Stock B, and a risk-free asset. Historical returns for each are listed below, along with the historical returns from the market.

Historical year	Stock A return	Stock B return	Risk-free rate	Market return
1	12.43 %	11.12 %	2.32 %	8.43 %
2	10.55	8.11	3.01	11.90
3	9.43	3.22	1.98	13.31
4	6.32	−2.11	2.31	6.43
5	8.43	−1.08	2.43	7.08

Suppose you have $24,000 in total to invest and you know you want to invest $8,000 in the risk-free asset. In order to get your desired risk level, how much of the remainder would you invest in Stocks A and B, respectively?

29. **Portfolio returns** You have had the following portfolio returns over the past 10 years. Also included are the market returns for the same period of time.

Year	Your return	Market return
1	14.43 %	21.04 %
2	17.90 %	−9.10 %
3	9.43 %	−11.89 %
4	7.09 %	−22.10 %
5	11.94 %	28.69 %
6	13.33 %	10.88 %
7	15.00 %	4.91 %
8	10.41 %	15.79 %
9	−2.54 %	5.49 %
10	−7.92 %	−38.49 %

You may assume that a market return in excess of 15 % is a boom market. Any negative return is a recessionary market. Everything in between is a normal market.

(a) The probability of an expansion next year is 15 %, while the probability of a contraction is 20 %. Based upon this, what is your expected return?
(b) Based upon these values, what is your historical standard deviation?
(c) Based upon these values, what is the probability your return next year will be less than 5 %?

30. **Portfolio beta** Consider the following historical returns for Stocks A and B, along with the returns for the market and the risk-free asset at the end of the last 4 years.

Year	Stock A return	Stock B return	S&P return	Risk-free
1	8.65 %	17.43 %	4.79 %	1.32 %
2	−4.32	3.74	−4.22	0.24
3	6.39	12.78	5.46	2.01
4	8.32	11.99	10.74	2.91

You have a total of $80,000 to invest. First, you will put $16,000 in the risk-free asset. You want a portfolio with a beta of .6. The covariance between Stock A and the market is 34.69 %. The covariance between Stock B and the market is 24.55 %. What percentage of your portfolio will go into A and B, respectively?

Chapter 8
This Is So WACC!

Thus far, we have done a great deal of preparatory work. In the remaining two chapters, we will finally get to reap the rewards of all this hard work. The efforts that have gone into calculating the various pieces of the puzzle are now going to pay off as those pieces begin to come together. There are two topics covered in this chapter. The first is the weighted average cost of capital, or *WACC* for short. Once we learn about the *WACC*, the second objective is to use this knowledge to examine capital structure theories. Upon accomplishing this, we can finally answer the question posed way back in Chap. 1 of how to maximize shareholder wealth.

8.1 The Cost of Capital

In beginning this chapter, we need to make a few points. First, firms need money in order to invest in projects that are expected to benefit the business. Second, this money does not come without cost. And, third, this cost will largely determine the success or failure of the projects involved. By now, you are aware there are two ways for a firm to obtain money: debt and equity. In previous chapters, we have learned how to solve for the price and corresponding required return for each independently. We have also discussed the notion that the return on each of these asset types is the cost to the firm. Further, it is this return that determines the current selling price.

Now, we want to use all of this knowledge to make some final conclusions. Consider a simple example of a project in which a company has decided to invest. The project is a building that requires $1,000,000 to get up and running. The firm has decided to borrow $300,000 and issue $700,000 in equity to finance the project. Thus, the firm has implicitly selected a capital structure of 30 % debt and 70 % equity. Recall from Chap. 2 that these values can be calculated with the leverage ratios.

M.K. Pyles, *Applied Corporate Finance: Questions, Problems and Making Decisions in the Real World*, Springer Texts in Business and Economics,
DOI 10.1007/978-1-4614-9173-6_8, © Springer Science+Business Media New York 2014

The entire text until this point has assumed a known capital structure. That is, we assume the company has chosen a capital structure for their existing operations; thus, we have left discussion of alternations to the structure out of the conversation. We first need to find a way to accurately and concisely reflect the existing structure before we ask the very pertinent question of whether funding allocation for future activities will deviate from this existing structure.

Once we have identified the sources of capital, we then turn our attention to calculating, or estimating in some cases, the cost of each source. A very important note to all this is that the cost of capital (k) depends on the risk of the investment rather than just the source. This is a bit difficult to understand at first since the issue is always approached from the source side. However, it should make sense if you put yourself in the shoes of the *lender* or the *investor*. So, pretend for a moment that you are an investor considering purchase of either a bond or a stock in Firm ABC. You know the firm is going to use the money you give them to finance a project. The riskier that project, the more return you are going to require. You are likely unconcerned about the breakdown of debt and equity the firm is using. In other words, you do not care what percentage of the project that your dollars are specifically funding. Rather, all you care about is that you are giving money to the firm in exchange for potential returns. The overall conclusion is that, ultimately, it is the use of the money that matters, not the origin.

The total cost of capital can be summed up as

$$\text{Total cost of capital} = \begin{array}{c}\text{returns needed to}\\ \text{compensate lenders}\end{array} + \begin{array}{c}\text{returns needed to}\\ \text{compensate shareholders}\end{array}$$

The "returns needed to compensate lenders" is the amount of money that we must pay in interest on the money we have borrowed. For example, if the annual interest rate on our debt is 5 %, then whatever we use the money for must have at least a 5 % return to pay back the money borrowed to finance the project. The "returns needed to compensate shareholders" is the amount of money the firm must make in order to generate enough reward for the shareholders to feel secure in their investments. So, if the shareholders require 5 % in exchange for the money they invest, then we need to make at least that amount on whatever the funds were used for. When we combine the two elements, we get the total amount needed to pay back the sources of funds. In addition, we need to generate money beyond that amount so as to increase shareholder wealth.

This is the basic idea, but we must now turn to details. In order to practically complete this exercise, we need to complete a four-step process:

1. Identify the sources of capital used.
2. Calculate or estimate the cost of each source.
3. Calculate the capital structure weights.
4. Complete the weighted average cost of capital.

8.2 Sources of Capital

The good news is that we have already done most of this, just in a very disjointed manner. We have spent considerable time on identifying each piece of the puzzle. Now we simply have to put the pieces together.

8.2.1 Existing Equity

The most obvious source of funds that a firm can use comes from their existing equity. When a firm issues stock, they obtain funds from the shareholders and are largely free thereafter to do with it whatever they wish. The ideal notion, of course, is that it will be used to advance the firm and create retained earnings. A portion of these retained earnings can then be plowed back into the firm. At first blush, it may appear that the cost of this capital is zero, since the firm already has the money and can simply choose to use it. However, this logic would be missing a huge link in the shareholder-firm relationship.

When investors spend money to invest in the firm, they do so with the belief it will be a profitable venture. As we now know, this can happen in two ways, either directly by dividend payments or indirectly via price appreciation. The most obvious way of paying back the shareholders is to issue dividends, and when the firm chooses to invest the retained earnings, they are doing so at the expense of higher dividend payments. This effectively reduces the amount of money the shareholders can *directly* receive. Had shareholders received the funds instead of the firm using them, they could have presumably invested the earnings in another market position. Therefore, the shareholders intrinsically expect the firm to generate a return equivalent to that which they would have earned with the dividends given to them. The question becomes: how do we estimate this return?

When we began to value common stock in Chap. 6, we discussed some of the difficulties associated with doing so. One of those difficulties is that it is almost impossible to observe an appropriate required return on equity before the market reveals the influences of current supply and demand. The only true way of identifying the return required by shareholders would be to ask each one of them and then trust their answers to be correct. This, unfortunately, is practically impossible. Thus, there is no great way to calculate the cost of equity. Rather, we must *estimate* it with some financial model. Luckily, we have already covered two such models in the previous chapters and will now use that knowledge to pursue a strategy of determining the cost of existing common stock, which we will label k_{cs}.

The first option is the Gordon Growth Model (GGM), which we covered, in depth, in Chap. 6. If you will recall, the equations look like this:

$$P_{cs} = \frac{D_0(1+g)}{k_{cs}-g} \text{ or } \frac{D_1}{k_{cs}-g}$$

As we learned in Chap. 6, if we rearrange a bit, we can solve for k_{cs} as follows:

$$k_{cs} = \frac{D_0(1+g)}{P_{mkt}} + g \text{ or } \frac{D_1}{P_{mkt}} + g$$

Remember that P_{mkt} is not the same as the P_{cs} calculated with the base GGM model. P_{cs} is the theoretical price assuming the appropriate application of discounted cash flow methodology, whereas P_{mkt} is the actual market value at the time of cost estimation. Since the goal of this chapter is to get away from being given values for important variables, let's continue that trend by thinking about different ways of estimating the growth rate. Remember the model assumes the growth rate of not only the dividend payments but the overall firm as well. While there are many ways of estimating g, we will discuss three.

We'll begin with the easiest method, which is basically to let someone else do the hard work for you. All over the world, there are people called **analysts** that are paid to create estimates of many facets of a firm's future financial capacities. Among many other things, these analysts create estimates of growth rates. So, one way of estimating a growth rate simply involves looking up an analyst estimate.

LOOK IT UP: Where can you find these values? You may want to experiment with a service known as Value Line, which creates reports (which include growth rates). They provide the Dow 30 stocks for free. See if you can find the estimated growth rate for General Electric (GE).

A second way of estimating a growth rate is also a reminder of something covered earlier in the text. Many practitioners simply use the **sustainable growth rate (*SGR*)** as an estimate of the firm's growth rate. If period-ending equity values are used, recall it is calculated as

$$SGR = \frac{ROE^{*}b}{1-(ROE^{*}b)}$$

where b is the **retention ratio**. As a quick example, consider Billy's Biker Bar, which has an *ROE* of 14.95 %. This year, the company is expected to generate a net income of \$748,000. They also plan to pay a total of \$300,000 in dividends throughout the year. Thus, they will retain the remaining \$448,000, which leads to a retention ratio of

$$\boldsymbol{b = \frac{448,000}{748,000} = 59.89\,\%}$$

Therefore, the *SGR* would be

$$\begin{aligned} SGR &= \frac{.1495^{*}.5989}{1-(.1495^{*}.5989)} \\ &= 9.83\% \end{aligned}$$

A third method of estimating the growth rate is simply using the historical record. Suppose that, on a per share basis, Billy's Biker Bar has issued the following historical dividends.

Year	Annual dividend	% change
1	$.24	–
2	.27	12.50 %
3	.31	14.81
4	.34	9.68
5	.36	5.88

The final column presents the percentage changes for each year. Notice the first year's growth rate is missing, since calculating the percentage change requires both a beginning and ending value. All other growth rates are calculated with the standard (*E-B*)/*B* convention.

Once accomplished, we then average the annual growth rates:

$$\begin{aligned} g &= \frac{12.50+14.81+9.68+5.88}{4} \\ &= 10.72\% \end{aligned}$$

It is also possible to calculate the geometric average. There are a couple of ways of doing this. First, we can consider the notion that we start with a dividend of $.24 and end with a dividend of $.36. It takes 4 years to get there. So, the average growth rate, compounded annually, can be computed as follows:

$$\begin{aligned} .36 &= .24(1+g)^{4} \\ g &= \left(\frac{.36}{.24}\right)^{1/4} - 1 \\ g &= 10.67\% \end{aligned}$$

One could also use the geometric average formula from Chap. 7. Feel free to prove that to yourself.

Unfortunately, there's no real way of knowing which of the above methods provides the best estimate of future growth. Therefore, it is often useful to do them all and find the average. Now we can return to our original discussion of the cost of equity. Continuing our examination of Billy's Biker Bar, we know the current (or most recent) dividend is \$.36. We have also estimated the sustainable growth rate to be 9.83 % and the historical rates to be approximately 10.7 %. Suppose we have looked up the analyst estimates for the growth rate and found them average 9 %. For the sake of simplicity, we can average these rates to get 9.84 %. Finally, let's pretend that we know Billy's current stock price is \$31.55.

Thus, with all of this knowledge, we can complete the GGM to solve for the cost of common stock, k_{cs}:

$$\begin{aligned} \boldsymbol{k_{cs}} &= \frac{\mathbf{.36(1.0984)}}{\mathbf{31.55}} + \mathbf{.0984} \\ &= \mathbf{11.09\%} \end{aligned}$$

Therefore, Billy's **cost of equity** is 11.09 %, at least according to the Gordon Growth Model. Before we move on, it is important to understand there are distinct shortcomings in estimating costs with any method and the DGM is no exception. The dividend growth model is heavily dependent upon the chosen growth rate and, more so, the requirement that it be a constant value. Thus, an error in estimation of this figure would result in a potentially large error in the final estimate. Perhaps an even larger issue is that the method doesn't work for a large percentage of firms, namely, those that do not pay dividends. Thus, we also need to recall the other method we have covered for estimating the cost of equity.

The capital asset pricing model (CAPM), as discussed in Chap. 7, is also a valid way of determining the firm's cost of equity. The formula, from the firm's perspective, can be written as follows:

$$k_{cs} = r_f + \left(E[r_m] - r_f\right)\beta_{cs}$$

β_{cs} is the beta of the firm's common stock. If we assume the current risk-free rate is 2.13 % and the return on the market is 10 %, all we need for the specific firm is beta. For Billy, let's assume that his beta is 1.17, indicating his firm is a bit riskier than the market. Therefore, his estimated cost of equity is

$$\begin{aligned} \boldsymbol{k_{cs}} &= \mathbf{2.13 + (10 - 2.13)^{*}1.17} \\ &= \mathbf{11.34\%} \end{aligned}$$

This method is also not without fault, however. Beta is an *estimate* of risk and is the primary determinant of the outcome of the CAPM estimation. Also, the expected return on the market is an unknown estimate, and failure to predict it in a relatively accurate manner would result in a large estimation error for the cost of equity.

8.2.2 Preferred Equity

Preferred equity is a relatively simple form of equity, primarily for one reason. The amount of the cash flow is constant. Thus, the formula is the same as always when dealing with an infinite stream of constant cash flows. The theoretical price of a preferred share of stock is

$$P_{ps} = \frac{D}{k_{PS}}$$

where D is equal to the dividend yield on the preferred stock multiplied by the preferred stock face value. A minor algebraic rearrangement results in the following alteration to solve for the cost of preferred stock:

$$k_{ps} = \frac{D}{P_{ps_{mkt}}}$$

To see how it works, suppose we have a preferred issue that pays a 5 % dividend on a $75 face value. The current price of the issue is $47.86. So, the current cost of preferred stock is

$$\begin{aligned} \boldsymbol{k_{ps}} &= \frac{\mathbf{3.75}}{\mathbf{47.86}} \\ &= \mathbf{7.84\%} \end{aligned}$$

8.2.3 New Equity

The material above, for both common and preferred stock, refers to calculating the cost of existing equity. The other possibility, of course, is to issue *new* equity. When doing so, calculating the price is similar, but not identical. When common or preferred shares get issued, they do so at a cost. And this cost is often significant. Thus, the actual value of the new shares must be discounted by this issuance cost. Thus, the formula for estimating the cost of new common stock is

$$k_{ncs} = \frac{D_0(1+g)}{P^*_{ncs}} + g$$

where P^*_{ncs} is the price of new common stock minus issuance costs per share. For example, suppose a firm issues 10,000 new shares of common stock. The firm just paid a dividend on their existing shares of $.20 and will do so for the new shares as well. The growth rate is 5 %. Finally, the firm estimates it will cost $1 per share to issue new stock and they will sell for $25. Thus, the cost of this new equity will be

$$k_{ncs} = \frac{.20\,(1.05)}{25-1} + .05$$

$$k_{ncs} = 5.88\%$$

The cost of new equity must be greater than the cost of existing equity, providing the dividend expectation, the expected growth rate, and the price are the same. This is typically the case. The same notion would apply to any new issuances of preferred stock:

$$k_{nps} = \frac{D}{P^*_{nps}}$$

P^*_{nps} is the net price of new preferred stock, calculated as the price minus the issuance costs.

8.2.4 Coupon Bonds

We already know from Chap. 5 that any calculations involving debt are relatively simple relative to those involving equity. The *YTM* is the cost of debt to the firm, and the return to the investor. Thus, we can replace *YTM* with k_{cb} in the bond equation and solve for the cost of coupon bond debt. Let's review the process with an example. Suppose Jenny's Embroidery Barn, Inc., has 2,800 bonds outstanding with a current price of $940.76 each. The bonds were issued 10 years ago as 25-year bonds. The coupon rate is 5.87 % and the payments are made semiannually.

Given this information, we can plug what we know into the bond formula. The coupon rate of 5.87 % translates to a semiannual payment of $29.35, so we have

$$940.76 = 29.35\left[\frac{1-\frac{1}{\left(1+\frac{k_{cb}}{2}\right)^{15*2}}}{\frac{k_{cb}}{2}}\right] + \frac{1,000}{\left(1+\frac{k_{cb}}{2}\right)^{15*2}}$$

and with the help of a financial calculator (see the TECH HELP box in Chap. 5), we can get the following as the cost of coupon bonds:

$$k_{cb} = 6.49\%$$

8.2.5 Zero-Coupon Bonds

We again have a familiar refrain. We already know how to do this but need to repackage the materials in a different context. Recall the formula for finding the price of a zero-coupon bond is

$$P_{zc} = \frac{Face}{\left(1 + \frac{k_{zc}}{m}\right)^{t^*m}}$$

which results in the following transformation to solve for the cost of zero-coupon debt:

$$k_{zc} = m\left[\left(\frac{Face}{P_{zc_{mkt}}}\right)^{\frac{1}{m^*y}} - 1\right]$$

It is fairly rare for corporations to issue zero-coupon debt, although it does occasionally happen. Suppose that Suzy's Skateboard Shack, Inc., is one of those rare companies and has zeros in their capital structure. They have a face value of $1,000 and 8 years left until maturity. The interest rate is compounded semiannually, which is relatively standard, and is selling for $561.24. Thus, Suzy's cost of her zeros is

$$\boldsymbol{k_{zc} = 2\left[\left(\frac{1,000}{561.24}\right)^{\frac{1}{2^*8}} - 1\right]}$$

$$\boldsymbol{k_{zc} = 7.35\%}$$

8.2.6 Private Sources of Capital

The vast majority of this text concerns public investments, from both the firm and investor perspectives. However, firms often undertake private investments as well. Private debt is a prime example. We will generically refer to it as "bank debt." This is particularly true when the required capital amounts are relatively modest. Private equity is also a very viable source option. Private firms are, naturally, comprised of private equity. Public firms also get involved in private equity, however. The so-named PIPE (private investment in public equity) is essentially an offering not made available to the public, but rather to a group of private investors. While not exceedingly common, this is also a possibility when firms need additional capital.

In each case, the cost of each type of private funding is a negotiated amount, generally driven, at least indirectly, by current market conditions. The most obvious example involves bank debt, where the borrower receives an interest rate that is usually based upon some type of benchmark rate (such as the prime rate) plus a borrower-specific spread. This spread would be based upon the risk of the borrower and the characteristics of the loan. So, unfortunately, there is no boilerplate equation that allows us to consistently estimate the cost of private debt. Rather, we must use estimates based upon the best information available. Things are even more complicated for private equity because the availability of details surrounding the obtainment of funds is limited.

Table 8.1 Sources and cost of capital

Source of capital	Cost of source
Common stock (existing)	$k_{cs} = \frac{D_0(1+g)}{P_{cs_{mkt}}} + g$ or $k_{cs} = r_f + (E[r_m] - r_f)\beta_{cs}$
Common stock (new)	$k_{ncs} = \frac{D_0(1+g)}{P^*_{ncs}} + g$ or $k_{cs} = r_f + (E[r_m] - r_f)\beta_{cs}$
Preferred stock (existing)	$k_{ps} = \frac{D}{P_{ps_{mkt}}}$
Preferred stock (new)	$k_{nps} = \frac{D}{P^*_{nps}}$
Coupon bonds	$P_{cb_{mkt}} = C/m\left[\frac{1-\frac{1}{\left(1+\frac{k_{cb}}{m}\right)^{y^*m}}}{\frac{k_{cb}}{m}}\right] + \frac{Face}{\left(1+\frac{k_{cb}}{m}\right)^{y^*m}}$
Zero-coupon bonds	$k_{zc} = m\left[\left(\frac{Face}{P_{zc}}\right)^{\frac{1}{m^*y}} - 1\right]$
Private debt	Negotiated between two parties
Private equity	Negotiated between two parties

Table 8.1 summarizes the potential sources of capital and the method through which we can estimate or calculate the cost of each.

8.3 Capital Structure Weights

When given a known capital structure, calculating the weights of each component is an exercise in redundancy. It may be helpful to recall the discussion in Chap. 7 of portfolio weights, for we are about to undergo the same process for our capital structure. If you recall, the weight of each asset in your portfolio is calculated as the percentage of your overall portfolio made up of each individual asset. Drawing from this, each **capital structure weight** is the percentage of the firm's overall capital structure comprised of each specific capital source. To begin, let's assume the firm only has two sources, common stock and coupon bonds. Specifically, consider the following example.

Gert's Guitar Hut currently has 2,200 bonds and 650,000 shares of common stock outstanding. Suppose we look up the current price of each and find the bonds are selling at $1,120.31 each and each share of common stock is selling at 23.96. We shall designate *CB* as the total market value of coupon bonds within the firm and *CS* to be the equivalent for common stock. Thus,

$$CB = number\ of\ bonds^*price\ per\ bond$$
and
$$CS = number\ of\ shares^*price\ per\ share$$

Since these are the only two sources of capital utilized by Gert, when we combine the values, we obtain the total market value of the firm, *V*:

$$V = CB + CS$$

Thus, Gert has the following capital structure values:

$$\begin{aligned} \boldsymbol{CB} &= \mathbf{2,200^{*}\$1,120.31} \\ &= \mathbf{\$2,464,682} \end{aligned}$$

and

$$\begin{aligned} \boldsymbol{CS} &= \mathbf{650,000 * \$23.96} \\ &= \mathbf{\$15,574,000} \end{aligned}$$

Combining the values, we find the total value of Gert's Guitar Hut to be

$$\begin{aligned} \boldsymbol{V} &= \mathbf{2,464,682 + 15,574,000} \\ &= \mathbf{\$18,038,682} \end{aligned}$$

To transform these values into percentages, we must divide each piece by the total value:

$$W_{cb} = \frac{CB}{V} \text{ and } W_{cs} = \frac{CS}{V}$$

For Billy, this works out to be

$$\begin{aligned} \boldsymbol{W_{cb}} &= \frac{\mathbf{2,464,682}}{\mathbf{18,038,682}} \\ \boldsymbol{W_{cb}} &= \mathbf{13.66\%} \end{aligned}$$

and

$$\begin{aligned} \boldsymbol{W_{cs}} &= \frac{\mathbf{15,574,000}}{\mathbf{18,038,682}} \\ \boldsymbol{W_{cs}} &= \mathbf{86.34\%} \end{aligned}$$

where W_{cb} and W_{cs} are capital structure weights. Notice they must sum to one, since Gert only has debt and equity as options for funding.

In reality, a firm is very likely to have more than two specific sources of capital. This could happen in two ways. First, they could have other types of capital, as outlined in the previous section. For example, they could have preferred stock or bank debt in addition to common stock or coupon bonds. Second, a firm can easily have multiple issues of the same capital sources. Firms often issue common stock at different times with different characteristics. Even more often, firms will have several issues of coupon bonds, differing in maturity, coupon rates, or any number of other characteristics. When these issues occur, the weight of each specific source is calculated according to the current number outstanding and current market price. It is possible for a firm to have dozens of specific sources of capital, each of which has its own weight and cost.

8.4 Weighted Average Cost of Capital

Before we put all of this together, there is the remaining caveat of the subject of taxes. We are primarily concerned with *after-tax* costs as they provide the most accurate measure of the true cost to the firm. We live in a world where taxes are a necessity and therefore have to be considered. While we will discuss this in a more theoretical framework in the next section, there are times when taxes certainly hurt (don't we all know!), but there are also times where taxes can help a firm.

Backing up a bit, recall the direct cash flow to equity holders is a dividend payment. This payment, since it is voluntary by the firm, cannot be deducted from taxes. It is a gift the firm chooses to give its shareholders and therefore cannot be viewed as a tax-deductible obligation. The indirect cash flow to shareholders is an expected increase in stock price, as evidenced by an expected growth rate. This too, naturally, cannot be a tax-deductible expense to the firm. On the other hand, when a firm enters into a debt arrangement, they are accepting a contractual obligation. The government recognizes this in much the same way that the IRS recognizes home interest expenses as personal tax-deductible expenditures. The ultimate impact of this understanding is that the after-tax cost of equity is exactly the same as the before-tax cost. However, the after-tax cost of debt is equal to

$$k_d(aftertax) = k_d(beforetax)^*(1 - T)$$

To revisit our example of Gert's Guitars, where T represents the firm's tax rate and d represents any type of debt financing. Suppose the estimate of the cost of both common stock and coupon bonds is 8 %. At first blush, this would seem to suggest the choice of capital source is irrelevant, since they cost the same. However, the 8 % estimated cost of equity has no tax implications. The 8 % cost of debt, however, can be deducted from the firm's taxes. Thus, it really has a net after-tax cost of 5.2 % if we assume the standard 35 % tax rate. While this is a subject of considerable significance, we will save thorough discussion of the ramifications to later in this chapter.

Getting back to the subject at hand, we can now calculate Gert's **weighted average cost of capital (*WACC*)** with the following equation:

$$WACC = W_{cs}k_{cs} + W_{cb}k_{cb}(1 - T)$$

You can now see why it's called the *weighted* average cost of capital. The actual overall cost of capital is a combination of the individual costs. These individual

Table 8.2 Jill's scooter shop capital structure

Capital source	Number of units	Price/unit	Cost
Common stock	400,000	\$17.87	14.76 %
Preferred stock	120,000	\$8.66	6.24 %
Coupon bonds A	740	\$965.15	8.42 %
Coupon bonds B	500	\$970.85	7.86 %

costs must be weighted, however, according to the firm's chosen capital structure. As such, the weighted average cost of capital is the average cost of each dollar obtained by the firm. The objective, which we have been discussing throughout the entire text, is to then use these dollars to advance the firm financially. This advancement will only occur if the funds are used on investments that generate more than they cost. Putting these notions together suggests that another definition of the weighted average cost of capital is that it is the return the firm must earn on new projects in order to maintain the current value of the firm. Any return earned greater than *WACC* is profit generating and consistent with the goal of the firm.

To finish with our illustration of Gert's Guitar Hut, his current *WACC* is

$$\begin{aligned}\boldsymbol{WACC} &= (\mathbf{.8634^*8}) + (\mathbf{.1366^*8^*.65}) \\ &= \mathbf{7.62\%}\end{aligned}$$

So, Gert's current capital structure costs 7.62 cents to obtain each average \$1 of financing. Assuming any new dollars would require the same cost suggests that Gert needs to earn a return in excess of 7.62 % in order to gain firm value. Moving away from this simple example, the general form of the weighted average cost of capital formula can be expressed as follows:

$$WACC = \sum_{e=1}^{N} W_e k_e + \sum_{d=1}^{N} W_d k_d (1 - T)$$

where e represents any equity source and d represents any debt source. To avoid confusion the equation is split by the two components so as to make clear the differing tax implications. Each specific capital source would have a weight and cost component, with each debt component having an additional tax factor. Consider a more extended example of Jill's Scooter Shop, which has four sources of capital, as outlined in Table 8.2.

Jill has two sources of equity capital and two sources of debt capital. The debt sources are both coupon bonds but differ in some undefined nature to the extent they need to be examined separately. We can approach this calculation in two ways. First, we can simply utilize the equation above:

$$\begin{aligned}\boldsymbol{WACC} &= (\mathbf{.7615 * 14.76}) + (\mathbf{.1107 * 6.24}) + (\mathbf{.0761 * 8.42 * .65}) + (\mathbf{.0517 * 7.86 * .65}) \\ &= \mathbf{12.61\%}\end{aligned}$$

An alternative method would involve calculating individual weights of debt and equity cumulatively and then going back to the simpler version of the *WACC* equation where there is only one equity and one debt component. For Jill's Scooter Shop, the process would be as follows:

$$\begin{aligned}\text{Weighted average cost of equity} &= \frac{CS}{CS+PS}k_{cs} + \frac{PS}{CS+PS}k_{ps}\\ &= \frac{\mathbf{7,148,000}}{\mathbf{8,187,200}}*\mathbf{14.76}+\frac{\mathbf{1,039,200}}{\mathbf{8,187,200}}*\mathbf{6.24}\\ &= \mathbf{13.68\%}\end{aligned}$$

$$\begin{aligned}\text{Weighted average cost of debt} &= \frac{CB_1}{CB_1+CB_2}k_{cb_1} + \frac{CB_2}{CB_1+CB_2}k_{cb_2}\\ &= \frac{\mathbf{714,211}}{\mathbf{1,199,636}}*\mathbf{8.43}+\frac{\mathbf{485,425}}{\mathbf{1,199,636}}*\mathbf{7.86}\\ &= \mathbf{8.20\%}\end{aligned}$$

Putting it together provides the same final answer:

$$\begin{aligned}\boldsymbol{WACC} &= \frac{\boldsymbol{CS+PS}}{\boldsymbol{V}}*\mathbf{13.68}+\frac{\boldsymbol{CB_1+CB_2}}{\boldsymbol{V}}*\mathbf{8.20}*\mathbf{.65}\\ &= (\mathbf{.8722}*\mathbf{13.68})+(\mathbf{.1278}*\mathbf{8.20}*\mathbf{.65})\\ &= \mathbf{12.61\%}\end{aligned}$$

The conclusion is that the average dollar obtained by Jill's firm costs 12.61 % in after-tax dollars. The extension is that any use of these funds should generate a return in excess of this number. The fallacy of these statements is that it is highly unlikely the cost of any *new* dollars used to finance *new* projects would be the same as the cost of the existing dollars. It is this significant discussion that is covered in the remainder of this chapter.

IN THE REAL WORLD

Dubarb Freeman arrived at 6:15 A.M. on the cool Monday morning of December 19, 2011. He was accustomed to arriving well before everyone else. He always believed he could get more done before the rest of the workforce showed up than he could over the other 9 hours combined. All that talking and interacting... Such a waste of time.

As he trudged down the long corridor, he was shocked to see light flooding from a doorway at the end of the hall. After checking his watch again to make sure he wasn't "late," he lightened his step as he moved towards the light.

Suddenly, he was startled by a shadow projecting from the lighted doorway. The shadow lengthened as the source approached the door, causing Dubarb's heart rate to elevate beyond a comfortable rate. Jane stepped from the lighted doorway, head down, looking at several sheets of paper in her hands. Looking up at the last moment, she avoided contact with Dubarb only by violently jerking her body sideways into the wall. However, the lack of physical contact was more than offset by the piercing screech that flew out of her open mouth.

"Oh my goodness," she said, leaning against the wall to catch her breath. "You scared me to death, Mr. Freeman."

"The feeling is mutual," he responded, hand over heart. "I almost decked you thinking you were a petty thief. What in the world are you doing here this early?"

"I couldn't sleep so I wanted to get an early start," Jane said, tugging the jacket of her business suit back into position. "We have a big decision to make in the next couple of days and I couldn't stop thinking about it."

"Yes, we are getting close to deciding on the plant, aren't we?" Dube said. "I've scheduled a meeting with Tyler and Lilly on Wednesday. What do you have there?" He pointed at the sheets of paper in her hand.

"Oh, this? I wanted to take another look at where we currently are with our capital structure and costs," she answered. "I know we're going to have to make some adjustments to it for the new funding, but I feel better when I know exactly where we are first."

"Well, you read my mind," Freeman responded. "That's what I intended to do as well. Why don't you bring that stuff on down and we'll check it out together?"

Jane followed him to his office door and waited while he fumbled with his keys. The key-in-the-lock process took on the difficulty of three-dimensional chess, but he finally got the door opened and flipped the switch to flood the room with light. He made room for Jane by moving a large stack of file folders from the seat of an ancient wooden office chair to the floor beside the chair. Jane perched gingerly upon it while Dubarb moved around behind the desk and sat heavily.

"Okay," he said, leaning forward. "What've got there?"

Jane started to speak, but Freeman had a late thought and stopped her with a raised hand. He shuffled around behind his desk for a few minutes before ripping out an oversized notebook, the kind that sit on easels for classroom examples. Another earthmoving project commenced on his desk, with the end result being a blue marker held aloft. He handed both to Jane.

"Here," he said, "let's write it down to keep it straight." He had another late thought and added, "Please."

"Okay, she said. "We have four basic categories of capital sources, the largest by far being our common stock. When you include the shares held by ownership, we have the six million common shares outstanding."

She paused and shuffled through the papers in her hand to find the one she was looking for.

"And as of close last Friday, we were selling at $59.15 per share."

"Okay, write that down," Freeman instructed. Jane dutifully obeyed.

"We've been doing our best to hoard earnings over the past couple of years until we are ready to roll out these new plants," Freeman added. "How are we doing there?" He knew the number very well, but preferred to ask over stating.

"I think well," Jane said. "As of last quarter's balance sheet, we have nearly $50 million in retained earnings. Of course, that figure is slightly inflated because we have some stuff for which part of that is already earmarked. Things like overdue raises and current facility maintenance."

"Okay, good," he said, "write that down."

"And then on the debt side," Jane said, talking as she wrote, "we have the bonds that now have a bit over 16 years left. They're selling for $961.58 each, again as of last Friday."

"Okay," Freeman mumbled as he ran his fingers through his bushy head. Suddenly it appeared as though he was completely removed from the conversation taking place. The tuffs of hair sticking out at obtuse angles resembled oddly assembled smoke stacks, releasing the exhaust of an overburdened brain.

"Write that..." he said, distractedly.

"Got it," Jane interrupted, having already done so.

"If I recall, we probably also have about eighteen million in other odd private debt, right?"

"Uhmm, yeah," Jane responded, glancing at the sheets, wondering how much of this he already knew. "Just about that."

She wrote it down without being instructed. Freeman appeared to be appraising a small square of the office wall that looked largely the same as all the rest.

Apparently, Freeman reached whatever conclusion he was seeking, as he shook his head slightly and returned his full attention to Jane.

"Welcome back," she said, smiling.

"What?"

"Nothing. So, here is what we have." She turned the board and placed it upon her lap for him to view.

Source	*Amount*
1. Common stock	*6,000,000 × $59.15*
2. Retained earnings	*$50,000,000*
3. Coupon bonds	*20,000 × 961.58*
4. Private debt	*18,000,000*

"Go ahead then," Freeman said. "Calculate our current capital structure."

He reached under his computer monitor, spilled a cup filled with pencils, and grabbed a calculator before passing it to Jane. It was neon pink with blue buttons. It could add, subtract, multiply, and divide. That was it. Jane stared at him as she took it from his outstretched hand.

He bowed his head to avoid her gaze and said, "It was free from my grandkid's open house at school."

Jane reversed the board without comment and started to work. Freeman went to the back corner of his office and rummaged around until he got the ancient coffee machine to begin its morning chore. They finished at the same time.

"Here we go," Jane said. She turned the board again to show the calculations.

Source	*Amount*		*Weight*
Common stock	*6,000,000 × $59.15* =	$354,900,000	80.27 %
Retained earnings	*$50,000,000* =	$50,000,000	11.31 %
Coupon bonds	*20,000 × 961.58* =	$19,231,600	4.35 %
Private debt	*18,000,000* =	$18,000,000	4.07 %
		$442,131,600	100 %

"Alrighty, then," Freeman said, "So we are mostly equity based. But we knew that already."

"Yes," Jane responded, "that is not atypical of a publicly traded firm. The real question now becomes how much this capital costs us, particularly as we begin to plan how to use some more."

"Well, we did some of that analysis just last month during the infamous firm birthday celebration. Look, I left it there." He pointed at the dingy gray board that hung on the wall. Scribbled on it were the CAPM calculations from the previous month's impromptu powwow in Freeman's office. The bottom line was the most important, so he pulled himself noisily from his chair and pointed at it to emphasize his point:

$$\begin{aligned} k_{cs} &= .12+(10 - .12)*1.19 \\ &= 11.88\% \end{aligned}$$

"The last month hasn't done anything to really change all those numbers, and since they are all estimates anyway, we'll just go with that for now." The coffee machine gurgled in the background, and Jane could see Freeman fighting the mental battle of whether to wait for it to finish before sitting down again. She decided to plow on.

"We can also take a second to estimate the cost of equity according to the dividend growth model. I'll do that while you get your coffee."

Freeman almost smiled as he turned to impatiently wait for the coffee to finish.

The company had continued their strategy of increasing the dividend by $.04 per year. So, in 2011 they had made all four quarterly dividend payments of $.22 per share. This annual dividend of $.88 along with the current stock price of $59.15 could be used to find another estimate of the cost of equity.

"What growth rate?" Jane asked Freeman.

"We can stick with the 5%," he said. The coffee was done and he carried it back to his desk. Jane was astounded to find he also brought a steaming Styrofoam cup to her as well. Was it clean? She decided to take the chance.

"Thank you," she said, gingerly taking a sip. It wasn't as strong as motor oil, but it was close.

"Perfect," she said. This time, Dubarb did smile.

Jane tapped a few buttons on the comical calculator and stood to write the answer in the last remaining space on the gray wall board:

$$\begin{aligned} k &= \frac{.88(1.05)}{55.19} + .05 \\ &= 6.67\% \end{aligned}$$

"Well, that's different," she said. "What do you want to do?"

"They're both estimates. Let's use them both," he responded with a shrug. Now that he had his coffee, he was back to his normal self. He leaned way back in his chair and crossed his sockless ankles on his desk.

"So, we'll use 9.28% as our cost of equity then," she said. "The debt side is easier, at least in a way. We know the price of the bonds implies a yield of 9.08%. But what do you want to do about the private debt?"

He gave it some thought while also studying the light fixture in the ceiling.

"Well, it would average to be higher than the public debt, I think. Let's use 10% to be safe."

"Sure," Jane said. "So, using our tax rate of about 35%, we can calculate our current WACC now."

"Uh hmm," Freeman agreed, staring at the ceiling. Jane began to wonder exactly what was in that coffee. She went ahead and did the basic math:

$$\begin{aligned} WACC &= .9158(9.28) + (.0435 * 9.08 * .65) + (.0407 * 10 * .65) \\ &= 9.02\% \end{aligned}$$

When she passed on the answer to Freeman, he replied, "Well, there you have it. That is our starting point. On average, every dollar of value we have costs us 9.02 cents."

Jane felt as though she was being dismissed, so she shuffled her sheets of paper together and sat the easel pad on the desk in front of Freeman. He reached over and tore out the top sheet she had filled.

"Take this and type it up in a prettier document," he ordered. "And bring it to the others during the meeting on Wednesday."

"Can do," she replied rising, "as soon as I get done with my scheduled interview with the Big Blue Bank."

"Let someone else do that," Freeman said. "You can assign it to one of them when they get here."

Jane was surprised with how much she enjoyed hearing that she could "assign" her coworkers to do something. She decided to leave on that note.

"Thanks for the coffee," she said.

"Hey, hey!" Freeman exclaimed. He pointed and extended an open palm. "That's mine."

Jane meekly returned the calculator and retreated out the door.

ALTERNATE ENDINGS

1. *Dubarb Freeman decided to take the easy route and just use the estimated 5 % growth rate for the dividend growth model. Suppose instead they use the sustainable growth rate, calculated from the Hack Back's 2010 Financial Statements (located in an appendix). How does using the SGR change the situation? What is the new estimated cost of equity? What is the new WACC?*
2. *Think about the number of shares outstanding for a moment. Four of the six million shares belong to Tyler and Lilly. Is it fair to assume their expected return is the same as all other shareholders, given their level of entrenchment with the company? For the sake of argument, let's assume it is not. In fact,*

specifically assume their expected return is only 7 %. How does that change the WACC? After you answer that question, think about whether it makes sense to separate the two groups of equity. Why or why not?

3. ***What if Freeman says, "The DGM is useless. It's completely driven by the assumption of that growth rate. Let's just ignore it." First of all, what are your feelings on this notion? Secondly, how would such a decision change the values calculated above?***
4. ***Notice in the WACC calculation that common stock and retained earnings are assumed to have the same cost. This is an important assumption, so think about it a bit. Why does that (or does it not?) make sense to do?***

8.5 Capital Structure Theories

8.5.1 M&M Proposition I

As with most things, before we venture into new territory, we should first go back and discuss why this new territory is worthy of exploration. In this instance, the motivation takes us back to the dawn of finance. The discipline we now know as corporate finance is a relatively young field. In fact, it is generally assumed to take shape somewhere around the mid-twentieth century. The first significant undertaking of the discipline was to evaluate **capital structure policy**. We have covered in detail throughout the text the notion that corporate finance primarily involves two issues: finding capital sources and funding projects with those capital sources. Thus, the general question of whether corporate finance matters is essentially the same as whether the choice between the different sources of funding (e.g., debt or equity) matters. The first to truly take an aggressive approach to evaluating this question were pioneers Franco Modigliani and Merton Miller, who in 1958 published a seminal piece of research that has since become known as **M&M Proposition I**.

M&M Proposition I simply states the firm's choice of funding is completely irrelevant. The idea of M&M Proposition I, although proven via a relatively complicated financial model, can be most easily described in the framework of the old-fashioned balance sheet identity. Recall

$$\text{Assets} = \text{Debt} + \text{Equity}$$

Thus, you have a dollar amount of debt along with a dollar amount of equity, and when they are added together, they make up the total value of the firm. This is equivalent to the value of all the firm's assets. M&M Proposition I says the distinction between the two dollar amounts doesn't matter, since in the end the same value of assets is obtained.

This can be referred to as the pie model in that it doesn't matter how you slice a pie, at the end of it all, you still have the same amount of pie. Figure 8.1 illustrates this notion. Notice that both firms have a capital structure of 70/30. One of them has more debt and the other has more equity. Does it matter to you which is which?

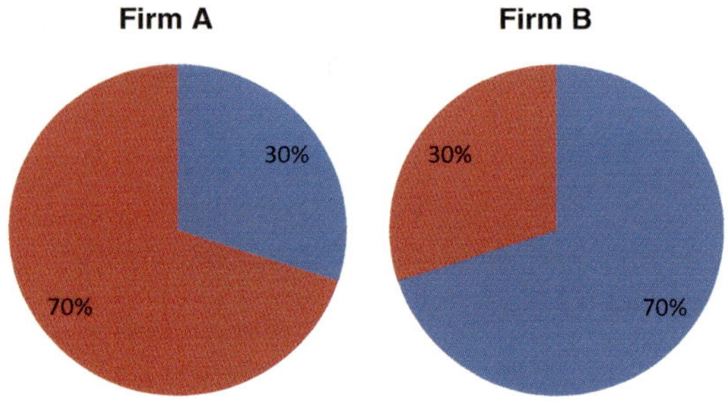

Fig. 8.1 M&M Proposition I

M&M says that it does not, as they are both the same size and the firm has the same value. To put it another way, assume that the picture below represents pizzas and the different allocations are pepperoni and sausage. If you are completely indifferent between the two, would you care how it was divided? No, of course not. This is the crux of the argument. If the firm is indifferent between the sources of funding (a dollar is a dollar is a dollar…), then the allocations are irrelevant.

If you take a moment to think on it, you'll realize that this extremely well-known work concludes that everything you have been learning is completely useless because at the end of the day, the choice between debt and equity financing is irrelevant. If they are interchangeable, the vast amount of work that you can put into the decision is mute. Don't lose heart, however. As you can probably imagine, this notion will change. Going back to the pizza example, what could make us *not* indifferent? What if sausage pizza cost double that of pepperoni? Would the allocation matter in that case? Of course it would.

The seminal work of M&M in 1958 made several qualifying assumptions, including zero transaction costs, efficient markets, and, perhaps most importantly, no taxes. Much of the discussion in the 50-plus years since publication of M&M Proposition I has been related to the topic of relaxing these restrictions.

8.5.2 M&M Proposition II

To add to this momentous finding, Modigliani and Miller developed another proposition that delved deeper into the firm's cost of equity. It is based primarily upon our earlier discussion of the weighted average cost of capital. Recall the simple version of the formula can be generalized as follows:

$$WACC = W_e k_e + W_d k_d (1 - T)$$

where e is an equity source (e.g., common stock) and d is a debt source (e.g., coupon bonds). Since one of the assumptions made by M&M is the absence of taxes, that can be dropped for now. And, if we use a little creative algebra to rearrange this to solve for the cost of equity (k_e), we get the following:

$$k_e = WACC + (WACC - k_d)\frac{D}{E}$$

Thus, the primary conclusion drawn by **M&M Proposition II** is that the cost of equity depends on three things:

1. The firm's overall cost of capital (*WACC*)
2. The cost of debt (k_d)
3. The ratio of the total firm debt (D) and total firm equity (E)

Recall that required returns are driven by the risk associated with the assets on which funds are used. Thus, the cost of equity depends on the risk of equity, which can be summed up mathematically with the right-hand side of the M&M Prop II equation. These pieces are often further divided into two types of risk. The *WACC* is a measure of total **business risk**, which represents the firm's current risk, given the existing capital structure. Since the underlying costs of this existing capital structure have been determined by the risk of business activities the firm has previously undertaken, the end value (*WACC*) can be interpreted as the risk of current business operations. Any current operation that fails to generate a return in excess of *WACC* is value reducing, which is very much inconsistent with the goal of the firm.

The second piece, which is

$$(WACC - k_d)\frac{D}{E}$$

can be referred to as **financial risk**. This is the risk that occurs with the issuance of additional debt (or, more specifically, a higher level of D/E). As the D/E ratio increases, the cost of equity will also increase with the elevated debt level within in the firm. Thus, it would be an error to examine only debt or equity independent of each other. As we move forward, we must examine not only the individual effects of the costs of debt and equity on the firm's capital structure and budgeting decisions, but the simultaneous effects as well.

8.5.3 M&M Proposition I with Taxes

While the notion of a tax-free world is certainly a nice fantasy, we all know it to be just that, a fantasy. There is nothing technically incorrect about M&M Proposition I or II. Given the assumptions utilized in the model, the choice of financing is completely irrelevant. However, we know this is not actually the case due to violations of those assumptions in the real world. Therefore, if capital structure matters (and you know it must), it is because of these violations of the assumptions. Therefore, it is these assumptions that we must examine in order to move forward with our discussion.

When a firm chooses to use debt in its capital structure, we refer to that firm as being **leveraged**. In society, debt often gets viewed negatively and often for a good reason. Debt represents a contractual obligation to future cash flows, for both individuals and corporations. Therefore, the higher that contractual obligation, the more risk of not being able to make your payments. Further, since debt is generally taken in order to secure additional assets for the firm, failure to make payments would result in removal of these assets and an upsetting of the financial budgeting of the entire firm. In short, too much debt has the potential to lead to very bad things, one of which will be discussed later in this chapter.

Thus, with that brief discussion completed, the logical first thought is that a firm should take on as little debt as possible and perhaps none at all. However, we have already discussed the positive side of debt, which is based upon the accounting fact that interest payments are tax deductible, while dividend payments are not. This can create a **tax shield**, which results from the reduction in taxes attributable to interest payments.

To illustrate, consider Firm OWW that just made a quarterly dividend payment of \$150,000 and, at the same time, just made an interest payment also of \$150,000. Assuming the firm's tax rate is 35 %, this means the actual (after-tax) cost of these payments is

$$\begin{gathered}\textbf{Dividends}:\textbf{\$150,000}\\ \textbf{Interest}:\textbf{\$150,000}*(\textbf{1}-\textbf{.35})=\textbf{\$97,500}\end{gathered}$$

resulting in a difference of \$52,500. Therefore, the debt costs the firm less than equity, all else equal. This example is the same as our discussion of *WACC*, wherein we concluded that the cost of debt financing needs to be adjusted by (1-*T*). In upcoming examples, we will continue to use the percentage cost rate, rather than dollar amounts, but the result will be the same. Given an equivalent raw cost of debt and equity, debt will always be cheaper.

Therefore, we have another simple, but important, conclusion: *taxes matter*. If we can see this, so too could the Nobel Laureates Franco Modigliani and Merton Miller. In fact, in response to this issue, M&M produced another seminal work in 1963 that addressed the influence of taxes on capital structure. We will refer to the resulting conclusion as **M&M with taxes**. Allow V_L to represent a firm that has some degree of leverage and V_U to represent an equivalent firm with a no debt (i.e., all equity) capital structure. M&M Proposition I with taxes concludes the following:

$$V_L = V_U + (D * T)$$

The *(D*T)* is the *PV* of the amount of the firm's tax shield from taking interest-bearing debt *D*. The firm's tax rate will never be negative, and the debt will also typically be no less than zero (unless a lending institution, which brings about a whole different set of circumstances). Thus, putting this together leaves the conclusion of

$$V_L \geq V_U$$

In short, adding debt adds value due to the accompanying tax benefits. So, debt *can* be a very good thing.

8.5.4 Financial Distress Costs

Financial distress is a bad thing. It means the company is having trouble paying their bills. This could be manifest in simple ways, such as an inability to pay leases or power bills, or in more advanced ways, such as missing coupon payments or being required to reduce or eliminate dividend payments. In the extreme, a company that has excessive financial distress can go **bankrupt**. While there are many definitions of bankruptcy out there and each has its own merits, there is really only one way to define it on a theoretical basis. If the firm's value of assets is equal to the firm's value of debt, then according to the venerable balance sheet identity, the value of the firm's equity must be zero. In this instance, the firm is economically bankrupt.

In our theoretical world, this is the worst thing that can happen to a firm. Since our only function is to maximize shareholder wealth, and shareholder wealth is a function of the value of the firm's equity, an equity value of zero is the worst-case scenario. Thus, a firm must do everything in its ability to avoid this situation.

Bankruptcy, or just the potential, can create two types of costs to the firm. The first, known as **direct bankruptcy costs**, is the sum of all costs that occur as the result of going bankrupt. When a firm becomes bankrupt, one of the first necessary reactions is to sell off pieces of the firm to generate cash flow. In a state of financial distress, the probability of receiving a fair market value is very low. Therefore, one example of a direct bankruptcy cost is the difference between the fair value and the necessary liquidation value. The more dire costs are those associated with the negative signal bankruptcy provides the market. As you may guess, the market does not joyously receive news of an impending bankruptcy, and stock prices generally respond negatively in kind.

The other type of cost, **indirect bankruptcy costs**, is those incurred in the effort to prevent bankruptcy. To repeat, the worst thing that can happen to a firm is bankruptcy, so it should be avoided if at all possible. Therefore, a company will expend considerable resources on things such as auditing, oversight committees, and insurance policies to insulate themselves from negative deviations in the firm's expected cash flows that could eventually result in bankruptcy.

So, why are we discussing financial distress in the context of capital structure theories? While bankruptcy is not a theory, per se—it actually fits very well into the discussion due to the relationship between debt levels and financial distress potential. The more debt you have, the riskier you become, which is an obvious fact to both the lender and the borrower. The result of excessive borrowing is that any additional borrowing will come only at a very high cost. The same is true of an individual who is already heavily mortgaged and goes back to the bank for more money. If the individual is able to receive additional debt funding at all, it will certainly be at an elevated cost.

To sum, the more debt a firm has in its capital structure, the higher the limitation on uses of the firm's future cash flows. This leads directly to a higher probability of future bankruptcy, which in turn leads to much higher cost of financing.

So, debt *can* be a very bad thing.

8.5.5 The Trade-Off Theory of Capital Structure

As you may have noticed, we have some dissenting views in the two immediately preceding sections. Is debt good or bad? Well, the answer, as you may imagine, is that it's both. Debt is good because it is cheaper than equity due to the tax benefits, but it is also bad because it increases the probability of bankruptcy. So, the million dollar question concerns how to find the point that creates an equal balance between the two sides.

The answer lies in the **trade-off theory of capital structure**. The beauty of this theory is that it builds upon the seminal M&M theories. We will describe the trade-off theory with a couple of graphs, as displayed in Fig. 8.2. The first relationship we need to address is that between the value of the firm and the firm's level of debt. The value of the firm is our primary concern, as to maximize the value is essentially the same as maximizing shareholder wealth. Also, the entire discussion of the optimal mixture of debt and equity can be summed up with a simple question. *How much debt should we take?* Whatever is left automatically becomes equity.

First, consider M&M Proposition I, which concludes the mixture between debt and equity is irrelevant. Thus, the firm has the same value no matter how much (or little) debt they hold. While we know this is based upon an unrealistic set of circumstances, it does provide a basis upon which to build. Second, consider M&M with taxes, which has the conclusion that adding debt adds value because the firm effectively obtains $1 worth of capital for less than a dollar (e.g., $65 cents, if the tax rate is 35 %). As the blue line on the top graph in Fig. 8.2 displays, this suggests the firm should just add debt indefinitely. But, naturally, this is ignoring the counterargument that debt increases distress costs and certainly cannot increase indefinitely. There must come a point where the elevated cost of obtaining debt funding disproportionally offsets the tax benefit.

Thus, the trade-off theory in the graph allows for this balance between the positive and negative aspects of debt. Adding debt is advantageous, at least for a while, because the tax benefits outweigh the increase in financial distress costs. However, after a while, this relationship must reverse and the additional risk becomes too much for the tax benefit to overcome. For example, suppose a firm could get debt additional financing but only at a rate of 30 %. Even with a 35 % tax relief, the 19.5 % after-tax cost is likely higher than any type of equity financing.

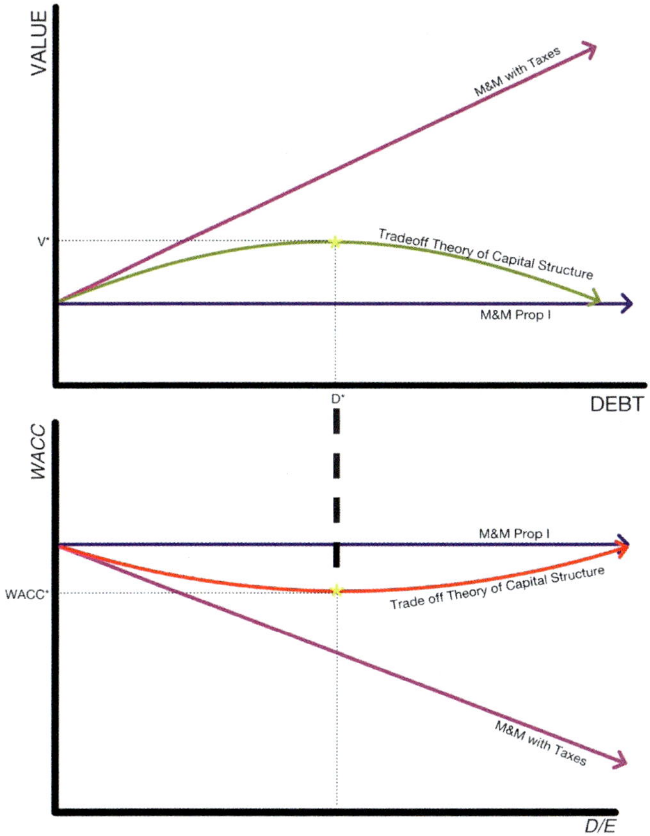

Fig. 8.2 Trade-off theory of capital structure

The optimal level of debt, which is that which maximizes the tax benefit under the constraint of increasing financial distress expenses, is indicated with the * and labeled D^*. More importantly, this corresponds to V^*, which is the highest value of the firm given these parameters.

Now sit back and take a breath. We are about to unveil the answer to the most important question in corporate finance. Let's review the reason we are taking this journey. Our goal is to maximize shareholder wealth. And, while that is a very pleasant sounding goal and certainly an accurate depiction of the motivation behind corporate finance, it has been thus far little more than that. The goal as stated represents an unsolvable problem as there is no quantitative framework on which to measure the maximum potential value of the firm. It is simply not available. To see why, ask yourself the following question. How rich can *you* possibly be? Can you answer that with a number? Yeah, me neither.

In fact, if you think about it for a moment, you can also see an obvious problem with "finding the optimal level of debt." Without a point of reference, we have no notion of the potential. To illustrate, consider trying to find the level of debt on a balance sheet without knowing the level of assets. It is impossible. The same is true here. So, let's take a look at the bottom graph in Fig. 8.2. Notice it relates the *WACC* to the debt-to-equity ratio. Examining the debt-to-equity ratio is more important than just examining the level of debt alone because it is crucial to understand there is a trade-off. Given a fixed capital structure, adding a dollar of debt automatically results in a reduction of a dollar of equity, and vice versa. Even when given an unfixed structure, choosing to use debt automatically means choosing to not use equity for that specific piece of funding. The point is that the two levels must be decided upon simultaneously, as M&M Proposition II suggests.

On the *y*-axis is the level of *WACC* that the relative capital structure entails. Notice that the conclusion of M&M Proposition I indicates that the cost is completely irrelevant to the capital structure chosen. When taxes are included, the capital structure certainly matters, as every additional dollar of debt funding (and corresponding reduction in equity funding) represents a lowering of costs. This again suggests the optimal capital structure would be 100 % debt, which of course is impractical given the constraints of financial distress. Thus, the trade-off theory again balances these issues. For a while adding debt is advantageous, as the tax benefit decreases the cost of funding. However, beyond a certain level, adding debt comes at increased cost, as the increased risk of financial distress overwhelms any tax benefit. The result is again an optimal level, represented by $(D/E)^*$, which corresponds to the minimum realistic value of *WACC* (*WACC**).

Most importantly, as the graph indicates, the capital structure that results in the minimum level of *WACC* will automatically also result in the maximum value of the firm.

BOOM!! There is it. We have been waiting on that answer for a long time. It bears repeating (and bolding):

To maximize shareholder wealth, the firm should identify the minimum weighted average cost of capital.

Although this took a lot of work to get to, on the surface it's not that difficult to understand. Consider your current life just as it is right now. And then suppose I offer you two options of financially bettering yourself over the next month. First, I would increase your pay by $100. Second, I will magically decrease the value of whatever you buy by $100. It wouldn't matter which I did. Either way, you would have $100 more at the end of the upcoming month. The same is true of a firm. The goal is to make money by generating a profit in excess of what they spend to generate the profit. Thus, the less they spend, the more the profit. Also, the cheaper the funds are to obtain, the more of them the firm can obtain and the more profit that can then be made. Doing so will continuously assure the firm maximizes shareholder wealth.

We are still left with a remaining question of how to actually do this, but before we move onto that, review Table 8.3, which summarizes the very important conclusions drawn from capital structure theories.

Table 8.3 Summary of capital structure theories

Theory	Conclusions drawn
M&M Proposition I	Capital structure is irrelevant
M&M Proposition II	$\uparrow$Debt = > $\uparrow$cost of equity
M&M with taxes	$\uparrow$Debt = > $\uparrow$value
Financial distress	$\uparrow$Debt = > $\uparrow$cost of debt and equity
Trade-off theory	Firms should borrow money to the point that the tax benefit of the additional debt is exactly offset by the increase in financial distress costs accompanying the additional debt

LOOK IT UP: The seminal trade-off theory is but one of the numerous theories that have been posited regarding capital structure choice. Two other very notable examples are the pecking order theory and the market timing theory. Both have very interesting implications for how a firm should decide between financing options when funding projects. What are they? For a more detailed exercise, do some research into what current literature says about the validity of all three theories in relation to actual financing decisions firms make.

8.6 Applications of the Trade-Off Theory

The conclusion drawn above should be an ever present concern. For each project the firm is considering, considerable care should be given to obtaining the cheapest possible capital with which to fund it. To do so would maximize the value of each project, and when done continuously, the value of the firm would also be continuously maximized. Consider the following example. A firm is considering a project that costs $10,000,000 to implement. They need to identify some way of obtaining the funds and have identified the following four potential options:

Option 1: Use 75 % equity and 25 % debt
Option 2: Use 60 % equity and 40 % debt
Option 3: Use 40 % equity and 60 % debt
Option 4: Use 25 % equity and 75 % debt

The situation is complicated by our understanding that the different capital structures will result in differing costs of debt and equity. Suppose the firm has discovered that the respective costs of each option are as illustrated in Table 8.4.

Notice that the costs increase in the expected manner. As debt increases, so too does the cost of both equity and debt financing. Adding debt adds risk, and this should be reflected by expected returns from both shareholders and creditors.

Table 8.4 Capital structures and costs

Option	W_e	W_d	k_e	k_d
1	.75	.25	9.4 %	7.4 %
2	.60	.40	9.5	9.2
3	.40	.60	10.2	10.6
4	.25	.75	10.7	13.2

Table 8.5 Dollar amounts of cost

Option	Average cost	Cost in $
1	8.25 %	$825,250
2	8.10	809,200
3	8.21	821,400
4	9.11	911,000

Recall that our objective is to minimize the cost of obtaining the funds by finding the minimum *WACC*:

$$WACC = W_E k_E + W_D k_D (1 - T)$$

There are five determinant variables in this equation, but only two that the firm has any direct control over. The cost of equity and cost of debt are determined by the shareholders and creditors, respectively. The tax rate is determined by tax law. Thus, the weights are the only variables the firm can determine and should do so in a way that minimizes costs. Assuming the standard 35 % tax rate, the *WACC*s for each option are as follows:

$$\begin{aligned} \boldsymbol{WACC_1} &= (\mathbf{.75 * 9.4}) + (\mathbf{.25 * 7.4 * .65}) = \mathbf{8.25\%} \\ \boldsymbol{WACC_2} &= (\mathbf{.60 * 9.5}) + (\mathbf{.40 * 9.2 * .65}) = \mathbf{8.10\%} \\ \boldsymbol{WACC_3} &= (\mathbf{.40 * 10.2}) + (\mathbf{.60 * 10.6 * .65}) = \mathbf{8.21\%} \\ \boldsymbol{WACC_4} &= (\mathbf{.25 * 10.7}) + (\mathbf{.75 * 13.2 * .65}) = \mathbf{9.11\%} \end{aligned}$$

Given the option, the firm should choose capital structure #2 because it allows them to obtain the necessary funding at the cheapest possible rate. The average dollar of financing costs 8.1 cents, as compared to the worst choice (option 4), which cost over one cent more per dollar to obtain. While it may seem silly to be concerned over fractions of pennies, remember that we are talking about a lot of pennies. To further drive this point home, consider Table 8.5.

The optimal capital structure of 60 % equity and 40 % debt costs the firm a bit over $809,000 to obtain the $10 million needed. This is calculated as follows:

$$\begin{aligned} \mathbf{Cost} &= [(\mathbf{.60 * \$10M}) * \mathbf{.095}] + [(\mathbf{.40 * \$10M}) * \mathbf{.092 * .65}] \\ &= \mathbf{\$809,200} \end{aligned}$$

Due to rounding the average dollar percentage cost (*WACC*) gives a close approximation of this number. So, choosing the optimal structure as opposed, in the extreme to the worst selection, saves the project and the firm over $100,000. Making such decisions on each and every project will ensure we are doing our absolute best to maximize shareholder profits.

Of course, in the case of an actual real-world application of these notions, the firm is not constrained to a fixed number of capital structure options. In fact, there are technically an infinite number of capital structures to choose from. For example, is a 61/39 better than the 60/40 above? What about 60.5/39.5? In such a case, the situation becomes infinitely more complicated, as we could spend the rest of our lives calculating all possible *WACC*s in an effort to determine the absolute lowest. Such calculations are best left for a computer program. The nearby TECH HELP box shows an example of doing this in Excel.

Another obvious potential complication is that the firm can have many different capital sources. Suppose the firm has three, common stock, coupon bonds, and preferred stock. The choice of optimal structure is fundamentally the same; we want the lowest *WACC*. The process of identifying this structure becomes much more complicated, however. A 1% increase in debt no longer automatically means a 1 % decrease in common stock. While it could mean this, it could also mean a 1 % decrease in preferred stock, or any combination of decreases in both that add to the 1 %. Again, a suitable computer program should be used to obtain the proper answer in such a situation.

8.7 Additional Details

There are a couple of very important caveats to this discussion. It would be easy to fall into the trap of believing that the cost of funds depends only or primarily upon the source of the funds. While this may be true in part, as evidenced by theoretical findings and practical anecdotes, source is not the primary driver behind the estimated costs. This is another important point, so we'll make it stand out a bit:

The cost of funds is determined by the risk associated with the use of the funds.

This means that riskier projects will generate higher costs of funding, while safer projects will come at a cheaper rate. It is up to the shareholders and/or the creditors to determine exactly how the level of risk gets incorporated into the expected returns. While we know that an increased debt level will almost certainly raise the cost of debt due to the increased probability of bankruptcy, we are unsure of exactly the degree. The increase should be proportionally larger if the money is being spent on projects that increase the overall risk of the firm. Such projects are those with the greatest chance of creating financial distress through lack of cash flow. But again, it is the lender (private or public) that must incorporate that knowledge into the pricing of the funds.

Rising debt will also likely raise the cost of equity as well, which is suggested by M&M Proposition I. This is a much more difficult relation to get a handle on, as there are many factors that come into play. Consider the two estimation methods available to us. First, the dividend growth model suggests the cost of equity is dependent upon the dividend payment, the current stock price, and the expected growth rate. All of these things could change as the level of debt rises, but there is no way to know the exact degree.

The second method, the CAPM, has similar problems. The only variable specific to the firm is beta, which is an estimate of the firm's movement along with the market. Again, the level of debt (and equity, of course) a firm has will likely affect stock price movements, although indirectly. Again, this is very hard to estimate. In fact, accurately measuring the effect of rising debt levels on the total required return (*WACC*) is impossible. It is determined by the risk of the project and the lenders' (or stockholders') perception of their required compensation for funding that risk. In short, there is no set equation to lean upon.

So, where does that leave us? In short, we will never know exactly how much funding will cost. We will never know exactly how much lenders will charge for future funding and how it may differ from past funding. Even more so, we will never know in advance the return that shareholders require to remain loyal in their holdings. Thus, it is the corporate finance employee's task to essentially estimate the unknown and attempt to obtain reasonable figures that accurately reflect expected costs. And, with all estimates, the true goal may not be to attempt perfection, but, rather, to attempt to minimize the possibility of significant error.

TECH HELP 8.1 Finding the Optimal Capital Structure in Excel

Consider the following question:
Firm ABC has a current capital structure of 75 % equity and 25 % debt. The current cost of equity is 7.87 %, and the current cost of debt is 7.08 %. The firm has a tax rate of 35 %. For every 1 % increase in debt (and corresponding 1 % decrease in equity), the firm's cost of debt is expected to increase by 5 basis points (.05 %), and the firm's cost of equity is expected to increase by 2 basis points (.02 %). Given this, what is the firm's optimal capital structure?

We first set up what we know in Excel. The screenshots below show an "Inputs" field, which includes the current capital structure weights and costs. The "Calculations" fields are those where the work is done, and the "Outputs" fields are where the answers are derived. The example below uses Solver, which is available as an add-in for Excel. Notice that you must reference the cells and put constraints on the levels of the "Output" variables. The answer to the question is an optimal capital structure of approximately 36.5 % equity and 63.5 % debt. This results in the lowest *WACC* of 6.87 %.

(continued)

(continued)

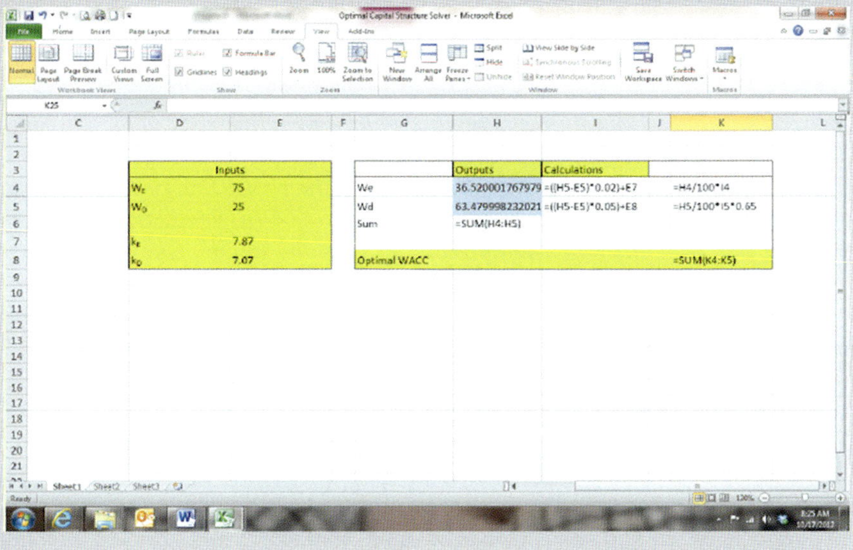

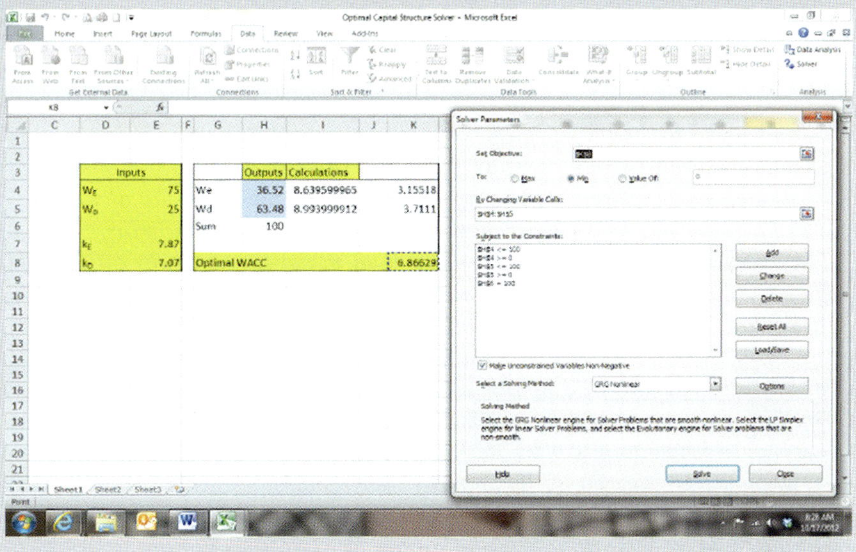

IN THE REAL WORLD

Jane had done as she had been instructed (as always) and had copies of the predawn report she and Freeman had compiled ready well in advance of the Wednesday meeting. Brandon had helped in drafting the report and was

graciously accepting of his role as interviewer of the private lenders they were considering. In fact, he thought that played more to his strengths of communication anyway.

The three were joined by Marilyn and Stewart 5 minutes before ten on Wednesday morning in the conference board room.

"What a mess!" Marilyn exclaimed as she came into the room. She was dressed to play volleyball in a tsunami, with head-to-toe rain gear. She quickly shucked her designer raincoat covered with some type of floral pattern and then kicked neon green rain boots into the corner of the room. She rummaged around in her massive purse until she pulled out a pair of 4-in. heels. Once she slipped them on her feet, she was finally ready to face the others. She turned to their stares.

"What?" she said. The weather outside was unusually nasty and put a damper on everyone's holiday spirit. The weather in Arizona was never very cold, even in the dead of winter, but over night the temperatures had drifted down to the low forties and there was a cold rain blowing across the city. While fully equipped for 100°, anything below 60 made the city grind to a virtual standstill.

"Aren't you from the Northeast?" Stewart said, removing his hat and gently placing it on the floor beside his chosen chair.

"Apparently, I still am," Marilyn said, making a beeline for the coffee machine humming quietly in the corner.

It took a few moments, but soon she was comforted enough to take her seat, and behind closed doors, they were ready to begin. Jane handed out the report and gave them a few minutes to examine what they were seeing.

"Tyler and Lilly will be around in a few minutes," Freeman said, "and when they get here, we will want to show them where we are. Since, for some bizarre, unexplained reason, the entire company is shutting down for the next week, this will be our last time to get their attention before the first of the year."

"Is there final word on when we want to make the decision on the plants, Scrooge?" Brandon asked. He earned smiles from his colleagues.

Freeman let the unflattering comparison pass and instead answered the question.

"As soon after the first of the year as we can. We've been dancing around everything for long enough and have answered as many questions as can be answered. It's time to make the decision."

"I hope we've covered all the details," Jane said nervously.

"I assure you that we haven't," he responded, garnering sharp glances from everyone, "but we have done the best we can. We can't predict the future, so there will be surprises, but I am confident our estimates are sound."

There was a firm knock on the door before it was opened. Tyler and Lilly strode in with cheerful looks on their faces.

"Happy Holidays, everyone," Lilly said, beaming.

"Are you ready for us?" Tyler added.

"Yes, sir. Have a seat," Jane said, handing each of them the report. They each began to flip through it, Tyler out of genuine curiosity and Lilly out of habit. Both knew they were going to be filled in on the high points.

"What you see here is the result of nearly a year's work." Jane continued after they refocused their attention on her. While they had been reviewing the data, she had begun a PowerPoint presentation and was standing with remote in hand. She pointed and clicked the forward button.

"As a little background, if you recall, Brandon and I were assigned the task of determining where we should get the money to fund the plants that we hope to break ground on very soon. When we got involved in doing that, we realized that a comprehensive review of our capital structure hadn't been done since the company had gone public. So, we began there. Brandon, do you want to go over the highlights of that?"

"Sure," he said, standing with Jane and accepting the offer of the remote. Using the laser pointer, he indicated the section of the first slide that detailed the current capital structure.

"As you can see, our existing capital structure is heavily equity weighted, with over 90 % coming from either common stock or retained earnings. The remaining eight-plus percent comes from our bonds and other miscellaneous private debt. The estimated cost of the equity is around 9.28 %. The bonds are currently yielding 9.08 %, and the other debt is about 10 % annually."

He switched the slide to show the calculated WACC.

"As you can see, when you put it all together, you get an average cost just north of 9 %."

"Okay, stop there," Lilly said. "Remember that you are talking to someone here that owns a company but doesn't come from a finance background. What exactly does that mean to me?"

"Great question," Jane said. "The best way to think about it is to remember that debt plus equity equals assets and that what you have just seen represents the value of the firm. So, each dollar of value comes at an expense whether it is direct. . ."

". . .like the interest on our debt," Brandon interjected and Jane nodded in agreement.

"Or indirect like the expected return of our shareholders," Jane continued. "In short, every dollar we have comes from somewhere and it cost something."

"And remember these are annual returns," Marilyn spoke up, "so each year we have to pay for these dollars of value. Shareholders don't just require the return once, they require it each year."

"And the same with the creditors," Tyler said. "I understand that, I believe, but I have a concern. I remember back when we were looking at discounting the future cash flows of the project, we used a 7 % discount rate. This seems to say that we were underestimating our costs then. Won't that make a large difference?

"Yes, of course it does," Marilyn said in her typically outspoken way, "That's why Mr. Freeman was so adamant that we go through the entire process before we make a decision."

This did nothing to reassure Tyler, but he reluctantly accepted the answer.

Lilly spoke up again. "I've got a follow-up... Is that good? Is 9 % a good number or is it too high?"

The question, as many of Lilly's, while framed with simplicity, gave the others pause. She was a much more qualitative thinker than the others and often asked such questions. Still, the room remained silent for a moment as they pondered an answer.

"I'll answer that," Freeman said. More and more, he was lying in the background and letting the younger folks run the conversations. But, when needed, he still enjoyed speaking up.

"In fact, I'll give you two answers and they are both correct. The first is that we have no idea if it is good or not. To say so would require a comparison to some other entity or time and that is not information we have available at this moment. If we could say, for example, that the cost was 10 % last year and only 9 % this year, then yes, that seems to indicate this is a good, or at least better, number."

"What's the second answer?" Lilly asked.

"When you asked if it needed to be lower, the answer to that is always yes."

"But you just said...." Lilly sputtered.

"I know what I said," Freeman said, holding up his hand. "We don't know if the number is good or bad relative to what it could be. But we always need to get that number lower if at all possible."

"Why?" Tyler said.

"Because," Jane said, jumping back into the fray, "the lower that number, the higher the value of whatever we are funding."

"In this case," she added, pointing at the screen, "we are discussing the entire firm. So, the lower that cost, the higher the value of the firm."

"Think of it this way," Brandon said, "the lower the cost of funds, the more funds we can get and the more that we can do with them."

"So, it's never low enough?" Lilly said.

"Well, we always want it to be lower," Freeman said, hedging slightly. Lilly seemed to accept the explanation but with a raised eyebrow.

"So, let's move on with it then," Tyler said. "We are here of course because we want to break ground on the new plants sometime next month. Am I correct in saying that to do so would cost us 9 %?

"Probably not," Jane said. "Not unless the funds that we use for these projects are obtained from the exact same capital structure allocations and the same costs of each of the sources."

"Which probably will not happen in either case," Brandon said, clicking for the next slide. "Recall the projects we are contemplating. Here are the summaries that Marilyn and Stewart put together in August."

High-tech plant			
	Year 0	*Years 1–14*	*Year 15*
Operating cash flows		*4,726,865*	*4,726,865*
Net capital spending	*−18,000,000*		
Change in NWC	*−5,000,000*		*5,000,000*
Total project cash flows	*−23,000,000*	*4,726,865*	*9,726,865*

Traditional plant			
	Year 0	*Years 1–19*	*Year 20*
Operating cash flows		*3,661,494*	*3,661,494*
Net capital spending	*−13,000,000*		
Change in NWC	*−3,000,000*		*3,000,000*
Total project cash flows	*−16,000,000*	*3,661,494*	*6,661,494*

Marilyn rose and took the remote.

"The part we are focusing on right now is that first column of figures," she said. "Those are the costs to get the project under way. Recall that we want to do two plants, so we need to double those amounts."

"Based upon the current WACC, obtaining the funds for the high-tech project costs around $2 million per year, and the funds for the traditional plant could cost about $1.44 million per year."

"But you just said those wouldn't be the costs," Lilly said.

"Right, that's where the real work sets in," Jane said. "Over the past several months, Brandon and I have been doing an extensive analysis designed to estimate our costs given the new funds we would be obligated to spend. The first job is to list the possible sources of funds."

"Starting with the obvious," Brandon said, clicking the remote. Marilyn had retaken her seat. "We can fund a large part of the projects with just our retained earnings if we so choose. We need $46 million for the high-tech and $32 million for the traditional plants. We probably have enough in retained earnings to cover that.

"I am very reluctant to use all of our safety net," Tyler said, "just in case we hit some hard times. And some of it is already earmarked to be used, anyway."

"Of course," Brandon said smoothly, "we all couldn't agree more. In fact, we decided we could perhaps feel comfortable with using as much as fifteen million, but no more than that."

The screen showed the $15 million subtracted from the required amounts.

High-tech plant	*Traditional plant*
*Cost $23 * 2 = $46 million*	*Cost $16 * 2 = $32 million*
Minus $15 million (RE)	*Minus $15 million (RE)*
Need $31 million	*Need $17 million*

"So where do we get the rest?" Lilly asked.

"We think there are three viable options," Brandon said. "First we can borrow some of it privately. We have had, over the past several months, conversations

with all the large banks in the area. They are all willing to lend varying amounts and at varying costs."

"Can we borrow all the rest?" Tyler said.

"We could," Jane said, clicking forward to the next slide and indicating the names listed. "These two banks are willing to lend up to the $31 million dollars but at considerable cost."

"What does that mean?" Lilly asked. "What are considerable costs?"

"If we borrow $31 million, the risk that entails would require the bank to only offer at a rate of 18 % annually."

"Ouch," Tyler said. "We can't do that."

"Again, we agree," Brandon said, "In fact, it's not only the debt that gets expensive. If we borrow that much, the shareholders would also notice and get very nervous."

"And increase their expected return as well," Jane added.

"Okay, so what other options do we have?" Tyler asked.

"Well, the second thing we can do is offer more bonds to the public." Jane walked to the computer and pulled up the current bond quotes. "The market is viewing our current bonds pretty favorably right now, and we feel new issues would be received fairly well. While we won't know the exact rate we would have to pay until we agree with the underwriters, we feel that we could easily borrow up to $15 or $20 million in public debt."

"Again, of course," Lilly said sardonically, "at an increasing rate."

"True," Brandon said, "and remember that issuing public bonds is not an easy process by any means and comes with considerable headaches. We have been discussing this prospect with several underwriters for several months and know that we can move forward with issuing some bonds, but we have to give careful consideration of how much we want to bite off."

"You said there were three more options," Tyler said, "I assume the last one is more equity."

"That is correct," Jane said. "We could again find an underwriter to use new shares of stock. The downside to this is again a long process at high costs."

"Define high costs," Tyler said.

"Our best guess is that it would cost about $5 per share. So, if they begin selling at the same price of our current stock, which is about $58, we could expect to get only about $53 out of each share."

"Look," Lilly said, "Tyler and I both are very grateful of the information and thank you for giving it to us. But I am getting the feeling that there is a bottom line we need to get to and that many of the details are too intricate for us to get in an hour meeting anyway. Am I correct?"

"Ah, young Ms. O'Grady," Freeman intoned from his seat in the back, "you never want to know how the sausage gets made, do you?"

"Yuck," she responded with a twisted face.

"In this case," he continued with a rare smile, "you are correct. There has been an incredible amount of work that has gone into what you are about to see

and believe me when I say that the youngsters have done an excellent job in getting to this point."

The "youngsters" stared in surprise at the blindsiding compliment. Brandon recovered first and handed two sheets of paper to the owners. Jane pulled the slide copy up on screen.

"These are our conclusions for each project," she said. "Here's what we did. First, we did as much research as we could on the cost of the sources of capital, particularly how we expect those costs to change as the allocation percentages change. Then, we fed all of this information into an advanced computer program and had it run several rounds of simulations. The objective was to minimize the cost of the funds given the changing allocation percentages. What you see in front of you is the conclusion of that process."

High-tech plant			
Source	*Amount*	*Weight*	*Cost*
Retained earnings	*$11 million*	*11/46 = 23.91 %*	*13.06 %*
Coupon bonds	*$20 million*	*20/46 = 43.48 %*	*9.16 %*
Private debt	*$15 million*	*15/46 = 32.61 %*	*10.87 %*

$$\begin{aligned} WACC &= (.2391*13.06) + (.4348*9.16*.65) + (.3261*10.87*.65) \\ &= 8.02\% \end{aligned}$$

Traditional plant			
Source	*Amount*	*Weight*	*Cost*
Retained earnings	*$13 million*	*11/32 = 34.38 %*	*12.17 %*
Coupon bonds	*$15 million*	*17/32 =53.13 %*	*8.36 %*
Private debt	*$5 million*	*4/32 = 12.50 %*	*9.77 %*

$$\begin{aligned} WACC &= (.3438*12.17) + (.5313*8.36*.65) + (.1250*9.77*.65) \\ &= 7.86\% \end{aligned}$$

The two owners took several long moments to soak in what they were seeing. Tyler jotted down a few notes of questions to ask. The finance team gave them all the time they needed. Finally, Lilly spoke first.

"So, I have some questions," she said. "First of all, how is it possible that we can get these new projects at a lower cost that we currently have? I thought adding these projects would increase the risk."

"That is a good point," Brandon said, "but it turns out that we were too reliant on our equity. Debt financing is not a bad thing, particularly given the tax benefit associated with it. So, the reason these costs are lower is that we propose taking advantage of the benefits of debt financing."

"It looks like debt is a lot cheaper," Tyler said, studying the information in front of him. "Why not go even farther in that direction?"

"We thought about it," Jane said, "but you have to remember that debt is a double-edged sword. Although it has a very positive side, adding too much gets away from those advantages and puts the firm in a very awkward situation. We don't want to commit too much of our future cash flows to interest in case we hit hard times. Does that make sense?"

They nodded, but then Lilly had another thought.

"How is it that it costs more to obtain funding for the high-tech plant than for the traditional plant?"

"It all boils down to risk," Brandon said. "When we approach the lenders, for example, they want to know what we are going to use the money for. The high-tech plant comes with considerably more risk because it is less vetted as a method of production. There are many more unknowns. The banks have to look at this as though there is an increased likelihood of default for those plants simply due to the risk they have."

"But what about the public debt and equity? How do you know those numbers?"

"We don't know any numbers, Lilly," Freeman interjected. "We are giving you our very best guesses. That is all we can do. The risk thing runs throughout everything. When the underwriters promote and sell our offerings, be it debt or equity, they have to tell the potential buyers what we are going to do with the funds. Thus, when they tell the investors we are going to use it for something riskier, like the high-tech plant, we have to assume they will require a higher return. We have to factor that in our estimates."

"What about the equity," Tyler said. "Since we are using money we already have, I don't see why the cost is so high."

"I'll take that one," Jane said. "Remember that all the equity is technically the shareholders and even the retained earnings are there to support their wealth enhancement. So, the cost of those funds is the same as if it were money in their pockets instead of ours."

"But the cost increases from where it currently is," Tyler said, glancing back at the current WACC calculation. "I assume that is because these projects increase risk, but how do you estimate the increase in risk?"

"We estimate how much we think the new projects will increase our beta," Jane said. "Specifically, for the high-tech project, we feel it will increase our beta to 1.31, and for the traditional plant, we think it could increase to 1.22. Those are based upon simulations ran with various scenarios involving our stock price. While we can't guarantee those numbers, we feel relatively comfortable in the estimates."

"Well, okay then," Lilly said. "I guess I am good with this."

After a long moment, Tyler nodded in agreement.

"Okay, then folks," Lilly continued, "what's the next step?"

Freeman stood, happy with the outcome of the meeting. A major hurdle had been crossed.

"You should be asking 'what's the final step?'" he said, stretching. "And the answer is that we will show you after the holidays."

ALTERNATE ENDINGS

1. ***The example above uses the CAPM as the estimate of the cost of equity given the increase in risk brought about by the new project. An alternative would be to use the DGM and assume either a higher expected growth rate or a higher required dividend payment. For the sake of argument, assume that Jane and Brandon used the DGM instead of the CAPM. For the high-tech project, they assumed the shareholders would expect a growth rate of 8 % (rather than the 5 % they have been using). For the traditional plant, they assumed a growth rate of 7 %. How would this change the estimate of the cost of equity?***
2. ***Building upon #1, what if they chose to use both methods of estimating the cost of equity. You may maintain the assumption of the firm's beta increasing to 1.22 and 1.31 for the traditional and high-tech plant, respectively. Also, you may maintain the assumption of 7 % and 8 % expected growth with the traditional and high-tech plant, respectively. If you use the average of the two methods, what is the new cost of equity for each project? What is the new WACC for each project?***
3. ***Notice that the chosen capital structures for the financing of the projects incorporate no new equity. Suppose that Jane and Brandon's research had indicated that new common stock was superior to coupon bonds. Replicate the WACC's in this instance. You may estimate the cost of new equity by using the dividend growth model. You may assume the issuance costs are $5. The expected constant growth rate is 8 % for the high-tech firm and 7 % for the traditional firm.***
4. ***Suppose Lilly asks "One final question. Since the WACC on the traditional plan is lower than the WACC on the high-tech plant, should we just conclude that the traditional plant is the better choice? Didn't you just say that we wanted to minimize the costs?"***

   This is a very good question. How do you answer it?
5. ***Suppose that Dubarb Freeman had chosen to approach the issue from a different perspective. He chose to only look at equity and debt as types of capital, thusly lumping retained earnings and common stock together and coupon bonds and private debt together. Doing so would result in the following current capital structure for Hack Back as a firm. The weights are rounded for simplicity:***

$$\begin{aligned} &W_E = 92\% \\ &W_D = 8\% \\ &k_E = 9.28\% \\ &k_D = 9.56\% \\ &T = 35\% \\ &WACC = 9.03\% \end{aligned}$$

   Instead of specifically looking at sources of funds for the project, he simply prefers to look at the optimal capital structure. They estimate that a 10 % increase in debt (and a corresponding 10 % decrease in equity) will result in a

1 % higher cost of debt. Also, the same 1 % increase would result in a .2 % increase in equity. Given this, what is the optimal capital structure? What is the WACC in this situation? (Hint: Use Excel)

Concept Questions

1. **Cost of capital** What is meant by the cost of capital? How does the concept apply to the financial operations of a firm, and why is it so important?
2. **Required returns** Discuss the relationship between costs of capital and required returns. Who cares about which and how do they relate to each other, both qualitatively and quantitatively?
3. **Equity** Your boss comes to you and says "why don't we just use all our retained earnings for the project. That's the company's money, not the shareholders." What is the fallacy of this statement, and how does your boss indicate his misunderstanding of the way a publicly traded firm operates.
4. **Growth rates** Why is estimating the growth rate of a firm so important? Discuss from both the shareholder and firm perspective.
5. **Cost of equity** What are the strengths and weaknesses of using both the DGM and CAPM methods of estimating the cost of equity?
6. **Debt sources** List at least three sources of debt capital. What are the characteristics of each?
7. ***WACC*** Describe in a sentence what the *WACC* tells the firm. Where does it come from?
8. ***WACC*** Discuss both the qualitative and quantitative implications and design of *WACC*.
9. **Cost of debt** How do taxes influence the cost of debt? Why? Can you create a personal financial analogy to extend the answer?
10. **Capital structure theories** Briefly describe the primary findings of the capital structure theories discussed in the text. How do we incorporate those findings into capital structure policies?
11. **Financial distress** Bob from accounting just barged into your office and screams "We're about to go bankrupt! Do something!" Why is Bob so upset? Why is financial distress such a concern for a firm? What does Bob want you to "do" about it?
12. **Source of funds** Evaluate the statement "the cost of funds depends upon the use of the funds." What does that mean? Assume you are talking to your supervisor in relation to a project you are planning that has a very high level of risk.

Problems

1. **Cost of equity** Kelly's Tiki Hut has experienced growth of 11 % per year over the past 15 years and expects this to continue indefinitely. Three years ago, they began paying dividends. The first dividend was $.90. The current price per share of Kelly's stock is $35.99. What would you estimate Kelly's current cost of equity to be?

2. **Cost of equity** Suppose ABC company has stock currently selling at $21.00 per share that just paid dividends of $1.75. They have a required rate of return of 12 %. We have the following data for their historical dividends. Calculate the cost of equity using the DGM approach.

Year	Dividends
1	1.10
2	1.20
3	1.35
4	1.55
5	1.75

3. **Cost of equity** You have just taken a position as chief financial officer of a large, multinational firm. Your first task is to find an appropriate cost of capital to apply to capital budgeting. Historically, dividend growth has averaged 3.12 % and the last dividend paid was $1.02. The current stock price is $12.25. The stock currently has a beta of .82 and the market risk premium is 9.8 %. The current T-bill rate is 3.2 %.

    1. What is the estimated cost of equity using the CAPM approach?
    2. What is the estimated cost of equity using the DGM approach?

4. **Cost of equity** Harry's Toupee Shop, Inc., has publicly stated they are going to pay dividends next year of $1.24 and then increase this amount by 4 % for the following 5 years. Following that, Harry is going to stop paying dividends forever after. According to the DGM, what should be the current cost of equity if Harry's stock price is $17.82?
5. **Cost of debt** Suppose Bob's Golf Cart Shop has 4,000 30-year bonds outstanding, each currently selling at $897.64. The bonds have 18 years left until maturity and have a coupon rate of 7.5 %. What is Bob's before-tax cost of debt if the bond pays semiannual coupons? If the tax rate is 35 %, what is the after-tax cost?
6. **Cost of debt** A firm has two types of debt in their capital structure. They have 200 coupon bonds selling at $986.68 each. They also have $200,000 worth of bank debt, which has an interest rate of 4.5 %. If the firm's weighted average cost of debt is 5.24 %, what is the YTM on the bonds?
7. **Taxes and costs** You need $530,000 and have decided to get it either from bank debt or from issuing equity. The beta on your firm is .35, the risk-free rate is 1.75 %, and the market risk premium is 7.45 %. If your tax rate is 35 %, at what rate would you be better off getting bank debt?
8. **Cost of preferred stock** Your firm has 250,000 shares of $50 preferred stock currently selling at $23.56 per share. If these stocks pay a 3.5 % dividend, what is the cost of these preferred shares?
9. **Cost of zero-coupon bonds** Consider a zero-coupon bond that has a face value of $100 and 13 years left until maturity. If the current price is $54.86, what is the current YTM of this bond?

10. **Capital structure weights** Firm X has a *WACC* of 9.43 %. They only have one type of debt and one type of equity. The cost of their debt is 8.4 % and the cost of equity is 11.3 %. What is the weight of debt in their existing capital structure? The tax rate is 35 %.
11. **Capital structure weights** If the debt-to-equity ratio for a firm is .38, what is the weight of debt in the firm's capital structure?
12. **Capital structure weights** Your firm has an odd capital structure made up of only coupon bonds and preferred stock. The coupon bonds have a YTM of 5.61 %. The preferred stock pays a dividend of $1.12 each year and is currently priced at $14.54. If the firm's tax rate is 35 % and their *WACC* is 4.95 %, what percentage of their capital structure is coupon bonds?
13. **Weighted average cost of capital** Your firm has two types of bonds. First, there are 3,000 bonds outstanding with a 7 % coupon rate and a yield to maturity of 6.5 %. These bonds are selling at $1,098.71. Also, there are 10,000 bonds outstanding with a 5 % coupon rate and a 4.5 % yield to maturity. These bonds are selling at $1,102.98. The remaining capital structure is comprised of 1.2 million shares of common stock selling at $34.00 per share. In addition, the firm just paid a dividend of $1.37, and the growth rate of dividends has averaged 5.6 % over the past 25 years.

    The covariance between your firm and the market is 16 %, while the variance of the market is 38 %. The expected return on the market is 12 %, and the T-bill rate is 3.21 %.

    1. What is the estimated cost of equity using the SML approach?
    2. What is the estimated cost of equity using the DGM approach?
    3. What is the firm's weighted average cost of capital using the SML estimate of the cost of equity? What about when using the DGM estimate of the cost of equity?

14. **Weighted average cost of capital** Suppose your firm has five sources of funding. They are as follows:

    - 400,000 shares of stock currently selling at $12.33 per share. The firm has experienced an average growth rate of 4 % for the past 50 years, and they expect this to continue indefinitely. Their next dividend will be $1.23.
    - 100,000 shares of preferred stock that pay an annual dividend of 3 % of face value, which is $25. They are currently selling for $18.77.
    - 3,400 corporate bonds currently selling at $1,223.90 and yielding 6.54 %. They have 13 years left until maturity and a coupon rate of 9.15 %.
    - 1,945 corporate bonds currently selling for $884.44. They have a coupon rate of 7.36 % and 14 years left until maturity. The bonds have a current yield to maturity of 8.83 %.
    - A bank loan of $1,000,000. The interest rate on the loan is 7.5 %.

    What is your firm's *WACC*?

15. **Optimal capital structure** Suppose a firm has four pieces of capital structure. They are as follows:

- Common stock that a beta of 1.21. In addition, the market risk premium is 9.1 % and the risk-free rate is 2.2 %. The stock is selling for \$13.00 per share.
- Preferred stock that has a cost of 5.4 %.
- Bond 1: Long-term corporate bonds with 10 years left until maturity that are currently selling for \$978.03 each. The coupon rate is 7.5 % and the face value is \$1,000. Payments are made semiannually.
- Bond 2: Long-term corporate bonds that are selling for \$1,004.87. The coupon rate is 8.41 %, and there is 17 years left until maturity. Face value is \$1,000, and payments are made semiannually.

Assuming the following represents the only available options, which is the optimal capital structure?

Weight of common stock	Weight of preferred stock	Weight of bond 1	Weight of bond 2
20	10	30	40
40	20	30	10
60	10	10	20
70	5	15	10

16. **Optimal capital structure** You are in charge of the finance department at Johnny's Kawasaki, Inc. The firm is considering expanding to Europe and will build a plant in London. The plant will cost approximately \$14 million. Your duty is to identify the optimal capital structure with which to pay for the \$14 million dollar project. After months of work, you have identified the following data.

		...you will have...	
Option	If you have debt of...	Cost of debt	Beta
1	\$2 million	6.67 %	.76
2	\$5 million	7.25 %	.81
3	\$7 million	8.19 %	.92
4	\$10 million	9.65 %	.98

In addition, the expected return on the market is 9 % and the risk-free rate is 3 %.

(a) Of these options, which capital structure is best?
(b) Given the optimal capital structure, how much will obtaining this \$14M in funding cost the firm?

17. **Optimal capital structure** Bobby's Beer Barn just paid a dividend of \$1.06 and has seen their stock price rise to \$27.48. However, they are attempting to purchase a new plant that needs capital of \$1.5 million. This capital will come

from common stock and bank debt. They have the following choices in terms of getting the capital:

Option	Wcs	Wpd (private debt)
1	.80	.20
2	.60	.40
3	.40	.60
4	.20	.80

If the firm uses option 1, the cost of debt is 5.87 % and the cost of equity is 6.10 %. The cost of equity is estimated based upon the capital asset pricing model assuming a market risk premium of 7.5 % and a risk-free rate of 1.5 %. However, for every 20 % increase in debt (and resulting 20 % decrease in equity), the cost of debt increases by 1 %. Also, for every 20 % increase in debt, the firm's beta increases by .4. This would then affect the cost of equity. Given a tax rate of 35 %, what is the optimal (of these four) capital structure?

18. **Optimal capital structure** Your current capital structure is made up of 500,000 shares of common stock and $4 million in private debt. The common stock is currently selling for $27.14 per share. The current T-bill rate is 1.1 %, and the expected return on the market is estimated to be 9 %. Currently your firm's beta is .78. The rate you pay on your private debt is currently the prime rate plus a spread of 3.75 %. Prime is currently 3.25 %.

    You are considering altering your capital structure (not adding money, just shifting). After thorough research, you have determined that a 1 % increase in debt (relative to equity) would result in an increase in your cost of equity of .02 %. In addition, the 1 % increase in debt would increase your cost of debt by .05 %.

    Given this, and the fact that you do not want to examine other forms of capital, what is your optimal capital structure? Your tax rate is 35 %.

Chapter 9
Capital Budgeting Decisions: The End of the Roads Meets the Beginning of Another

As promised, we are at long last to the end of our journey. After the long, tedious task of determining the *WACC*, we now just have to use it. While the hard part is over, arguably the most important step is yet to come. As stated several times, in order for a company to flourish financially, they must maximize shareholder wealth, which they do, in part, by ensuring company growth. This growth most often comes about as a result of the company undertaking new projects. Thus, we have to decide which projects to accept, and which to reject, in order to maximize shareholder wealth. As you can probably ascertain, a large part of this goes hand in hand with the discussion of cost of capital completed in the previous chapter. To put is as simply as possible, the objective of this chapter is to find the best possible projects, conditional upon the optimal capital structure used to finance said project. We are finally combining the concepts of capital structure and capital budgeting.

9.1 Capital Budgeting Tools

There is a myriad of capital budgeting "tools" that have been developed all with the same goal: to make an accept/reject decision on a given project. However, there are other things to be considered for each tool. We are going to examine five of these tools throughout this chapter. For each tool, after defining the method, we will discuss the calculation. Then, most importantly, we will then discuss the decision rule and advantages and disadvantages of each method. As with any "tool," the effectiveness is limited to the user's understanding of and ability to use it. Also, the effectiveness is strongly contingent upon the inputs into the model. Let's use the example of a hammer to drive the point home (hardee har har). A hammer is perhaps the most effective tool ever designed by man. However, if one chooses to drive the nail with the handle, it will become very ineffective. Likewise, if one attempts to drive a rubber nail, they will be sorely disappointed. Our objective in this chapter is to make sure we are all firmly ahold of the handle and the rubber nails are quickly cast aside.

M.K. Pyles, *Applied Corporate Finance: Questions, Problems and Making Decisions in the Real World*, Springer Texts in Business and Economics,
DOI 10.1007/978-1-4614-9173-6_9,

9.1.1 Payback Period

The first capital budgeting tool we will examine is the payback period (PB). Perhaps the simplest technique, the **payback period** is defined as the length of time it takes to repay the initial net investment (i.e., the *NINV*). As covered in Chap. 3, the *NINV* is the summation of the amount of spending on fixed assets and the change in *NWC* required to bring the project to operation. The payback period is based upon the fact that time is a crucial ingredient of financial planning. All else equal, a project that is paid back quicker than an otherwise equivalent project is superior. The quicker the project's net outlay can be redeemed, the quicker the firm starts to earn a profit on their investment. From our knowledge of the time value of money, we know that receiving money sooner rather than later is preferred. This process encourages successful financial planning and facilitates growth.

If the expected net cash flows (*NCF*s) are constant, calculating the payback period is relatively straightforward:

$$PB = \frac{NINV}{NCF}$$

For example, consider a project that has an estimated *NINV* of \$128,000. The expected cash flows are \$37,000 per year for 5 years. Given these data, the project's payback period is

$$\begin{aligned} \boldsymbol{PB} &= \frac{\mathbf{128,000}}{\mathbf{37,000}} \\ &= \mathbf{3.46\ years} \end{aligned}$$

Thus, this project takes almost 3.5 years to pay back. The natural follow-up question concerns whether this is a good or bad number. We will discuss that in a moment. First, however, we must discuss the alternate calculations required when the expected *NCF*s are not constant. Let's now consider the following expected cash flow stream:

Year	Exp. *NCF*
1	\$45,000
2	50,000
3	35,000
4	25,000
5	30,000

Unfortunately, there is not a neat little formula to calculate the payback period when dealing with nonconstant cash flows. Instead, we have to take the cash flows one step at a time. The first step involves adding all the cash flows for each consecutive year until you arrive to the cash flow just prior to the one that will take you above the *NINV*. In the above example, this would take the form of

$$\textbf{Try 1}: \mathbf{45,000 + 50,000 = 95,000}$$
$$(\text{Yr.1}) + (\text{Yr.2})$$
$$\textbf{Try 2}: \mathbf{45,000 + 50,000 + 35,000 = \$130,000}$$
$$(\text{Yr.1}) + (\text{Yr.2}) + (\text{Yr.3})$$

So, we know it takes more than 2 years, but less than three, to pay back this initial cash flow of this project. Further, we can see that it is going to be almost 3 years, since the total of the cash flows for the first 3 years is only $2,000 more than the amount required to cover the *NINV*. However, we need to be more specific than this. So, we first determine the remaining cash inflow needed during the third year in order to meet the *NINV*:

$$\begin{aligned} NCF \text{ Needed in Yr. 3} &= (NINV - \text{Total } NCF\text{s through first two years}) \\ &= \mathbf{128,000 - 95,000 = \$33,000} \end{aligned}$$

Then, we find the fraction of the year it takes to generate the needed *NCF*:

$$\begin{aligned} \text{Fraction of Yr. 3} &= \text{Needed Amount/Yr.3 Expected } NCF \\ &= \mathbf{33,000/35,000} \\ &= \mathbf{.94} \end{aligned}$$

So, putting this together, we find the payback period for this project to be 2.94 years. This approach assumes the annual *NCF* is spread evenly throughout the entire year. While this may not be true, unless we have more specific information, it is the most likely assumption. Now that we know how to calculate the payback period, we can return to the question posed a bit earlier. How can we tell if the calculated payback period is acceptable or not? In other words, what is the decision rule?

We need a two-step process:

Step 1: Pick some target *PB* period.

Step 2: If the project $PB <$ target PB ▸ Accept.

If the project $PB >$ target PB ▸ Reject.

In other words, if the project "pays back" faster than the firm requires, it is a good project. Otherwise, the project is unacceptable, at least according to the *PB* period rule. For the above example, suppose the firm has a target payback period of 4 years. Therefore, the project's calculated *PB* period is less than the target payback period, indicating an acceptable project.

As with most things, there are advantages and disadvantages to the *PB* period method of determining the acceptability of projects. The first advantage has already been mentioned, simplicity. The payback period requires nothing more than basic mathematical skills and requires no real understanding of finance. Another advantage is a bit more technical. The *PB* period biases the firm towards liquidity in their capital budgeting decisions. While there is a limit (see Chap. 2), liquidity is generally regarded as a good thing for a firm. The more liquid the firm, the lower the probability of financial distress. Thus, increased liquidity is beneficial to a firm, and this is a positive attribute of any method that facilitates it.

On the other hand, there are several disadvantages to the *PB* period method. The first is the arbitrary nature of the target *PB* period. Perhaps the term "arbitrary" is a bit misleading. This is not to say the value is simply pulled from thin air. Hopefully, careful analysis determines an appropriate target *PB* period. We title it an arbitrary *PB* period because there is no known way to accurately calculate it. It is entirely up to the individual firm. Although it is unavoidable, we are cautious of any decision made based upon an arbitrary value.

The second disadvantage is that the payback period ignores cash flows beyond the target payback period. In other words, cash flows beyond the target payback period are not accounting for in the overall project evaluation. A third disadvantage is that the *PB* period may provide more than one answer when there are unconventional *NCF*s. Consider the following project *NCF*s:

Year	Exp. *NCF*
1	\$10,000
2	15,000
3	−10,000
4	10,000
5	15,000

If the project has *NINV* of \$25,000, the *PB* period is simply 2 years. Right? Right, but wrong as well. If we keep going, we find the payback period is also 4 years. So, which one is correct? Good question.

A final disadvantage that we will mention is the lack of time value of money content. Notice these values have not been adjusted for time or discount rate. The opportunity cost of waiting for some of the money longer than the rest is not accounted for. The process assumes that all cash flows are equal, which we know to not be the case. The raw values of the expected *NCF*s cannot really be compared to the raw value of the *NINV*, although that is just what the payback period does.

We are left with a method that has a couple of positive aspects, but these are offset with several negative aspects. Thus, the natural conclusion is that there must be better methods available to us.

9.1.2 Discounted Payback Period

One improvement upon the *PB* period method is simply done by incorporating the time value of money. The **discounted payback period** first discounts each of the future expected net cash flows back to time zero before the payback period is calculated. By doing so, we then have created an apples-to-apples comparison in relation to the *NINV*. Recall our previous nonconstant cash flow example. If we assume a discount rate of 6 %, compounded annually, we get the following discounted values:

Year	Exp. *NCF*	Discounted *NCF*
1	\$45,000	\$42,452.83
2	50,000	44,499.82
3	35,000	29,386.67
4	25,000	19,802.34
5	30,000	22,417.75

Then, we would calculate the *PB* period exactly as we did earlier:

$$\begin{gathered}\textbf{Try 1}: \mathbf{42,452.83 + 44,499.82 = \$86,952.65}\\ (\text{Yr}.1) + (\text{Yr}.2)\end{gathered}$$

$$\begin{gathered}\textbf{Try 2}: \mathbf{42,452.83 + 44,499.82 + 29,386.67 = \$116,339.32}\\ (\text{Yr}.1) + (\text{Yr}.2) + (\text{Yr}.3)\end{gathered}$$

$$\begin{gathered}\textbf{Try 3}: \mathbf{42,452.83 + 44,499.82 + 29,386.67 + 19,802.34 = \$136,141.66}\\ (\text{Yr}.1) + (\text{Yr}.2) + (\text{Yr}.3) + (\text{Yr}.4)\end{gathered}$$

The project's DPB period must then be between 3 and 4 years. Continuing, we find:

$$\begin{aligned} NCF \text{ Needed in Yr. } 4 &= (NINV - \text{Total Discounted Exp } NCF\text{s through first three years})\\ &= \mathbf{128,000 - 116,339.32 = \$11,660.68}\end{aligned}$$

Then, we find the fraction of the year it takes to generate the needed *NCF*:

$$\begin{aligned}\text{Fraction of Yr. } 4 &= \text{Needed Amount/Yr. 4 Discounted Exp } NCF\\ &= \mathbf{11,660.68/19,802.34}\\ &= \mathbf{.59}\end{aligned}$$

So, the discounted *PB* period is 3.59 years. Notice this is more than the basic *PB* period, which will always be the case since the present values of the expected *NCF*s must be less than the raw values. The decision rule is the same as earlier. So, even though the discounted *PB* is larger than the basic *PB*, the project would be accepted since the value is still less than 4 years.

9.1.3 Average Accounting Return

The next method for examining the acceptability of a project requires us to venture once again into our sister discipline of accounting. The **average accounting return (*AAR*)** is based upon values pulled from pro forma accounting statements and, as such, will be subject to the same interpretations and limitations as with any financial statement we have encountered to this point. We will begin with the generic formula for the *AAR*:

$$AAR = \frac{Some\,measure\,of\,average\,Accounting\,profit}{Some\,measure\,of\,average\,Accounting\,value}$$

The most popular variation, and the one that we will use, will take the form

$$AAR = \frac{Average\,net\,income}{Average\,book\,value}$$

The numerator will come from a series of pro forma income statements that depict the firm's expectations for income to be generated solely from the project in question. For illustration purposes, let us suppose that has already been done and the following data have been pulled from those statements:

Year	Projected NI
1	$52,000
2	60,000
3	72,000
4	82,000
5	75,000

Therefore, it is a straightforward exercise to calculate the average net income from these:

$$\begin{aligned}\textbf{Average net income} &= \mathbf{(52,000 + 60,000 + 72,000 + 82,000 + 75,000)/5}\\ &= \mathbf{\$68,200}\end{aligned}$$

Calculating the average book value can be made relative simple if you make a couple of assumptions. First, we will assume that the project will be depreciated straight line over the life of the project. Second, we will assume the project has zero salvage. To complete our example, let's assume the project we are examining has a net investment of $200,000.

If that is the case, we would have the following schedule of book values:

Year	Projected NI
0	\$200,000
1	160,000
2	120,000
3	80,000
4	40,000
5	0

Notice that we have simply subtracted \$40,000 in depreciation for each year of the project, which provides the final book value of \$0. Thus, the average of these values is:

$$\begin{aligned}\textbf{Average book value} &= \mathbf{(200,000 + 160,000 + 120,000 + 80,000 + 40,000 + 0)/6} \\ &= \mathbf{\$100,000}\end{aligned}$$

Actually, we didn't have to do all that work. Any time we assume straight-line depreciation and zero salvage, the average book value will work out to be exactly half of the *NINV*. This makes the task at hand considerably less burdensome. If these assumptions are not made, the proper process would involve creating pro forma balance sheets for each future year of the project, incorporating the depreciation for each upcoming year, and then averaging the resulting book values. Regardless of how you arrive at the average book value, once you have it, we can complete the calculation of the *AAR* with a simple calculation:

$$\begin{aligned}\boldsymbol{AAR} &= \frac{\mathbf{68,200}}{\mathbf{100,000}} \\ &= \mathbf{68.2\%}\end{aligned}$$

So, for every \$1 invested in the project, we expect to have an accounting return of 68.2 cents. Is that good? Just like with the payback period, it depends on the target. So, we should now discuss the decision rule for the *AAR*. Again, we have a two-step process. The first is that you must decide upon a target return. Once this is decided upon, the accept/reject decision is made based upon the following:

- If Project *AAR* > Target *AAR* ▸ Accept.
- If Project *AAR* < Target *AAR* ▸ Reject.

Solely for the sake of completion, let us assume the target *AAR* for the above project is 50 %. Therefore, we would accept this project since the calculated *AAR* is greater than the target. Unfortunately, there are several flaws to the *AAR* method of capital budgeting selection. The first is the aforementioned arbitrary nature of the target. The reasons are much the same as they were for the payback period, but in case you don't want to flip back a couple of pages, we'll go over it again: we are highly skeptical of any decision made based upon a value that has no quantitative validation.

Other disadvantages surround the fact that the values included are accounting in nature and, as such, have the same limitations as in previous chapters. Specifically, the numbers are projections, based upon rigid accounting guidelines, and have no adjustment for risk and no consideration of the time value of money. As such, the resulting answer really has no financial content. That is not to say that it does not have its uses but rather to suggest that it should not be used as a primary determinant of capital budgeting.

9.1.4 Net Present Value

We will now discuss the crème de le crème of capital budgeting techniques. Known as the **net present value (*NPV*)**, this technique is without fault and should be the primary determinant of a project's acceptability. Sound impressive? Well, it is. In fact, this is the point that we've been trying to get to all semester. It's taken a lot of stops along the way, and a few detours, but this is where it all leads. Hopefully you'll see why soon.

The design of the *NPV* is not a new idea. Let's back up a bit. Starting from step one, we know the only appropriate goal of the firm is to maximize shareholder wealth. We do this by ensuring firm growth, which we do by choosing projects that facilitate growth. Projects that fit these criteria have to be *worth more than they cost*. Now, while that's a pretty simple idea, we know by now that it's not quite so simple to apply. Luckily, we already know how to find both the cost and the benefit of projects, due to our hard work in all nine previous chapters.

The cost of a project is simply the net investment (*NINV*) of the project. If you can't remember the details, see Chap. 3 for a complete discussion of how to calculate the *NINV*. Rather than deal with those details again, however, we shall just say that we know the *NINV* for a project is \$380,000. The "worth" of a project requires a bit more work, but we've already covered that as well. In fact, we've covered the notion several times throughout the text. The benefit, or value, of anything is simply the present value of the expected cash flows generated. Thus, for any project, once we've determined the expected future cash flows, we simply have to discount each of them to time zero, and sum. Of course, the appropriate discount rate is crucial to accurate estimation. But, once again, we already know how to do that as well. As discussed in Chap. 8, the appropriate discount rate is the firm's *WACC*, which should be minimized by their choice of capital structure. See, I told you we were eventually going to put all this together.

So, let's make up a project. Imagine a firm by the name of Stars and Stripes, Inc. is considering purchase of a machine that is expected to generate the following cash flows over the 5-year life of the project. You should assume we went through that entire process from Chap. 3 to calculate these.

Year	Expected CF
1	$85,000
2	90,000
3	100,000
4	105,000
5	115,000

In addition, let's say we've already done all the work associated with calculating the *WACC* and have come up with a value of 7.9 %. Hopefully, you now see why it was crucial that we learned how to calculate all these different pieces (expected cash flow, capital spending, net working capital, *WACC*, etc.) throughout the text. In fact, once we've done all that, the work is pretty much over. The formula for *NPV* is

$$NPV = \underbrace{\sum_{t=1}^{T} \frac{CF_t}{(1 + WACC)^t}}_{\text{Part A}} - \underbrace{NINV}_{\text{Part B}}$$

where Part A is the "benefit" of the project, whereas Part B is the "cost" of the project, both as previously defined throughout our discussions thus far. Both values, once the expected future cash flows are discounted, are in time 0 values. Once we subtract Part B from Part A, we can find the value of the project in today's dollars. If we break down the individual cash flows, we can find the answer with the following:

Year	Expected CF	Discounted CF
1	$85,000	$78,776.65
2	90,000	77,303.58
3	100,000	79,604.14
4	105,000	77,464.64
5	115,000	78,630.42

Thus, the sum of the discounted cash flows is $391,779.43. Therefore, the *NPV* of the machine is

$$\begin{aligned} \boldsymbol{NPV} &= \mathbf{391,779.43 - 380,000} \\ &= \mathbf{\$11,779.43} \end{aligned}$$

So, this project, very simply, is *worth* $11,779.43 more than it *costs*. That's the simple beauty of *NPV*. It is the only capital budgeting technique that tells us exactly how much better off we would be as a firm for taking on a project than we would be should we reject it.

Due to this, the decision rule is very intuitive. Unlike the payback period and the average accounting return, there is no arbitrary target upon which to base our judgment on the acceptability of the project. With *NPV*, the target isn't arbitrary at all. Should a project's *NPV* be calculated to be anything greater than zero, the project is acceptable. Anything less than zero warrants rejection. A positive *NPV* project would benefit the firm by facilitating growth, which should, in turn, increase shareholder wealth. On the other hand, should a negative *NPV* project be accepted in error, shareholder wealth would ultimately decrease. The decision rule of the *NPV* is entirely consistent with the goal of the firm. In the numerical example above, Stars and Stripes should implement the project, because it is expected to generate value for the firm. In fact, they should accept every positive net present value project for which they can obtain funds. Since we naturally live in a resource-constrained world, when faced with limited funds, the firm should invest in the project with the highest *NPV*.

There are a number of other benefits to the *NPV* method of capital budgeting. For example, each cash flow is included, no matter the life of the project. Thus, we get an accurate depiction of the actual value to the firm. Also, the *NPV* adjusts for risk by including the *WACC* as a primary variable in estimation. The WACC depends on the risk of the investment, so its inclusion automatically makes the resulting answer "risk-adjusted." Finally, the largest advantage of *NPV* as a capital budgeting technique is that is has *no disadvantages*. While that sounds a silly statement, it drives home an importantly point. The process is perfect, without error. Make sure to understand that it *is still possible* to make a poor decision with the *NPV*. However, this would not be due to the *NPV* method but rather with the inputs or user error.

If you recall from Chap. 4, there are two types of multiple cash flow situations: equal or unequal. If the cash flows are equal (and meet a few other requirements), it creates an annuity. An annuity has an equation that may significantly shorten the time it takes to calculate *NPV*. In fact, if the expected cash flows from a project are the same during each period of the project, the equation is

$$NPV = CF\left[\frac{1-\frac{1}{(1+WACC)^t}}{WACC}\right] - NINV$$

To illustrate, let's revisit the Stars and Stripes project just above and flatten the cash flow stream so that the raw expected cash flows add evenly to \$495,000 over 5 years. So, instead of the cash flow schedule as presented above, let's just assume that each year's expected cash flow is \$99,000. Thus, we would calculate the *NPV* as

$$NPV = 99,000\left[\frac{1-\frac{1}{(1.079)^5}}{.079}\right] - 380,000$$

$$= 396,322.29 - 380,000$$

$$= 16,322.29$$

So, in this case, the project is worth $16,322.29 more than it cost. As a quick reminder quiz, can you tell why this value is higher than the other, given that we have the same total of raw cash flows?

These calculations are very important in corporate finance and, as such, are incorporated into easy-to-use financial tools. A nearby TECH HELP box illustrates the process for calculating *NPV* with both a financial calculator and Excel.

TECH HELP 9.1: Net Present Value

Using the Financial Calculator

As always, set the calculator to the appropriate compounding cycle (annually in this case) and clear the stored cash flow values. You do the latter by first pushing the [CF] button and then [2nd] [CE|C]. Then, you can begin inputting the cash flows:

Step 1: (CFo) 380,000 [+|-] [ENTER] [⇓] (inputs the *NINV* and then moves to the next CF)
Step 2: (C01) 85,000 [ENTER] [⇓] (inputs the first cash inflow and then moves to the frequency)
Step 3: (F01) 1 [ENTER] [⇓] (tells the calculator the $85,000 occurs only once)
Step 4: (C02) 90,000 [ENTER] [⇓]
Step 5: (F02) 1 [ENTER] [⇓]
Repeat for remaining three cash flows. When you have imputed all the cash flows, quit the process by [2nd] [CPT]
Step 6: [*NPV*] (this will pull up the requirement for a discount rate)
Step 7: (I) 7.9 [ENTER] [⇓] (this returns you to *NPV*=)
Step 8: [CPT]

You should get the $11,779.44 answer as in the main text. For practice, compute the *NPV* with the alternative of five equal cash flows of $99,000.

Using Excel

The formula in Excel is "=*NPV*(rate, values)". The rate is *WACC*, and the values are all positive cash flows. Note that Excel views the column as being

(continued)

(continued)

placed in the order of receipt, starting at time period 1. Thus, you cannot include the *NINV* as part of the =*NPV* equation.

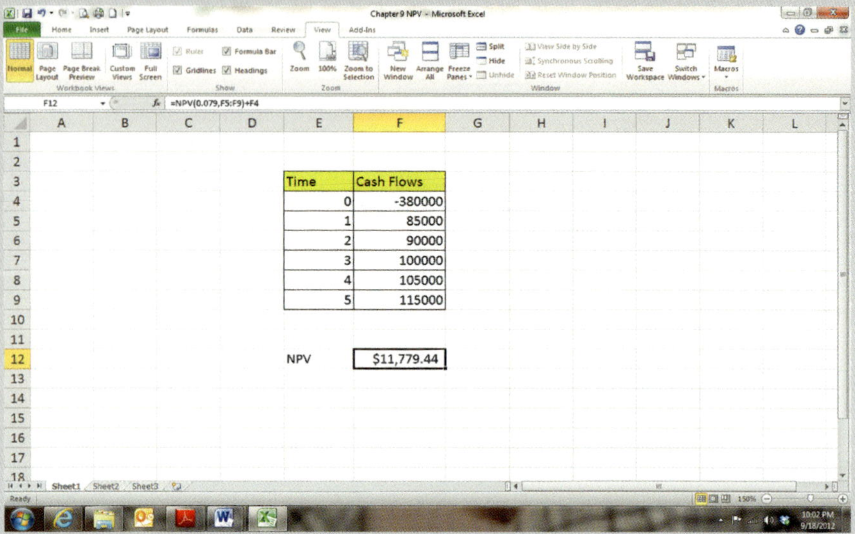

9.1.5 *Profitability Index*

The *NPV* is the best, so covering other methods is akin to being the act that comes on after Pavarroti or becoming Mariano Rivera's replacement as Yankees closer. The natural question is: why bother? If we have identified a method with no obvious faults, why should we identify others? The answer is twofold. One, the world uses these other methods, and as a member of the finance profession, it would be expected that you know them as well. Second, there is value in each of the methods that, while not better than the answers provided by *NPV*, provide additional information the firm can use to make the best decisions possible.

We'll start with something known as the **profitability index (*PI*)**. Similar to the *AAR*, the *PI* is a ratio. However, unlike the *AAR*, the values used to compute the *PI* are financial rather than accounting in nature. The *PI* can best be described as a benefit-to-cost ratio. If you followed the discussion of *NPV* just above, then the discussion of *PI* will be a relatively painless task. Recall

$$NPV = PV \text{ of Benefits} - PV \text{ of Costs}$$

The *PI* uses the same set of numbers but turns this equation on end:

$$PI = \frac{PV \text{ of Benefits}}{PV \text{ of Costs}}$$

Putting the individual variables into this gives us the formal equation of *PI*:

$$PI = \frac{\sum_{t=1}^{T} \frac{CF_t}{(1 + WACC)^t}}{NINV}$$

For the Stars and Stripes project, this results in the following:

$$\boldsymbol{PI} = \frac{\frac{\mathbf{85,000}}{(\mathbf{1.079})} + \frac{\mathbf{90,000}}{(\mathbf{1.079})^2} + \frac{\mathbf{100,000}}{(\mathbf{1.079})^3} + \frac{\mathbf{105,000}}{(\mathbf{1.079})^4} + \frac{\mathbf{115,000}}{(\mathbf{1.079})^5}}{\mathbf{380,000}}$$

$$= \mathbf{1.031}$$

This indicates that for every $1 the firm expects to spend to implement the project, they expect to receive $1.031 in return, or a $.031 profit. Thus, for a $380,000 cost, they expect a (380,000*.031) $11,780 profit. This is a bit different from the *NPV* calculated earlier due to rounding, but the point is made. In most instances, the *PI* tells you the same thing as the *NPV*, but in a different way. In fact, if you have already calculated the *NPV*, you can save yourself a shortcut by calculating the *PI*:

$$PI = \frac{NPV + NINV}{NINV}$$

As an added exercise, find the *PI* in the alternative example where the expected cash flows are equal in each of the 5 years. You should find the answer to be 1.043.

Any *PI* with a value in excess of 1 is acceptable, as $1 of costs will return more than that $1. Doing so will add to firm value and, ultimately, shareholder wealth. Also, a positive *NPV* project will also have a $PI > 1$, and we must be consistent with the conclusions drawn from the *NPV*. The *PI* has many advantages. It considers all cash flows, adjusts for risk with the inclusion of the *WACC*, and naturally incorporates the time value of money. A disadvantage is that it is possible for the *PI* to provide an incorrect answer in the case of mutual exclusive projects. In such a situation, the company cannot accept both projects as the redundancy would be value threatening. Since the *PI* is a ratio, there are two ways to get a higher value. One can increase the numerator or one can decrease the denominator. Thus, consider the following.

Project A is expected to run for 5 years and has a cost of $1 million. The expected cash flow for each of the 5 years is expected to be $300,000. Project B is also expected to run for 5 years and has a cost of \$9 million. The expected cash flow for each of the 10 years is expected to be \$2.5 million. Assume an 8 % *WACC* for each. Thus, the *NPV*s can be calculated as follows:

$$\begin{aligned} NPV_A &= 300,000\left[\frac{1-\frac{1}{(1.08)^5}}{.08}\right] - 1,000,000 \\ &= \$197,813 \end{aligned}$$

$$\begin{aligned} NPV_B &= 2,500,000\left[\frac{1-\frac{1}{(1.08)^5}}{.08}\right] - 9,000,000 \\ &= \$981,775 \end{aligned}$$

If the projects were not mutually exclusive, and if the firm can obtain the funds, they should accept and incorporate both. However, since they cannot do so, the *NPV* rule says to accept Project B, as it returns fivefold that of Project A. However, look at what happens when we calculate the *PI*:

$$\begin{aligned} PI_{\mathrm{A}} &= (197,813 + 1,000,000)/1,000,000 \\ &= 1.198 \end{aligned}$$

$$\begin{aligned} PI_{\mathrm{B}} &= (981,775 + 9,000,000)/9,000,000 \\ &= 1.109 \end{aligned}$$

According to the *PI*, Project A is preferred because it returns more *per dollar* of investment than does Project B. Depending on the financial constraint of the firm (i.e., how much money they have/can obtain), this may be a very important factor. If they cannot readily obtain the \$9,000,000 needed to obtain the higher *NPV*, then Project A is naturally the best for them. However, recall that in order to get to this point, the firm should have estimated the *WACC* based upon expected costs of obtaining the funds. Thus, if they can obtain the funds, in this example, at 8 % for either amount, the result is the same. The firm should take the project that is expected to make the most money, which would be Project B.

9.1.6 Internal Rate of Return

Another, very popular capital budgeting method is the **internal rate of return (*IRR*)**. This method again usually tells us the same thing (in terms of acceptability) as the *NPV*, but they do it in very different ways. As the name implies, the *IRR* is a

percentage, as opposed to a dollar amount. In fact, it is the discount rate that equates the present value of the project's expected cash flows to the project's *NINV*. In simpler terms, it is the rate that makes *NPV* equal to zero. Thus, you would find the rate such that

$$\sum_{t=1}^{T} \frac{CF_t}{(1+IRR)^t} = NINV$$

Unfortunately, there is no formula to solve for this. You may recall that in Chap. 4 we discussed solving for an interest rate with multiple cash flows and concluded the only way to do it was trial and error. The same applies here. Let's once again illustrate with the Stars and Stripes example. So, we have cash flows throughout the 5-year project and a *NINV* of \$380,000. This creates the following situation:

$$\mathbf{380,000} = \frac{\mathbf{85,000}}{(\mathbf{1}+\boldsymbol{IRR})} + \frac{\mathbf{90,000}}{(\mathbf{1}+\boldsymbol{IRR})^{\mathbf{2}}} + \frac{\mathbf{100,000}}{(\mathbf{1}+\boldsymbol{IRR})^{\mathbf{3}}} + \frac{\mathbf{105,000}}{(\mathbf{1}+\boldsymbol{IRR})^{\mathbf{4}}} + \frac{\mathbf{115,000}}{(\mathbf{1}+\boldsymbol{IRR})^{\mathbf{5}}}$$

There is no magic formula for this. Try a percentage and see if it works. Then adjust and try again. And again. And again. . ..

You get the point, so I'll save you the work. You should obtain approximately 9 % for your *IRR*. There are, naturally, faster ways of doing this, using a financial calculator or spreadsheet. See a nearby "TECH HELP" box for instructions. You should, of course, get the same answer.

TECH HELP 9.2 Internal Rate of Return

Using the Financial Calculator

The process for using the TIBAII plus to calculate the *IRR* is very similar to that for solving for *NPV*. The first five steps when inputting all cash flows are the same.

Step 6: [*IRR*]
Step 7: [CPT]

You should get the 9.0 % answer as in the main text. For practice, compute the *NPV* with the alternative of five equal cash flows of \$99,000. In the latter case, you should get an *IRR* of 9.51 %.

Using Excel

The formula in Excel is "=*IRR*(values, guess)". Thus, you simply put the raw cash values into the sheet, type the formula in a blank cell, and highlight the column. Make sure you put the cash flows in the correct order, as Excel uses

(continued)

(continued)

the input order as the discounting pattern. The "guess" is optional and generally not required for the calculation to successfully complete.

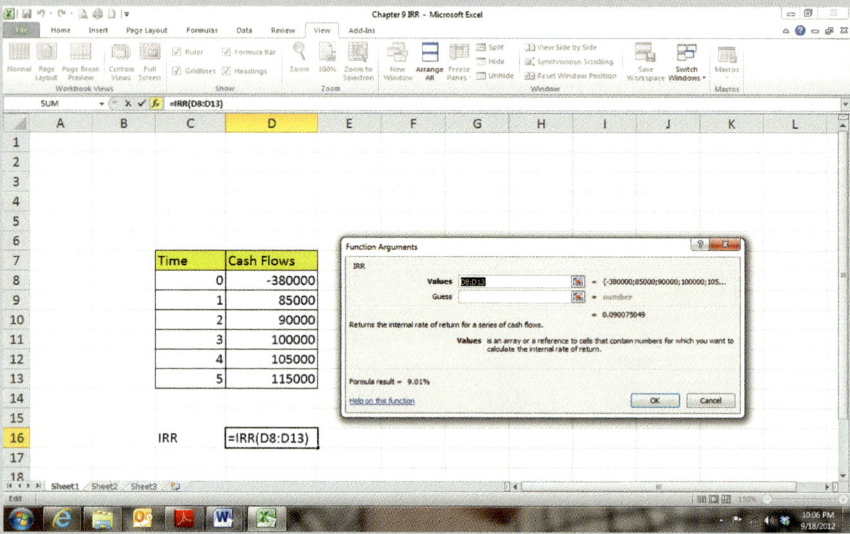

An *IRR* of 9 % means the annual return on this investment is implied to be (by the cash flow values provided) approximately 9 %. We now need to focus on how to make use of this number. The decision rule with the *IRR* is as follows:

- If *IRR* > *WACC*, ▸ Accept.
- If *IRR* < *WACC*, ▸ Reject.

It makes sense that, in order to make a decision, we need to compare a rate to another rate. But why is the appropriate comparison to the *WACC*? The *WACC* can be defined as the return the firm must generate in order to avoid losing money on a project. It is the cost of the funds, on an annual basis, to get the project to operation. In order to benefit the shareholders, we must make a return on the project in excess of this cost. Therefore, the *WACC* represents the lowest boundary on the return the firm can accept for a project. Anything less would be inconsistent with the goal of the firm. Therefore, it is logical to accept only projects where the *IRR* (the calculated project return) is greater than the *WACC* (the firm's required returns on project).

Perhaps the most important thing to know about the *IRR* is that, given conventional cash flows, it will always provide the same accept/reject decision as the *NPV*. You can begin to see why by understanding we use the same formula for both and essentially just solve for different variables. The primary advantage of the *IRR* is that it is a percentage rather than a number. This is appealing to many for a myriad of reasons, including ease of comparison. Also, since it uses the same basic form as *NPV*, it also adjusts for risk, particularly in the decision rule, and incorporates all cash flows.

A shortcoming is that the *IRR* can provide multiple answers should the cash flows be unconventional. This is a similar criticism to that of the payback period and should be acknowledged when using this capital budgeting technique. Also, despite the fact that is uses the same setup as *NPV*, it fails (like the *PI*) to provide a value of just how much better off the shareholders will be.

LOOK IT UP: The reason the *IRR* will provide multiple answers when faced with multiple negative cash flows is related to the way the cash flows are assumed to be reinvested. This creates problems when there is more than one outflow. Excel has a fix for this situation, and looking it up will probably also give you some insight into the problem itself.

9.2 A Note on the Capital Budgeting Tools

To sum, we have provided discussion pertaining to six capital budgeting tools. Each has strengths and most have weaknesses. We can summarize the findings in this chapter by ranking the tools by quality in meeting the goal of the firm. They fall within four categories, as illustrated in Table 9.1.

To drive the point home again, the *NPV* is the best capital budgeting tool due to one very simple reason: it is the most consistent with the goal of the firm. However, since the *PI* and *IRR* are methods that are based upon the same premise as *NPV*, they are also relatively high-quality tools. The difference between these latter two and *NPV* is the method in which it provides an answer. Both the *PI* and the *IRR* generally do a good job of providing the correct accept/reject decision. They help us determine which projects are good or bad. However, they stop short of telling us *how good* or *how bad* the project is. Let's ask a question. Suppose you have just been offered a job at a prestigious financial advisory firm. Which of the following would you rather hear?

Statement A: Your salary will be greater than the industry average.
Statement B: Your salary will be $25,000 higher than the industry average.

If we assume that your requirement to accept the position is that your salary be above industry average, both of these answers are acceptable. Statement A is akin to the *PI* or the *IRR*, while Statement B is akin to the *NPV*. You naturally prefer the specificity of Statement B, just as the shareholders would prefer knowing exactly how much better off the project is expected to make them rather than a generic statement. As a note, it is possible to obtain the specific information from the *PI* or the *IRR*, but you would need additional information. In the Stars and Stripes example, if you are told the *PI* is 1.04 *and* the *NINV* is $380,000, then you can

Table 9.1 Capital budgeting tools

Highest quality	Net present value (*NPV*)
High quality	Profitability index (*PI*)
	Internal rate of return (*IRR*)
Lower quality	Discounted payback period (*DPB*)
Low quality	Payback period (*PB*)
	Average accounting return (*AAR*)

figure out the *NPV*. However, that is the advantage of the *NPV* in a nutshell. You need nothing other than the answer.

The discounted payback period is a level below the top three tools due to the fact that it does not include all cash flows. As such, it does not tell the firm how much the project is supposed to return: only that it will generate a profit in a certain amount of time. However, since the discount rate is the *WACC*, it has the benefit of appropriately discounting the future cash flows. Finally, the last two methods are put in the lowest quality category due to the differences between the answers they provide and the goal of the firm. The payback period has the shortcoming of not incorporating major facets of finance (such as the time value of money), while the AAR utilizes accounting data to make financial decisions. They are not without value, however. For example, the payback period is often used as a tiebreaker of sorts. If two projects have similar *NPV*s, and we can accept only one, it probably makes sense to accept the one that pays back faster. And the average accounting return is useful due to the fact that a larger percentage of business professionals are more knowledgeable with accounting concepts such as net income than they are with financial concepts such as cash flows.

Finally, an important point needs to be made. In all likelihood, all methods will give the same accept/reject decision. However, if there is any disagreement among the methods, there is a very simple rule to follow: Always go with the NPV!

LOOK IT UP: Do you wonder which of these methods are actually used by corporations and financial executives? This may come as a shock to you, but academia and the corporate world do not always agree on which methods to use. See if you can find some research on the relationship between academic perception of the quality of the capital budgeting tools and the real-life implementation of these tools.

9.3 Sensitivity Analysis

It is very important to remember that we are dealing with estimates in every aspect of this process. The sales were an estimate, as were everything else on the pro forma statements, resulting in estimated net incomes. The cash flows were then estimated based upon these estimates. The *WACC* is also an estimate. So, with all of this estimation, there is one thing that we know for virtual certainty; our answers will be wrong. We just hope they aren't *too* wrong. If we believe the NPV is $200,000 and it turns out to only be $180,000, we aren't too upset because we still are benefitting the firm. If it turns out to be $-20,000, then we are very upset because we are going against the goal of the firm and indirectly harming the shareholders. Of course, there is also the much more pleasant possibility that we may underestimate our cash flows.

Thus, once the initial calculations are completed, it is important to do sensitivity analysis on the estimates to see how wrong we can be before we make a huge mistake. There are several ways of doing this. One standard way is to simply adjust the expected cash flows by a certain percentage. For example, suppose we chose to do a 15 % sensitivity analysis on the Stars and Stripes project. Therefore, the expected cash flows would be as follows:

Year	Expected CF	15 % More	15 % Less
1	$85,000	$97,750	$72,250
2	90,000	103,500	76,500
3	100,000	115,000	85,000
4	105,000	120,750	89,250
5	115,000	132,250	97,750

These values would result in the following net present values for the optimistic (15 % more) and pessimistic (15 % less) cases:

$$\begin{aligned} \boldsymbol{NPV_{Optimistic}} &= \mathbf{450,546{-}380,000 = \$70,546} \\ \boldsymbol{NPV_{Pessimistic}} &= \mathbf{333,013{-}380,000 = \$\text{-}46,988} \end{aligned}$$

Naturally, the optimistic scenario looks good and improves the situation. Unfortunately, the same cannot be said of the pessimistic scenario. If our expected cash are overestimated by 15 %, then we will make a large mistake. This understanding leads to the natural follow-up of whether this is acceptable, and the answer depends on the individual firm. Most firms have a sensitivity range in which they are comfortable and a deviation outside of that range is unacceptable. Of course, this leads to the much more difficult question: how likely are we to be off by 15 %? There is no easy answer to this, as it depends on the number of variables at play and the flexibility in each of them.

Of course, we could want to be even more specific than this. Rather than impose a percentage of increase or decrease in our estimates, we may wish to find the value that provides the breakeven point. In finance, the logical breakeven would be to find the level of cash flows that results in $NPV = 0$, since this is the lowest point where we at least do not *lose* money. Unfortunately, if the cash flows are uneven, this is difficult, if not impossible to do, unless the cash flows increase based upon some quantitative relationship (e.g., if sales increase 5 % each year). If the cash flows are equal, it becomes an easier problem to solve. To illustrate, let's again revisit the alternative example of the Stars and Stripes project where the cash flows are expected to be $99,000 in each of the 5 years.

In this scenario, we can identify the level of expected cash flow that would make expected benefit equal expected cost by

$$\mathbf{0{=}CF}\left[\frac{\mathbf{1}-\frac{1}{(1.079)^{5}}}{\mathbf{.079}}\right]-\mathbf{380,000}$$

where we would solve *CF* to be $94,922.75. So, our estimate could be off by a bit over 4 % and still be in the acceptable range. If 4 % is deemed an acceptable deviation, then the project would still be acceptable. Otherwise, we would explore other projects in the effort to identify those with a wider range of error.

Recall also that the expected cash flows are primarily a product of sales. So, in many cases, the firm would like to continue this analysis to see the necessary error in sales projections to generate a negative *NPV*. This would be accomplished by reversing the process of creating pro forma income statements. This gets to be a burdensome process, particularly in the event where estimates differ over the years of operation. Such activities are generally best left to software packages, such as Excel.

IN THE REAL WORLD

It was a BIG day for Hack Back and due to the heavy gravity of the situation, Tyler and Lilly decided to class it up a bit. Tyler knew the finance department had been pulling overtime to get everything ready for the meeting, so he decided to reward them. Rather than the traditional board room meeting, he and Lilly splurged for a private room at the Tall Oaks Golf Clubhouse.

The members of the finance team were dressed in their business best and were eager to impress the board members who had shown up for the meeting. It wasn't a tough sell to get the members to arrange their schedule to come to the picturesque course. The spacious room was filled nearly to capacity, and the tasty lunch helped put everyone in a good mood. The view from the large picture window was of the eighteenth green, where scratchers and duffers alike were finishing up their rounds. It was a beautiful day, and the site of the golfers struggling on the toughest hole on the course was enough to keep everyone's attention. If the golfers knew the number of eyes staring through the heavily tinted third-story window, their self-imposed pressure would magnify greatly.

"All right," Freeman said, clearing his throat, "are we about ready to get started with this thing?" While he certainly understood the need for team moral, the current surroundings were much out of his comfort level and the fact that he had been required to wear a sports coat had ruffled his feathers. He had had about enough of this tomfoolery.

"Sure, Dube," Lilly said. She was looking particularly at home, choosing to wear golfing clothes rather than her typical business suit. There was no way she was going to let a trip to the Oaks go by without getting in nine holes. In fact, she

was just as ready to get business under way. A quick glance at her watch said her tee time was in a couple of hours

"Why don't you go ahead and start?" she encouraged Freeman.

The room reluctantly turned away from drama unfolding over a very competitive dollar bet on the green below. Golfer A had three-putted; Golfer B was trying to "save" his double bogey with a three footer. The group behind the tinted window turned to face business just before the ball sank home, and Golfer B unleashed a vigorous fist pump to the sky.

Freeman got things started by pointing at Jane, who had become the unquestioned* de facto *leader of the group. The others were willing to follow. She was willing to work harder than they were and was a fair leader.

Jane rose from her chair and smoothed her skirt nervously before beginning. "You all have the full reports in front of you," she said, motioning to the thick bound documents lying near the center of the tables. In unison, the board members, Tyler, and Lilly each retrieved a copy. Brandon, Jane, and Stewart didn't need one, as they could recite it nearly from memory. Freeman didn't need one because he could recite it entirely from memory.

"Most of this is a fully detailed analysis of the projects that we want to get under way as soon as the weather is suitable in the locations. Just to remind you all, the working plan all along has been to fund, develop, and operate two additional plants. After a long process, we have decided the best locations for these plants were in Salina, Kansas, and Macon, Georgia. Pages 3-22 document our reasons for these conclusions, which have been thoroughly vetted and approved internally."

Tyler and Lilly both nodded, having been convinced several months previously that the necessary homework had been done on deciding the best locations. The board members flipped through the referenced pages and found nothing to argue about.

"After that, Marilyn and Stewart went through the exhausting process of estimating expected cash flows from the plants in question. Would either of you like to elaborate on that process?"

"The primary question is one of design," Stewart offered. "We are completely convinced that both plant proposals, the high-tech and traditional designs, are fully capable of producing the supply we need to gain market share across the USA."

"There is a trade-off in every area," Marilyn added. "The high-tech plant will be much more modernized and will put us on the cutting edge of the industry. But, it is also much less vetted than the traditional plant. The risks are much larger, and that is reflected in every aspect of our analysis. It also will cost much more to maintain from a resource standpoint, due to the intricacies of the machinery and software in use."

"The traditional plant will require less general manpower, as machines will be of somewhat less use in that design. We were left with a multilayered question of what we want and what is best for the company in the long run. While everyone likely has an opinion on which route they feel is best. . .."

A quick look around the room confirmed this to be true, as several board members nodded, while a few smiled slyly knowing they had been caught in their thought process.

"...we decided the best route would be to just let the numbers decide. So," Marilyn paused while picking up a copy of the report, "pages 23 through 55 detail the assumptions made, the research on which those assumptions were based, and most importantly, the resulting values that were derived from the process. What you see on page 51 is the summary of the expected cash flows, which we are convinced are the best available with the information we have."

High-tech plant			
	Year 0	*Years 1–14*	*Year 15*
Operating cash flows		*4,726,865*	*4,726,865*
Net capital spending	*−18,000,000*		
Change in NWC	*−5,000,000*		*5,000,000*
Total project cash flows	*−23,000,000*	*4,726,865*	*9,726,865*

Traditional plant			
	Year 0	*Years 1–19*	*Year 20*
Operating cash flows		*3,661,494*	*3,661,494*
Net capital spending	*−13,000,000*		
Change in NWC	*−3,000,000*		*3,000,000*
Total project cash flows	*−16,000,000*	*3,661,494*	*6,661,494*

There were several questions asked regarding the details of the numbers, but each were easily answered by Marilyn or Stewart. A short 10 minutes later, the board was satisfied by the values and ready to move on. Jane turned the floor over to Brandon, who elegantly buttoned his double-breasted suit as he stood. He was freshly shaved, coiffed, and had bought the new suit for just this occasion. He was in his zone.

"Jane and I have been spending the last several months trying to come up with viable funding options for each of the plant designs. When you consider that we need to obtain funding for two such plants, we had a relatively large undertaking. Pages 56 through 78 detail the process. In there you will notice the record of our in-depth discussions with all viable private lending partners, along with various underwriters for potential public bond or equity offerings. Also, I believe it is on page 60 or so that we start examining the potential costs of these funds, particularly how they relate to the return our shareholders will expect."

The room went abuzz with the sound of licked fingertips and page turning. Ever the considerate presenter, Brandon gave them time to absorb the information. As always, one or two of the board members had examples of firms they did not see included usually due to some type of inside "connection" the member claimed to have. In these instances, Brandon artfully deflected the criticism by assuring the member that they institution had either been contacted or had very good reasons why they weren't. Again, in the end, the members seemed satisfied by the estimates of costs for each project. More importantly, they seemed to

believe that the estimates provided by Jane and Brandon were probably the best available.

Throughout all of this, Freeman sat stoically and let his team work. It could have been assumed that he wasn't paying attention, but that would have been a misleading belief.

"Page 76 presents the summary of our findings," Brandon said.

High-tech plant

Source	*Amount*	*Weight*	*Cost*
Retained earnings	*$11 Million*	*11/46 = 23.91 %*	*13.06 %*
Coupon bonds	*$20 Million*	*20/46 = 43.48 %*	*9.16 %*
Private debt	*$15 Million*	*15/46 = 32.61 %*	*10.87 %*

$$WACC = (.2391*13.06) + (.4348*9.16*.65) + (.3261*10.87*.65) = 8.02\%$$

Traditional plant

Source	*Amount*	*Weight*	*Cost*
Retained earnings	*$13 Million*	*11/32 = 34.38 %*	*12.17 %*
Coupon bonds	*$15 Million*	*17/32 =53.13 %*	*8.36 %*
Private debt	*$5 Million*	*4/32 = 12.50 %*	*9.77 %*

$$WACC = (.3438*12.17) + (.5313*8.36*.65) + (.1250*9.77*.65) = 7.86\%$$

Tyler took the opportunity to convene a short break while everyone considered the mass of information. A couple of the board members perused the report, looking for potential weaknesses, while everyone else went back to the game of watching golf below the window. The courses dining room sent up a tray of brownies and fresh coffee, which everyone attacked as though it had been more than an hour since lunch. The desire for free food, instilled as a child, is never lost.

Finally, the meeting resumed, with Jane again at the helm of the presentation.

"Okay, so now that we have briefly discussed all the prep work, we are ready to discuss the conclusions. Please turn to page 80 of the report in front of you. Listed there are the tools we used to evaluate each project."

Payback period
Discounted payback period
Internal rate of return
Profitability index
Net present value

"I'm sorry," Dr. Collison, the board member most recently a mutual fund manager, said, "but it has been a long time since I had a finance course. I am not familiar with all of these."

Jane nodded. "Of course. If you will look at pages 81 through 90, you can see that we outline the entire process of calculating, interpreting, and troubleshooting each method. I know that is a lot of take in at the moment, but we believe all the information you will need is there."

She was right, of course, and the board members, along with Tyler and Lilly, spent several minutes reviewing what they were about to hear. Everyone was finally satisfied, and Tyler indicated that Jane could move forward.

"What you see on page 105 is the summary of the calculation of each of these methods," she said, "but I would like to take a moment to look at each of the methods separately, beginning with the payback period. That begins on page 91.

"The payback period for the high-tech project is 4.87 years, which means that we will not fully pay off the investment until nearly 5 years into the project. The traditional project pays off slightly faster in a bit less than four and a half years."

"The quicker the better, right?" Lilly queried.

"Well, all else equal, yes," Jane said, "but as you can see here not all else is equal. So, we can't really go by this for our final conclusion."

"For now," Brandon said, cutting off further questions, which were rising up the throats of the members, "just stock this away as information. We'll get back to it momentarily."

This satisfied the board members for the moment, as they settled back to listen to Jane continue.

"We also want to look at how quickly we pay back the project based upon the cash flows discounted by the cost of obtaining the funds."

"Am I correct in assuming the cost is the WACC for each respective project?" Susan Harding questioned. During her long tenure at Apple, she had been part of the review of many projects and was familiar with the process more so that many of her colleagues.

"Yes, exactly," Jane responded. "When we just look at the raw cash flows, we are essentially saying the funds come at no cost, which, of course, is not a true statement. Please turn to page 93."

She paused a moment while everyone did as asked.

"Once the cash flows have been discounted, they are worth less, naturally. That results in a discounted payback of 6.42 and 5.57 years, for the high-tech and traditional projects, respectively. So, the gap widens, which is not surprising, given the higher discount factor for the high-tech plant."

"Now," Jane said, drawing a deep breath, "we get to the real heart of the decisions. The following three methods are more complete and comprehensive evaluations of the projects, and as such, we put much more weight on their conclusions. You can read the summaries for the methods for a full discussion of why I say this."

Brandon again stood to relieve his partner.

"The internal rate of return is important because it tells us the implied return that each project will generate annually. It is based upon our expected cash flow figures. For the high-tech plant, it works out to be about 19.41 %. For the traditional plant, it works out to be 22.57 %."

"These numbers are then compared to the WACCs of each project," Jane added. For each project, we can summarize that as an average annual excess return. Which is about 11.39 % for the high-tech firm and 14.71 % for the traditional firm."

"That sounds like a no-brainer," Bobby Dennison said. Dennison was a member of the board primarily for his golf business acumen rather than his knowledge of finance, but he had a sound logical and analytical mind. "The traditional plant is better. And, once that money comes in every year, we can invest the excess in new projects things."

"Yes, that is entirely true," Brandon said, but held up an open palm as a gesture of patience, "but we also have to remember that percentage returns are based upon the amount of money involved."

"Ah, I understand," Dennison responded, quickly catching the point, "and since the high-tech firm has a larger investment and larger expected cash flow returns, we need to see exactly which of those returns warrant the highest dollar return."

His condensed analysis made sense to everyone and had the room nodding in agreement.

"That is exactly correct, Mr. Dennison," Jane said. "We need to do a bit more on that end, but let's first look at the profitability index. Page 101 please."

"If you sum up the discounted cash flows for the entire 15 and 20-year time periods, you get those following values," Brandon said, pointing at a column on the page.

$$PV\ of\ Expected\ Cash\ Flows\ (High - Tech\ Project)$$

$$\sum_{t=1}^{T} \frac{CF_t}{(1 + WACC)^t} = \$41,981,978$$

$$PV\ of\ Expected\ Cash\ Flows\ (Traditional\ Project)$$

$$\sum_{t=1}^{T} \frac{CF_t}{(1 + WACC)^t} = \$36,987,282$$

"And if you take that and divide by the cost of each project," Jane said, "you get the profitability index."

$$PI_{Hi-Tech} = \frac{41,981,978}{23,000,000} = 1.82$$

$$PI_{Traditional} = \frac{36{,}987{,}282}{16{,}000{,}000} = 2.31$$

"You can interpret these as a dollar spent will generate $1.82 and $2.31 in return."

"So, we're seeing a pattern," Dennison spoke up again, "but that still could be misleading. It depends on how many dollars is spent, and we know the high-tech project will cost more than the traditional."

"That is true, but it's easy from this point to tell if the extra cost is worth it," Brandon said. "If we are planning to make $.82 for each dollar spent and we spend 23 million, then we will make, or expect to make, around $19 million on the high-tech project."

"And nearly $21 million from the traditional project," Jane said, with emphasis. That number had been in hiding for a long time, and it was great to have it out in the open.

"Since there is some rounding in those numbers," she added, "you can see the exact calculations on page 103.

$$PVA_{Hi\text{-}Tech} = \left[4{,}726{,}865 \left[\frac{1 - \dfrac{1}{(1.0802)^{14}}}{.0802} \right] + \frac{9{,}726{,}865}{(1.0802)^{15}} \right] - 23{,}000{,}000$$

$$= \$18{,}981{,}975$$

$$PVA_{Traditional} = \left[3{,}661{,}494 \left[\frac{1 - \dfrac{1}{(1.0786)^{19}}}{.0786} \right] + \frac{6{,}661{,}494}{(1.0786)^{20}} \right] - 16{,}000{,}000$$

$$= \$20{,}987{,}286$$

"Let me see if I understand what you are showing us," Susan Harding said, thoughtfully, "both projects are viable in that they both are expected to generate more than the costs of those projects. But, given that there is no need to take both projects, the traditional plant is better. It returns the cost, plus an excess of nearly $21 million."

"That is it in a nutshell," Jane said.

The room digested this information for a moment before Brandon spoke.

"If you will now turn finally, to page 105, you can see the summary of our results."

Capital budgeting tool	*High-tech*	*Traditional*	*Conclusion*
Payback period	*4.87 year*	*4.37 year*	*Traditional is better*
Discounted payback	*6.42 year*	*5.57 year*	*Traditional is better*
Internal rate of return	*19.41 %*	*22.57 %*	*Traditional is better*
Profitability index	*1.82*	*2.31*	*Traditional is better*
Net present value	*$18,981,975*	*$20,987,286*	*Traditional is better*

The room fell silent as the board members thought about what they were seeing. The finance team was confident in both their work and their presentation. All that was left was the approval by the board, and ground could be broken on the plants.

"Does anyone have any questions for the finance team?" Tyler said, addressing the board members.

No one did.

"Okay, folks," Tyler said, "great work. Could you please excuse us while chat about this for a moment?"

"Sure," Freeman said, surprising everyone by speaking for the first time in 2 hours. "Let's go kids."

The board unanimously agreed to accept the recommendation of the finance team. Two months later, ground was broken in Salina, Kansas. A month after that, the same occurred in Macon, Georgia.

ALTERNATE ENDINGS

1. ***The finance team decided to not show the results for the average accounting return (AAR). However, if you review Chap. 3, you will find the necessary information to complete the calculation. What is the conclusion drawn by the AAR?***
2. ***While you are reviewing Chap. 3, recall that the numbers used in the base calculations are based upon a relatively simple set of assumptions about the cash flows. In the Alternate Endings of Chap. 3, we posed several potential alterations to those assumptions that required redesigning the expected cash flow process. Now, based upon those alternative scenarios, calculate the answers for the capital budgeting tools. Do the results change in any meaningful way?***
3. ***Suppose Ms. Harding had said, "Both projects are viable, in that they both have positive NPVs. Why don't we just do one of each and see which works out better?" What do you think of this statement? What are the positive and negative results that could come from following this advice? What does corporate finance theory say regarding this statement?***
4. ***Suppose the remaining member of the board, Dr. Steven Austin, still has reservations about what he has just seen and says:***

   "I'm sorry, but maybe I'm missing something here. Isn't the point to get the most money flowing into the firm? If it is, aren't you telling me that, even on a discounted basis, the high-tech plant will bring in $5 million more than the traditional plant. I understand what you are saying about profit-per-dollar, but we can get the money to fund the high-tech project. Why not do so and get the extra $5 million in cash inflows?"

   Man, I hate tough questions! How do you answer that?
5. ***Dennison is a numbers guy and is concerned about returns. What do the NPV and IRR say about annual returns, specifically as they relates to shareholders? What about that excess return (IRR – WACC) that they were talking about? How do you explain what that means to him and the others?***

6. ***The discussion above leaves out reference to any sensitivity analysts, which surely must have been completed. Suppose Tyler says the following:***

   "I am worried about these estimates and the emphasis we are putting on them being correct. What happens if we are off by 10 %?"

   How do you answer him?
   Now, suppose he chooses to really be a pain about it and says:

   "What is the bottom line sales figure we have to reach each year to break even on these projects?"

   He's your boss. You have to answer him.

Concept Questions

1. **Capital budgeting and capital structure** Discuss the relationship between the capital budgeting and capital structure decisions. Are they made independently or simultaneously? Why? How?
2. **Capital budgeting tools** Your boss, Mad Man Mike, just said that you screwed up because the *NPV* calculation that you provided turned out to be wrong. How do you respond to this?
3. **Payback period** What are the strengths and weaknesses of the payback period method of capital budgeting?
4. **Average accounting return** What are the strengths and weaknesses of the average accounting return method of capital budgeting?
5. **Net present value** Your brilliant finance instructor just made the following comment: "The *NPV* incorporates everything we have done all semester long." Is she/he crazy? Why would she/he make such a statement?
6. **Profitability index** You have the *NPV* of a project. In order to get the *PI*, what other piece of information do you need? What does this tell you about the two methods?
7. **Profitability index** What are the strengths and weaknesses of the profitability index method of capital budgeting?
8. **Internal rate of return** You have calculated an *IRR* of 8.5 % on a project. What does this mean? If the *WACC* is 7.5 %, what is your decision based upon the *IRR*?
9. **Internal rate of return** What are the strengths and weaknesses of the internal rate of return method of capital budgeting?

Problems

1. **Payback period** Suppose you have a project that has a *NINV* of $825,000. The project is expected to generate net cash flows of $76,000 each year for 20 years. What is the payback period?
2. **Payback period** Joe's Beef Barn is planning to purchase a new meat grinding machine. They have two options. Option A is expected to generate net cash flows of $35,000 for the next 10 years and has a *NINV* of $270,000. Option B is

a 7-year project that is expected to generate the following net cash flows: \$14,000 at the end of time one, 13,800 at the end of time two, 11,430 at the end of time three, and 17,200 at the end of times four through seven. Project B has a *NINV* of \$95,000. Joe makes all of his capital budgeting decisions based upon the payback period. Which project is better?

3. **Discounted payback period** A firm is considering a 15-year project that is expected to return *NCF*s of \$12,000 in each of the first 7 years and then \$8,000 in each of the remaining 8 years. If the *NINV* is \$75,000, what is the discounted payback period? The firm's *WACC* is 7 %.
4. **Discounted payback period** Netty's Cow Barn, Inc. is considering a new milking system. They have calculated the *NPV* of this project to be \$68,524. The project is an 8-year project where each year is expected to generate the same *NCF*. The project requires no addition to *NWC*, so the only *NINV* is the *NCS* on the machine itself, which is \$35,563. The machine will be depreciated straight line until zero salvage. What is the project's discounted payback if the firm's $WACC = 8\ \%$?
5. **Average accounting return** Consider a project that is expected to generate \$45,800 in net income for each of its 10 years. In addition, it is going to cost \$389,000 to get started. What is the average accounting return?
6. **Average accounting return** The AAR of a project has been calculated to be 98.43 %. The project is a 5-year project and is expected to generate net income of \$126,440 in each of those 5 years. If the project is depreciated straight line to zero salvage, what is the *NINV* of the project?
7. **Average accounting return** A firm is considering a 3-year project. It is believed that the first year's sales will be \$21,000 and that this number will increase by \$2,000 (over each previous year) in each of the remaining 2 years. Costs are estimated to be 46 % of sales, and depreciation will be \$3,000 each year, based upon straight-line depreciation. The firm's tax rate is 35 %. The project has a *NINV* of \$24,000; what is the project's AAR?
8. **Net present value** What is the *NPV* of a project that is expected to generate *NCF*s of \$450,500 each year for the next 32 years? The project has a *NINV* of \$6 million and *WACC* of 7 %.
9. **Net present value** Suppose you are considering a 3-year project that is expected to generate *NCF*s of 24,000 in each of the first 2 years and then \$36,000 in the last year. If the *IRR* is 6.47 % and their required rate of return is 4.61 %, what is the project's *NPV*?
10. **Net present value** An investment project has an installed cost of \$518,297. The cash flows over the 4-year life of the investment are projected to be \$287,636, \$203,496, \$103,802, and \$92,556, respectively. What is the *NPV* of this project if the discount rate is 0 %?
11. **Net present value** Suppose you have a project with *IRR* of 11.3 %. The project is expected to generate *NCF*s of \$44,900 in each of its 8 years. What is the firm's *NPV* if their *WACC* is 10.4 %?

12. **Net present value** Hattie's Hat Company, Inc. is considering a project that has a *NCS* of \$256,000, an increase in *NWC* of \$125,000, and *NCF* of \$85,542 during each year of the project. Hattie has calculated a *PI* of .89 times. What is the project's *NPV*?
13. **Internal rate of return** Billy's Bean Barn is thinking of purchasing a new shucking machine that costs \$126,000. They expect to generate *NCF*s of \$26,000 each year for the 7 years of the project. What is the *IRR* of this project?
14. **Internal rate of return** Suppose a project is expected to have a 2-year life and is expected to generate net cash flows of \$10,000 in year one. In year two, the cash flow decreases to \$8,000. If the project has a *NINV* of \$16,000, what is the internal rate of return (*IRR*)?
15. **Internal rate of return** Consider a project that is expected to generate *NCF*s of 75,000 in each of the 4 years of the project. In order to get the project up and running, the firm will have to have net capital spending of \$205,000 and must increase *NWC* by \$89,000. At the end of the project, the firm will be able to recover 60 % of the increase in *NWC*. What is the firm's *IRR*?
16. **Breakeven analysis** Suppose you are evaluating a 4-year project, where each year is projected to be identical. The *NINV* of the project is \$897,000, and the company's *WACC* is 7.6 %.

    a. What level of net cash flow each year would be the breakeven amount, where the project would have *NPV* of \$0?
    b. Assume you know the depreciation each year is \$56,000, costs of goods sold are 46 % of sales, and the firm has a 35 % tax rate. Given this, what level of sales would generate the breakeven cash flow level?
    c. If you have calculated the *NPV* to be \$145,000, what level of sales is your best estimate?

17. **Net present value** You are considering a 4-year project that has the following pro forma statement:

Pro forma income statement (annual)	
Sales	\$2,056,280
COGS	1,205,000
Depreciation	86,000
EBIT	765,280
Interest	52,000
Taxable income	713,280
Taxes (35 %)	249,648
Net income	\$463,632

In addition, you have estimated the project will require an increase in net capital spending of \$1.8 million and an increase in net working capital of \$450,000. If the firm's *WACC* is 8 %, what is the net present value? Should you accept or reject?

18. **Sensitivity analysis** In #18 above, suppose you wanted to conduct sensitivity analysis where actual sales can deviate by +/− 10 % from those projected. What is the "best"-/"worst"-case scenario for the *NPV* if they are defined by this 20 % range?
19. **Capital budgeting tools** Scotty's Pickle Factory is considering purchase of a new machine to supplement his operations. After a long, drawn-out process, his financial team has come up with estimates regarding the project. First, they think the initial addition to net capital spending will be $657,000. In addition, they believe they will have to change their level of net working capital from $109,000 to $176,500. They have created the following pro forma statements for each year. Scotty's required *WACC* is 6.74 %.

	Year 1	Year 2	Year 3	Year 4
Sales	900,000	960,000	1,025,000	650,000
COGS	350,000	373,333	398,611	252,778
Depreciation	218,978	291,971	97,367	48,684
EBIT	331,022	294,696	529,022	348,538
Taxes (35 %)	115,858	103,144	185,158	121,988
Net income	215,164	191,552	343,864	226,550

(a) What is the project's payback period?
(b) What is the project's discounted payback period?
(c) What is the project's net present value?
(d) What is the project's profitability index?
(e) What is the projects internal rate of return?

Appendix 1

In the Real World Epilogue

IN THE REAL WORLD

It was Spring 2014 and the plant in Salina had been running for a month. Hack Back had been a publicly traded company for over 6 years and was among the industry leaders. It had the market cornered on injury-reducing golf equipment and the newest version of the "Dice Q" hybrid clubs were a huge success. There was even talk that the PGA tour was going to allow Hack Back clubs to be used during tour events. In short, things were going well, thanks in large part to an aggressive, but sound, financial strategy.

The last piece of the current plan had just fallen into place, with the grand opening of the Macon plant happening that day. Tyler and Lilly had flown the entire finance team down to see the results of their work. The day had been a success. The Mayor and Governor were in attendance and the crowd of future employees, town well-to-dos, and the Hack Back administrative staff was in a joyous mood. The ribbon feel gracefully to the ground as pictures were snapped and confetti fell.

It was late evening and the sun was setting. It was already warm in central Georgia, so the finance team, along with Tyler and Lilly were having an after-dinner drink on the deck of a local restaurant.

"Well, there are my all-stars!" The booming voice came from the doorway. Eli Eldridge slid his ever-growing girth through the door and pulled up a chair. He sat down loudly and jostled the ice in his drink as he thumped it on the table.

"Eli!" Lilly said. "What a pleasant surprise. Were you at the grand opening?"

"Of course, dear," Eli said, "I have to check out my competition."

"Competition," Tyler scoffed, "unless you've changed your business plan, we are a long way from being each other's competition."

"We supply. You retail," Lilly added. "You're not thinking of starting to produce, are you?"

"Oh, of course, not," Eli said, "but I have a different idea for you."

M.K. Pyles, *Applied Corporate Finance: Questions, Problems and Making Decisions in the Real World*, Springer Texts in Business and Economics, DOI 10.1007/978-1-4614-9173-6, © Springer Science+Business Media New York 2014

"Ahh, there it is," Freeman said, from his corner seat. He was nursing his drink as he watched birds flitter around tree to tree in the open expanse beyond the deck. "Eli Eldridge is always thinking business."

Eli released a thunderous fit of laughter.

"You know me well," he chuckled, but then quickly sobered up quickly, "but seriously, I have a plan that I am going to propose to you guys first and then, if you're not interested, I'll go elsewhere."

Tyler and Lilly stared at each other. They hadn't expected to be talking business tonight, but they'd be fools to not hear him out.

"We're listening," Lilly said.

"It's this new club made out of a brand new material. A combination of aluminum and titanium, calling it tillumium."

"Is anyone but you calling it that?" Freeman said with a half-smile.

Eli was so into his pitch that he didn't even hear the comment. "It's the next big thing. Has the durability and performance of titanium combined with the weight of aluminum. Suppose to reduce the weight of the club by 15 %, which adds 20 yards to every shot. Next big thing, I'm telling you. I've got the plans for a whole set, starting with drivers and woods. Had my engineering team draw up the whole shebang."

With that, he pulled a series of design prints from his back pocket and smoothed the wrinkles on the dusty table-top.

"All I need is the facility, the workforce, and someone to help with the funding."

Tyler looked thoughtful and Lilly's eyes took on an aggressive tint.

"The lighter weight would likely reduce the possibility of injury," Tyler said, half to himself. "We'd have to get some studies done, but it could fit into our business plan."

"And you know we've talked about getting more into mainstream development, Tyler," Lilly said.

They both turned to the finance team, huddled around their table, watching and waiting.

"Do you folks think you can get started on seeing about this?" Tyler said.

"Give it the full works?" Lilly added.

"All you've got," Eli added needlessly.

"Sure, we can," Jane said confidently. "We'll get started when we get back to the office Monday." She had a belated thought and turned sheepishly to Dubarb Freeman.

"Of course, if it is okay with you."

Freeman smiled, perhaps the largest smile he had ever shown the group.

"Young lady," he said, "it is more than all right with me. In fact, this is the perfect time to tell you all something that I've been waiting a long time to say. Tyler and Lilly brought this old dog out of the yard to help get this company to a new level and I hope that I've done that."

"What are you talking about, Dube?" Tyler asked, puzzled.

"Today was the culmination of me doing all I can for you. The kids are ready. They know the whole process and are probably better at it than me."

He paused and pointed at Jane before looking back at the owners. "And you have a ready-for-action new CFO right here."

Jane blushed while the others smiled and nodded. Marilyn reached over and patted Jane's hand in support.

"You're quitting?" Lilly said incredulously.

"Yep, you don't need me anymore."

"But, what will you do?"

Freeman raised his glass, and drained the remainder before sitting it back down on the table. He rose to his feet.

"I'm moving with my honey bun to San Diego. Got surfing lessons all lined up." With that, he walked out the door without looking back. The rest of the crowd sat in stunned silence.

Finally, Eli Eldridge spoke.

"If wetsuits could talk," he said, turning up his cup, "they'd be crying right now."

ALTERNATE ENDINGS

1. *Suppose, instead of surfing, Dubarb Freeman and his "honey bun" take up roller blading.*

   Discuss.

Appendix 2

Hack Back's Daily Stock Prices

Date	Price	Date	Price	Date	Price	Date	Price
12/14/2007Open	40.00	3/6/2008	55.84	5/28/2008	48.18	8/18/2008	35.90
12/14/2007	49.25	3/7/2008	52.84	5/29/2008	48.17	8/19/2008	35.91
12/17/2007	49.07	3/10/2008	52.34	5/30/2008	48.18	8/20/2008	35.95
12/18/2007	50.81	3/11/2008	52.85	6/2/2008	46.31	8/21/2008	36.27
12/19/2007	48.51	3/12/2008	51.48	6/3/2008	45.08	8/22/2008	37.43
12/20/2007	49.02	3/13/2008	50.25	6/4/2008	45.69	8/25/2008	36.30
12/21/2007	50.74	3/14/2008	51.50	6/5/2008	47.69	8/26/2008	37.07
12/24/2007	56.09	3/17/2008	51.02	6/6/2008	40.74	8/27/2008	36.93
12/26/2007	50.90	3/18/2008	49.82	6/9/2008	42.56	8/28/2008	37.47
12/27/2007	53.51	3/19/2008	51.19	6/10/2008	43.15	8/29/2008	36.62
12/28/2007	54.38	3/20/2008	51.06	6/11/2008	39.86	9/2/2008	36.77
12/31/2007	54.08	3/24/2008	49.46	6/12/2008	40.83	9/3/2008	36.71
1/2/2008	54.68	3/25/2008	49.78	6/13/2008	41.19	9/4/2008	35.55
1/3/2008	52.33	3/26/2008	51.58	6/16/2008	41.13	9/5/2008	36.20
1/4/2008	54.49	3/27/2008	52.52	6/17/2008	40.57	9/8/2008	39.22
1/7/2008	55.39	3/28/2008	53.54	6/18/2008	39.75	9/9/2008	36.00
1/8/2008	55.25	3/31/2008	51.48	6/19/2008	41.27	9/10/2008	36.80
1/9/2008	55.18	4/1/2008	51.79	6/20/2008	39.54	9/11/2008	37.34
1/10/2008	54.57	4/2/2008	50.63	6/23/2008	40.09	9/12/2008	37.40
1/11/2008	55.25	4/3/2008	50.74	6/24/2008	39.95	9/15/2008	36.78
1/14/2008	56.52	4/4/2008	48.09	6/25/2008	40.19	9/16/2008	37.25
1/15/2008	57.36	4/7/2008	48.82	6/26/2008	39.56	9/17/2008	33.68
1/16/2008	56.91	4/8/2008	47.45	6/27/2008	38.77	9/18/2008	36.38
1/17/2008	58.54	4/9/2008	45.72	6/30/2008	40.65	9/19/2008	37.49
1/18/2008	54.88	4/10/2008	45.90	7/1/2008	40.19	9/22/2008	35.44
1/22/2008	56.19	4/11/2008	47.33	7/2/2008	39.71	9/23/2008	34.49
1/23/2008	57.24	4/14/2008	46.84	7/3/2008	39.89	9/24/2008	34.82
1/24/2008	58.48	4/15/2008	47.26	7/7/2008	39.74	9/25/2008	35.32
1/25/2008	58.21	4/16/2008	49.89	7/8/2008	40.29	9/26/2008	35.48
1/28/2008	58.18	4/17/2008	49.03	7/9/2008	38.00	9/29/2008	34.56

(continued)

M.K. Pyles, *Applied Corporate Finance: Questions, Problems and Making Decisions in the Real World*, Springer Texts in Business and Economics,
DOI 10.1007/978-1-4614-9173-6,

(continued)

Date	Price	Date	Price	Date	Price	Date	Price
1/29/2008	58.51	4/18/2008	49.22	7/10/2008	39.25	9/30/2008	36.82
1/30/2008	61.93	4/21/2008	48.92	7/11/2008	38.43	10/1/2008	35.98
1/31/2008	62.55	4/22/2008	48.81	7/14/2008	38.02	10/2/2008	35.61
2/1/2008	63.40	4/23/2008	47.61	7/15/2008	37.68	10/3/2008	35.61
2/4/2008	59.98	4/24/2008	48.70	7/16/2008	38.04	10/6/2008	34.59
2/5/2008	63.03	4/25/2008	50.83	7/17/2008	38.06	10/7/2008	32.10
2/6/2008	57.29	4/28/2008	47.05	7/18/2008	38.12	10/8/2008	33.41
2/7/2008	58.14	4/29/2008	47.56	7/21/2008	37.78	10/9/2008	30.78
2/8/2008	57.87	4/30/2008	46.54	7/22/2008	38.48	10/10/2008	32.33
2/11/2008	57.94	5/1/2008	48.50	7/23/2008	39.05	10/13/2008	38.08
2/12/2008	56.44	5/2/2008	48.21	7/24/2008	37.69	10/14/2008	35.90
2/13/2008	56.80	5/5/2008	47.62	7/25/2008	38.13	10/15/2008	32.54
2/14/2008	55.48	5/6/2008	49.61	7/28/2008	37.75	10/16/2008	34.33
2/15/2008	58.98	5/7/2008	47.48	7/29/2008	37.55	10/17/2008	33.92
2/19/2008	56.45	5/8/2008	48.68	7/30/2008	38.01	10/20/2008	34.19
2/20/2008	53.90	5/9/2008	48.29	7/31/2008	36.63	10/21/2008	33.72
2/21/2008	54.56	5/12/2008	48.50	8/1/2008	36.79	10/22/2008	32.08
2/22/2008	53.39	5/13/2008	47.74	8/4/2008	36.89	10/23/2008	32.97
2/25/2008	54.06	5/14/2008	48.27	8/5/2008	37.11	10/24/2008	32.74
2/26/2008	55.34	5/15/2008	48.42	8/6/2008	37.84	10/27/2008	31.95
2/27/2008	55.09	5/16/2008	48.50	8/7/2008	35.49	10/28/2008	35.97
2/28/2008	56.33	5/19/2008	48.98	8/8/2008	36.53	10/29/2008	34.17
2/29/2008	54.53	5/20/2008	47.41	8/11/2008	36.98	10/30/2008	35.15
3/3/2008	54.80	5/21/2008	47.51	8/12/2008	35.35	10/31/2008	34.57
3/4/2008	53.68	5/22/2008	48.18	8/13/2008	36.03	11/3/2008	33.41
3/5/2008	56.89	5/23/2008	47.79	8/14/2008	37.27	11/4/2008	37.04
3/6/2008	55.84	5/27/2008	48.06	8/15/2008	36.19	11/5/2008	31.77
11/7/2008	33.21	2/10/2009	34.81	5/12/2009	45.44	8/11/2009	46.60
11/10/2008	32.92	2/11/2009	35.04	5/13/2009	44.62	8/12/2009	48.60
11/11/2008	32.47	2/12/2009	35.17	5/14/2009	46.48	8/13/2009	48.19
11/12/2008	31.08	2/13/2009	34.96	5/15/2009	44.58	8/14/2009	48.03
11/13/2008	33.53	2/17/2009	34.78	5/18/2009	48.04	8/17/2009	46.35
11/14/2008	30.07	2/18/2009	34.72	5/19/2009	46.81	8/18/2009	47.72
11/17/2008	30.97	2/19/2009	34.57	5/20/2009	46.42	8/19/2009	47.22
11/18/2008	32.50	2/20/2009	33.83	5/21/2009	45.36	8/20/2009	48.45
11/19/2008	30.25	2/23/2009	33.89	5/22/2009	45.39	8/21/2009	49.76
11/20/2008	30.05	2/24/2009	38.56	5/26/2009	46.75	8/24/2009	49.01
11/21/2008	33.10	2/25/2009	35.97	5/27/2009	45.84	8/25/2009	50.63
11/24/2008	33.30	2/26/2009	36.00	5/28/2009	47.72	8/26/2009	50.40
11/25/2008	31.73	2/27/2009	35.96	5/29/2009	47.30	8/27/2009	50.64
11/26/2008	34.11	3/2/2009	35.95	6/1/2009	48.21	8/28/2009	50.11
11/28/2008	33.64	3/3/2009	34.81	6/2/2009	47.01	8/31/2009	49.65
12/1/2008	31.10	3/4/2009	35.31	6/3/2009	45.76	9/1/2009	47.07
12/2/2008	32.20	3/5/2009	34.63	6/4/2009	48.03	9/2/2009	48.12
12/3/2008	32.04	3/6/2009	34.89	6/5/2009	46.77	9/3/2009	48.33
12/4/2008	31.92	3/9/2009	33.84	6/8/2009	47.19	9/4/2009	49.65

(continued)

(continued)

Date	Price	Date	Price	Date	Price	Date	Price
12/5/2008	33.60	3/10/2009	36.94	6/9/2009	47.41	9/8/2009	49.34
12/8/2008	34.79	3/11/2009	35.83	6/10/2009	45.39	9/9/2009	49.53
12/9/2008	34.41	3/12/2009	37.40	6/11/2009	47.19	9/10/2009	49.67
12/10/2008	35.34	3/13/2009	35.71	6/12/2009	46.57	9/11/2009	48.74
12/11/2008	34.79	3/16/2009	36.06	6/15/2009	42.56	9/14/2009	49.21
12/12/2008	35.06	3/17/2009	38.58	6/16/2009	44.15	9/15/2009	49.31
12/15/2008	33.24	3/18/2009	38.16	6/17/2009	42.43	9/16/2009	51.23
12/16/2008	36.26	3/19/2009	35.54	6/18/2009	44.09	9/17/2009	49.79
12/17/2008	34.95	3/20/2009	35.99	6/19/2009	43.56	9/18/2009	50.41
12/18/2008	35.03	3/23/2009	40.25	6/22/2009	39.67	9/21/2009	50.06
12/19/2008	35.14	3/24/2009	38.20	6/23/2009	42.70	9/22/2009	50.53
12/22/2008	34.46	3/25/2009	38.53	6/24/2009	42.29	9/23/2009	48.98
12/23/2008	33.67	3/26/2009	39.22	6/25/2009	44.94	9/24/2009	49.95
12/24/2008	34.15	3/27/2009	38.11	6/26/2009	42.71	9/25/2009	49.72
12/26/2008	34.17	3/30/2009	37.96	6/29/2009	43.32	9/28/2009	51.54
12/29/2008	34.15	3/31/2009	38.65	6/30/2009	43.09	9/29/2009	49.49
12/30/2008	35.64	4/1/2009	38.54	7/1/2009	42.96	9/30/2009	49.66
12/31/2008	35.48	4/2/2009	39.42	7/2/2009	41.65	10/1/2009	46.45
1/2/2009	35.48	4/3/2009	39.16	7/6/2009	43.41	10/2/2009	47.57
1/5/2009	34.95	4/6/2009	39.45	7/7/2009	41.43	10/5/2009	49.64
1/6/2009	35.43	4/7/2009	38.21	7/8/2009	40.64	10/6/2009	49.70
1/7/2009	33.29	4/8/2009	39.45	7/9/2009	42.60	10/7/2009	49.96
1/8/2009	34.17	4/9/2009	40.53	7/10/2009	42.19	10/8/2009	50.37
1/9/2009	33.55	4/13/2009	40.09	7/13/2009	43.76	10/9/2009	50.30
1/12/2009	33.66	4/14/2009	39.06	7/14/2009	43.35	10/12/2009	50.50
1/13/2009	33.78	4/15/2009	39.58	7/15/2009	46.06	10/13/2009	50.32
1/14/2009	32.68	4/16/2009	38.93	7/16/2009	45.13	10/14/2009	52.74
1/15/2009	34.86	4/17/2009	40.64	7/17/2009	44.94	10/15/2009	51.69
1/16/2009	34.58	4/20/2009	38.41	7/20/2009	46.88	10/16/2009	50.92
1/20/2009	33.71	4/21/2009	40.22	7/21/2009	46.66	10/19/2009	51.59
1/21/2009	35.74	4/22/2009	39.91	7/22/2009	45.77	10/20/2009	50.72
1/22/2009	33.61	4/23/2009	39.93	7/23/2009	48.08	10/21/2009	49.94
1/23/2009	35.43	4/24/2009	42.08	7/24/2009	47.66	10/22/2009	51.55
1/26/2009	34.83	4/27/2009	41.02	7/27/2009	46.88	10/23/2009	49.65
1/27/2009	34.83	4/28/2009	41.35	7/28/2009	46.93	10/26/2009	49.69
1/28/2009	36.31	4/29/2009	45.46	7/29/2009	46.36	10/27/2009	48.74
1/29/2009	34.35	4/30/2009	43.10	7/30/2009	48.70	10/28/2009	48.43
1/30/2009	33.50	5/1/2009	43.47	7/31/2009	47.76	10/29/2009	50.90
2/2/2009	35.55	5/4/2009	47.36	8/3/2009	48.47	10/30/2009	47.06
2/3/2009	34.77	5/5/2009	46.00	8/4/2009	48.33	11/2/2009	48.53
2/4/2009	33.72	5/6/2009	46.07	8/5/2009	47.66	11/3/2009	49.38
2/5/2009	35.31	5/7/2009	45.93	8/6/2009	47.27	11/4/2009	48.80
2/6/2009	35.25	5/8/2009	46.37	8/7/2009	48.82	11/5/2009	50.41
2/9/2009	35.29	5/11/2009	44.53	8/10/2009	47.99	11/6/2009	50.03
11/9/2009	52.23	2/10/2010	46.18	5/12/2010	51.01	8/11/2010	55.99
11/10/2009	51.43	2/11/2010	46.81	5/13/2010	51.16	8/12/2010	55.85

(continued)

(continued)

Date	Price	Date	Price	Date	Price	Date	Price
11/11/2009	51.40	2/12/2010	45.86	5/14/2010	48.78	8/13/2010	55.98
11/12/2009	47.91	2/16/2010	47.45	5/17/2010	49.38	8/16/2010	56.19
11/13/2009	49.71	2/17/2010	45.41	5/18/2010	48.79	8/17/2010	58.01
11/16/2009	50.29	2/18/2010	44.48	5/19/2010	51.21	8/18/2010	57.32
11/17/2009	50.17	2/19/2010	45.66	5/20/2010	47.84	8/19/2010	55.45
11/18/2009	49.72	2/22/2010	44.72	5/21/2010	51.86	8/20/2010	55.95
11/19/2009	48.23	2/23/2010	43.25	5/24/2010	49.78	8/23/2010	55.55
11/20/2009	48.73	2/24/2010	43.84	5/25/2010	51.31	8/24/2010	54.78
11/23/2009	49.32	2/25/2010	42.72	5/26/2010	49.67	8/25/2010	55.13
11/24/2009	49.29	2/26/2010	43.46	5/27/2010	52.72	8/26/2010	56.22
11/25/2009	49.56	3/1/2010	45.17	5/28/2010	50.36	8/27/2010	57.54
11/27/2009	47.50	3/2/2010	45.05	6/1/2010	49.30	8/30/2010	55.32
11/30/2009	48.95	3/3/2010	45.03	6/2/2010	53.02	8/31/2010	56.57
12/1/2009	49.97	3/4/2010	45.05	6/3/2010	51.95	9/1/2010	57.55
12/2/2009	47.98	3/5/2010	46.71	6/4/2010	49.47	9/2/2010	57.57
12/3/2009	48.07	3/8/2010	46.34	6/7/2010	49.83	9/3/2010	58.99
12/4/2009	48.52	3/9/2010	46.34	6/8/2010	51.03	9/7/2010	58.24
12/7/2009	48.50	3/10/2010	46.33	6/9/2010	51.00	9/8/2010	58.50
12/8/2009	47.70	3/11/2010	47.33	6/10/2010	52.71	9/9/2010	58.54
12/9/2009	48.20	3/12/2010	45.70	6/11/2010	52.14	9/10/2010	57.35
12/10/2009	48.32	3/15/2010	45.92	6/14/2010	51.92	9/13/2010	58.13
12/11/2009	48.37	3/16/2010	47.18	6/15/2010	53.66	9/14/2010	57.50
12/14/2009	48.45	3/17/2010	47.09	6/16/2010	53.05	9/15/2010	58.36
12/15/2009	48.26	3/18/2010	46.13	6/17/2010	52.77	9/16/2010	58.43
12/16/2009	48.37	3/19/2010	46.43	6/18/2010	52.75	9/17/2010	57.78
12/17/2009	47.75	3/22/2010	47.27	6/21/2010	51.52	9/20/2010	59.43
12/18/2009	48.04	3/23/2010	47.23	6/22/2010	49.58	9/21/2010	59.28
12/21/2009	48.18	3/24/2010	46.71	6/23/2010	51.45	9/22/2010	58.93
12/22/2009	48.17	3/25/2010	45.33	6/24/2010	50.75	9/23/2010	58.78
12/23/2009	48.24	3/26/2010	46.29	6/25/2010	51.46	9/24/2010	59.62
12/24/2009	48.41	3/29/2010	46.64	6/28/2010	50.82	9/27/2010	59.06
12/28/2009	48.39	3/30/2010	47.10	6/29/2010	49.25	9/28/2010	60.69
12/29/2009	48.43	3/31/2010	47.03	6/30/2010	47.78	9/29/2010	60.18
12/30/2009	48.57	4/1/2010	47.19	7/1/2010	53.03	9/30/2010	59.41
12/31/2009	47.72	4/5/2010	48.27	7/2/2010	52.16	10/1/2010	60.95
1/4/2010	49.81	4/6/2010	47.78	7/6/2010	53.43	10/4/2010	60.33
1/5/2010	49.43	4/7/2010	47.22	7/7/2010	56.11	10/5/2010	61.51
1/6/2010	49.36	4/8/2010	48.33	7/8/2010	54.57	10/6/2010	60.99
1/7/2010	49.86	4/9/2010	48.21	7/9/2010	53.80	10/7/2010	61.05
1/8/2010	49.73	4/12/2010	47.99	7/12/2010	55.28	10/8/2010	61.21
1/11/2010	49.97	4/13/2010	48.46	7/13/2010	55.26	10/11/2010	61.41
1/12/2010	50.05	4/14/2010	50.05	7/14/2010	54.76	10/12/2010	61.37
1/13/2010	50.49	4/15/2010	48.72	7/15/2010	53.70	10/13/2010	62.16
1/14/2010	50.47	4/16/2010	43.51	7/16/2010	52.35	10/14/2010	62.04
1/15/2010	49.71	4/19/2010	46.80	7/19/2010	54.36	10/15/2010	62.24
1/19/2010	50.25	4/20/2010	48.04	7/20/2010	54.23	10/18/2010	62.32

(continued)

(continued)

Date	Price	Date	Price	Date	Price	Date	Price
1/20/2010	49.73	4/21/2010	47.95	7/21/2010	53.73	10/19/2010	60.35
1/21/2010	48.53	4/22/2010	49.46	7/22/2010	56.87	10/20/2010	63.70
1/22/2010	47.63	4/23/2010	48.32	7/23/2010	55.82	10/21/2010	62.94
1/25/2010	48.32	4/26/2010	48.82	7/26/2010	56.18	10/22/2010	62.00
1/26/2010	47.97	4/27/2010	43.11	7/27/2010	56.64	10/25/2010	61.78
1/27/2010	48.19	4/28/2010	47.16	7/28/2010	55.78	10/26/2010	59.55
1/28/2010	46.52	4/29/2010	49.56	7/29/2010	55.82	10/27/2010	59.87
1/29/2010	47.13	4/30/2010	48.25	7/30/2010	56.08	10/28/2010	61.32
2/1/2010	48.31	5/3/2010	52.43	8/2/2010	57.73	10/29/2010	60.44
2/2/2010	48.25	5/4/2010	47.17	8/3/2010	57.21	11/1/2010	62.05
2/3/2010	46.49	5/5/2010	47.84	8/4/2010	57.21	11/2/2010	61.25
2/4/2010	44.22	5/6/2010	46.51	8/5/2010	57.06	11/3/2010	61.72
2/5/2010	46.21	5/7/2010	47.15	8/6/2010	56.77	11/4/2010	63.61
2/8/2010	45.69	5/10/2010	50.17	8/9/2010	57.36	11/5/2010	62.92
2/9/2010	47.47	5/11/2010	49.06	8/10/2010	56.91	11/8/2010	61.28
11/9/2010	61.07	2/9/2011	66.25	5/11/2011	63.57	8/10/2011	55.52
11/10/2010	62.54	2/10/2011	67.04	5/12/2011	65.41	8/11/2011	60.28
11/11/2010	63.16	2/11/2011	66.97	5/13/2011	64.74	8/12/2011	60.79
11/12/2010	60.03	2/14/2011	67.10	5/16/2011	63.88	8/15/2011	63.19
11/15/2010	60.82	2/15/2011	67.51	5/17/2011	65.24	8/16/2011	62.05
11/16/2010	59.46	2/16/2011	68.89	5/18/2011	63.81	8/17/2011	62.24
11/17/2010	60.61	2/17/2011	68.91	5/19/2011	65.34	8/18/2011	59.00
11/18/2010	62.24	2/18/2011	68.14	5/20/2011	65.09	8/19/2011	57.65
11/19/2010	63.47	2/22/2011	65.19	5/23/2011	64.81	8/22/2011	59.24
11/22/2010	62.78	2/23/2011	65.95	5/24/2011	64.67	8/23/2011	60.79
11/23/2010	61.22	2/24/2011	66.62	5/25/2011	66.52	8/24/2011	62.24
11/24/2010	63.97	2/25/2011	67.84	5/26/2011	66.29	8/25/2011	60.38
11/26/2010	63.02	2/28/2011	68.18	5/27/2011	66.26	8/26/2011	62.93
11/29/2010	63.44	3/1/2011	63.54	5/31/2011	67.79	8/29/2011	65.43
11/30/2010	63.37	3/2/2011	66.48	6/1/2011	65.18	8/30/2011	63.87
12/1/2010	66.43	3/3/2011	67.55	6/2/2011	64.33	8/31/2011	64.60
12/2/2010	66.55	3/4/2011	66.12	6/3/2011	63.59	9/1/2011	63.74
12/3/2010	65.95	3/7/2011	65.93	6/6/2011	62.59	9/2/2011	60.59
12/6/2010	65.89	3/8/2011	64.92	6/7/2011	62.96	9/6/2011	60.66
12/7/2010	65.02	3/9/2011	66.35	6/8/2011	62.84	9/7/2011	65.01
12/8/2010	65.00	3/10/2011	63.14	6/9/2011	63.30	9/8/2011	60.05
12/9/2010	65.80	3/11/2011	65.45	6/10/2011	62.52	9/9/2011	59.45
12/10/2010	66.20	3/14/2011	63.64	6/13/2011	63.42	9/12/2011	60.27
12/13/2010	66.11	3/15/2011	63.95	6/14/2011	65.86	9/13/2011	61.25
12/14/2010	66.15	3/16/2011	63.62	6/15/2011	61.89	9/14/2011	61.42
12/15/2010	66.18	3/17/2011	65.53	6/16/2011	64.40	9/15/2011	65.35
12/16/2010	66.38	3/18/2011	66.43	6/17/2011	63.61	9/16/2011	63.89
12/17/2010	66.56	3/21/2011	67.08	6/20/2011	63.71	9/19/2011	64.29
12/20/2010	66.27	3/22/2011	65.81	6/21/2011	64.36	9/20/2011	64.37
12/21/2010	67.07	3/23/2011	65.86	6/22/2011	63.71	9/21/2011	62.40
12/22/2010	64.27	3/24/2011	66.29	6/23/2011	63.78	9/22/2011	61.02

(continued)

(continued)

Date	Price	Date	Price	Date	Price	Date	Price
12/23/2010	65.09	3/25/2011	67.24	6/24/2011	62.57	9/23/2011	61.97
12/27/2010	64.75	3/28/2011	66.63	6/27/2011	63.18	9/26/2011	64.99
12/28/2010	66.57	3/29/2011	67.13	6/28/2011	64.90	9/27/2011	63.91
12/29/2010	64.62	3/30/2011	66.61	6/29/2011	64.33	9/28/2011	60.92
12/30/2010	64.73	3/31/2011	64.55	6/30/2011	66.56	9/29/2011	61.83
12/31/2010	64.92	4/1/2011	65.56	7/1/2011	65.95	9/30/2011	58.81
1/3/2011	65.24	4/4/2011	65.77	7/5/2011	64.75	10/3/2011	57.50
1/4/2011	65.12	4/5/2011	64.68	7/6/2011	66.24	10/4/2011	61.08
1/5/2011	66.96	4/6/2011	64.69	7/7/2011	66.07	10/5/2011	63.58
1/6/2011	65.83	4/7/2011	63.55	7/8/2011	64.47	10/6/2011	63.54
1/7/2011	66.29	4/8/2011	63.78	7/11/2011	63.72	10/7/2011	62.95
1/10/2011	65.83	4/11/2011	63.63	7/12/2011	64.23	10/10/2011	67.51
1/11/2011	64.66	4/12/2011	62.80	7/13/2011	62.18	10/11/2011	66.22
1/12/2011	66.19	4/13/2011	62.91	7/14/2011	62.84	10/12/2011	66.31
1/13/2011	66.12	4/14/2011	63.10	7/15/2011	61.85	10/13/2011	66.13
1/14/2011	66.49	4/15/2011	63.25	7/18/2011	63.12	10/14/2011	67.53
1/18/2011	66.30	4/18/2011	62.68	7/19/2011	64.37	10/17/2011	65.13
1/19/2011	65.12	4/19/2011	63.06	7/20/2011	62.91	10/18/2011	67.44
1/20/2011	65.40	4/20/2011	65.94	7/21/2011	64.73	10/19/2011	65.96
1/21/2011	66.29	4/21/2011	65.14	7/22/2011	64.29	10/20/2011	66.44
1/24/2011	66.49	4/25/2011	63.59	7/25/2011	64.24	10/21/2011	68.60
1/25/2011	66.29	4/26/2011	65.29	7/26/2011	65.27	10/24/2011	67.52
1/26/2011	67.18	4/27/2011	65.77	7/27/2011	61.66	10/25/2011	66.57
1/27/2011	66.92	4/28/2011	65.54	7/28/2011	60.36	10/26/2011	67.03
1/28/2011	64.11	4/29/2011	66.50	7/29/2011	60.90	10/27/2011	67.53
1/31/2011	64.57	5/2/2011	65.90	8/1/2011	60.82	10/28/2011	66.92
2/1/2011	64.06	5/3/2011	65.66	8/2/2011	56.94	10/31/2011	64.40
2/2/2011	64.12	5/4/2011	64.74	8/3/2011	59.35	11/1/2011	64.82
2/3/2011	66.84	5/5/2011	64.96	8/4/2011	56.14	11/2/2011	65.26
2/4/2011	66.33	5/6/2011	64.78	8/5/2011	56.75	11/3/2011	66.49
2/7/2011	66.29	5/9/2011	65.36	8/8/2011	53.79	11/4/2011	64.59
2/8/2011	66.47	5/10/2011	66.89	8/9/2011	59.66	11/7/2011	65.22
11/8/2011	66.93						
11/9/2011	64.22						
11/10/2011	65.16						
11/11/2011	66.86						
11/14/2011	66.17						
11/15/2011	65.90						
11/16/2011	64.47						
11/17/2011	63.74						
11/18/2011	65.96						
11/21/2011	63.42						
11/22/2011	63.77						
11/23/2011	60.95						
11/25/2011	59.39						
11/28/2011	64.34						

(continued)

(continued)

Date	Price	Date	Price	Date	Price	Date	Price
11/29/2011	62.89						
11/30/2011	65.63						
12/1/2011	64.88						
12/2/2011	63.67						
12/5/2011	64.13						
12/6/2011	63.80						
12/7/2011	62.67						
12/8/2011	59.45						
12/9/2011	61.49						
12/12/2011	58.01						
12/13/2011	58.93						
12/14/2011	58.78						
12/15/2011	58.58						
12/16/2011	59.15						
12/19/2011	56.07						
12/20/2011	60.06						
12/21/2011	57.94						
12/22/2011	57.98						
12/23/2011	58.24						
12/27/2011	58.02						
12/28/2011	57.85						
12/29/2011	58.52						
12/30/2011	58.22						

Appendix 3

Hack Back's 2009 and 2010 Financial Statements

Hack Back, Incorporated		
Income statement for years ending December 31, 2009 and 2010		
	2009	2010
Sales	327,890,500	402,456,525
Cost of goods sold	244,606,313	327,599,611
Depreciation	37,435,864	41,385,900
EBIT	45,848,323	33,471,014
Interest	1,743,800	2,015,435
Taxable income	44,104,523	31,455,579
Taxes (35 %)	15,436,583	11,009,453
Net income	28,667,940	20,446,126
Dividends	2,400,000	5,040,000
Addition to retained earnings	26,267,940	15,406,126

Hack Back, Incorporated					
Balance sheet as of December 31, 2009 and 2010					
Assets			Liabilities		
	2009	2010		2009	2010
Current assets			Current liabilities	20,435,135	27,349,500
Cash	37,970,869	51,581,987	Long-term debt	28,197,000	30,125,346
A/R	17,976,050	19,341,907	Total debt	48,632,135	57,474,846
Inventory	102,987,500	140,891,891			
Total current	158,934,419	211,815,785	Equity		
				2009	2010
Fixed assets	147,505,203	118,872,674	Common stock	223,200,000	223,200,000

(continued)

M.K. Pyles, *Applied Corporate Finance: Questions, Problems and Making Decisions in the Real World*, Springer Texts in Business and Economics,
DOI 10.1007/978-1-4614-9173-6,

(continued)

Hack Back, Incorporated					
Balance sheet as of December 31, 2009 and 2010					
Total assets	$306,439,622	$330,688,459	Retained earnings	34,607,487	50,013,613
			Total equity	257,807,487	273,213,613
			Total liabilities and equity	$306,439,622	$330,688,459

Appendix 4

Competitor and Industry Composite Financial Statements

Bubba's Golf Equipment, Incorporated

Bubba's Golf Equipment, Incorporated	
Income statement for year ending December 31, 2010	
Sales	914,598,785
Cost of goods sold	583,971,324
Depreciation	142,432,424
EBIT	188,195,037
Interest	22,345,402
Taxable income	165,849,635
Taxes (35 %)	58,047,372
Net income	107,802,263
Dividends	24,569,000
Addition to retained earnings	83,233,263

Bubba's Golf Equipment, Incorporated			
Balance sheet as of December 31, 2010			
Assets		Liabilities	
Current assets		Current liabilities	68,454,454
Cash	178,970,498	Long-term debt	224,869,342
A/R	94,341,907	Total debt	293,323,796
Inventory	170,979,371		
Total current	444,291,776	Equity	
		Common stock	636,120,000
Fixed assets	610,605,363	Retained earnings	125,453,343
Total assets	$1,054,897,139	Total equity	761,573,343
		Total liabilities and equity	$1,054,897,139

M.K. Pyles, *Applied Corporate Finance: Questions, Problems and Making Decisions in the Real World*, Springer Texts in Business and Economics,
DOI 10.1007/978-1-4614-9173-6, © Springer Science+Business Media New York 2014

PLC Golf, Incorporated

PLC Golf, Incorporated	
Income statement for year ending December 31, 2010	
Sales	284,567,934
Cost of goods sold	156,142,425
Depreciation	31,834,343
EBIT	96,591,166
Interest	12,434,523
Taxable income	84,156,643
Taxes (35 %)	29,454,825
Net income	$54,701,818
Dividends	31,834,334
Addition to retained earnings	22,867,484

PLC Golf, Incorporated			
Balance sheet as of December 31, 2010			
Assets		Liabilities	
Current assets		Current liabilities	19,843,542
Cash	46,834,334	Long-term debt	29,454,324
A/R	70,352,534	Total debt	49,297,866
Inventory	56,654,656		
Total current	173,841,524	Equity	
		Common stock	204,600,000
Fixed assets	125,510,685	Retained earnings	45,454,343
Total assets	$299,352,209	Total equity	250,054,343
		Total liabilities and equity	$299,352,209

Industry Composite

Industry composite	
Income statement for year ending December 31, 2010	
Sales	653,343,346
Cost of goods sold	397,755,429
Depreciation	94,313,080
EBIT	161,274,837
Interest	23,856,512
Taxable income	137,418,325
Taxes (35 %)	48,096,414
Net income	$89,321,911
Dividends	26,454,235
Addition to retained earnings	62,867,676

Industry composite			
Balance sheet as of December 31, 2010			
Assets		Liabilities	
Current assets		Current liabilities	56,435,423
Cash	155,547,894	Long-term debt	165,454,324
A/R	88,994,234	Total debt	221,889,747
Inventory	127,589,745		
Total current	372,131,873	Equity	
		Common stock	641,700,000
Fixed assets	569,910,214	Retained earnings	78,452,340
Total assets	942,042,087	Total equity	720,152,340
		Total liabilities and equity	$942,042,087

Index

M.K. Pyles, *Applied Corporate Finance: Questions, Problems and Making Decisions in the Real World*, Springer Texts in Business and Economics,
DOI 10.1007/978-1-4614-9173-6, © Springer Science+Business Media New York 2014

Printed by Printforce, the Netherlands